FOURSCORE YEARS

CAMBRIDGE
UNIVERSITY PRESS
LONDON: BENTLEY HOUSE
NEW YORK   TORONTO   BOMBAY
CALCUTTA MADRAS: MACMILLAN

PRINTED IN GREAT BRITAIN

FOURSCORE YEARS

An Autobiography

BY

G. G. COULTON

CAMBRIDGE

AT THE UNIVERSITY PRESS

1943

To

MY HOSPITABLE FRIENDS
IN CANADA & THE UNITED STATES

In whose gardens so many of these pages were written

CONTENTS

Preface   *page* vii

Chapter I   Wensleydale and Oldham   1

II   Apron Strings   8

III   Dame's School   12

IV   Victorian Lynn (1)   20

V   Victorian Lynn (2)   28

VI   St-Omer   39

VII   The Grammar School   48

VIII   Pentney   55

IX   The Public School   68

X   The Chrysalis Stage   80

XI   Cambridge in 1877   91

XII   College Small-beer   99

XIII   St Catharine's   111

XIV   Malvern Wells   127

XV   Llandaff   141

XVI   Parish Work   151

XVII   Fresh Woods   158

XVIII   Wales (1)   168

XIX   Wales (2)   179

XX   Heidelberg   186

XXI   Sherborne   200

XXII   Sedbergh   206

XXIII   Dulwich College   218

XXIV   Lausanne and Naples   226

XXV   Sorrento and Amalfi   236

XXVI   Homeward Bound   246

XXVII   South Lynn   252

Chapter XXVIII A Bee in the Bonnet *page* 265

XXIX Winter Sport 282

XXX Thurlestone 295

XXXI First Books 302

XXXII Cambridge Again 311

XXXIII History and Controversy 317

XXXIV An Extreme Case 329

XXXV Soul's Ease 338

Appendix 351

Index 355

PLATES

I At the University of Wisconsin, April 1941 *Frontispiece*

II Aged four: About the time of the Royal Marriage (1863) *facing* 16

III The old mulberry tree in the garden of Tower House, Lynn. 17
'Rick', 'Essy', 'Etta', Edmund, Gordon (the author)

IV Pentney, from the Green Drive 58

V The author's father, John James Coulton 59

VI Moonlight at Pentney: from a drawing by the author 144

VII Rothenburg: from an etching by the author 145

VIII The author and his wife in 1904 288

IX 'Gordanus Shelfordiensis'. From the original cartoon by G. R. 289
Owst, now in the Library of St John's College, Cambridge

X View from the author's rooms at St John's College, Cambridge 304

XI Signing the records at Queen's University, Kingston, with the 305
Cardinal Archbishop of Quebec, after presentation for the
degree of Doctor of Laws

PREFACE

LOOKING BACK here and now, this early summer day in America, upon nearly eighty years of memories, I am comforted to realize how all my places of abode come out in sunshine. The garden at Lynn is wreathed in great purple Morning-Glory convolvulus, while the shadows from mulberry and pear tree lie cool upon the grass. At St-Omer, on our long and dusty afternoon walks, the little school-boy trudges in tears amid the alien corn, but under a blue French sky. At Pentney, sunshine broods over hay field and fruit garden and our careless rustic abundance of roses; sunshine over the school playing fields at Felsted and the elms and river at Cambridge. At Malvern, where first I earned my living, Bredon Hill basks before me under the midday sun, while Tewkesbury and Gloucester, with Cheltenham and the Cotswolds, swim in the distant heat-haze. So again do the Welsh valleys and hills, beyond their cool green pastures in the foreground. Thence to the cherry orchards of Heidelberg; the great Rhine plain and the Neckar valley; Dorset pastures next. So is it even with the Sedbergh Fells, in one of the rainiest corners of England; with Dulwich, a village green set in the midst of Greater London; even with Eastbourne, where by an effort I recall the biting east winds, but remember far more naturally the 'multitudinous billows...in the universal sun'. Then lastly, Cambridge once more, with this present extension of University work into Canada and the United States, where everybody is at this moment acclaiming the sunniest May in living memory. Even in far-off 1879, coldest and wettest of all my life, when crops rotted as they stood, I see myself nestling warm-blooded among the sandhills at Hunstanton, and gloating over Shakespeare's 'thy eternal summer shall not fade'. Without actual optimism perhaps, but in impenitent meliorism I can quote here again from the Sonnets, with the change of only one word:

> To me, fair Earth, you never can be old,
> For as you were when first your eye I eyed,
> Such seems your beauty still...

—not, indeed, in forgetfulness of what is now around me, but in effort to turn away from the irrevocable and to face only remediable things. As I write at this moment (May 30), bad news comes almost daily, and who knows what may be yet to come? But this is Memorial Day in the United States, and the chimes from Harkness Tower are rippling down into the gardens at its foot, reinforced for this special occasion by *Nun danket alle Gott* and by what to me is *God Save the King*, though others may call it '*My Country, 'tis of Thee*'. Thus Clough comes into my mind: 'Say not, the struggle nought availeth'; and again: 'It fortifies my soul to know that, though I perish, Truth is so'. Democracy will win in the end, whether or not in my lifetime and in that of those whom I have left at home. Meanwhile, my job is to plant my cabbages here.

Therefore I venture to add one more to the existing multitude of life stories, in the conviction that all such have some interest of their own, so long as they are honestly told.

Aiming at frankness for myself, I have used the same freedom— or even more, human nature being as it is—about others. But I have tried to write here nothing which I have not already said in print, or in public discussion, or at least more privately face to face. In many cases I have silently changed the real names, where they were immaterial. In important matters I give the real names, for I hope for general agreement that, in proportion as a man is really great, he can afford the truth, alive or dead, and would with the better part of his nature have welcomed such truth.

It dates me, of course, that I have often given way to the luxury of quotation; but, in memory of occasional pathetic pleas from past readers, I take pains here to append translations.

My special thanks are due to three who have generously under-taken, under present wartime difficulties of correspondence, to prune a too discursive volume and see it through the press; Mr H. S. Bennett of Emmanuel College, Mr F. H. Kendon of the University Press, and my daughter Mary.

G. G. COULTON

NEW HAVEN, CONNECTICUT

30 *May* 1941

CHAPTER I

WENSLEYDALE & OLDHAM

I COUNT myself fortunate within the limitations of Solomon's ideal: 'Give me neither poverty nor riches.' My father's earliest recorded ancestor was Ewan Coulton, a yeoman farmer in Wensleydale, Yorkshire, in the sixteenth century. A couple of generations later the name occurs in the will of Judge Fell, an upright and influential squire whose widow married George Fox, and thus gave a great impulse to Quaker prosperity. He bequeathed £10 to 'William Coulton, my menial servant', whom I like to think of as an ancestor. My great-grandfather, the Rev. James Coulton, was the first of the family to outgrow the tiny hamlet of Burtersett or Burterside, where they were settled. Exercising the traditional freedom of an eldest son, who might choose between the farm and a liberal education, he studied at St Bees, became (I believe) curate at Morpeth and domestic chaplain to Lord Lonsdale, and finally came south into Norfolk. There he became assistant curate at Castle Rising and Roydon, kept a small school at King's Lynn, and died in 1834, at the age of 74, as incumbent of North Wootton, midway between Rising and Lynn.

Yet on the village green, as I like to think, he met his villagers on truly Wordsworthian terms, with his 'reception of young and old, rich and poor, in feast and merrymaking on his birthdays'. Moreover, he had practical warnings against extreme political conservatism. Castle Rising was one of the most notorious 'pocket boroughs' of the yet unreformed Parliament. Two members were there chosen by a constituency of fewer than twenty persons, in the days when Manchester, Sheffield, Leeds and Birmingham had not a single representative between them. Even at Lynn, the two members were painfully unrepresentative of the whole population. Freemen alone had votes; and freedom of the borough was jealously limited to sons, or sons-in-law, or apprentices of freemen. James Coulton's ecclesiastical and educational status gave him here no voice whatever. My father himself, in 1831, stood through the night with the crowd on the Tuesday Market Place, awaiting the news of that decision which, by a single vote, pledged the House of Commons to reform itself and thus to avert the danger of civil war. Of Lynn elections in post-Reform days, I shall speak later.

John James Coulton, my grandfather, became a solicitor at Lynn. He was a presentable and intelligent man, and married into a Lincolnshire family which was growing from prosperous merchant status to something like country squire. Their name was Calthrop (earlier, Calthorpe) and they were perhaps connected with the Lady Parker whose crayon portrait by Holbein is one of the famous series at Windsor. He died of consumption in his prime, leaving seven children, the eldest of whom was my father, John James the Second, born in 1818. The family filled, or a little more than filled, a small house in Austin Street, facing the precinct wall and gate of the old Austin Friars. When my father, in his boyhood, began to read Gibbon, he had to secure the necessary quiet by lying under the dining-room table. He looked forward to Cambridge, where his uncle, Henry Calthrop, was a Fellow of Corpus Christi College. This man was something of a reformer for his day and his environment; one of his few surviving colleagues told me, in 1880, how it had been proverbial at Corpus to answer 'Let Calthrop come!' in the face of any complaint of abuse. The physician, however, could not heal himself. He was next in seniority for the Mastership, or at least in expectation, when the lucrative College living of Braxted fell vacant. The reigning Master was little older or less healthy than himself; therefore Henry Calthrop burned his boats by accepting the benefice. Upon this the Master suddenly died; and it was to this disappointment that his family attributed a severe and prolonged mental breakdown. It must be remembered that, in those semi-monastic days of celibacy and Holy Orders for almost all University Fellowships, such restrictions were apt to breed within those small, close corporations a nexus of rivalries and jealousies as intricate as those of any medieval abbey. For the Master had much of an Abbot's practical irresponsibility and hierarchical pre-eminence, with freedom of marriage to boot. J. W. Clark's *Reminiscences* describe how College Heads with their wives invited each other to dinner, with Professors and other smaller fry to come in later and dance attendance at tea.

My father had a far severer stroke of fortune; his father's health broke down, and all thought of Cambridge had to be given up. As it was, he was only just in time to complete his articles and pass his examinations, and step into the office without any actual break of continuity between the firm of John James senior and John James junior. The burden of a family thus came upon him early in life: but he made good, and brought up his own eight children no less loyally when the time came.

Old 'Grandmamma Coulton' was a formidable figure to all of us: she lived to nearly eighty-five. The Calthrops of that generation had exceptional vitality. Their mother, Mary Gordon, had lived to ninety-six. They numbered thirteen brothers and sisters. Two died in earliest childhood; another, in early manhood, was killed at the bombardment of Algiers (1816): a cannon-ball took his head clean off just after he had quoted exultingly from Byron's *Corsair*

> Much has been done, much still remains to do;
> Their galleys burn, why not their city, too?

Excluding those three, the remaining ten reached an average age of nearly eighty-four, although the eldest of them came only to about ninety. Priscilla, my grandmother, I never remember to have seen except in black silk or something almost equally solemn. She had something of the monumental rigidity of Queen Victoria; she seemed made of other clay than the rest of us; and Aunt Ellen (the only unmarried one left) was her submissive but not unhappy subject. Though less than a quarter of a mile distant from us in space, she entered scarcely at all into the lives of us children, whether for good or for evil. It seemed quite natural that she and her defunct partner should be commemorated on our dining-room wall by a pair of black silhouette portraits. The grandfather's silhouette was eloquent also of other things. He stood there mending a quill pen, in just the dress and attitude of the 'Honest Lawyer' at the South Gates. There, the first inn that confronted a traveller from London or Wisbech bore this sign, unique so far as I know: 'This Honest Lawyer bore his head not on his shoulders, but tucked under one arm'; the innuendo being that when we meet a lawyer in that guise we may be assured of his honesty. But, to my childish mind, that inn sign seemed personal and symbolical. Our own silhouette resembled the inn sign so closely, apart from that one eccentricity of the portable head, that I claimed the compliment, at least in some mystic sense, for my own ancestor.

One figure of my grandparents' generation was more living to us than our grandmother. This was James Maher, District Surveyor of Roads; he had been a pupil of Macadam himself, the pioneer of modern road-making. He was a handsome, stately, and witty Irishman, commonly dressed in fashionable sporting costume, who had been a close friend of my grandfather, and (it was whispered darkly to us as we grew up) something too much of a friendly boon companion. In mellow age he was one of my father's closest friends; whenever Mr Maher came to dinner the Staunton chessmen of boxwood and ebony were brought out, as a sequel to the port and walnuts. He taught my brother Richard to love and manage horses; it was a great sight to see his gig going at a spanking trot along the fenland roads which stretched westwards from the little house which he had across the river. Here too was delicious fruit to which we were sometimes invited, and rooms full of china, collected with life-long care. Once, when I dropped a rare piece from my hands, to my father's violent indignation, the old man interceded for me with a 'Well, well, it would have been all the same a hundred years hence!' My eldest brother was a vigorous and ebullient boy. Old Maher's comment once ran: 'Well, there are worse fellows than Jim Coulton —but they don't let 'em go loose.'

My mother's family were also north-country folk, this time from

Lancashire. Her grandfather was a colliery owner at Oldham, one Samuel Lees, who married three times. First, his own cook; then, with circumspection, a lady of good family; but finally in more random fashion than the first. From the second was descended Beatrice Lees, History Tutor at Somerville College, Oxford. By the first, he had a son who died of consumption in early manhood, and a daughter Elizabeth, my grandmother. To each of his numerous children he was able to leave a comfortable portion; and my grandmother was wooed by her cousin, James Radley, a young Oldham solicitor. She had another suitor, named Copeland, whom, as she frankly confessed in old age, she preferred. She kept, and we still preserve, Copeland's reproachful letters; for she had actually given him her promise. Why, then, had she taken her cousin? 'Eh, my dears, he wanted me—he wanted my money—and I was sorry for him!' This, without altogether dispelling the mystery, was not unintelligible to those who knew 'Mitty', as we called our grandmother by Lancastrian pet name for 'mistress'. Her rôle was passive all life long, whether at Leamington, whither she retired in widowhood with four children, or in Canada, where she lived for a while with her son at London on the Thames, or at Lynn, where she and Aunt Sophia lived to ripest old age on the remnants of their inheritance. 'Mitty' was by nature unadventurous and querulous: to all us grandchildren she was a living embodiment of Law on its negative side: 'touch not, taste not, handle not!' Sitting on the grass would spell rheumatism; boys who made faces were 'struck so'; and he who lost his temper and smote the table with his hand broke a 'guider' of his wrist; again, the direst results had been known to follow upon the swallowing and internal growth of cherry stones. But I cannot remember that all this had the least effect upon our spirits. Both she and Aunt Sophia were excellent cooks, and it was a treat to go and bespeak from them a meal of 'offal': tripe and onions, or stuffed bullock's heart, or pig's fry, or trotters. Aunt Sophia's face bore considerable resemblance to Benjamin Franklin's; and she had much of his common-sense and ready choice of *le mot juste*. She had inherited the larger share of my grandfather's collection of engravings —mezzotints by Earlom and Smith, portraits by Houbraken, and even a Dürer or two. For 'Grandfather Radley', however merciful it may have been for the family that an apoplexy carried him off in full manhood, had been an intelligent collector in a small way. When, therefore, we children had put away the desire of eating and drinking after our Homeric feast of offal, it was a great delight to turn over these treasures under the stimulus of a glass of sherry with sugar and boiling water.

My mother was the youngest of the family; and she made a memorable sacrifice, which she never hinted to us boys, though the girls knew it. Her favourite was the second sister, Mary Ann. When, in process of time, Mary Ann became engaged and her portion of £2000 was not enough to marry upon, my mother contributed her own £2000. Mary Ann's husband died early of consumption, leaving two children, whom she brought up, with the help of contributory relatives, in something of her own mother's mildly querulous and indefinite fashion.

My grandmother and aunts had help in later life through the generosity of my grandfather's nephew James, whose industry and ability had raised him at last to the ownership of two or three collieries. Among his many benefactions, he made up to my mother, in later life, the £2000 which she had sacrificed to her sister. In addition, he supported two of his brothers. One of them, Stephen, was among those people who never really grow up. His features were regular, but he was stunted in body and mind, and incapable of work. Though he lived with James and upon James, nothing in the house ever pleased him. The morning porridge, especially, gave him daily opportunities for grumbling. One day, however, he faced his little porringer in only silent discontent. James was rash enough to ask, 'Well, Stephen, nothing wrong with the porridge this morning?' Stephen answered, 'They are na poured out right'. Porridge, be it noted, is a plural noun among old-fashioned folk in Scotland and northern England.

John was my father's next brother; and this alliance thus introduced John James to Sarah Radley. He was better able than John to bear the burden of a family, and the pair were married in 1849. As he waited on the platform for the train which was to take him to Leamington and to his bride, a friend accosted him with 'Why, Coulton, they tell me you are going to be married'. My father replied, 'People will say anything!' and sought the farther end of the platform.

CHAPTER II

APRON STRINGS

MY FATHER'S first child was born in the old Austin Street abode; but he soon moved to Tower House, a roomy old Georgian building of grey brick facing the theatre and the Greyfriars' Tower. As with many Lynn houses of the period, nearly all its rooms were on one front, with nothing but passages and stairs behind. Unlike many of them, this front faced due south; so that one attic window faced east and another west. The garden was of comfortable size, one of the largest of any within the actual town; and it had one great advantage, that it was not overlooked. We on the other hand, by climbing our trees, could look eastwards upon Theatre Plain and the street, and westwards over corners of our neighbours' gardens. In one corner, only, the blind wall of Drake's pottery-yard rose to about 20 feet, and shut out our view. In this Tower House seven of us were born and grew up. I was number six, born in 1858; and Richard, from his height of four years older, blighted me once with a quotation from Macaulay's *Lays*: 'False Sextus, that wrought the deed of shame.' I do not think we were more mischievous than the average; at any rate, not much more. But our vantage-ground in this garden tempted me and my younger brother Edmund to what we called 'cad-fishing'. For the wall towards the theatre was broken by old, high carriage gates, permanently closed. Through the great keyhole of these gates one of us would slip a slender shoot from the lilac bushes, and wave it about to attract notice. Some passing boy—sometimes perhaps even some incautious grown-up—would take the bait and grasp the twig, which we then withdrew at a rate which must have added considerable physical discomfort to the obvious mockery. One day, however, the intended victim grasped our bait so firmly, and pulled so vigorously, that it was Edmund's hands which were chafed. In his childish surprise—he was nine or ten years old—he applied his eye to the keyhole, just at the moment when the victor-victim pushed the twig insolently back. Thus my brother came within a hundredth of an inch of being blinded, and 'cad-fishing' interested us no more.

Another painful instance of class distinctions occurred about the same time. It was while the memory was still fresh of one of the greatest floods ever known in the basin of the Ouse: viz. the bursting of the Middle Level Drain. My two elder brothers went out for a long day among the fenland marshes, and dragged weary, mud-beplastered legs home in the summer sunset. During their last quarter of a mile, a rabble of small boys gathered round them and hooted them home to the chorus of 'Yer've bin to the Middle Level, Yer mucky little devil!'

We had one such *déclassé* among us later, when I came again to the Grammar School. His father, if I remember rightly, was a roadmender. Unluckily, poor Langwade had nothing in himself to redeem his ancestry. He left at sixteen or seventeen and became a shunter on the railway. There, after a few months, he ignored one train while looking at another, had both his feet cut off, and was taken to the common hospital. A few hours after the amputation, he regained consciousness and murmured to his nurse that he felt pain in his feet. 'Feet!' she replied, 'you ain't got none.' He shut his eyes and gave up the ghost quietly: and when we heard of it, I think class distinctions were for one moment obliterated.

Even earlier than this—for it happened when I was at Croad's—I had a strong revulsion from traditional snobbery. I was trudging to school, and (I don't know why, unless it were in an unusually strong fit of unwillingness) by way of St John's Church and the station. Just round the corner on the left, a house had been pulled down or building was beginning: at any rate, the whole corner was littered with heaps of bricks and rubbish. There stood two young fellows—I should now judge, nineteen and seventeen—of whom the younger had just been flung down, and was rising to his feet. He stood there facing his antagonist; his poor shoddy trousers were horribly torn at one knee, and one cheek-bone was badly cut, the blood oozing through the dust in an untidy way which seemed more pathetic than whole spouts of clean blood from a clean face. It was the first time, too, that I had ever seen a face literally ashen-grey with pain and rage. He stood there with half a brick in his hand, threatening his antagonist again and again. The other, clean and well dressed, faced him in insolent triumph. The 'cad', after one or two convulsive jerks, lost heart and dropped his brick. Years afterwards, reading the story of Steerforth and the usher in *David Copperfield*, I saw this Lynn scene again in sickening realism. I cannot claim to have been more compassionate than most boys of my age; and there is painful truth in La Fontaine's 'cet âge est sans pitié'. But this experience did take me, early in life, a little way beyond the traditional political liberalism of our household. Almost all of us were too insensitive to the just claims of the 'under dog'; but I cannot remember ever having been tempted to look upon poverty as an insuperable law of nature. The mention of Croad's School, however, compels me to give another side of the picture here. Our Headmaster, one day, rebuked us with solemn emphasis for growing unpunctuality, or even truancy. He told us how, when he was at our age, there had been a man hanged at a town six miles from his home. His schoolfellows had deserted *en masse* that morning to see the execution, but Duty and Conscience had compelled this good little Croad to attend school and miss the execution. I told my parents, at lunch, how old Croad had boasted his strange self-sacrifice, and was surprised at the laughter which greeted my naïve question, '*Do* you *believe* him?'

One of my earliest clear and datable recollections (Plate II, p. 16) is the wedding of the Prince of Wales, afterwards Edward VII (March 1863). He brought his 'Sea-King's daughter from over the sea' down to his newly furnished Sandringham Hall, among the pines and fern and heather, between Lynn and Hunstanton. They came down in a tiny special train of their own, all white, and wreathed in white flowers. At Lynn, the royal pair deigned to halt their train for an hour or so, and drive up to the Town Hall for a loyal address. The people did not take their horses out and drag the coach with their own hands; they had done that recently for Queen Victoria, with a tumultuous and possibly alcoholic exuberance which kindled the Queen to outspoken disgust. But we saw, from our own house, a far better sight than that. The passage window opposite our nursery door commanded Theatre Plain and a hundred yards of St James' Street, through which the coach came. We children had this all to ourselves; for the elders had another window. We heard the trumpet-blasts, and then saw a surging crowd, and then the outriders: great life-guards bearing tabards and silver trumpets hung with em-

broidered banners; and Edward and Alexandra waving acknowledgement to the crowd.

Those were the days in which I saw more of my mother as housekeeper, if only I had had sense enough to take it fully in, than ever
before or after. For about two years, while Edmund was in the
nursery and Beatrice still unborn, I was the youngest walkable child,
and easiest to keep out of mischief by continual companionship.
The mists lift capriciously after all these years, and show me half a
dozen scenes of no special interest now, or perhaps even then, except
that they are typical. The great cupboard in one corner of the
dining-room, opened by a large key from the capacious key basket,
from which all kinds of delicacies were ceremonially dealt out to the
kitchen, and one lump of sugar to myself; strictly no more than one,
for sugar was then an expensive and jealously guarded luxury. Our
Tom, a big cat of old English tabby pattern, more aged than the
three youngest of us, is at the fireplace, with his hands hanging over
the fender almost like one of ourselves. The cupboard is locked, and
we go out shopping. We want groceries. Sugar and most other
things we can get from (literally) next door, at the corner. But my
mother is more particular for her cheese. We thread St James' Street
and give a wide berth to the grocer opposite the 'Three Pigeons',
whose weekly tallow-boilings infect the whole town with their
odour, and whom we patronize only for candles or kitchen soap.
We turn at St Margaret's and push far on into High Street, to the
principal grocer of the town. His window makes a grand show with
cheeses and bacon, raisins and citron peel, and (if Christmas be near)
boxes of crackers. We enter, and two or three great cheeses are produced for our choice. The assistant inserts his gouge, and brings out
a round plug of fresh moist cheese, with a small biscuit for each of
us; and my mother (I seem to remember) is never content to try
fewer than two or three. Then, in summer, to the fruiterer's, as
rich a show as any in England, for our Fenland soil is among the
best. The sight and scent of it all are unforgettable.

CHAPTER III

DAME'S SCHOOL

SO FAR, I was but a step removed from the cradle and the nursery. The next advance was to the dame's school. This may have been hastened by two incidents which cannot be omitted here, if I am to write 'un livre de bonne foi'. Of the first I have no personal recollection; for the second my memory vaguely supports my mother's. One day, I was so exasperated by some stroke of parental discipline as to fly to the open window and scream out to a passer-by: 'Man! come and kill my mother!' The second matter concerned my first nurse, Hunnybun by name, doubtless a corruption of Honeybourne. She was a charming girl, and my mother felt in her a treasure. But she was attached to a sailor; gradually she lost her spirits, refused all comfort, and quitted us altogether. She wept bitterly at the parting, and for weeks I was inconsolable, crying daily for 'Hunny-bunny'. My mother used to confess that her own affection for the girl could never entirely conquer maternal jealousy, or guard her from the natural feeling that my passionate devotion to the handmaid separated me, if only by a hair's breadth, from the rest of the family, so rightly dependent upon her. She would have justly resented any idea that she loved one more than another; but looking back now, I think she instinctively left me more to my own devices than the other seven.

At any rate, to the Misses Thompson I went at four or five, after picking up some of my letters at home. They lived in one sense next door, though one had to go half round the block to get at them. Their little garden was back-to-back with ours, divided only by a few feet. But the front door opened upon Stonegate Street,[1] and led to a Georgian building which would be worth untold sums at present-day Williamsburg, brick for brick and beam for beam, let alone its neighbours by the side of the muddy little Fleet which creeps down under Lady Bridge into the Ouse. The street door led—

---

[1] More properly, plain 'Stonegate'; but the nineteenth century had forgotten that gate was a common medieval word for way, and had therefore added this pleonastic Street to a little thoroughfare which had indeed been paved, but had never had a vestige of gate in the modern sense.

and still leads, I hope—into a small court, with pilasters and admirably proportioned members in the best eighteenth-century style. The house opened originally from both sides of this court, east and west; but even in my day it had been partitioned off into two, the Thompson ladies occupying only the western half. Their hall and staircase were the most beautiful portions of the house; but they had also admirable wainscoted dining- and drawing-rooms, and a few square yards of garden enclosed by a brick wall two centuries older than the house, and ripened by time almost to a mulberry purple. A similar wall, by the way, formed the western bounds of our own garden; both were probably remnants of the merchants' warehouses which had been built beside or near the Fleet in prosperous medieval times. So far as I can remember, the ladies left us very much to ourselves: I can only see myself sitting at the drawing-room window with some sort of simple book. In later days, two literary friends have given me their recollections of the Misses Thompson and their school. Thomas Seccombe[1] remembered mainly one meticulous habit: whenever they licked a gummed envelope, they laid it on the carpet and stood on it long enough to ensure perfect adhesion. The comic side of this superstitious ceremony impressed him deeply; but to Francis of Caius, the Assistant University Librarian (1877), the memories of Stonegate Street were tragic. His parents, who lived in Suffolk, had sent him thither as a boarder; he had no specific complaint against the place, but his homesickness was incurable. He lay awake at nights listening to chime after chime from the eight bells of St Margaret's, which count among the finest in the kingdom; the result was that, even at eighty, the mellowest church chimes were still odious to him.

There was probably a gap between the Miss Thompsons and further schooling; for how else could I have such vivid memories of the 'Walks' and the morning bun? The Walks are a public promenade, stretching from Greyfriars Tower to Guanock Bridge and Postern and the Red Mount; they are bordered by a double avenue of fine chestnuts, rich in autumn fruit. It was only a couple of hundred yards from Tower Place to the iron gates; and, on the way, were two most attractive halting places. Mr Thew, with one leg

[1] Author, among other things, of *Lives of Twelve Bad Men*, which would have scandalized the old ladies sadly.

shorter than the other, was licensed to keep his ambulatory booth at the southern corner, with every conceivable kind, colour, and flavour of 'rock', home-boiled from old-fashioned brown sugar. The piquancy of his sweets was enhanced, to our Liberal Party mind, when we were old enough to think we thought about politics, by the knowledge that he was own cousin to the great J. D. Thew, Jupiter Tonans of the aristocratic *Lynn Advertiser* and mainstay of the Tory Party—that he was own cousin, and the knowledge was irksome to the Tories, or at least to the small unfledged Tories with whom we exchanged occasional abuse, and who sucked their rock from the same stall. Exactly opposite, at the north corner of St James' Street, was Mrs Bush, as lame as Mr Thew but for very different reasons. Even if her buns had not been the best in the town, she was wonderful to us children as a victim of a memorable railway accident on the Hunstanton line. That line, built in the late fifties, was (I have been told) the cheapest ever yet constructed, costing only £3000 per mile. It ran all along the flat margin of the Wash; no tunnels, scarcely even a cutting anywhere; the land largely heath or fern, of no agricultural value. But, with almost its first train (August, 1863), there came what to the little Lynn world was a famous disaster. A few stray cattle broke the fence and wandered down the line, and a single bullock got into the way. It was 'bad for the coo', as George Stephenson said, but worse for the train; the engine was overturned, seven passengers lost their lives, and Mrs Bush lost a leg. We always longed to ask after her experiences, but never dared. Armed each with one of her buns, very sticky and curranty, we toddled to the Walks and looked for chestnuts, which lay on the ground in splendid abundance. Here was one of our first lessons on the vanity of human wishes. The disgust generated by that contrast between the newborn chestnut of to-day and the dry chestnut of the morrow was almost as great as the later contrast, at Yarmouth, between a pebble fresh from the sea and a pebble dried. I say *almost*; for at Yarmouth it took only half an hour to fade into the gloom of common pebbledom.

The morning bun did not blunt our appetite for dinner: far from it. At that midday meal there was hearty fare, welcomed daily without sense of monotony, for the present at least. A hot potato, baked in its jacket, was at first allowed in bed, until it was found that we nursed it too long, and overlay it in our sleep. For supper, hot milk and a special nursery biscuit, known in those days as 'German rusk', whereby hangs a tale pretty exactly datable. My father looked up one day from his paper at breakfast, and said with unusual violence that Ruskin must be mad. This was doubtless in 1862 or 1863, when *Unto this Last* shocked orthodox Liberals, and threatened to ruin *The Cornhill Magazine*, by preaching a political economy which should return to the ethical standards of the past. To my childish mind, it seemed tragic that a man with that delightful name should be such an outcast.

After supper, warm bed and last kisses: and then firelight dancing upon the nursery ceiling for a few minutes before dreamless sleep. My mother was even more solicitous, I think, to keep us from cold than from hunger. That is what I always feel in recalling the story of the boy whose poor mother could supply no bedclothes, but only one or two old boards to protect him from wet and cold, and who asked once: 'How do poor children do whose mothers have no boards to put over them?'

When morning came, Edmund and I were as yet too young to slip down and hunt for pears in the dewy grass. For we had a splendid tree of Jargonels, sweetest of pears, almost unprocurable nowadays because they bruise on the way to market, and last only a day or two at best. That shortlived perfection, however, was no practical drawback to us, in a family of eight children. Our mulberry, again (Plate III, p. 17), was the oldest I have ever seen except Milton's at Cambridge. Unlike that famous tree, it was very large and almost undecayed, until one great arm broke off and fell with a crash in the hot summer of 1868. In that year, the scare of cholera put this tree upon the list of fruit forbidden, though not, I must confess, altogether untasted. My uncle Anthony Allinson, our family doctor, was very fond of the berries, which were certainly big and luscious beyond anything that I have since seen. In ordinary years, he would come and dine solemnly with us and bring his own gadget, a broken-footed wineglass fixed upon the top of a sort of fishing rod. With this he would elaborately tickle a chosen berry until it slipped, unbruised, into the glass and thence into the voluptuous purse of his lips. It was an exhibition of ripe and patient professional skill which impressed me even more than anything he ever did to my sick ear. For in this early paradise of mine there was one cruel serpent: earache, far worse than any toothache I have since had. It came, as so often, after measles, in my fourth year; an abscess which almost altogether destroyed the left ear-drum. My mother, in such time as she could spare, would read to me from some story book: there was a child stolen by gipsies, and, again, one who fell (or was warned by his parents against falling) into a bottomless pond. I couldn't understand how it could possibly have no bottom, not even if it ran through to the other side of the earth; for, if so, why didn't all the water run out? By uncle Anthony's advice, I was taken to London for examination by the great Toynbee, father to Arnold and grandfather to the present London Professor. We reached Shoreditch (the Great Eastern had not yet extended to Liverpool Street) as a cold, wet night was falling: the mile or more of houses by the side of the railway, mostly poverty stricken and ill-lighted, yet generally without blinds and open to the traveller's curiosity, impressed me greatly. Toynbee, of course, began by inserting an otoscope for examination. The thing looked so like those metal dibbles which I had watched the grocer wielding against our Lynn cheeses, that I felt sure its function must be some wholesale and immediate scooping, and my poor mother had much ado to keep me reasonably quiet.

Through those early memories stalks the figure of old Dr Hunter. My impression is that all doctors, in those days, were still bound to the professional tradition not only of the long coat and tall silk hat, but also of the walking-cane, knobbed with silver or ivory. Certainly Dr Hunter was, and his hat, of prodigious size, was always tilted to the back of his head. He lived in one of the least fashionable streets, near the fishers of the North End, and had, I fancy, serious difficulties in keeping above water. I am not sure that I could ever have named any patient of his. His eccentricities were notorious, and they included astrology. 1858 was a famous comet year; and he predicted fame for all who were born under that favourable conjuncture, so that my mother had a natural prejudice in his favour. But, somewhere about 1868, this unbalanced doctor met with a still more unbalanced patient. The man, I believe, was literally crazy: unless rumour lied, poor Hunter scarcely escaped with life from his own surgery: and certainly I saw him abroad with almost as much sticking plaster on his brow as my cousin Calthrop Allinson, who, about that same time, had a similar misunderstanding with a pet monkey which gnawed suddenly upon his forehead. By that time I was at the Grammar School, and my masters' reports were not such as to give my mother special confidence in the astrological influence of that comet of 1858.

I have spoken of 'dreamless sleep'; but one exception must be made here. In general, we children probably answered to what was once said to me by the mother of my school friend Alfred Stable: 'If I had laid a penny upon his temple as he lay asleep, it would have been there next morning.' But there was one period, perhaps a year or more, when that peace was broken. It must have been before my thirteenth year; for we were still at Tower Place. Like most children, I was very much afraid of the dark; and our big roomy house had many dark corners of stair or passage between room and room. It was not, indeed, quite the atmosphere of E. M. Geldart's youthful home some ten years earlier, where he used to gloat upon a hymn beginning

> My thoughts on dreadful subjects roll,
> Damnation and the Dead.[1]

But there were ghost stories in the bound volumes of *Saturday Night*, forbidden but accessible; and once a children's party at South Lynn Vicarage afforded me two or three hours in a solitary corner with *The Night Side of Nature*, stories of unrelieved horror and unhealthy fascination. Finally, my father possessed, and we unearthed, a full report of the fairly recent Kent murder, committed by a jealous girl upon her small brother. Though these particular horrors were not traceably reproduced in detail, yet they may have been the main source of my distempered dreams. Once, I was lying prone upon a bed, under a great marble slab which had a steel spike running through my body. Another time, a terrible figure chased me out of bed: I sped madly down the passage to my father's dressing-room where he should properly be shaving, burst the door open with a cry, and he was not there! But the worst of all, the more

[1] See *A Son of Belial*, by Nitram Tradleg (i.e. Martin Geldart): a rare and most illuminating book, which I have not here at hand in America. The author was a distinguished Unitarian minister, Balliol scholar and father to a still more distinguished Law Professor at Oxford.

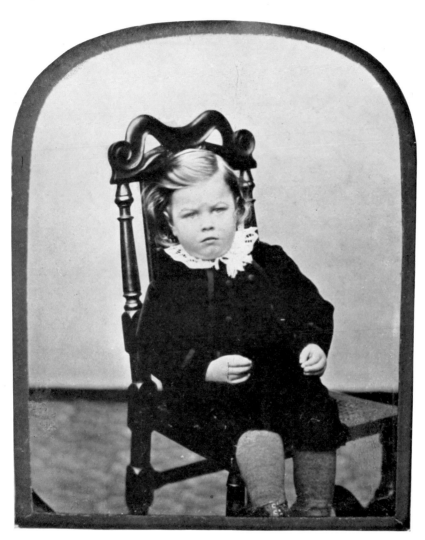

Plate II.   Aged four: about the time of the Royal Marriage, 1863
(see p. 9)

Plate III.   The old mulberry tree in the garden of Tower House,
Lynn (see p. 14)

'Rick'   'Etta'   'Essy'
Edmund   Gordon (the author)

horrible because most inexplicable, was one which recurred at intervals, perhaps half a dozen times in all. It was a great rolling sphere, of which I could note confusedly that it was in fact a congeries of spheres, fitted like the layers of an onion and each with its own independent revolutions. It grew under my view with immense rapidity: imagination saw no limit to its possible size. I was not afraid that it would roll upon me: it did not seem material enough for that. The horror was not in anything it might do to me, but only in the thing itself and what it was doing to itself: and yet neither at the moment nor afterwards could I explain why it should not have been what it was or seemed to be, and why it should not have done its own doings. Nor was there anything about it that could be called hideous in form. I can only ask the reader to believe that the disgust and loathing of those moments were proportionate to the impossibility of analysing the apparition, whether asleep or awake. But its recurrence drove me to open rebellion. I made up my mind that, next time it came, I would defy it as a thing of nothing, and rend that veil of sleep behind which the foul phantom masqueraded. The effort was completely successful; and that has been of great value to me in the confidence it has given of control over sleep itself, within reasonable limits. I may almost boast that all my subsequent nightmares have been in traceable conformity with the law laid down by a Victorian board-school boy in his examination essay on Dreams: 'Dreams are the last thing you have eaten before you went to bed. If it was meat or fried fish, they are very bad.' This belief in will as master of sleep has been a great friend to my work, even if there be no more in it than the Virgilian 'possunt, quia posse videntur'.[1]

Much of our activity and our thoughts was taken up, during these rudimentary years, by the State of Troy. Who first gave it that name, and when or why, I never discovered. We younger members accepted it by tradition. I remember that it had laws, in theory at least; but I don't think I ever understood them, except in so far as they were obvious laws of nature. 'Natural Law' worked with us very much as I suspect it worked in the Middle Ages, apart from academic theories. Richard, being four years older than I, was to that extent in the right: being four years younger than Jim, he was in the wrong. I was two years righter than Edmund; and all four of

[1] 'They can, because they think they can.'

us were righter than our four sisters, except where the disparity of age was too great, or they had definite parental decrees to back them up. The economics of Troy were as vague, and as far subject to the fluctuations of Natural Law, as its political theories. We had a currency, it is true, based upon H.M. General Post. My father had joined the Volunteer levy from the first. In those muzzle-loading days, each man had his own mould for making bullets, and his punch for cutting neat round wads from a sheet of thin felt. These were about the size of a shilling, and the punch could thus be used to cut a postage stamp from an old envelope, in excellent resemblance to a coin. His waste-paper basket gave us plenty of stamps; but I cannot remember any attempt at scientific discrimination of values: nor, again, would I venture to assert at this distance of time that any but imaginary values were ever exchanged for this imaginary coinage. Troy currency might be legal tender for cornelians found at Yarmouth, ranging in size from a pea to a bean, and dazzling in lustre when moistened with saliva in memory of their baptismal seaside innocence. But I fear that untold Troy pennies would never have commanded any appreciable fragment of Thew's rock.

Troy, however, was a very valuable factor in our education. Geographically, it was most favourable: a large unfurnished attic immediately above the nursery. We were in nobody's way, and nobody in ours. An exactly similar attic, at the west, was used as a servants' bedroom. Between the two was some fifty feet of desert, nominally forbidden ground, but actually approached by a door from Troy. This desert had no floor: nothing but open joists, with intervals of plaster through which any erring foot would plunge into some lower room, and one long narrow plank from end to end, by following which authorized explorers might find empty trunks, discarded draught screens, rolls of carpet, whenever any emergency should recall these to civilization. Troy's one window looked east, straight upon the theatre and Greyfriars' Tower, if the view had not been partly blocked by a great chimney stack, broad enough to contain the flues of three rooms beneath us. This window being in the slope of the roof, one could creep out over the sill and sit in a sort of pocket, perfectly secure, and puffed up with superiority over ordinary folk creeping like insects below. From the back of the room itself nothing could be seen but this broad, flat chimney of time-stained grey brick, with flickering cloud shadows in chequered weather. One day, however, these shadows assumed special significance. I was alone, very possibly with a bad conscience, but certainly I had a hallucination optically clear and distinct, though psychologically far more vague. A black shadow passing slowly over this chimney curtain seemed like an exact silhouette portrait of Satan, as depicted in *Pilgrim's Progress* and other similar sources. It lasted, of course, for less than a second; so that the mind could not so much say 'that *is* distinct' as 'that *was* distinct'. Still, with this modification, distinct it was, and carried conviction. It scared me at the moment, and made me shy of going alone again into the room for a little time; but not, I think, for long. For one thing, there had been no suggestion of attack or menace; I had seen the devil, but he had shown no sign of seeing me. At the worst, this was Satan going about his daily business and seeking whom he might devour; a warning that this is a dangerous world, but nothing more immediate than we were constantly hearing around us. In one child, that kind of suggestion may breed haunting terror; with another, or the same at another time, there may be as little terror as the little fish shows for a pike, so long as the monster is not evidently concerned with him.

What Troy did for us, was to ease a great deal of family friction; for, though the girls might show great patience, we boys did not. The free room and undisturbed occupations enabled us to learn much for ourselves. It taught us the valuable lesson of using our own hands for the fulfilment of our own wants. For instance, we had a large number of wooden bricks, wholes and halves and quarters, cut into uncompromising parallelograms, with which we had to build arches and solve other small engineering problems. Thus our wishes and our fancies were tempered with realism. No schoolmaster, and few parents, can show a child its own mistakes so clearly as its personal experience does. Tell a boy that his argument is illogical, or his ambitions are foolish, and he will not believe you: but you do not need to tell him where he has failed to make a box as neat and efficient as the one his brother is making. Mark Twain has written somewhere a golden sentence of autobiography: 'When I was 14 years old, I thought my father an old fool; but, when I had grown to 21, it seemed to me that the old man had learned an extraordinary amount in those 7 years.'

CHAPTER IV

VICTORIAN LYNN (1)

IN EAST ANGLIA, as in Massachusetts, Lynn looks across the bay to Boston. In the Middle Ages it was the more important town of the two. It was then under the lordship of the Bishop of Norwich—*Lenna Episcopi*; but under Henry VIII, by a forced exchange, it became *King's Lynn*. To all faithful natives, in my boyhood, it was Lynn pure and simple in ordinary speech: the one and only Lynn. Even now, we suspect a cockney or a foreigner in the man who adds 'King's'. It may be that, in these more literate modern days, the full and formal name is beginning to prevail even among the inhabitants of Lynn, just as 'Huns*tan*ton' prevails over the immemorial pronunciation of 'Hunston', and perhaps some day men may even speak of Wy*mond*ham' and 'Cholm*ond*eley'. But in this chapter I write of the days when we lived in Lynn pure and simple.

Of this simplicity—as apart from purity, which is an ambiguous word—a memorial remained in the north-east corner of the Tuesday Market Place. Here was the last, or nearly last, burning on record for the crime of 'petty treason'; it was (and is?) marked by a cross cut in the plaster of the wall. To compass the King's life was, of course, High Treason; but it was Petty Treason to compass that of one's immediate lord and master; for the *servus* to attempt against his *dominus*. A miserable servant-girl had abetted her lover in burgling a house; he also killed the owner, and the girl was burned for her treason.

This, I think, is typical of the old-fashioned spirit which had hampered Lynn even in the days when one of her two parliamentary representatives was always Sir Robert Walpole, representative of moderately progressive Whiggery. After Walpole, the political barometer fell (or rose, if the reader prefers) into almost unbroken Toryism: to that I shall come later. Meanwhile, here is a story from my father's experience. Mr Mickle was a respected ironmonger, as several generations of Mickles had probably been. Then came two brothers Micklethwaite into Lynn, pushing men from the north, I think. At any rate, they set up nearly opposite to Mickle, and soon cut very heavily into his custom. Mickle discussed this matter one day with my father, either professionally or in ordinary friendly talk. Sales were diminishing, and stock was rusting on his hands. My father suggested some mild form of clearance sale; a yearly and even monthly phenomenon nowadays, but then fairly novel even in more advanced business centres than Lynn. To Mickle, this seemed revolutionary. 'What, sell at a loss! And who's to pay me interest on all these things that I've had for so many years?'

That was at the turn of the sixties; let us pass now to the turn of the twentieth century. The Librarian of the Stanley Public Library was promoted to a similar post at Luton, a thriving manufacturing town in Bedfordshire. One of his new acquaintances asked him, 'Do they still eat snails at Lynn?' 'Why, did they ever eat snails there?' 'Oh yes, very fond of them; only I hear now they find the snails too fast for them.'

This kind of backwater existence was fairly common among the middle-sized or under-sized ancient boroughs of those days: Lynn, in 1861, had 15,981 inhabitants. When my father first remembered, the mail from Lynn to Wisbech or vice versa (13 miles) went through London, 98 miles off, and paid mileage. Thus, apart from the appalling waste of time (for railways were then non-existent) the correspondents were charged for 196 miles traversed by each letter. Two other of my father's stories may come here without too great irrelevance; I give them as he used to tell them, without possibility of checking them here from documentary evidence. Soon after Parliamentary Reform, the Commons began to take Municipal Reform in hand. In some cases, at any rate, the Borough Corporations had become mere cliques, self-perpetuated by co-operation. The Bill naturally prescribed real public elections; and the Wisbech Corporation took its measures accordingly. Two Radical candidates were in the field, X and Y, among a majority of Tories. Shortly before election day, X received a courteous official letter appointing him Borough Auditor, while Y received a similar letter of appointment to the office of—I forget what, let us say Registrar. Both offices had become mainly or purely formal; both were unsalaried; and in both cases refusal carried with it a fine of £10. The two Radicals, both poor men, pulled a long face and paid the fines, commenting freely upon the shabby trick. By return of post, Y received an appointment to the auditorship, and X to the registrarship. The second fine was beyond their resources; election day was at hand, and thus the Wisbech Corporation was saved from any intrusion of independent thought.

Poole, one of the most notoriously corrupt boroughs in the kingdom, outdid even this. The Town Clerks of Britain had sufficient political influence to procure an insertion in the Bill of a clause protecting jealously their vested interests. Each existing Town Clerk was to be secured in his office for life. Or if, at any time, the town wanted to get rid of him, and could produce no conclusive evidence of his unfitness, he was to receive his full salary until death. At Poole, the 'old gang' took advantage of this clause to dismiss their Town Clerk without reason assigned, and appoint his son as successor. Thus the ratepayers were doubly taxed for the benefit of a corrupt gang.

These things must not be forgotten when we are tempted to lay disproportionate stress upon the defects of our own age. Without for one moment overlooking or palliating these, let us take a longer view. Two hundred years ago, the elder Pitt made an epoch, it may. almost be said, by refusing to rob the officers of the two Services to the extent of £30,000 a year. His predecessors had regularly withheld the pay for a whole year, enjoying meanwhile interest upon the vast sums invested in their name. Rapacities and dishonesties within the Anglican Church were almost as scandalous in those days, here and there, as in the Church of Rome during the Middle Ages. Whereas, before 1832, many reasonable men feared that this partial democratization of the House of Commons would open floodgates of dishonesty and vulgarism, yet, on the whole, how can we now doubt that its main effect has been to let in fresh air? This is our best justification for frank and microscopic examination of the records of the past. Only thus can we escape from the agnosticism with which I once heard a distinguished historian close a discussion: 'We shall never know anything about those people.'

Lynn was not so very far superior, in those ways, to Wisbech and Poole. The first parliamentary election I remember was that of 1868. I was not quite ten; but the family was politically minded, since my father was Agent for the Liberal Party in the borough. That job, in a predominantly Tory borough, was far from a sinecure.

At a not very distant date, in 1852, a sort of semi-Liberal had indeed been elected, in the person of Lord Jocelyn, who sat until his death in 1854. Feeling ran so high then that my mother had to smuggle Lord Jocelyn out by a back door into a dark court of St James' Street. She believed to her dying day that she had saved his life; and it is pretty certain that she did save him from something of the indignities recorded at Eatanswill in *The Pickwick Papers*. For there was as yet no Ballot Act. Votes were recorded verbally and openly at the 'hustings', a public platform where one teller sat for each party, to record them. Messengers ran backwards and forwards to the respective committee rooms, carrying news of the mounting totals, which were at once placarded, to the encouragement or discouragement of the respective parties.

Lynn, after all, was a typical middle-sized, old-fashioned borough.[1] Disraeli, the year before, had 'dished the Whigs' by bringing in a further extension of the franchise; we had now practically household suffrage, probably ten times wider than the old 'freeman' limitation of before 1832. But a large proportion of these new voters were painfully deficient both in political education and in political morality. Bribery, therefore, was rampant. For, in the first place, the briber had a certain amount of public security: there was the open record; the bribee delivered the goods over the counter. In the second place, the legislation with regard to corrupt practices was still very imperfect. It was not as now, when a single case of bribery, whether by a candidate or any of his agents, ruins his case. One had to prove enough to give a reasonable presumption that bribery had actually swayed the election; and, in fact, this Lynn contest of 1868 gave rise to an immensely complicated and costly trial. The whole district beyond St Nicholas Church, the 'North End', was a fishermen's quarter: and that was the main hotbed of electoral corruption. Lynn was not quite so bad as Yarmouth, where the nautical element was even stronger, and the borough was disenfranchised at least twice, in punishment for the scandals disclosed. But it may be said of the Lynn fisher folk that, even more than other wage earners, they were tempted to sell their vote, to drink away the proceeds, and thence

[1] Trollope's *Rachel Ray* gives an admirable picture, in quiet naturalistic fashion, of the kaleidoscopic changes in social relations wrought by a disputed election in a small borough.

to fight away the fumes of liquor. My eldest brother, who was now nearing the end of his teens, and already registered as 'able seaman', took me round the Tuesday Market Place to count the broken windows and the pools of blood—only from noses, of course, but sufficiently impressive on the pavement. As we came to the corner where St Nicholas Street debouches from the North End, there came out a huge virago ·of 13 or 14 stone, with the picturesque fisher-woman's shawl over her head, not so much disguised as enveloped in liquor. She saw the blue Liberal rosettes in our buttonholes; and, without a word, she smote my brother full on the nose, and mingled his blood with the rest.

That election, though Lynn returned two Tories as usual, was fateful for the country. Britain as a whole returned a sweeping Liberal majority, which remained five years in power and wrought changes which seemed then almost revolutionary. The Ballot Act, compulsory education, abolition of purchase in the army, disestablishment of the alien Protestant Church in Ireland, abolition of religious tests in our universities, competitive examinations for the Civil Service, were all brought in between 1868 and 1874. Then ensued, of course, the great reaction of 1874, when Disraeli could point the finger of scorn at his rivals, now aligned on the Opposition Bench, as 'a range of exhausted volcanoes'. Meanwhile those revolutionaries had earned me probably my first black eye at school from an older cousin who heard daily at home that the policy of universal education for rich and poor would be fatal to British character: while I at my home heard the contrary every morning, but probably knew or thought as little about the matter as my cousin. One reaction to that Bill deserves serious attention; it shocked the out-and-out individualists who held that no good can come out of compulsion, anywhere or at any time, and who in effect were more ready to face eternal failure through the apathy of the multitude than to succeed at the price of abandoning their traditional shibboleth. It was not every Liberal who answered with Macaulay, in face of those who argued in 1847 that Voluntarism would do all that was necessary for popular education, 'if we will duly wait with patience. Wait with patience! Why, we have been waiting ever since the Heptarchy! How much longer are we to wait? Till the year 2847? Or till the year 3847?' I am glad to remember that my father had an unshaken belief in popular education, and in his later years was less and less inclined to hope for improvement anywhere on the hard-and-fast principle of *laissez-faire*.

During all the rest of our time at Lynn, two Tories were nearly always returned. The senior member, Lord Stanley, afterwards Earl of Derby and a Cabinet Minister, was firm and unshakable; the only chance of a real fight was round the second seat. Lord Stanley's succession to his father's title left Mr Bourke as senior member, and brought in Lord Claud Hamilton, son of the Duke of Abercorn. Finding myself once, at an official dinner, side by side with his elder brother, Lord George, I was obliged to confess that, some thirty years earlier, I had joined in the election chorus of

> Young for ever!
> Hamilton in the river!
> A knife in his heart, and a fork in his liver!

But Toryism was too strong, and Young was beaten; yet the minority was less than thirty, and he could have counted on fifty more from the fishermen's quarter, but for a foul wind which kept them out in the Wash. Those were the days when house-to-house personal canvassing by the candidates was *de rigueur*.[1] At the corner of Athenaeum Plain stood a butcher's shop, kept by Mr Massingham, first cousin to H. W. Massingham, the famous journalist. Lord Claud was a slender, rather pale, figure in long frock coat and fault-less silk hat. Later on, as Chairman of the Great Eastern Railway, he showed great business qualities, and was mainly responsible for the remarkable revival of that almost moribund Company. But, to the ordinary spectator, he looked almost a stage caricature of the drawling aristocrat. Massingham was well known as a militant Liberal, and Lord Claud approached him in hail-fellow-well-met fashion: 'Why, Mr Massingham, I see you have nothing but blue meat here, and I always take yellow meat.' 'Wall, my Lord, if that yaller meat don't dew ye more good than that seem to dew, I should advise ye to take to our blew.'

Lynn has enough genuine traditions to dispense with two false-hoods which were current in my boyhood and are very likely re-peated to-day. In St Margaret's Church are several slabs of Purbeck

[1] Here, again, Trollope gives a most faithful picture in *Rachel Ray*.

marble which show the sockets from which funeral brasses have been torn. This vandalism has been attributed to Cromwell's soldiers: but in fact the richest of those stolen brasses was still existing, a little more than a century ago, when the antiquary Gough, fortunately for us, took an impression from it in printer's ink. It was stolen, I believe, by a fraudulent sexton of the church. Again, the caretaker of the Red Mount chapel was wont to show, in the southern wall of the basement vault, an arched doorway which, now obstructed, was said to have formerly opened into a passage leading to Rising Castle, three and a half miles distant in an almost due northerly direction. The fact is that my great-grandfather used to lead his pony in and out by that door. For it is subterraneous only in the sense that it is below the top of the little mount: one would need to clear only four or five yards of earth away, to find the doorway on the level of all the surrounding turf.

An old pupil, who came up to Cambridge just after the Armistice, writes to remind me that his own children will see a world differing as much from that of my father, born in 1818, as the world of that year differed from that of our Tudor ancestors. In no external matter has that change been greater than in locomotion. My father in his boyhood never saw a railway engine, nor heard of the electric telegraph till shortly before he was married. Until I had come to half the Psalmist's span of seventy years it was illegal to use any mechanically propelled vehicle upon the roads of Great Britain at more than three miles an hour; and, even so, the machine must be preceded by a man waving a red flag as warning to horses and their drivers. In my childhood, the wooden velocipede, the 'bone-shaker', could be seen as a rarity at the Crystal Palace. Then came the 'penny-farthing', upon which a good rider could do fifteen miles an hour on a good road, while horses shied into the ditch, or turned tail in terror. At Pentney, even our very sober old pony had often to be held in as soon as we saw a cyclist coming. The rider was balanced above the high front wheel; my brother Rick had one of 60 inches' diameter: I was content with a modest 56. The equilibrium was so delicate that, downhill in the dark, a little loose stone in the road might send us headlong over the handles. Rick, who had an unhealthy taste for medical books, convinced himself for a month or two that one toss of this description had torn his liver in half, on

the strength of some such accident which he found recorded. Even
the railroad was rudimentary by modern standards. Ernest Foxwell
of St John's, somewhere about 1870, I believe, while still in his teens,
wrote an enthusiastic booklet upon future railroad possibilities, and
sent a copy to Ruskin. The great man replied: 'Young man, you are
doing the Devil's work, but you have done it d—— well.' The
first excursion trains to Yarmouth often contained three or four
primitive third-class coaches, mere wooden boxes without windows,
half-sheltered by a roof on iron supports. One of my schoolfellows
had seen a passenger truck that was destitute even of roof. It was
in 1880 that some girl cousins came to us from Surrey, and told us
that, in those advanced semi-metropolitan districts, it was becoming
socially respectable for ladies to travel third class. About the same
time came rudimentary heating in winter by means of 'foot-warmers'
filled with hot water, about a yard long and shaped like a flattened
sausage. One had often to tip a porter to get this luxury. In the early
eighties, during a recrudescence of Fenian terroristic explosions, a
villager on one of the Kentish railways found in his compartment
this strange mass of metal, too hot to touch; he seized it by the
handle, threw it out of the window, and stopped the train to report
how he had got rid of the infernal machine.

CHAPTER V

VICTORIAN LYNN (2)

ONE could mark at Lynn age-long conservatism in the arrested development of the building areas. Within the sluggish ditches, or 'fleets', which with the great river formed almost the only defences Lynn ever had, there were large open spaces, mainly half-forgotten relics of the four different monastic precincts: Greyfriars, Blackfriars, Austin Friars and Whitefriars. The whole of London Road, from the Greyfriars field to the South Gates, was mere modern jerry-building with the exception of a few old houses hidden behind, and clustering round, South Lynn Church. It seemed characteristic, though no doubt it was merely fortuitous, that Bardell and Snodgrass should have been next-door neighbours on London Road; and behind, in the little petrified nucleus, the first three publicans who were ever fined by the magistrates for breach of the brand-new Early Closing Regulations: Benjamin Wagg, Elizabeth Jagg, and Solomon Spragg. Benjamin Wagg was our milkman, and our German rusks at Tower Place were dipped in milk from his cows.

The cattle market, again, did and still does mark the wide precincts held by the Dominicans, 'till they decayed through pride'. A few cows or sheep grazed habitually among thistles and nettles round Greyfriars, or 'The Old Tower', as it was called *par excellence*. Along the riverside, on the other hand, houses still jostled each other, as they had done in past centuries, for elbow room; and even the most stately had seldom as much garden as we were lucky enough to enjoy at Tower Place.

When people mentioned, as a great curiosity, that butter was sold by the yard at Cambridge, my father would reply that at Lynn beer was sold by the pound. The underlying truth of that quip referred to one of our medieval survivals, from the days when there had been no hard-and-fast distinction between urban and agricultural life. Not far inside the South Gates, we had a great open field which had once been the site of the Whitefriars' Monastery and its precincts. At one corner of this field stood the 'Scots Grey' public house; and, next door, the Pound, for the reception of stray cattle until their owners should redeem them with a fine.

The Tuesday Market Place, with the broad King Street leading up to it on the river side, gives an excellent idea of mercantile prosperity in the past. The 'Duke's Head', with its imposing seventeenth-century façade, was originally built for one such family: so again with Bank House and another on the west side; again with two or three in King Street, which for practical purposes is a continuation of the market square. 'Allen's House', opposite St Nicholas Church, was too stately to find any suitable occupant in my day: its marble chimneypieces and heavy mahogany woodwork and hangings of stamped Spanish leather were then out of place on the edge of what had become a mere fishermen's quarter. So again, with that at the other extremity of the river front, which my doctor-uncle, Anthony Allinson, now shared with Mr Garland, the shipping agent, several doorways being built up to secure privacy for both households. There, again, all the woodwork was of splendid solid mahogany, and the staircase almost palatial. Most of the larger Lynn houses, including our own on Tower Place, as I have said, had nearly all their rooms in front, with nothing but passages and offices behind. But few were so well oriented as Tower House had the luck to be, straight in the eye of the midday sun. For the Lynn builders showed what Erasmus, long before, had branded as one of the weak points of English town life: 'They never consider towards which quarter of the heavens their windows or doors look.' Insufficient use was made even of such limited space as could be obtained. In Queen Street is a beautiful doorway with twisted pillars, of the early seventeenth century, leading into a diminutive garden court and thence to a brick tower which rises a couple of stories above all the buildings round. It is built upon a fifteenth-century cellar, with stone vaulted roof. From the antiquarian and picturesque point of view, this house is a gem; but it is so cramped that the owner is always glad to moderate the rent for any tenant who can be trusted to keep it in order. Thus, as railway and highroad conditions improved, the richer urban families moved more and more into the country. From being merchant princes in a small way, they became a sort of country squires. I remember the last generation of one of these, lingering on in the town as a dying class: let us call them the

Bantocks. Two old maids lived near the church, worked embroidery for it, exercised quiet Anglo-Catholic pressure upon successive vicars and curates, and finally bequeathed their money to it. One brother, childless, lived in a country rectory; to all who came to look at his church he boasted of the Lynn 'prince merchants' his ancestors. His brother, the youngest, had been (I think) a junior officer in the navy: his popular nickname was 'Commodore Bantock'. At the 'Three Pigeons', his perpetual evening resort, the company often enjoyed their own favourite diversion with him. He was challenged to walk round the room with a sixpenny piece balanced on the edge of his glass of gin and water. A tiny spot of cobbler's wax, placed by some wag at the bottom of the coin, kept it safely in place, while the 'Commodore', tacking heavily from side to side, suspected nothing in the storm of applause which greeted his performance.

There were others who clung to the past with even more limpet-like tenacity. Along Priory Lane, beside St Margaret's churchyard, ran a narrow row of medieval buildings which, until the Dissolution, had been inhabited by Benedictine monks from Norwich Cathedral. This Priory figures conspicuously in the medieval autobiography of Margery Kempe.[1] These buildings had been partitioned off into sections of some twenty feet long, in which humble tenants, artisans or labourers or pensioners, lived like so many hermit crabs each in its borrowed shell. One jobbing tailor, at any rate, managed to rear a family in those narrow quarters; and another became quite familiar to me when I had struck up a friendship with its inhabitant, Martin Dean, an ex-sailor who had charge of the public baths. Professionally, Martin was grim; when one older schoolboy attempted to show by his watch that we were not exceeding the statutory half-hour, he replied, 'I don't care for your old tin kittle of a watch; but, if yer don't git out, I'll pitch yer in.' In private, however, he was the essence of kindness; and his monastic cell was crowded with all sorts of sailors' marvels: a three-masted ship inside a gin bottle; a little rum cask formed from the single joint of a great bamboo; a centipede six or eight inches long, capable of killing countless human beings, but now suspended in a long chemist's phial of alcohol. This, when our friendship had ripened for weeks

[1] *The Book of Margery Kempe*, ed. S. B. Meech (Early English Text Society), 1940.

and months, he gave to me, and it added greatly to my family importance. He wore his white beard plaited into the form of a cravat, which he tucked into his Guernsey vest. The family invited me to come and see him in his coffin. It was good to have seen death first in such a quiet and honest shape.

But most crustacean of all was a citizen of my father's standing. Thomas Moody owned one of the old houses, inhabited once by Dr Burney, father to the lady novelist and friend of the great Dr Johnson. Moody had been born in it, had inherited it from his father, and possessed no other occupation in life beyond inhabiting it. He was some ten years younger than my father, so that his four children answered pretty exactly to the four youngest of our family. There was much interchange of sociabilities; but Mr Moody himself was almost always shut up in his 'office', busy with mysterious nothings. He did not drink, he did not smoke; he did nothing, so far as we or his own children knew, beyond killing time at this 'office', and taking a vague objectless walk in the morning, with another in the afternoon. A remark or two caught here and there between my father, usually so reticent, and my mother, let us know that 'Tommy' Moody was unfortunate in having inherited just enough to keep himself without the necessity of any real business. His wife and children, pretty plainly, felt the same. He was kind-hearted, and they met him with Victorian obedience; but there seemed little depth of respect. Then, suddenly, came a real tragedy. We ourselves had left Lynn by that time, and I was out of my teens. One morning (I believe, with little or no previous warning) Moody announced to his wife that they must give up the old house. Family expenses had been mounting from year to year; one son was now half-way through his University course; he himself had been silently spending from capital, and the old house must now be sold. They moved into another, much smaller and less commodious; and Mrs Moody, a brave woman and excellent housekeeper, declined to accept the position of a *déclassée*. But for Moody there was no longer any refuge of 'office' or 'business'; and he felt himself fallen to rise no more. His solitary walks filled now a greater part of the day, and were even more aimless, except for one unbroken resolution. During the ten or twelve years that remained to him, he never saw the old house again. It was, literally, no more than a stone's throw from his present abode; but, from whatever part of the town he came, he always chose side streets which avoided that heart-wrench. It had almost the tragic leaden significance of that line in Wordsworth's *Michael*:

And never lifted up a single stone.

Another eccentric figure was Miss Garrod, who owned the house in King Street which now belongs to the Girls' High School. It possessed the enchantment not only of a garden on the river, but of a bridge which spanned Ferry Lane and led to another garden beyond. She and her brother had inherited a considerable fortune; the brother had died in early manhood, and her talk always ran pathetically upon his brilliant gifts and his sainted memory. She herself was a typical bluestocking, and suffered from frequent headaches. These, she used to tell us, could be most efficiently dispelled by balancing her Swiss musical box on her head, and playing it through from end to end. This story always delighted us by its evident providential moral; for she was markedly dolichocephalic, of that 'mallet-headed' type which Aubrey describes in the philosopher Hobbes; and in imagination we could always see the box resting securely upon that tableland of cranium.

Few indeed were such gardens on the actual riverside; but, on the other hand, the quays were full of busy interest to our primitive provincial minds. In much later years, when my eldest brother was a very prosperous doctor in South Africa, I tried to persuade him to take a year's holiday and come back to Lynn. He replied: 'It would break my heart to go down to the riverside where we used to see timber ships building, and find nothing there but tin carcasses.' That was only too comprehensible; yet Lynn's antiquarian interest has endured and is likely long to endure, if the buildings survive this present war. Quite apart from the magnificent churches, and that Custom House which is a seventeenth-century gem and is fragrant with the memory of the explorer Vancouver, the whole quayside at Lynn presents a mass of buildings claiming, almost without exception, the veneration of centuries. True, daylight falls now upon the Devil's Alley, which once ran under cover from Nelson Street to the quayside, and showed at its darkest point a queer cobble in the pavement shaped like a gigantic human foot.

Here and there, again, in different parts of the town, I have seen masses of ancient mulberry-coloured brick pulled down and sold to mend the roads, no Cambridge College having had the foresight to buy those priceless materials for its own uses, until these last days when they are already grown almost unprocurable. But there still remain fourteenth-century stone doorways in St Nicholas Street and New Conduit Street; carved oak doors of the fifteenth in St Nicholas Street and Nelson Street; and the sculptured corner post of the 'Gallant Sailor' inn; and the old Tolbooth arches reverently transported to safety close beside the Greyfriars Tower.

My father's office was at first in the back rooms, numerous and roomy, of Tower Place itself. There was a tin speaking-tube from his room above to the clerks below, delightful for us to practise upon, until it was once abused by pouring a glass of water down upon the hearer: thenceforward the upper room was out of bounds.

My father would seldom talk business; but occasionally I got interesting glimpses. The iron garden railings at East Gates House began to suffer from periodical vandalism, for no ascertainable reason. At last the criminal was found; a blacksmith who lived exactly opposite was bribing a tramp to do the job, and thus bring profit to himself for the mending. My father had to go and interview the tramp at the workhouse. He told his history: he had been an Etonian and Fellow of King's College, Cambridge. 'Then you are a clergyman.' 'Yes, certainly.'

A farmer client drove one of the smartest gigs in the county, and was inordinately proud of his steed as 'the 'oss that killed the lawyer'. This previous owner, I believe, had aspired to honours in the hunting-field, but with fatal results. Another farmer could not write, yet was ashamed to make a bare cross, and therefore carried a little card in his waistcoat pocket, with J. FOX in block capitals, which he would imitate with infinite pains. One day he had forgotten his model, and was driven to extemporize; the result was J. FXO. Another had gone through the retreat from Russia in 1812. Born in North Italy, he had been conscripted by Napoleon: after Waterloo he became courier to a rich English family, married the lady's maid, and kept an inn at Downham until his death at the age of more than a hundred. I read his obituary in the paper and pointed it out to my father as a remarkable fact: his only answer was, 'Didn't you know that? You might often have seen him at the office.' It was a bitter disappointment that my father's silence should have deprived me of the boast of having seen such a link with the past. Another client had been all but drowned; he described the process itself as not wholly unpleasant, though resuscitation was infernal. 'The water was quite smooth, and I lay there on the sand, watching the stars in the sky and wondering who would feed my chickens that evening.' At Felsted, I had a somewhat similar experience in a very small way. A bigger schoolfellow was resolved to drag me away from the table, and I was resolved to cling on. He pulled me by the scruff of my neck, with consequent semi-suffocation as I held out stubbornly. Then I felt a rather pleasant sensation, as the blood gathered in my head; almost a sort of alcoholic exhilaration. My next consciousness was of lying on the floor while my antagonist told me 'not to sham'.

I wish that I had seen for myself the Scotch woollen pedlars of whom my father used to tell. These men came down for a whole season with such a stock of cloth or hosiery as they could lay in; the bulk came by wagon or luggage train, and the pedlar divided this into parcels which he carried on his own back from town to village, from village to town. These loads were such as to strain physique and resolution almost to breaking-point. Over one of the more ordinary local pedlars there hung a romantic mystery. He was seen one evening riding in the cart of another man fairly well known in the district. Nobody ever saw him again; and, apart from the crude fact of this inexplicable disappearance, there was no reason to suspect foul play. My father was once betrayed by this into his only unprofessional lapse that I can remember. He was asked to give a few reminiscences on the occasion (I think) of the opening of our Public Library in its new glory which the Carnegie Endowment had created. He told the story, adding incautiously the actual name of the cart owner, who had naturally been examined on suspicion at the time. He was much pained, though in no way surprised, that it brought him a strong letter of protest from a descendant.

I cannot separate Lynn from Yarmouth. It was not only the same fisher folk and rich Norfolk dialect (only even more so), and heavy ripe Norfolk fruit on the market stalls, and bloaters of a size and quality unknown to less favoured counties, but also because the one came as a natural and inevitable sequel to the other. For Yarmouth was our yearly holiday place, until the years when we left Lynn for the country, and in that sense everything became holiday. The 'Rows', those narrow parallel lanes which took their shape and extent from the fishing-net which the family had been wont to spread out for drying on the sands, gave Yarmouth town a character quite unique in its way, which will soon become merely traditional, even if the present air raids have not already obliterated the ancient landmarks. There we could gloat upon the tobacco shop in the main Row, with its Highlander opening a snuff-box for a pinch: a figure as large as life, gaudily coloured, and standing outside upon the pavement like one of ourselves. Again, the deep yellow sands were a Golconda to us, with amber, jet, cornelians, and agates. These, as the tide receded, we sought with eager rivalry for size and for lustre, and always with the sustaining hope that one or other of us might find a specimen worthy of being made into an actual brooch or scarfpin by the man whose little shop on the parade advertised him as THE ONLY WORKING LAPIDARY in the town. We felt what a gulf there must be between this man and the vulgar horde who did indeed expose polished stones in their windows, but who did not work.

Trains came down from London, and steamboats from Margate, bringing trippers—and, tell it not in Gath, their attendant fleas—to those hot, swarming, August sands. The retreating tide left delicious little pools, with opportunities for all sorts of ambitious hydrostatic engineering. But the most Yarmouthy of all Yarmouth things were the seaside minstrels, black or white. There were songs which, since then, I have hardly ever heard, and in this twentieth century never at all.

But this attempt to recapitulate in detail leaves me all the more sensitive to the overwhelming impression of Yarmouth in its totality upon our infant minds. A Bishop of Oxford, Dr Paget, once recounted his own experience with a Mothers' Union excursion from his large urban parish to the seaside. Next day, he asked one of the oldest how she had enjoyed the day. She said, 'Oh, Sir! that took me quite aback! I sits there and I says to myself: "Well, here's the first thing I ever seed in my life as there's enough on for everybody."' To us, during a few weeks yearly, Yarmouth was such a type of God's own plenty.

Our most distinguished Lynn citizen, from the seventies to the nineties, was Harvey Goodwin, son of a local lawyer. Born in that house with the iron railings close by the East Gate, he became Second Wrangler and Second Smith's Prizeman at Cambridge; then a University Preacher of unusual popularity; and eventually Bishop of Carlisle. When he revisited the town in 1884, he stayed with the then head of the firm, living in the same old house, and still cherishing the same old cellar. My father and I were among the guests at dinner, where we finished up with a glass of Waterloo port; a vintage celebrated in its own year of 1815, and so carefully treasured by these owners that there still remained something of its strength and bouquet.

In these Canadian days, three thousand miles away from Lynn, there comes a recurrent dream which never visited me at home. I find myself wandering about there and peering into out-of-the-way corners, and discovering things that my waking hours had never seen. The place melts into just such a dream-city—*alterthümlich Niederländisch*—as Heine saw while he leaned over the gunwale in the North Sea. The Puck who plays with our sleeping brains, the monkey who plays with our colours and our canvas when the master has quitted the studio, takes me to the north-eastern corner of that narrow dingy lane which runs parallel to St James' and New Conduit Street; a mean passage darkened all along the southern side by high windowless walls. At that corner stood a mean public house, with one door on the street and another on the lane: double outlet fit for dubious deeds. One dark night, more than sixty years ago, the owner of an opposite house in the street was awakened in the small hours by a horse pawing almost under his window, and then clattering madly over the cobbles towards the South Gates. Some days later, a body turned up at the Cut Bridges, bloated with drifting up and down the tides, and gashed horribly across the forehead. This was a man who had last been seen alive at the little inn. Nothing beyond this could be elicited at the inquest or afterwards; but my brother, whose legal work introduced him to many secrets, told me once 'There was a woman in that job' and refused to go further. Here, then, my Puck starts me, and presently shows me,

not quite things that never were on sea or land, but sights com-
pounded from a hundred impressions at home or abroad, woven
into a coherent phantasmagoria much as Thackeray created his
Captain Costigan out of 'a hundred scraps and heel-taps of character'.

I find myself walking warily at first between that sinister side
door and the blind wall, as apprehensive as when I once tried a short
cut, with wife and children, from Aldgate Station to Liverpool
Street, and found myself entangled in slums swarming with squalor
and disquieting faces. But gradually the blank brickwork on my left
changes into relics of the old Greyfriars' convent, far loftier and
more intricate in lacework of hewn stone than it ever could have
been in reality. The restorer has disengaged half of this from its
parasitical modern accretions, and has revealed a structure almost
rivalling Mulciber's palace in *Paradise Lost*:

> Out of the earth a fabric huge
> Rose like an exhalation.

It might really owe something to distant memories of Milton read
in class at Felsted; at any rate, it swallows up instantly the mean
background of actual Lynn. This dream-palace is half in ruin; but,
as at Tintern and Melrose and Castleacre, and a dozen other dis-
mantled abbeys, the half is almost greater than the whole, and we
wonder whether the building was ever quite so beautiful in its in-
tegrity. So this revelation fascinates me in my dream, as my last
visit to Ghent, in 1914, fascinated me with what had been done,
since the first in 1880, to disengage the Château des Comtes from its
degrading slum-encumbrances. Lost in wonder that I had never
seen all this before, I drift on westwards and cross the High Street,
the old Mercer's Row, and plunge into Baker Lane. The little fourteenth-century house at the corner is still there, but presently the
lane narrows and deteriorates into a squalid passage, untouched by
the sun, with nameless filth on the pavements and repellent faces
at half-open doors, like Butter Canal Street at Antwerp in 'the
unreformed' seventies, or similar slums at Rouen and Naples and
Ravenna. Hastening onwards, I emerge with infinite relief upon
King's Staith Quay.

Another dream may take me northwards, past St George's Hall
and the Tuesday Market into the fishermen's quarter. Here I find

great stretches of town wall with commanding towers and bastions, woven from memories of old Cologne, but broken off, as at Lynn, and intermingled with modern patches. Here, again, I find a great medieval mansion, definitely reminiscent of the Overstolzen-Haus at Cologne, only that it is in our home-bred English Perpendicular style, instead of the thirteenth-century German. Many other such splendours I have seen in these dreams, more than I can remember; there is no hard and fast pattern in their recurrence. But always there is that familiar illusion of dreamland: 'How queer! I thought all this had been fancy, but here it is now in reality!' And of course there is always the same disillusion, and these architectural glories vanish no less tantalizingly than my magnificent and incredible windfalls among the book barrows of Farringdon Street or of some foreign market place; dream-children of my Library. 'In sleep, a King; but, waking, no such matter.'

Yet 'dreams are true while they last, and do we not live in dreams?' If the theory be true that our sleeping fancies are broken forecasts of our coming experiences, then it is pleasant to dwell upon mine as heralds of some future day when I shall again see the Cambridge that we love with unbeclouded eyes, and drift lazily down by river, in June sunshine, to an old Lynn rather dignified than disfigured by the scars of war.

CHAPTER VI

ST-OMER

IN MY seventh year, my father tried sending me to the Grammar School, which was less than a stone's throw from our door, and whither my two elder brothers had gone in due course. Very soon— I think, after a few weeks—my handwriting was found to be so unformed that he transferred me to Croad's, one of the two private schools which laid themselves out for more commercial and utilitarian education. Here again, however, my stay was brief. The 'Coal' in my name tempted my schoolfellows not only to nicknames—'Coal-heaver', 'Coal-hole', etc.—but also to what might be described as a practical pun. I was bundled, neck and crop, into the great schoolroom coal-box, and the lid put down upon me for what seemed a suffocating time. So it was finally decided that I should join my brother Rick, four years my senior, in France. One of the great Tuesday Market Place buildings was Bank House, the Cresswell abode. The reigning Cresswell had married a daughter of Lord Calthorpe, who at some moment of condescension had admitted to my mother the possibility that our own Calthrops might be distant branches of her family. The son, George Cresswell, would naturally reign next; so his father had the foresight to equip him with a foreign language. For this, St-Omer in the Pas-de-Calais enjoyed a certain reputation: thither George Cresswell went and, after his example, Rick and I. In the sixteenth and seventeenth centuries, the city had been conspicuous, side by side with Douai, for its zeal in training politico-theological missionaries for the conversion of England. It was now one of the places where English folk could live cheaply, so that, like Boulogne and Calais, it had its little colony of residents escaping from high prices at home, or perhaps sometimes from creditors. Thus the Lycée Impérial de St-Omer had always an average of twenty or thirty English pupils, of whom a few were advanced enough to take their place in ordinary class, but the large majority were, like ourselves, come just to pick up the language.

Thither, then, at Easter 1866, went two little urchins of eleven and seven. Rick had already been there for one term, but that was

not very much help to either of us. Our father saw us off from
St Katharine's Wharf, by London Bridge, on a little tramp steamer
for Calais. The start was dismal; but in half an hour we were wildly
interested in the swarm of Thames shipping; and, as the river widened,
our world opened out into infinities even more imposing than
Yarmouth. About sunset, we were off Southend Pier, more than a
mile long. My next memory is of climbing into one of the lifeboats
and nestling into such comfort as I could, with the resolve of telling
everybody how I had crossed the Channel in a rowboat. Next, the
lights of distant Margate, and one single alternate twinkler from more
distant France. Then open sea, with all its attendant disquietudes,
and immediate abandonment of our lifeboat or other boastful ambitions. Then, under next morning's chilly dawn, Calais harbour
with its long stretch of slimy sandbanks, and a sudden puff of
wind which blew away my new 'Muller hat'[1] beyond all hope of
recovery.

As the pride in my new Muller had gone some way to soften the
pain of parting from home, so its ignominious loss increased tenfold
the seasick and homesick sadness of landing on this foreign shore.
We had some hours to wait for the St-Omer train. We bought some
uncooked Normandy pippins at a grocer's, and munched them about
the streets. This left us still time and pence enough to go up the old
lighthouse tower, where there was a collection of rare moths and
birds which had dashed themselves against the glass at night. That
afternoon, we were charitably entertained with hot chocolate and
brioches by the family of the Censeur, or second in command, at
the Lycée; let me gratefully record his name of Bastien, and also
that he had a daughter of sixteen or seventeen with eyes as black as
sloes, such as I had never seen in England, who poured us out a
second cup. Désiré, also, the staff janitor, let me commemorate not

[1] The Muller hat is so nearly forgotten nowadays that it may be worth while
to write its epitaph. The story is of a railway crime, still fresh in those Easter
days of 1866. A comparatively wealthy traveller named Briggs, if I remember
rightly, was alone in his compartment when Muller got in, stabbed him with
a pair of tailor's shears, rifled the corpse, and slipped out at the next stop.
But he had the imprudence to steal Briggs' felt hat also, only attempting to
disguise it by paring off half the width of brim. This hat led to his capture and
execution; and it embalmed his memory, for some years at least, in the name
given to a new fashion in hats.

only for his pleasant name but for occasional little kindnesses during our time at school.

Next morning we found ourselves in charge of Monsieur Legrand, who was supervisor over us foreigners. He took us in two divisions, one of which was generally writing or preparing while he dealt orally with the other. The younger division, naturally, enjoyed comparatively little individual attention. The text-book was Ollendorff's *French Method*, supplemented by little paper-backed volumes of Voltaire's *Charles XII* and St-Pierre's *Paul et Virginie*. I believe we never travelled, in class, outside those three volumes. But in both cases we were in at the death; for my clearest recollections are of the bullet in Charles' eye, and Virginie's corpse. Most of our work, however, was the mere memorization of rules and lists of exceptions from Ollendorff. As ill-luck would have it, our grammar in use at Felsted later on followed the opposite principle: *fou, clou, verrou* were treated as normal in the one, and *pou, chou, hibou* as exceptions, while in the other these exceptions became normal and vice versa. Thus those later years, nominally of study, brought only confusion here and in other matters which depend upon grammatical memorizations. Outside the classroom I remember looking at only two French books. One was a prose translation or summary of the *Iliad*, from which I took a sympathy for Hector which has never changed. The other was some sort of pornographic manual which a French schoolfellow put into my hands for a few minutes, and which contained a description of 'la courtisane'. I may say here in passing that, although this Lycée under the Second Empire had a definite clerical tinge, and auricular confession was habitual if not compulsory for our French schoolfellows, the moral level was practically that of a small and ordinary English Grammar School. At Felsted, later on, I found a much healthier atmosphere. Of English books we had scarcely any at St-Omer. Rick had brought from home Mayne Reid's *White Chief,* and I had Albert Smith's *Ascent of Mont Blanc*, with its fascinating but impossible picture of a caravan threading its way over a cone of polished glass. Those we read and re-read until we knew them almost by heart.

I think Legrand was lazy, and certainly I was. Rewards and punishments were on a methodical basis. Corporal punishment was nominally non-existent. It may possibly have been legally permitted on the rarest occasions and with the greatest solemnity, but I never heard of any such case. Yet in practice I often suffered at least as much as under an English caning. Legrand had bristly red hair on his head, and long red hair on the back of his hands, almost to the finger-tips. Without ever striking or (so far as I remember) showing anger, he would take me by the ear and remonstrate with elephantine playfulness: 'Ah, petit polisson', etc., screwing all the time at the ear. The skin would sometimes give way and form a bleeding crack; sometimes I suffered thus from both ears at the same time.

The statutory recognized punishment was 'détention'—extra work beyond school hours. Against this there might stand an 'exemption'—a formal printed slip, about three inches by two, coloured and priced according to its negotiable value. If I remember rightly, the highest was No. 10, on white satin-glazed paper: there was also a salmon and a light pink, and the commonest, No. 1, was on ordinary white paper. The number denoted value in terms of detentions. Rick hoarded some at least of his, including one satiny white, which my mother used to turn up occasionally afterwards, from lowest deposits in her ancient wardrobes. With mine, I lived from hand to mouth, and found myself more than once in the debtors' prison. This, I believe, was the extremest statutory punishment before final expulsion, and the modern reader may be more impressed by it than a boy of eight was, consciously at least.

The detention room was about 10 feet square, quite bare except for a straw-bottomed chair, a small table, and what in England is called a commode. A tiny square window, perhaps 2 feet by 2 feet 6 inches, high up in one wall, just under the ceiling, looked out upon a corner of the gravelled playground. One Spaniard, imprisoned for smoking, once earned our admiration by appearing at that window with a fresh-lit cigar in his mouth; his name was Delgado, and we felt that it rhymed aptly with 'bravado' and 'desperado'. I myself, in one of my two imprisonments, climbed up to that window-sill, and found it to be a repository of nameless defilements. I have a vague impression that, on the second occasion, a pallet was brought in and I was kept all night. I cannot remember any inherent horrors in this solitude; it may indeed have been rather a relief from Legrand's hairy fingers. But the authorities evidently had their own natural misgivings; for at last, when my small stock of 'exemptions' had been squandered and my 'détention' debts had risen again to bankrupt proportions, I was put into solitary confinement in the music room. This was spacious, airy, well lighted, on the terrace overlooking the whole playground: moreover, it was good sport to climb up from shelf to shelf until one reached the violin cases at the top. Here were so many fiddle-bows that, by spacing one's depredations over the whole collection, one could collect enough long horse hairs for a whole fishing-line, to be utilized on our next walk to the Cistercian ruins of Clairmarais by the riverside. Towards the end of our time at the Lycée, perhaps seventy-four years ago to the very moment as I write these lines, music room and prison witnessed a small political tragedy. We Lower School boys were loafing about on a summer day, in our gravelled playground, dominated at one end by a terrace upon which opened the *salle de musique* and other classrooms. Suddenly, through the open doors, came loud sounds of a piano and a tune which caught even my unmusical ear, and made others turn round at once to stare. Then the *pion*—the usher who was on disciplinary duty during play hours—rushed headlong towards the terrace, the tails of his black frock-coat fluttering in the wind. He plunged into the *salle de musique*; the piano ceased with that remorseless suddenness with which we switch off our wireless nowadays; and the *pion* emerged dragging one of my schoolfellows by the collar. In a sudden daredevil fit, the boy had struck up the 'Marseillaise', that song which had been the French National Anthem in former days, but which was far too Republican to be permitted at a Lycée Impérial under Napoleon III. That tune, therefore, was almost as dangerous to the performer in 1867 as it would be now in the St-Omer of 1941. My schoolfellow was hauled off straight to the school prison, and we small boys never heard the final dénouement. Certainly he did not, like Delgado, flaunt his impenitence at the little window.

For sport, we had rounders within our playground, or elementary running games such as prisoner's base. On Sunday afternoons, and on the Thursday half-holiday, we had long walks in our stiff-padded and gold-laced military uniforms. St-Omer, as a frontier town in Louis XIV's day, had been fortified by Vauban; so we marched in step past the Cathedral, and through the long underground passage that threaded the ramparts; thence we emerged at once into open country, peeled our coats, and broke step. After three miles or so, at Arques, our most usual destination, there was a chocolate factory which could be smelt for a hundred yards; fifty gaping nostrils snuffed the air as we passed. Then Sept Écluses, where the canal made such a change of level that seven lock gates rose there in succession above each other, though nowadays a huge hydraulic lift raises or lowers the barges at a single leap. More rarely we went to fish at Clairmarais; and here my memory suggests that the fish's brain showed itself more active than ours. From all walks, however, we came home hungry and thirsty to our bread and milk.

For the first day's chocolate and brioches were no true sample of Lycée diet. Breakfast was bread and milk. For dinner, at noon, soup as a matter of course, but such soup as lends all its point to the ancient story of *Distinguo*. A certain Roman Catholic seminary student rendered himself conspicuous by the hard subtlety of his logical distinctions: never plain 'Yes' or 'No', but always, 'That depends'. The bishop, interested in this peculiarity, seated the youth by his side when he next came to the seminary, and began: 'Monsieur l'Abbé, I hear that you are a subtle and accurate casuist. May I put a thorny case before you? Is it permissible to baptize an infant at the last pinch, in soup?' '*Distinguo*, my Lord. In your soup, *no*: in the seminary soup, *yes*.' Of our Lycée soup it can only be said that it had at least one advantage over the ensuing meat dish: it was almost tasteless. We stigmatized those ragoûts as horseflesh; but, having since occasionally patronized a *Boucherie Hippophagique* in Paris, I have often wondered whether they had ever given us anything so respectable at the Lycée. On Wednesdays and Fridays, under this pious ecclesiastical régime of Napoleon III, we fasted on vegetable dishes and cheese. This was nearly always Gruyère, so ancient and fish-like that its multiplicity of vacant spaces was almost a relief. The most welcome dish for those days was the crown artichoke, far more daintily cooked than most of our other dishes. The first time I heard Désiré pronounce *artichaut*, in answer to my hungry question, I thought he was sneezing. But the ecclesiastical calendar had its good sides also, since Sundays and red-letter saints gave us chocolate instead of plain milk for breakfast and supper, with proportionate ameliorations for dinner. The steady absence of butter was certainly the worst gap in our dietary. When, at the very end of our time, our parents came to fetch us away, and put up at the 'Porte d'Or' and had us to breakfast, we practically cut slices of butter and spread them thinly with bread. Here, as I write, I can almost feel the rich, creamy mouthfuls going down my throat. There was, indeed, one 'goûter' which I have omitted: a 'pistolet', or halfpenny roll, at four o'clock, with a drink of water from the play-ground tap. But if twilight may be described as darkness made visible, that four o'clock twi-meal was hunger made sensible. Ever since, when the Apocalypse says 'They shall hunger no more, neither thirst any more', it is not the emptiness before a Lycée meal that comes back to me, but the aching void that followed upon the last mouthful of our 'pistolet'. Once a week, we had a drawing-hour. Each had a great sheet of paper, a *fusain* of vine charcoal, and a piece of stale bread for rubbing out or toning down our designs. My first proceeding was always to eat that bread: what followed for the rest of the hour is blank in my memory.

Pocket money we had to the extent of 50 centimes a week for the two of us; the equivalent of nearly 3*d*. each. The Christmas week of 1867—for we stayed in the Lycée all through that vacation— was cheered by five francs, a tiny gold coin sent by my father between two visiting-cards in a letter. This went almost entirely in oranges, from which every scrap of peel was finally baked on the schoolroom stove and eaten: no scent takes me back to old days more immediately than this. On Christmas Day itself, Bastien, the charitable Censeur, again entertained us at his own table.

Our usual work was, I think, very unsystematic: or was it our idleness and unwillingness that rendered all system purgatorial? I have vague recollections of written exercises which were hardly ever free from blunders; of exceptional moments when, on the contrary, Legrand said reproachfully that he wished all might be like this, and of painfully frequent condemnations for criminal negligence. One incident stands out a little more clearly than the rest. My memory has always been capricious: I remember things I don't know why, and forget others where memory is a matter of duty or of plain self-interest. I could never score heavily in 'repetition' lessons, nor can I to the present day trust myself to recite off-hand a dozen consecutive lines of poetry. But at St-Omer I sat often half-bored, half-amused, to hear the older section repeat their grammar by heart while we were supposed to be preparing our own task. The rules for the agreement of the past participle were exceptionally unintelligible, and therefore more curiously interesting, especially Legrand's frequent expostulation: 'Le régime est en avant, animal!' In due time, the Inspector of the Département came down and in his examination probed even down to our irregular class of English boys. As ill-luck would have it, he enquired into the agreement of the past participle, with pitiful results. Legrand lost his temper, and said, 'Why, here is an urchin in the lower class who can put you to shame!' Put thus upon my mettle, I did in fact rehearse the grammatical matter sufficiently to pass muster; and for a little while there was peace between me and Legrand. The Inspector passed on to Arras, where two of my sisters were then at school. He noticed the similarity of the names, and told them the story.

There was no more bullying than was to be expected among twenty or thirty boys jumbled together all day long. As youngest and smallest, I had probably more than my share, and Rick was not old or strong enough to resist this. From the French boys we had no interference whatever. It was probably clear enough that, in any such case, we should have stuck together like one, and there would have been a major scandal in the school. On the other hand, I retain one most vivid illustration of the motto *Gallus Gallo lupus*—'the Frenchman is a wolf to his fellow-Frenchman'. One boy of fourteen or fifteen was of that type which one often finds here and there: greedy, bloated, yet not to the point of actually impairing his physical activities. A quarrel broke out between him and another of about his own age. With us, it would have been a more or less chivalrous fight, with fisticuffs, under recognized rules, and with a ring to maintain them. Here, however, we saw mere jungle law. They began with a wrestle: 'Bloatie' had far the greater weight, and soon fell uppermost. Bearing then with all his load of flesh upon his prostrate foe, he raised his right elbow and brought his fist down with all his force upon a head which, resting on the hard gravel, lay literally between the anvil and the hammer. The blood spurted; grisly groans came from the vanquished, and the victor rose and swaggered off. It was brute force almost in its crudest animal form;

like a spider swelling visibly as she drinks the blood from her prostrate fly.

One of our masters I must not forget; the only one with whom I had any real human intercourse, apart from those necessarily rare kindnesses from the remote Bastien. The *pion* who arrested that revolutionary pianist was named Jullien; I dare say he was not yet out of his teens. During the last few weeks of our time he took pleasant and friendly notice of us, talking humanly while he was on duty, and even treating us sometimes to a stick of chocolate. In 1890, he was dead, but his memory was still fresh at the school; and then I regretted not having visited the Lycée much earlier, when I might have thanked him as he deserved.

In these conditions, our three terms at the Lycée did no more than to teach us French pronunciation and give us a certain rudimentary familiarity with the language which survived even the neglect of our English schooling during the next ten years.

In June, 1867, my father and mother came over for the great Paris exhibition, the first of a series which continued, at intervals of ten years, down to 1937. A week later, they came to fetch us, and stayed at what was then a well-known hostelry, the 'Porte d'Or'. In 1890, I stayed there on my way home from Italy, and found characteristic French courtesy. Some game of cards was started in the evening, in which I joined with very imperfect knowledge. I took an extreme risk at one point, and lost several francs at one stroke. Mine host resolutely refused to admit this; the others bore him out, and my rash decision was cancelled by common consent. Nobody deigned to pluck such an ignorant pigeon as this English wayfarer. At my last visit, in 1936, the 'Porte d'Or' had ceased to exist. But if any reader cares to trace its story back to the early sixties, he should get hold of one of the most entertaining among English travel stories. This is *A Cruise upon Wheels*, by C. A. Collins, who was an artist of the Pre-Raphaelite school and brother to the famous author of *The Woman in White* and *The Moonstone*. He and his companion started from the 'Porte d'Or' with a gig and a dog, and the book follows their adventures from day to day, across Burgundy to Geneva. It was first published in 1862, and has been republished by Peter Davies in 1926.

CHAPTER VII

THE GRAMMAR SCHOOL

EARLY in the sixteenth century, one Thoresby was Mayor of Lynn. He founded there a 'collegium', or endowed community, of priests. The old dark brick building still stands there in Queen Street, with its inner quadrangle, its great gate, and its carved oak door from which 'Pray for his soul' has been rudely cut away and obliterated. Yet it was precisely for his soul's sake that Thoresby had founded his college: the priests were to pray for him, they and their successors in unbroken order, until the end of time. A further clause directed that here, as in many other similar foundations, one of the priests should keep school. The foundation escaped from spoliation by Edward VI's commissioners; other small benefactions flowed in as time went on; and thus Thoresby's School has had a continuous existence to the present day.

At times it may have been dormant; and indeed it was nearly so in my father's day: otherwise the little town would not have had room both for the Rev. James Coulton's school and for that of Mr Beloe, whose son became my father's junior partner and my own antiquarian guide. Even in the fifties, the Headmaster was negligent and the scholars few. On one Sunday walk my father, with Jim holding to his hand, passed by the Headmaster's garden, and Jim enquired, 'Is this the Garden of the Sluggard?' My mother had familiarized him with that picture from Proverbs, as she did all of us: for the ghosts she most feared were Bankruptcy and Drink. (My father, in old age, would spread his hands to the fire after a good day's work and say to us, 'Look at your mother: always busy about something! There isn't one lazy bone in her whole body.') This Sluggard's Garden, then, had not become a perfect seminary even in the autumn of 1867, when I began my three and a half years' pupilage there. If I describe it unsparingly, it is mainly for the sake of encouragement to be drawn from the contrast of its later development, through the generosity of the late Sir William Lancaster, on a fine site outside the town.

In my day, it was ruled by the Rev. Thomas White, who had

come out from St John's College, Cambridge, as 13th Wrangler in
1852. This was a good degree; in 1854, Robert Campbell earned
his Fellowship at Trinity Hall by a 14th place and Leslie Stephen
by a 20th. We nicknamed him 'Pinkie', for which there were two
competing derivations. Either it was in tribute to his 'red and raging
eye', as the poet Robert Montgomery puts it, or it was a corruption
of 'pig's eye'; for certainly he had the 'little peepy eyes' which
Dickens so aptly describes in Henry VIII. Otherwise, there was no
similarity of face or figure. His long visage and pointed nose were
far more reminiscent of John Knox; and his limbs were as lean as
his cheeks. His wife and sister-in-law were of the same ungenial
north-country type. They had no children. He was an excellent
business-man and advertiser. Thus he had always from twenty to
thirty boarders in addition to the many day boys: his diligence and
discipline were respectable according to the standard of his time, and
he was a fairly prominent figure in town life.

The school itself was situated in an ordinary house in St James'
Street, facing the theatre and the 'Old Tower' (Greyfriars). A narrow passage from the street door led to the playground behind,
gravelled and about sixty feet square. This was squeezed in among
other houses; but its eastern side was mainly taken up by the schoolroom, a sort of shed perhaps forty feet long. Inside, it was furnished
with two desks at the south-east and south-west corners, for the
Head and Second Masters, and a third at the north-east for the
usher or the Modern Language Master. I do not think there were
ever more than three teaching there at the same time; sometimes,
indeed, only two; for the Head was often taking a class in his own
dining-room, which looked out upon the street; and modern languages were comparatively occasional. In 1867 they were taught
by one Borngiesser, and later by Goebbels, both German-Swiss, and
both pronounced in Lynn after the fashion of Stratford-attë-Bowe,
Bong-gesser and *Go-bèlls*.

Not only had the whole premises the inconvenience that they
were divided from some of our neighbours by no more than moderate
and easily scalable brick walls, but by others we were actually overlooked. One case, at least, was very scandalous. The north end
of the schoolroom was lighted high up by a window, of ordinary bedroom size, which had another bedroom window exactly opposite,

across a very narrow lane. That house, as it happened, became one of notorious ill fame; and on one occasion a naked female appeared at the window, beckoning across to ours. I heard of this only afterwards, and no doubt White heard and reported it to the police; but the thing in itself was typical of the unsuitability of our premises for efficient modern education.

On the other hand, my criticisms must clearly mark my own point of view. From the scholastic standpoint, I was an idle schoolboy and an idle undergraduate. It was not until I became my own master that I thoroughly enjoyed anything that can fairly be called scholastic work. The compulsion did me good in the long run, but I was too undeveloped to take long views. Later experience has taught me the value of compulsory virtue: I wonder whether any more specious falsehood was ever invented than the flattering parrot cry that nothing good has ever been done under compulsion. Therefore I have no grudge against the dullness of many classroom hours; there, the clay was as much at fault as the potter, the boy as the teacher. Dr Johnson noted how men are seldom more innocently employed than when they are making money; and boys are seldom doing things better than when they listen to older folk struggling to impress older folk's ideas. Great is the importance of merely listening to what we do not immediately understand; how many grown-up people do we meet who have really learned to listen to each other? There is a deep psychological truth in the cry reported from one modern boy, weary of a modern school which deifies originality: 'Must I always do just what I like?' And I admit myself grateful to those who, in the classroom, dragged me through paths of Greek and Latin which I should never have trodden by mere unforced choice. Let us do everything possible to soften the harshness of compulsion, and to procure unity of direction between the master's will and the pupil's natural impulses. Much has been done in that direction during the past seventy years. Much, no doubt, still remains to be done. But we cannot truly advance, rather shall we relapse into ignorance and stupidity, by ignoring nature's distinctions between childhood and maturity. Goethe asked once: 'Could we ever get a perfectly wise society?' and answered: 'Not unless everybody could be born thirty years old.'

Our Grammar School of the sixties bore still certain unregenerate

Dotheboys characteristics. Mrs White served clammy and cloying treacle puddings before the meat. The usher had not the full privileges of humanity; he could not rely on White to back him up. I remember one scene, disgusting even to those of us who, by nature, looked upon all masters as natural enemies. A dead cat had been thrown over the wall by some neighbour, and it lay near the schoolroom door. The usher, Mr Wallis, stood by to watch us go in. William Gamlyn, the school pugilist, picked the corpse up and flung it in Wallis' face. The victim only said: 'Gamlyn, you are no gentleman!' It was practically Steerforth and the usher in *David Copperfield*, but on an even more sordid scale.

Within the schoolroom, again, there was little discipline. The mere multiplicity of classes produced unavoidable confusion; and White was generally elsewhere with the older boys. The room was heated by a single iron stove at the end of the two senior desks, while draughts poured in from the ill-fitting door and windows. Much of our work was done on slates: these we cleaned with spittle, and then claimed the right of drying them at the stove. By judicious delays, one could heat one's slate to about 150 degrees, and then take it back to sit upon for the next five minutes.

Caning, of course, was frequent. White, I think, kept a monopoly there; at least I cannot remember suffering from anyone else. But quite a considerable proportion of us managed to earn this distinction once or twice a week. One, Jary, was caned thrice in a single day, and White proclaimed that, if there were a fourth provocation, he would expel him. Alan Hardwick, one of the oldest boarders, was a favourite of Mrs White and in many ways privileged. He was good-looking, high-spirited, and as mischievous as a monkey. Once at supper, tempted by 'Bos' Baker's bovine inertia and expanse of flabby face, he applied a whole slice of hot treacle tart to his cheek and left it to stick: the resultant wild rush of his victim became legendary at the school, and added emphasis to his nickname. Alan, as we all knew, had sworn by the nine gods that he would never take the cane. But at last there came some obviously canable transgression, and we were all agog to see what would happen after prayers next morning. He appeared with a heavily bandaged hand; he had cut it that morning in breaking an indispensable bedroom utensil. White would take no such excuse; Hardwick must hold out his left. He held it out for a moment; then started aside like an unbroken colt and ran out of the schoolroom. In the face of expulsion, he at length submitted and accepted a few formal cuts.

Another time, however, it was the culprit who won. He was the youngest child of a worthy citizen of conspicuous musical talent. Their yard lay back to back with our playground: desperadoes like Hardwick and Sandford used to climb the brick wall and make love in twilight hours to the boy's adolescent sister; deep holes had been made in the brickwork to facilitate such visits, and the authorities must have closed one eye. Charlie was a pampered little urchin dressed with artistic taste; and my only surviving memory shows him in the middle of the schoolroom, whimpering, while the Head bent over him cane in hand. 'What are you saying?' thundered White: 'What? if I cane you, your father will take you away from the school? We shall see, we shall see!' But in fact Charlie was sent back to his place. Authority took care not to risk another such rebuff: and there was much envious murmuring among us who knew that our home would always be ready enough to endorse the sentence of the school.

White, however, was not without his own grim sense of humour. Shortly before my time, when the elder Gamlyn was still at school, that eccentric youth advertised his conversion to the Church of Rome, and sealed it with a mustard plaster, which of course gave him a neat tonsure. White sentenced him to a hundred lines a day until the hair should grow again.

Our studies were as might have been expected from the general tone of the school. Arithmetic, of course; but when I left after three and a half years I was not yet quite sound on the multiplication table. English meant ordinary spelling, dictation, rules of grammar, and a little learning by heart. French meant Ollendorff again; and here of course I marked time, at best. German was a nightmare, for we had to learn the detestable cursive script, and here again the classic was Ollendorff in his most baldly mechanical exercises for beginners. One relief, however, I secured after some time. Goebbels permitted me to write my exercises by dictation to my eldest sister, whose writing was fine and clear even in German. With a little dishonest pressure, it was possible to coax one's amanuensis into helping with brain as well as with pen. With Greek my acquaintance was almost equally distant. My father put me through a little Anacreon, and on Sundays we had to do a few verses from the Greek Testament: but, as Jim remarked, the Authorised Version was here of great assistance. For Latin, I had got into Cornelius Nepos before I left, and done a good many, if not all, of Virgil's *Eclogues*. Those last were taught by White himself, who had obtained a third class in the Classical Tripos. He had in his desk an old eighteenth-century edition, with English prose translation on alternate pages, and an elaborate copperplate engraving of Tityrus teaching the woods to re-echo the charms of Amaryllis. We sometimes burgled that desk with a skeleton key, and handled also the master's store of canes.

The *Eclogues*, at least, I had begun to enjoy; and in the Autumn Term of 1871 I must have begun to wake up. Our ancient, muzzy, incompetent Second Master had now left, and had been succeeded by Mr Kershaw, who afterwards became Head of a Grammar School in Essex. He might be described in terms of Calverley:

> Old Poser snorted like a horse...
> His manner, when excited, coarse...

but he took his job seriously and made us work. As a result, I got the Fifth Form Prize that Christmas.

Our Lynn speech days had quite their share of leather and prunella. To begin with, we had to live up to a new honour. The Prince of Wales, future Edward VII, settled now at Sandringham, was appealed to for patronage, and gave an endowment for presenting a silver medal to the best pupil of each year. In 1869, he even condescended to come and give the prizes, as an appendage to his formal opening of the Alexandra Dock. A town boasting two Members of Parliament could always count upon one of them. In 1868, for instance, when Rick and I were only beginning to forget what we had learnt at St-Omer, and were put on to declaim a scene from *L'Avare*, White received imperturbably Lord Stanley's public compliment to a school where French was so well taught.

In the summer of 1871 my father bought a country residence, while still practising in Lynn. At one time, he had thought of sending me up to compete for a foundation scholarship at Eton. There was a distant neighbour, a clergyman called Everard, whose son was already a prominent Eton master, and, as my father fondly believed, had been tutored to this success by his own parent. That belief had painful fruits for us both; for my father undertook to coach me in Latin verse. We began, of course, with the traditional 'nonsense verses'. But the procedure, simple enough in itself, was painfully complicated by the pupil's want of zeal and the teacher's impatience. My heart was in the open air, and he himself was weary after an honest day's work. Those hours were among the most painful and unremunerative of all my school days; and my father was probably as much relieved as I when this experiment was frankly abandoned.

CHAPTER VIII

PENTNEY

THE background to all the rest of my school and college life was our home at Pentney, eight and a half miles from Lynn on the Norwich road.

In 1870, while we were still living in Lynn, my father bought a second-hand phaeton and what my horse-loving brother Rick regarded as a third-hand pony, Jack. I would like to think that the patient beast found us the least exacting of his masters. Looking back, I can find in my mind nothing but gratitude to him, and I do feel also that we were taught to treat him with consideration. We hailed this acquisition enthusiastically, with its extension of social and picnic facilities for the family; but, at first, we little realized how momentous was the change which this first step implied.

One special sultry day comes back to me, in a sandy lane beyond Gaywood, when my mother was in command and Edmund was with us. The Franco-German War had just been declared—possibly that very day—and we two boys were all agog with unhealthy excitement. Like the citizen in *Faust* on Easter morning, it was a comfort to us to feel that other folk were killing each other while we were so well off. St-Omer had given us no love for France, and our sympathies were for Germany: so, I believe, was the general feeling of our friends and our environment.

In the summer of 1871 it was announced that we were all going a long distance for a picnic of unusual magnificence. Some were to go by road, others by train. We met at a little belt of wood, some two hundred yards by eighty, half a mile from the station. There we found wild raspberries, and even one small bush of wild currants; delightful ferns and mosses; fungi and birds' nests. The lunch was an epic feast. My mother had made an enormous sponge cake for the occasion. She was past-mistress there, as in many other culinary matters: it was a pivot of her creed that whatever Lancashire did in cookery in her day would be done, after an inferior fashion, in Norfolk to-morrow. On this occasion, for the only time that I remember, the sponge cake refused to rise in the oven, and came out in a rubbery consistency which thenceforward gave special point for me to the witches' words in *Macbeth*—'thick and slab'. But 'cet âge est sans indigestion'; and we found even an added flavour in this great doughy cake. From lunch we were led across the road, where, behind a screen of tall beech trees, lay a crescent-shaped sheet of water about half the size of the wood, with an island in the middle (Plates IV and VI, pp. 58 and 144). A lawn sloped down to this from a small old-fashioned sort of farmhouse, backed by stables and a great barn. Towards the east stood two enormous old trees, an oak and an elm: in the space between them and the house there wandered an old-fashioned profusion of roses, growing at their own will like bramble bushes, of a tender pink and a scent that seemed perfectly to match their colour: in so far as I have since been able to identify them, they are now called 'Ophelia'. Farther away to the east and the south were other small strips of wood; and, a few yards farther to the south, the little river Nar, navigable for barges with some difficulty as far as Narborough. Westward, beyond a kitchen garden and small orchard, was an ancient horse chestnut, as big as the elm and the oak. The garden lake was kept moving at that end by a sluice which let water out to the village, while at the other it was filled from a tiny stream which bubbled up from the sands in a wood four miles away, and ran thence over gravel to form one boundary of this little territory, and to fall finally into the Nar. The whole extended to about thirty acres of land; that is, about an average holding for a typical peasant farmer of the Middle Ages or for an 'habitant' of modern French Canada. Much of this we could observe that afternoon, between lunch and a riotous high tea and the drive home westward in the golden afterglow. We younger children wondered a little why this particular place had been chosen for our picnic, and who was the lord of this ground, so delicious and yet so deserted. But, here again, 'cet âge est sans prévoyance', and we munched the gooseberries and raided the unripe plums in the garden without greatly heeding the Tree of the Knowledge of Good and Evil. Only bit by bit, as days and weeks went by, it filtered out that this was to be our real home from October onwards. This was doubtless a touch of my father's secretiveness, like his 'People will say anything' on Lynn platform and on his way to be married.

Some thirty years later, just about the turn of the century, the

Westminster Gazette appealed to readers for their judgment: 'Which is the most pathetic line in all literature?' I remember a few: La Fontaine's 'Quittez le long espoir et les vastes pensées'; King Lear's 'He hath no daughters, Sir'; the Psalmist's 'No man can redeem his brother'. My father did not write to the paper, but said aloud from Horace: 'Cedes coemptis saltibus et domo'—'Thou shalt quit [some day] the woods and the house that thou hast bought.' He always carried a Horace in his office bag backwards and forwards to Lynn, and the words came instinctively to his lips. In those thirty years, his thirty acres had grown into his soul; in no spirit of vulgar jealousy, but in something of the mood of the old peasant proprietor. Here was the most natural rest from office work: here was God's plenty of rustic ease; here was a Norfolk incarnation of Virgil's *Bucolics*. His bread work had been plodding and monotonous, with the burden of a family of brothers and sisters before he was out of his teens. With an excellent memory for most things, he could seldom name even approximately the year in which this or that event had happened; he had no personal pegs to hang such memories on; all had been uniform. Now, then, Lynn and Pentney supplied the healthiest pair of uniformities. Without much interest in games, he had always been fond of exercise; and now it was his daily interest to go round the pastures waging war against thistles, or to roll lawn and gravel with a heavy roller. This he did daily before breakfast, in almost every possible weather, with empty stomach and naked breast. He was very insensitive to cold, never using overcoats till he was past seventy, and wearing under his black frock-coat nothing but a linen shirt, his long beard filling the place of collar and cravat. Before breakfast, the shirt itself was commonly absent. My mother once caught a fragment of dialogue at dawn between the gardener and cook: 'Pore man! and him without a shirt to his back in this bitter cold weather!' She enquired further, as for some villager needing charitable help. Cook, much embarrassed, confessed that she was speaking of 'the Master'.

It was a very small house at first for so many of us, although I was sent off to board at the Grammar School until Christmas and then to Felsted, while Edmund went to the County School and Jim had long been at sea. Even though my father added to it from time to time, the additions were not always labour-saving in themselves, quite apart from disturbances while workmen were about the place. Only in later years did I realize even a little of what all this meant to my mother, with only one village maidservant at first, and two later on. At a *Mayflower* celebration some half-century ago, an eminent American confessed that, the more he studied the actual records, the greater admiration he felt for the Pilgrim Mothers. In those earliest days budgetary problems were serious: but neither children nor friends found lack of good fare at our table. Londoners, indeed, assured us that my mother's sausage rolls had no rivals even in the Modern Babylon; and my 'poor threadbare octogenarian soul' can still believe this. Not, however, that we could quite hold our own with one or two neighbours who, in that respect, kept up almost the traditions of Chaucer's Frankeleyn. Such, especially, was Mr Paul, the gentleman-farmer under whom Rolfe the poacher worked as a boy, to whose kind treatment he pays a tribute, but from whose pigeon cote, later on, he took as heavy toll as from my mother's peahens. Once my mother had occasion to criticize the wastefulness of a maid who had previously worked for the Pauls. The servant drew an unfavourable contrast: 'Miss Paul, she never bothered about the milk; and as for the eggs, she reglar chucked 'em about.'

But, with all this, my mother was a country-lover, perhaps even more than my father: and our multiplicity of cats and peacocks, swans and ducks and guinea-fowl, added much to her solace and little to her labour. Our first and best cat had been saved from the garden of a friend in Northamptonshire, who maintained a whole posse for protection of his extensive strawberry beds. He contrived long wires in parallel lines about six feet apart: each wire had a sliding ring, to which a cat was attached by its collar and a few feet of cord. The cats fed themselves quite handsomely by this arrangement. One tabby kitten was so charming that my mother begged for her, and she became ancestress of innumerable generations. My father had no liking for pets. Jim met one night in the streets of Calcutta a stray kitten, half Siamese, which he pocketed and brought back to the ship. It was a dainty little creature, and slept habitually across his neck, under his beard. He brought it home and left it at Pentney. His leave was very short; and the first evening after his departure left the cat comfortless; but, after all, there was my father

Plate IV. Pentney, from the Green Drive (see p. 56)

Plate V.   The author's father, John James Coulton

enjoying his regular after-supper sleep, and the resourceful mouser
crept into his beard. An hour later, he started up in great perplexity.
But his heart was soft at that moment; and, for the only time I can
remember, he tolerated an animal about his person. Under shelter
of long white beard and hair, he had, indeed, cut off all superfluity
of collar and cravat, and from there he went on to abjure waistcoats.
Only towards the end of his life did he possess an overcoat. But
one night, on the last train from Norwich, he narrowly escaped
being snowed up. Thus he bought a good coat, and was occasionally seen to use it. He was, in his humbler way, of the school
of the late Latin Professor at Cambridge, 'Johnny' Mayor, with
whom for a while he corresponded. Both, in their later years, were
vegetarians, except that my father abhorred neither eggs nor fish.
This troubled his conscience, and he wrote to consult Mayor as
to a purer title for the fraternity. 'Let us choose not a Latin name
but a Greek, and call ourselves *Aζοöphags*.' At that point, the correspondence broke down: no answer ever came from Mayor. And
yet, names apart, the practice itself was one to which Mayor had
devoted—his nephew, Robin Mayor, would have said, sacrificed—
all the latter part of a long life. In my undergraduate days, he put
out a pamphlet entitled *Modicus cibi medicus sibi*. He reinforced
this by the story of two heroic abstainers in the past, the Venetian
senator Cornaro (who probably inspired some of the Second Part
of Goethe's *Faust*) and the Jesuit scholar Lessius. Mayor himself,
report said, was living then upon sixpence a day: brown bread,
bananas, and water. He started a little Food Reform Shop in the
curious building which stands anomalously at the junction of Corn
Exchange Street and Pembroke Street. He employed his cook or
housekeeper to compound a very excellent home-made marmalade,
which was appreciated as it deserved. The good lady used for this
purpose a collection of second-hand jam pots from every quarter.
Therefore, shortly after I went down there appeared in some Cambridge and other papers an advertisement to something of this effect:
'Be it hereby known that I, John Eyton Bickersteth Mayor, do most
humbly apologize to Messrs Keiller and Sons, of Dundee, for selling
marmalade in vessels distinguished by their trade-mark; and I thank
them for accepting this confession in lieu of legal proceedings.'
Mayor kept his vegetarian faith to the last, but condescended to all

sorts of complicated special dishes in Hall. The College cook, I am told, would sometimes whisper in confidence: 'Professor Mayor, Sir, 'e thinks 'e eats nothing but vegetables: but we allus puts something in to keep 'im up.'

My father allowed himself to become a sort of common carrier between home and Lynn. His bag was burdened with small parcels, and his conscience with small commissions: but the six hundred yards to and from Narborough station formed an integral and healthy part of his daily exercise. Sometimes, partly by our fault, he ran the train very close. Once it was already in sight, and we were beginning to trot, I in my thirties and he in his seventies. A man stopped my father some hundred yards from the station, to warn him that 'all medical men forbid running after forty'. It needed a second repetition to overcome my father's deafness; but then his gesture was eloquent. He never swore: but his hand said this time, 'Get thee behind me, Satan!' Another time we went slowly and gingerly over a frozen road. A villager saluted us with what, here again, needed double or treble repetition before my father could take it in, ''T ain't sweatin' weather, Guvnor!'

Once seated in the train, my father always made a point of saluting the rest of the compartment before settling down to the newspaper. One day we found ourselves facing a cheerful apple-faced old lady, to whom he remarked, 'A very severe winter, Madam!' She eyed his long white hair, and said, 'Ah, Sir! it 's many and many a winter as *you've* seen!' He replied in a rather patronizing tone, 'And you yourself not a few, Madam.' 'Oh, only eighty-three, Sir.' This was a year beyond his own age, and his deflation was very entertaining to behold.

His mind was judicial; but this taught me early to observe the frequent psychological distinction between judiciality and strict impartiality. He wished to hear both sides of the question; but then his decisions had all the force which Victorian tradition allowed to the Paterfamilias.

One morning my aunt Ellen came into the office, and said, 'James, I was with Miss —— an hour ago, and she told me the doctor had just left her. He had told her to close her right eye, and when she did so, she found she couldn't see with her left. So, without thinking, I shut mine: and I found *I* couldn't see with my left, either!' At this, my father instinctively closed his, with precisely identical result: those three old people made the same discovery within an hour of each other. For some years my father avoided operation, mainly because, in Gladstone's recent case, that had happened to be followed shortly afterwards by an operation for cancer. At last, on his eighty-seventh birthday, he was successfully taken in hand by Professor Flemming, and given nearly three years more of sight, until within a few months of his death.

Pentney had brought health to him, and it was very healthy for us boys, though for the girls, as they grew up, its social seclusion was a plain disadvantage. It was what is called an 'open' parish: no squire or considerable landholder; therefore none of the patriarchal tradition which redeemed Victorian England from many faults. The village consisted of just three or four groups of cottages scattered over a space of three miles. Therefore it was not a very happy field for the parson, especially as the income even of the combined parishes was extremely small. Changes were fairly frequent; but at no time did the Church fail to fulfil at least this mission for which nothing has yet been found to replace it, that it formed a natural and healthy focus for all good works in the parish. We generally had men with a little money of their own, retired from school or from some greater parish. The Sunday School scholars may be fairly measured by one intelligent little girl's answer to my sister's question on the Psalmist's frequent allusions to the dragon. 'Are there any dragons now, Lizzie?' 'Notsamany now, Miss', with an obedient curtsey.

Round about us were delightful walks and pilgrimages, especially from the antiquarian point of view. Pentney lies in what Dr Jessopp christened 'The Holy Land of Norfolk', where sixteen monasteries were once crowded into the basin of the little river Nar. Pentney 'Abbey' itself was, strictly speaking, a Priory of Austin Canons; there remains a very fine stone gateway with a hundred yards or so of the precinct wall; and all the older houses or cottages in Pentney are built partly with great Abbey stones, often showing their sculptured pattern. Just across the river, among the pastures of Marham, are the ruins of a nunnery. Shouldham and Blackbrough and Wormegay have perished almost completely; but Westacre shows considerable ruins, and Castleacre has one of the finest façades in England. All those are within a radius of six miles; and so is Swaff-

ham with a large and splendidly proportioned church, and one of
the great Norfolk angel roofs of oak, and the famous Pedlar sculptured at one bench end, and his dog at another. Swaffham itself
is on the 'Peddar's Way', the old Roman road to Brancaster, which
may still be traced for scores of miles as a grass-grown lane. This
Pedlar legend is one of those which, in different forms, crop up in
the folklore of a dozen countries. Again, it is one of the many
hanging round old London Bridge, which, overbuilt with houses like
the Ponte Vecchio at Florence, was counted among the wonders
of the world not only in England but in Scottish poetry of the
fifteenth century.[1]

John Chapman, pedlar, of Swaffham had a dream which bade him
go up to London Bridge and find a pot of gold there. It came three
nights running: therefore John was not disobedient unto the heavenly
vision. He trudged up with his staff and pack and dog, as shown
on the bench ends to-day, and in the painted windows until about
a hundred and fifty years ago, and ferreted in every hole and corner
of the famous Bridge. This he did three days running, but to no
effect. On the evening of the third, an inquisitive inhabitant asked
the reason of this strange behaviour. John, heartily disgusted by
this time, told him the whole story and sheepishly confessed his folly.
'Folly indeed, young man. Why, if I believed in that sort of dream,
I should have wandered off long ago on a wildgoose chase into
Norfolk. I had just such a dream as yours: I was to go to a place
called Swaffham, and to the house of one John Chapman, and dig
for a pot of gold at the foot of his apple-tree.' This was plain enough;
and with part of the gold in that pot John Chapman built Swaffham
church, and left his record in sculpture and stained glass.

To return to Pentney proper. A wide and scattered village like
this, with neither squire nor resident policeman (for our nearest
constable lived between Narborough and Narford) was a natural
field for poachers. This, indeed, was almost officially suggested
when the Hall and Manor of Narborough, our next village, were
put up for sale. The auctioneer's advertisement, an imposing foolscap
pamphlet, contained a clause to the following effect: 'The estate is

[1] See Dunbar's panegyric on London City:
'Upon thy lusty Brigge of pylers white
Been Merchaunts full royall to behold.'

not itself preserved: but it adjoins the well-stocked coverts of other neighbours'. In that parish, on the Pentney side, was a picturesque bit of wild land, Bradmoor, on the very verge of the parish, where heath and swamp and wood stretched to the borders of Westacre. Here, in a cabin on the waste edge of the wayside, lived one labourer who did no work and took no wages. But he always carried half a crown in his pocket, lest any policeman should class him as having no visible means of subsistence; and in his hovel he had a gun. Moreover, we had one other, Rolfe, who deserves international fame; for his freak autobiography[1] is a precious human document which I am able to verify in every important particular.

Two poaching dramas occur to me as I write this. Somewhere in the eighties, in a hard frost, a man slipped on the kerb in Lynn High Street on a market-day; he fell heavily to the ground and exploded, drenching the pavement in blood. He was a poacher who had taken a common poacher's risk, and ill-fortune had found him out. He carried his gun unscrewed, barrel in one capacious pocket, and stock in the other. The barrel was loaded for instant use. To keep the charge from damp, he had put a cap on the nipple; and, to secure the cap, he had let the hammer gently down upon it. But his fall struck the hammer so violently as to discharge the whole barrel into his body.

The other was within three or four miles of Offley, when I was living there. A poacher was let out at last after a long term of penal servitude, and here was what I heard from those who remembered his trial and sentence. Luton, already a busy manufacturing town, was making rapid strides in Victorian times. Just outside was a thinly populated district of grassland and woods, almost wild, with several large and aristocratic parks. To put it with epigrammatic exaggeration, while the town swarmed with hand-to-mouth operatives, the countryside was full of game and gamekeepers. One of the most notorious poachers was a stonemason, X, of sturdy physique and formidable temper. One night there was a worse affray than usual, with perhaps a dozen combatants on each side. X either grappled with the muzzle of a keeper's gun, or took his own by the muzzle to club an opponent. It went off, and blasted a great hole in his thigh. The police, in response to an urgent call,

[1] *I walked by Night*, edited by Miss Haggard.

came an hour or two later and traced him by his blood to a barn, whither his fellows had carried him, having done their best meanwhile to plug the gaping wound with a wisp of barley-straw! The man's physique was so marvellous that he survived even this, and was well enough, some months later, to stand his trial at the Assizes. As he was carried into the court room in his litter, he looked round upon the double file of policemen, and said, 'I should like to get a day's shootin' among ye all.'

But I must come back to Pentney proper. I need not dwell upon the intoxication of free life for us children among thirty acres of sandy pasture and woodland, too poor agriculturally to generate any strict law of trespass. Once, my father tried barley in one of the fields; but it produced little beyond a blaze of Norfolk poppies, which my father persistently called 'red-weed', in obedience to the bucolic dialect of our county. Those little pedantries were all that he ever learned of farmer lore; and in his franker moments he once confessed to a steady yearly loss of £30. Here, however, he got his money's worth in health and amusement.

So the whole family revelled in this life, which had all the charm, with none of the exhausting labour, of Virgil's or of Horace's peasant. My father's few acres were as stony and marshy as those of Tityrus; they earned him the polite scorn of real farmers in our parish; but they were all he wanted. Ours was the scent of the hayfield; the lark's nest, the brow dripping with honest sweat, were ours; even the scythe work, which we were allowed to play at, discovering for ourselves what my farmer schoolfellow Willie Marshall once described, 'That wrings you into all sorts of shapes.' Even beyond our teens it gave to our pleasures a tinge of childlike— often, of childish—simplicity. We spent whole mornings fishing in the gravel bed of the little crystal brook for microscopic barbel and loach and 'miller's thumbs'. We made elaborate architectural mud-pies with the white marl of which there was a small vein at one end of the pond. And Edmund brought us once into real public notice. He constructed a lighthouse, of flower-pot piled upon flower-pot like a Chinese pagoda, on the sandbank where the water was only about six inches deep. This he lighted one winter's evening with due solemnity: and that night my father had to placate with half a crown a dank and dripping police constable, who had groped his way after this friar's lantern in the supposed interests of public safety. For myself, I can remember enjoying such puerilities even after, having donned the academic gown, I could claim my place among 'those noblest of their species, called emphatically Man.'

Old men forget: yet all shall be forgot, but my sister Beatrice and I, sole survivors now from that little Eden, remember with advantages the luscious fruit to which our neighbour, Ben Young, would admit us with a 'Take as much as you can, my dears.' He had great shining carthorses on which he let us ride in the cornfields and at hay-carting time. 'Bonnie' and 'Brag' were two of them; 'Brag' a black and 'Bonnie' a bay. Just behind his farm, in a meadow, our old gardener, Adams, ended his days. We had had him in Lynn; to us, as to Cardinal Newman, one of the earliest child memories was to hear the whetting of his scythe under our bedroom windows, while the dew was on the grass and the half-awakened birds began their song. He came to Pentney with us, having still twenty years of work in him. He was small of stature, with a slightly Jewish cast of face, reminiscent of Lord Beaconsfield, and with a great fund of peasant experience and wisdom behind his didactic manner. He would discourse learnedly about his flowers, and especially his favourite gladiolus, 'that do grow so plentifully about Jerusalem'. Once he forgot his usual care, and left his scythe lying in the long grass at the end of the drive. My father stumbled upon it next morning, barefooted except for his low shoes, and cut himself rather badly. That evening he showed Adams his bandaged foot, and explained solemnly, 'Dr Allinson tells me that it was almost within a hair's breadth of severing the anterior tibial artery'. Adams, didactic as usual, said, 'Yes, Sir, I should 'a thought as much'. On another occasion I watched the two making a concerted effort to pitch a little sluice-door across to the other side of the ditch for which it had been constructed: 'Now, Adams, we'll swing both together: I shall say "one", "two", "three", and then "go".' That phraseology lacked, it will be seen, strict legal precision. Adams did not see (so to speak) the inverted commas at 'go'. He interpreted the word as an imperative following upon 'three', and cast at that point with all his might. My father, who still held fast to the other end, was taken off his legs within an inch of the ditch. His account of the incident at breakfast was rather forensic than judicial, as I was obliged to point out from my detached standpoint of spectator. But my father always recognized that Adams, take him for all in all, was worth his weight in gold so long as he could stand up to his work. As a small boy, he had begun with odd jobs; among them, the driving of turkeys to market. This he always remembered with horror; for, unless you got your flock to its destination before sunset every bird of them would fly up for safety into the nearest tree and nothing would bring them down until dawn. Other tales there were of hard work and the pinch of poverty; but his hair was black, with only a sprinkling of grey, until his death at 98.

I have spoken of my father's attachment to his thirty acres of stone and sand and swamp; but my mother's was still deeper and more instinctive. Every fibre vibrated in her to the nature of that most natural place, where our own labours had rather guided than ruled the flowers, and the water reflects free unlopped trees, and most of the living creatures went their own way without molestation. I cannot resist transcribing here two characteristic entries from the diary of my sister, who sometimes jotted down the words almost from my mother's mouth, interlarded with the Lancashire ejaculations of her childhood. She was then close upon eighty, and even the morning's uprising was becoming a labour, until the garden sunshine should bring back something of the lizard's placidity.

Feb. 4, 1904. 'How I should like to be a dormouse! Eh! I wonder if there comes a spring when the dormouse feels older than he did when he went to sleep! Eh, yes! And one winter he would roll himself up and wouldn't unroll any more.'

A few days later, in March: 'Eh! how they do go! Poor little February has quite gone—with its little Mart and everything—it has taken its little Mart all packed away on its back and run away—and it will never come back! Eh! This is such a beautiful day from the very beginning: it says "Eh! do make the best of me, I am going, and I shall never, never come again! There may be better, prettier ones, but never me again!"' She had never read Dante: ' *Pensa, che questo dì mai non raggiorna* ',[1] but it was the inevitable touch of the same natural chord. The Mart had been, even in my boyhood, a great yearly event at Lynn. In the Middle Ages, it had been a springtide Fair of national importance; and even I can remember

[1] *Purg.* XII, 84.

how some folk awaited it, month after month, for their purchases of silk or woollen or linen or cutlery and household utensils.

Thus at Pentney we were country mice almost in the strictest sense, except for my brother Jim who shared little in all this life until 1883, when he resolved to quit the sea and qualify as a doctor. We seldom came within the orbit of London, even for a night or two, or a few hours at a time.

CHAPTER IX

THE PUBLIC SCHOOL

FELSTED, in Essex, is a typical example of the ancient Grammar School improved and enlarged in the nineteenth century until it attracted pupils from all parts of the country. In January, 1872, it had only one day boy, who lived about a mile from the school. We had contemptuous pity for this person who had no holiday home as a change from the treadmill of school.

Richard Lord Rich, a successful courtier under Henry VIII, played a conspicuously mean part in the tragedy of St Thomas More, and became one of the most shameless profiteers by the Dissolution of the Monasteries. He built himself a lordly mansion, much of which still stands, on the site of Leighs Priory; and at Felsted, some three miles distant, he founded a charity to which he devoted a fraction of the monastic spoils. In 1554, a chaplain was endowed there to pray for his soul and to keep school. A schoolhouse was built on the roadside to the south of that church where his sumptuous marble monument stands in a chapel of its own. On the upper floor was the great schoolroom, whose oaken beams are now carved with the names of many generations. On the ground floor, to the east, the Master dwelt, while the western side of the main gateway still shows arches once dedicated to periodical doles of bread and herrings for the poor.

In Stuart times, this small Grammar School attained a certain celebrity and, what is better, solidity. Two of Oliver Cromwell's sons, Richard and Robert, were taught there; so, later on, was the famous Isaac Barrow, Professor of Mathematics and Master of Trinity, and an almost equally renowned mathematician, John Wallis, of Emmanuel, who afterwards became Savilian Professor at Oxford and one of the founders of the Royal Society. The lands of the original endowment gradually increased in value, and in 1860 the Trustees found themselves able to start upon an ambitious building scheme. They built a schoolhouse with dormitories and class-rooms for some two hundred boys, flanked by a Headmaster's lodge at one end and a Second Master's at the other. Felsted now became the principal school in the Eastern Counties. The Head was the Rev. W. S. Grignon, a personal friend of Dr Thring, who was at that time converting the similar small foundation of Uppingham into one of the best-known Public Schools. Grignon had also been contemporary, at Trinity, Cambridge, with my father's cousin Gordon Calthrop, from whom I gathered later that they had been not only fellow students but something of boon companions. Under Grignon the school throve, and deserved it; for, with all his little peculiarities, he was a born schoolmaster.

In stature he was only 5 feet 4 inches, and this once saved his life. He was a keen volunteer, with military second-line rank as Captain of the School Cadet Corps. Just before my day, when the rifles were still old-fashioned muzzle-loaders, he was commanding a firing exercise, in the tall silk hat which he habitually wore. As he gave the word 'fire', his hat left his head and settled in a hedge behind; one cadet had forgotten to extract his ramrod. Such accidents, by the bye, were naturally not infrequent. In one of our field days on Galleywood Common near Chelmsford, we 'captured' some prisoners of an 'enemy' battalion; one of them was found to have ball cartridges left over from his last day at the butts and mingled with the blank in his pouch.

If that ramrod's parabola had been three inches lower, Felsted and England would have lost a gallant little gentleman. He fought a good fight in his last year at the school, when he felt that vital principles were at stake. Meanwhile, for the first half of my time at Felsted, he kept us in order by a system which was watchful without degenerating into espionage. The conditions were favourable. The buildings are on the crown of a gentle hill, with wide prospect all round, and open to all the healthy breezes. It was no mere imagination which made us taste salt on our lips when the wind had blown steadily for two or three days from the east. The village was scarcely more than a mere appendix to the school. The nearest town, Dunmow, some five miles distant, was itself scarcely more than a village: it was out of bounds for all but the prefects. London was more than forty miles off by rail, and our little side-line had small and infrequent trains. The air was vigorous and bracing: nearly all of us were from homes of moderate means; and the diet was Spartan without sinking to the extremes of St-Omer. Our numbers, again, running from two hundred to two hundred and fifty, were not such as to create any difficulty of control for a Head who took his duties seriously. Soon after my arrival there had been unusually loud complaint of trespass from the farmers around. Grignon assembled us all in the Big School, and intimated that this must cease. He spoke in quiet well-calculated tones of omnipotence, omniscience and almost omnipresence. At the top of the main tower (he explained) he had a quiet study of his own, and a powerful telescope. Through the optic glass, like the Tuscan Artist, he often entertained himself with a view of the country round: and any Felstedian who gave fresh cause for the farmers' complaints might well find his transgression as publicly revealed as if it had been committed 'here in this very schoolroom'. We were thus plainly forewarned. I never heard of any trespasser being caught by this particular method; but for some time, at least, birds'-nesting was more cautious and sporadic; and that was all that Grignon himself would have anticipated. My contemporary, Sir Hugh Beevor, to the end of his life, chuckled at the recollection of his boyish mind haunted by this all-seeing telescope.

It was a great advantage to us that those Essex districts, better wooded than most of East Anglia and yet less plagued with gamekeepers, afforded an outlet for other activities than those of naked athleticism. The school's cricket performances were up to the average standard of our size, and our football was definitely above the average: two of my schoolfellows became Internationals, and the two brothers King succeeded each other as Captains of Association Football at Oxford. But there was room also for natural history after our schoolboy fashion: butterflies, birds, and especially eggs. The hunt for kestrels' and sparrow-hawks' nests was a kind of royal sport. In one spinney was a tree one of whose branches told then, and perhaps tells still, of a romantic story. It was about half-way up a big oak, perhaps the biggest in the wood. F. E. Sinclair, who was in the Upper Fifth and a good athlete, was able to swarm up that tall and difficult trunk. But the nest could also be attacked in the flank from a much smaller oak, one of whose horizontal branches stretched out to touch those of its neighbour: and Gale had courage enough to make that hazardous crossing. Hence a duel to the death, in which Gale had the advantage of a Lower-School boy, who could get out from afternoon school an hour earlier. Sinclair, therefore, sawed the branch of his own tree half through, and warned his rival that there was now no passage. Gale disregarded the warning, and took the risk; Sinclair felt that he deserved the prize, and accepted the defeat. The half-sawn branch was still conspicuous next year, when I first visited that wood. And that same year came a fight, which for some time was equally famous, between Gale and his nesting-partner Offin. Those egg pirates slipped out together one morning at sunrise; but they quarrelled at their return over the division of the spoil. Sixteen spectators—for it was one of the two greater dormitories—were treated to a long and exciting contest: but Gale's pluck could not prevail against Offin's superior length of arm. As we others hurried down the corridor from our own dormitories to early school, we peeped in for a moment to see eighteen incarnadined washing-basins, and the bloody trails along the floor.

Into this society I was admitted in January, 1872, and put into the Upper Fourth, lowest of the Upper School. Thus, and from the fact that I had to live at Rowe's for want of a vacancy in the School House, I escaped the worst hardships of a small Felstedian. Those hardships were similar, in a more moderate form, to those at Marlborough twenty years earlier, as described by Sir Courtenay Ilbert in *The Marlburian* of a generation later. In the Upper School, each had the room of his own class as some sort of refuge, but the Lower School had no classrooms; they were all herded together in Big School, where two open coal fires struggled against the draughts which flooded sideways from two open doors, and downwards from the lofty roof. The fireplaces, of course, were completely beset with bigger boys, some of whom were almost among the oldest in the school, for there was no superannuation rule in those days. One of these, in my time, called out from his place to a very small new boy who was flitting disconsolately about in the background, 'What's your name? How did you get that crooked nose?' The new boy, Ralph Beevor, who became Head Boy in the year after I left, explained meekly, 'My nurse neglected me, and I trod upon it', leaving his questioner to puzzle over this curious accident.

In jotting down notes for these Felsted days, I am rather scandalized by the trivial nature of the things which come first, and often most clearly, to my mind. My father was spending upon me more than he could have afforded for all three brothers at once. I was now, at last, in what might be called the main stream of Victorian education, even though we were far from the central and the strongest current. Is it my fault, or that of Felsted School, that certain of the villagers are more firmly rooted in my memory than some of my masters, and the woods or meadows than the classroom? On reflection, it seems merely to corroborate what others also have remarked to me during my thirty years of vagabond teaching after leaving Cambridge. I worked at those teaching jobs, on the whole, more steadily than the average of my colleagues, and I could not help feeling—the boast is not great—that I had a wider literary background than the average. Yet I seemed to see in my own classroom, as in others when we were set to exchange examinations, that there was disappointingly little difference in result between teaching done under a strong sense of responsibility, stimulated by ambition to rise, as compared with the go-as-you-please teaching of men who had come back (let us say) to their own school; men whose vouchers were almost as much in the athletic field as in the intellectual, and who thus had very little idea of what was done or might be done in other schools, but had passed by sheer weight of seniority into the lucrative House Masterships, and remained little more than grown-up schoolboys to the end. These men, of course, often possessed the one thing which might be most lacking in the busy and self-righteous colleague; they had instinctive sympathy with boyhood; they were not struggling to drag their pupils up into any rarefied atmosphere; they did not need to labour in rivalry, because all the comforts of life came to them without labour. But that consideration leaves untouched the main fact—if fact it be—that God's rain falls with comparative impartiality upon the field of the 'just' and the 'unjust' teacher. It is true that, from the mere examination point of view, the gulf is often immense. But, from the standpoint of human development, the difference may seem very small. Here, again, we must remember the wise carpenter's remark recorded by William James: 'There's very little difference between man and man, but it's just this that makes the difference.' Such decisive variations may come as much from imponderable influences as from organized method, and sometimes even more.

What Felsted gave us, as compared with other schools of the

same class, was a sort of healthy freedom. We were far from the mechanical pressure of some greater and more famous foundations, where even spectatorship at the games had been, to a certain extent, organized. 'Jas' Barker's cobbler's shop, at the parting of the roads just outside the village, was to many of us almost as regular a haunt as the two tuck shops. He had been a prominent Radical; he would distribute old numbers of Cobbett's *Weekly Register* to all who cared to read them: he had not been to church for forty years, and would not now, until he should be carried feet first. Nonconformity flourished in the village, under Mr Cox, a high-and-dry vicar who made a point of entering no Nonconformist door.

In 1876, the vicar raised money for the restoration of the parish church, giving liberally also from his own patrimony and from that of his wife, a lady of county family whom he had married after many years of bachelorhood. This restoration I was able to watch in detail even more closely than the contemporary work of the kind at Lynn and the two Dunmows. Two of these were under the direction of Sir Gilbert Scott, most renowned of Victorian architects in his own creations, and among the most merciless in his treatment of the old work. But Felsted, which was not his work, answered even better than Lynn to Ruskin's memorable phrase, 'utterly restored'. The Rich chapel had no historical connection whatever with the south aisle; therefore time and money must now be spent in joining them together. A beautiful fourteenth-century altar-tomb stood in the way of this reconstruction; I watched the workmen dislocating the stones of the sculptured canopy for transportation to another part of the church, and breaking many in the process. Even to a boy of seventeen, this vandalism was not fully compensated by the intense interest of watching the re-sculpture of the ruined portions and talking with the carver at his work. The old east window, again, was of a height which displeased the vicar: he therefore cut it down by three or four feet, thus ruining its proportions. On the other hand, two excellent funeral brasses were discovered under the flooring; also part of a wall-painting representing Avarice seized by devils and cast down into hell. There was real excuse for destroying this, since, in its fragmentary state and its lurid colours, it must have been more distracting than edifying to modern worshippers. But I drew it faithfully, in all its crudities of form and colour, for a copy of

Morant's *Essex* which the aunt of my friend H. J. Landon was 'grangerizing'; and I find it still one of my most illuminating lantern slides for showing the medieval Church walls as 'the Bible of the Poor'.[1]

My father's junior partner, the Lynn antiquary E. M. Beloe, had initiated me long ago into some of these mysteries. I had carved clumsy Norman doorways in chalk or wood, copied many pages of details from Rickman's *Gothic Architecture*, and vaguely dreamed of making my living by that profession. At Felsted came a further stimulus, from Peachey the innkeeper, who dealt also in furniture, and had in his backyard a shed crammed with unconsidered trifles which he had picked up in every direction. I still possess a charming little writing-desk candlestick in bronze which I bought for ninepence. Just after I had left, he sold me half a dozen painted glass 'carrels' from the Bishop of London's ancient palace of Much Hadham.

H. J. Landon, my exact contemporary, had much the same tastes: and together we tramped all round from church to church, rubbing brasses and collecting. It goes almost without saying that I would have sold my soul at any time to become a first-rate cricketer; and, on the other hand, that I now treasure those tramping memories beyond the fame of a 'W. G.' or a Bradman. One of them comes back most vividly, on a whole-holiday, such as we enjoyed three or four times a year, when the school had a cricket match away from home. That day we went to Thaxted, a famous pilgrimage church for modern antiquaries, but then in a state of disgraceful neglect. We resolved to cut across by Stebbing, and found the broom in full glory on a steep wild slope to the west of the village. It was not mere gorse, but golden broom six or seven feet high, such as intoxicated Burns in Scotland:

> O the broom, the bonny bonny broom,
>   The broom of the Cowden Knowes!
> And the bonny lassie, sae sweet as she sang
>   In the bught, milking the yowes!

By that cross-country route, taking Thaxted spire as a landmark from afar, one passes through Lindsell, where a bewitchingly pretty

[1] Reproduced in black and white in my *Art and the Reformation*, p. 310.

little church and farmyard are almost smothered in great trees and roses. There, as usual, the church was shut; but we soon found the parsonage and the key. When we restored it, the parson himself was in the hall, and invited us in to a biscuit and a glass of sherry, the usual welcome for visitors in that day. Unfortunately, he addressed me first, and I was too shy to accept. Landon declined also; but no sooner had we got out into the garden than I felt a severe kick in the pants. 'You ass! why did you refuse?' The mere *tu quoque* was no good: it was I who had set the evil example, and I knew it. On a bench in the Church Inn at Thaxted, we had nine miles in our legs, and fourpence each for food and drink, with a little bread and cheese from school. Yet when, more than thirty years later, I found myself alone on that same bench, with three or four sovereigns in my pocket and a raging tooth in my head, this led me to philosophize on the mutability of human fortune.

Next to Landon and antiquarianism, the greatest rival to the cricket field was in Ned Fuller. He was a wonderful combination of poaching, tippling, and fundamental good nature. In 1875, just after Easter, we had an epidemic of scarlet fever, and I was among the first victims. A mortal quarrel between Headmaster and Matron was then raging, with disastrous results for our comfort in the infirmary: at times we were scandalously neglected, especially in our hungriest convalescent stage, when dinner might come an hour late. Then, at last, two or three useless hussies were discharged, and this loafing labourer was put on to do the whole housemaid work of the infirmary. He was tall, broad-shouldered, and muscular, with a big, round, flat face that glowed all over like Bardolph's nose. He wore loosely the traditional poacher's shabby green velveteen coat, with pockets enough for one or two casual hares or rabbits. With us, he was never the worse for drink; and he slaved like the drudging goblin of *L'Allegro*. 'Seven maids with seven mops' could scarcely have kept pace with him. Then, when we began to get about and could do more for ourselves, he would sit and talk with us after work. The crown of his many poaching feats was to have baled out the pool below the bridge of the Chelmer. With half a dozen comrades, one summer night, he dammed the little stream just above the pool: thus the shallows below soon ran dry, and then all buckets plied to drain the pool itself. I forget how many pails full of fish they carried off: trout, pike, perch and roach. He taught us the art of snaring pike with a wire noose at the end of a rod: a proceeding more sportsmanlike, by the natural standard of artistic difficulty, than fishing with spoon-bait. In his lifetime, he had tried practically every village job: the most laborious of all, apart from harvesting, was in the brick pits, where the clay had to be kneaded underfoot. But that had entirely cured the corns that once crippled him.

Arthur Sidgwick, some fifty years ago, gave a lecture on 'Stimulus' to a large and select body of educationalists. He began by explaining the limitations of his direct experience, concluding: 'Of science I know nothing; I have not even taught it.' This alluded to the Arnoldian tradition that each Form Master should teach his own pupils in nearly all their subjects; a tradition surviving to some extent almost at that same moment at Haileybury, for instance, where, under a Rugbeian Head of energy and distinction, my friend A. V. Jones, an excellent Classic, was responsible also for the French of his form. He regularly began each scholastic year at the beginning of Edmond About's *Roi des Montagnes*. At the end of the twelvemonth, they had done about half the book; and Jones, in later life, never pretended to know any French word that did not occur in the first half of About. I have heard another Form Master pronounce French by the stolidly British rules which Mr Churchill, in these his present war speeches, applies to the German tongue. An exceptionally successful preparatory school Headmaster, on one festive scholastic occasion, quoted French across the crowded table to the Irishman whom he employed to teach the language: 'Is that not correct, Mr O'Grady?' 'Quite right, Sir, barrin' the pronunciation.' O'Grady himself claimed to speak French 'like a native'; and 'begorra, he did'—like a native of Cork.

When I first went to Felsted, Grignon was perhaps a little luckier in his Gallic assistant than the average. Monsieur Paul Dubois, some years after leaving us, became Professor at a provincial university, and his son became more successful still. But with us Dubois was a beginner, learning his job, and curiously combining the sinning with the sinned-against. In all our forms, marks went by the primitive system of 'taking places'. Questions went down the form till a right answer was given: then the answerer went up to the place at which the question had first been started; finally, at the end of the hour, we 'numbered up', starting from the bottom boy, while the master recorded our place. Once, in the middle of the term, 'Mons. Porl', as we called him, lost his mark-book. His ingenious resource was to 'make marks', by numbering and recording three or four times in the hour. Another term he began in similar difficulties: no mark-book to be found: where, therefore, was each boy to start, with no record from the term before? This time his expedient was even more frankly immoral. One boy was son to the Chelmsford solicitor who acted as Clerk to the School Trustees; another had been one of 'Mons. Porl's' most difficult subjects. 'Meggy, your father 'Ed Trustee; you go up top! Peck, you 'aive monkey face; you go bottom!' He was capable of equally off-hand methods with his colleagues. His rooms were just above those of Scott the mathematician, whose pet evening occupation was to tend the mignonette and nasturtiums of his flower box, while Dubois, at his own window, preferred the meditative pipe. One evening Scott suddenly found himself greeted by a moisture which was not dew from heaven. In white-hot rage, he burst open Dubois' door and sputtered out a half-articulate protest. The only satisfaction he could get was 'Ye fool, ye knew ah was thair!' On the other hand, Dubois might justly have filled his own memoirs with even sharper criticisms than those of the contemporary 'Max O'Rell' in his *John Bull and his Island*. We had a rhyme that ran

> This is Mons. Porl:
> 'Ah can't 'aive it at all!
> Zey veessle and blaw
> Through ze 'oles of ma door,
> And ven ah am vext
> And vonder, vat next?
> Ze boy that am fat[1]
> Puts stones in ma 'at.'

With all this, Dubois prospered sufficiently to achieve promotion elsewhere and probably to deserve it. Certainly we had reason to regret him under his successor, whom I will name by the decent obscurity of *X*. This man had a remarkable artistic facility in a small way: he could draw dozens and dozens of French soldiers, blue

[1] Pelly, scion of a family with an honourable military and naval record.

coats and red pantaloons, with wonderful life and rapidity; small boys thronged his room to admire them. But suddenly, after a few weeks or months, X was seen no more, and his very name became unmentionable. His successor was even more mysterious in his beginning than X had been in his end. I never even heard of this man's existence until after I had left the school. He arrived one Saturday night, and was discovered on Sunday morning dead-drunk in the pigsty behind the chapel. Then, about a year before the end of my time, came a young fellow of pleasant manners and evident good intentions, whose main failing was that he knew scarcely any English. By that time, an ambitious scheme was on foot for giving even the Sixth Form an hour of French per week. We brought in our J. R. Green's *Short History of the English People*, and this man's business was to help us translate it (or more often translate it himself in the last resort) into his own tongue. The section he chose was that which Green headed *The Faerie Queen*. Week after week, he steadily rendered that title as *La Belle Reine*, without protest on our part: for why should we object? Either he outlasted my time, or his successor laboured under similar disadvantages. For years afterwards, when I was exposing Public School Modern Language teaching, I wrote to Ralph Beevor for his recollections from 1877 to 1878. He replied, 'There is only one thing which I can reproduce pretty exactly. He asked us once in class, "Zees vob, from whom do she derivate himself?"'

Of German there was no pretence; I doubt whether anybody in the school could read it except perhaps J. H. Backhouse, the Second Master, who had written and published a book on Church History. He was a real scholar, but painfully guileless, and very weak in discipline. The form masters of the two lowest forms changed almost as often as the Frenchmen. One, named Wood, I remember as a very pleasant, good-looking B.A., and an excellent athlete; he was therefore an immediate favourite with the boys. After a few terms, in 1877, he left for some better post. His own class was then inspired to raise a parting present; an undertaking unprecedented for the Second Form. The very modest subscriptions were entrusted to two of the most active agents, who procured a pass to Dunmow for the last half-holiday of term. They came back with a large and sumptuously bound Bible, furnished on the flyleaf with illuminated spaces for registration of Wood's future wife and children. It was a touching ceremony: Wood gave his form a moving address on the text of 'The Bible is a good Book; and this is the best Bible I have ever seen'. Only next term did it transpire that the two delegates had succumbed to temptation at Dunmow, spent the collected shillings at the confectioner's, and ordered the Bible to be debited to Wood's account.

CHAPTER X

THE CHRYSALIS STAGE

ALL this while, how was I getting on in the two languages to which, officially, almost all my time was devoted and which were to constitute my key not only to some learned profession but also to the mysteries of life? I will try to tell the facts fairly, and had better begin by indicating the point of view from which I regard them after nearly seventy years. For the vexed question of Boarding School versus Day School, after experience of both, as pupil and as teacher, long consideration has slightly inclined me to the latter so far as the present day is concerned. With regard to the future, it seems plainly accordant with democratic principles that pupils should not, normally, be separated from their homes, or from their fellow-citizens by what amounts, in fact, to a class-barrier, since the Boarding School must always be far more expensive than the other. On the other hotly debated question of the value of Latin and Greek, I feel far more strongly. In the world as it was, I am heartily grateful for a Classical education; but during the last half-century I have become increasingly convinced that it should be a matter for specialists, and that those advantages of thought and style, which are commonly claimed for Latin and Greek, can be taught through the Modern Languages, some knowledge of which must become increasingly necessary in a world which will emerge from this War with such a striving towards sane Internationalism as will make an epoch in history.[1]

These generalities being now cleared away, it may be of real interest to some future student of educational history to trace the operation of what I may call the Victorian system upon what ranked as a 'Public School' in the select sense, although it was among the least wealthy, aristocratic, or conspicuous.

The Upper Fourth and Lower Fifth at Felsted were taken by A.W. Rowe. He was an excellent disciplinarian, with that shaven upper lip and abundant dark beard which gives a suggestion of iron will even

[1] See my *Public Schools and Public Needs* (Simpkin Marshall and Co. 1906).

to an ordinary face. He reminded me of Mr Murdstone in *David Cop-perfield*. He was not a first-rate scholar; during the term when he was acting Headmaster we caught him out half a dozen times in Sixth Form lessons. Once (to be frank) I thought I did so, but only exposed myself. For the year and a half that I spent in those two forms I smarted under his lash and, I still think, his occasional injustices. Yet, even at the time, I could not resist a certain gratitude towards the strong hand which took me by the scruff of the neck and carried me through pages of Herodotus and Thucydides, Aeschylus and Sophocles, Virgil and Horace and Livy and Cicero, which I should never have had half the courage and perseverance to attack by myself. For the first time in scholastic life, and almost for the last, I was here under a control irresistible within its own limitations. I respected Rowe then, and respect him even more after sixty-nine years, for doing his job so efficiently in spite of the frequent deficiencies on my own side. I even respected the fact, and took it as a kind of compliment, that he caught more easily in my case at the opportunity of sending me down to the bottom for any definite indications of idleness or carelessness, and thus seriously handicapping me for the Term's total. This reminds me of an incident which will probably interest Latinists, and which others may take warning to omit.

We were always allowed to prepare the morrow's work in pairs, and generally did so. My usual partner was G. F. Colborne, who is still alive and hearty at Newport (Mon.), in retirement from a successful life at the law, and surrounded by innumerable grandchildren. He was the model of the Good Apprentice. When, towards the end of our time, a prize was instituted for the worthiest figure in the School, he was the general choice. But once, in the Lower Fifth, he suffered heavily for our partnership. We were at Livy, XXI, 10 where Hanno tries to dissuade his city from war: 'Aegatis insulas Erycemque ante oculos proponite, quae terra marique per quattuor et viginti annos passi sitis'.[1] It was probably I who had excogitated the absurd translation of that sentence, but Colborne, as it happened, was put on to construe it, and he thus rendered the words: 'Set before your eyes the Aegatian Isles and Eryx, which

---

[1] 'Set before your eyes The [case of] the Aegatian Isles & Eryx; [consider] what [disasters] you have suffered for 24 years, both by land and by sea.'

suffered thirst by land and sea for four-and-twenty years.' He was sent down ignominiously, and it took him several lessons to work his way up again to first or second.

In those days, the gift most coveted was that of Latin versification: not quite with the idolatry of Eton or Shrewsbury, but still with the reverence of ancient tradition. Towards the end of my first Half, Rowe sent me up with one or two others to try for a Junior Exhibition. We were set a piece of hexameters; and, with the help of tags dragged in from the *Eclogues*, I managed to put together three or four lines. This counted more for me than all my deficiencies as a newcomer to Herodotus; and, counted in afterwards with the Upper Fourth examination, it put me first: a demoralizing success.

At Midsummer, 1873, J. H. Backhouse left and Rowe was promoted to take the Upper Fifth: he took us up with him. That Christmas there was an unusual batch of promotions; in favour of Colborne, T. W. Haddon (afterwards Scholar of University College, Oxford, and Sixth Form Tutor at City of London School) and myself. I was thus cast into the freedom of the Sixth Form at an inauspicious moment. For Grignon was already in difficulties; moreover, he was devoting most of his attention to the few Scholarship candidates; so he left us mainly to work out our own salvation. We were to read for ourselves the books in which our elders had already a term's start: the *Frogs* and some Lucretius, and I forget what else. Superficially, that resembled what G. G. Bradley had done at Marlborough with conspicuous success: he had turned his best boys loose in his study with the *Corpus Poetarum* and the *Poetae Scenici*; and his own intervention had been to a great extent Socratic. But Grignon intervened very little with us three, and this furnace of liberty soon distinguished between the gold and the dross. Haddon was a year older and had exceptional initiative: he forged definitely ahead. Colborne worked with his usual steadiness, and made a good second. I lapsed into childish idleness, and played a bad third. It was my worst record until my head was turned by the similar plunge from patriarchal Felsted into the liberty of a Cambridge 'man'.

Our Sixth Form Tutor was 'Vinegar' Jones, an exact scholar but unsympathetic teacher. I finally invented a technique of shirking his lessons; he gave me up as a bad job, and I have now only the vaguest memory of autumn, 1874, and the spring of 1875. My scarlet fever lost me the whole summer months of 1875: then came Grignon's dismissal and Rowe's appointment as acting Head pending the new election. Under Rowe I had to work decently again; but until that, for some eighteen months of my school life, I have scarcely anything to recall beyond a little verse or prose contributed to *The Felstedian*, and a speech or two in the recently formed Debating Society.

In January 1876 came our new Head, D. S. Ingram, and we were again in careful and sympathetic hands. Twice during that year he secured remarkably good Sixth Form assistance, but each time for a few weeks only. Tancred Raven, a Shrewsbury man and a great favourite of W. E. Heitland, came to fill up the time until he should be called to Sherborne. Then we had an even abler scholar, F. G. Selby, until at Christmas he was appointed to the headship of a college in India, from which he passed in due course to become Director of Public Instruction, and Vice-Chancellor of the University of Bombay. Haddon had now gone up with an £80 scholarship to University College, Oxford; and it was Selby's advice that Colborne and I should try our luck at his own College of Wadham.

The preliminaries of such a trial, at this very College, are admirably described by the late Humbert Wolfe in his autobiographical sketch, *The Upward Anguish*. Colborne and I, on our short journey from Felsted, had no such adventures as he had on his way from Bradford. At Oxford itself, by exception, my memory suggests no sunshine: only November gloom and the very opposite of *possunt, quia posse videntur*. True, I had once had some Greek verses commended by Raven; Selby, again, had directed me to Buckle and Mommsen, and made me think a little: but the immediate effect upon my raw mind was that which Mark Pattison describes in his *Memoirs*: 'A very feeble germ of intellect was struggling with a crushing mass of facts, ideas which it could not master, and with the tyrannical force of more powerful intelligence in the persons around me. Instead of starting, as I saw other men do, with a buoyant sense of mental vigour and delight in the masterful exercise of intellectual weapons, I was wearily nursing a feeble spark of mind, painfully conscious of its inability to cope with its environment.'[1] Even in the direction

[1] *Memoirs*, p. 325.

where my future really lay, I found at first rather the desperation of
sin than hopes of salvation. In that year, 1876, Sir G. O. Trevelyan's
Life of Macaulay appeared. I was then School Librarian, and thus
had indeed the first taste of the book, but always with

> Time's wingéd chariot hurrying near,

and a dozen ravenous schoolfellows gaping for their turn. This was
the first book to give me a feeling, not indeed that I was a man, but
that I might be. Here was what all the cultivated public had been
long looking forward to; here was what they, like us, had clutched
at; and (as I thought then, and am convinced still) what not one of
them read with more exalted feelings than I did in this little Essex
village. My own liqueur glass, like their great goblets, was full to
the brim.[1] It was one of my greatest pleasures, in later days, to buy
the new revised edition for Felsted Library in exchange for that
old tattered copy of 1876.

Yet the very height of this ideal enthusiasm contrasted with the
squalor of my actual state. I enjoyed Buckle and Gibbon; I was not
altogether discouraged even by the multitude of tribes and strange
names with which Mommsen begins; but I was conscious how
little, after all, I had managed to digest from all those pages.
Humbert Wolfe, many years later, tells in his Autobiography
how he approached the Wadham examiners with the buoyancy of
an elect and predestined soul. I sat before them in the consciousness
of sin.

And yet my friend Haddon had done much to pave my way. He
had a Manchester friend and future brother-in-law two years his
senior, and therefore three years older than I. This was A. J. Ashton,
then Scholar of Balliol and finally Recorder of Manchester, whose
tale of his own life is full of psychological and historical interest.[2]
Haddon asked him to dinner and to take me out for a walk next day;
we went round by Mesopotamia and Headington; and he gave me
wise advice. He had come up from Manchester Grammar School
in the days when Gladstone could say 'that there were two school-

---

[1] Carlyle, as I have since found out, judged at the time that the Biography
would 'long outlive anything that Macaulay himself had written' (*Carlyle in
Old Age*, by D. A. Wilson and D. W. MacArthur (1904), p. 401).

[2] *As I Went On My Way* (Nisbet, 1924). I shall quote this as *Ashton*.

masters in England, Bradley [of Marlborough] and Walker [of
Manchester]'.[1] Reading his book now again to refresh my memory,
I realize even more than in 1876 my own ignorance for all Scholarship purposes, in comparison with contemporaries from the first-rate
schools. His description of Walker's methods forms a document
of first-rate value for future historians of Victorian education.[2]
Walker, it seems, advised candidates to read Browning's *The Bishop
orders his Tomb* 'because they are sure to ask you about the Renaissance'.[3] Ashton did not pass this advice on to me; but, even if he
had done so, it might have been useless. For next day our General
Knowledge paper contained a question upon what it called the
'Renascence'—a quite recent form popularized by J. R. Green,
whom at that time I had scarcely dipped into.[4] For the 'Renaissance'
I was fairly equipped by familiarity with Macaulay's *Essays*, and
by having come across Roscoe's *Lorenzo de' Medici* in the school
library: but what was I to make of this unfamiliar 'Renascence'?
If I confused it with 'Renaissance', would not that be a pitfall as
fatal as to confuse 'Jacobite' with 'Jacobin'? So, to my disgrace,
I left that severely alone. Here was a bad fault of omission. But my
faults of commission were worse. I have no recollection now of the
Essay subjects: I only remember sitting in that ancient hall, one
of the most beautiful in England, and wondering how any man
could imagine that I knew anything whatever about these particular
three which were here offered for my choice. Even Selby, in his
short reign, had given us little practice in the formal essay; and my
own conception of the job lingered still in the childish stage of pure
Macaulay worship. However, I plunged into one of the three, much
as Caliban in Browning's poem plunges at one or other of the crabs.
But, after a few lines, there came a paralysing reflection. I had begun
a sentence: 'The Greek, for all his cosmopolitanism, ...' That
sounded well; but, as ill-luck would have it, I paused to reflect
whether the Greek spirit could truly be called cosmopolitan. In this
kind of examination, the essayist who hesitates is lost, unless he be
one of those rare boys of eighteen who have actually something to

[1] *Ashton*, p. 11.   [2] *Ibid.* pp. 16 ff.   [3] *Ibid.* p. 17.
[4] The *Oxford English Dictionary*, giving 'Renaissance' as early as 1840, has
no examples of 'Renascence' (in that sense) earlier than Matthew Arnold, 1869,
and J. R. Green, 1874.

say. In due course, the Wadham authorities notified Selby that I was evidently meant for Cambridge: so to Cambridge, in due course, I went. To Colborne they offered an exhibition of £30 which he did not care to accept, and has never had reason to regret. For, as a successful lawyer and man of business, he has earned the same tranquillity and respect in the world as had been promised by his career at school. Ashton I never saw again, to my great regret: my wandering life never threw me at all in his way, and very little in Haddon's.

Believing, as I do with increasing conviction, that life is an experiment, a test of character, and that the Self has to make its own mosaic from a staggering choice of alternatives set before it, I cannot now regret my failure at Wadham; nor, after the first moments, do I remember ever to have done so. The variations between Oxford and Cambridge are healthy, corresponding to natural differences in the human mind; and I think I should not have fitted well into the more elaborate and intricate educational pattern of the older university. As a merely personal calculation, I feel happy in not having been moulded under a system which culminated in Jowett's consummate tutorial mastery. There is something also in this fact, that Oxford walls and gardens appear to me now *sub specie aeternitatis*: very much as Charles Lamb saw them. It is good to have worked at Cambridge; but it is glorious to wander about Oxford courts, and to look down from Boar's Hill upon 'that sweet city with her dreaming spires', or upon 'the line of festal light in Christ Church Hall'. How much do we not all owe to the unattained and unattainable! If Dante had married Beatrice, where would the *Commedia* have been? The reality may well be better than the dream; but it is good, while we live the reality, to dream the dream.

After Christmas, there came to Felsted the best of all my schoolmasters: E. G. Hardy, Fellow and future Principal of Jesus, Oxford. He well knew the value of persistence; for six Oxford colleges had turned him down before he won a scholarship at Exeter, after which he justified the choice by his First in Mods and in Greats. His sympathy and help were unfailing, to the just and the unjust. Under him I gained some real confidence, and went to Cambridge that Easter as a candidate for Trinity Hall.

The Senior Tutor of that College was the Rev. Henry Latham,

familiarly known as 'Ben'. Under a not very clerical dress or manner, he had a deeply religious mind. If not true, it is *ben trovato*, that, when a parent once asked him whether his correspondence was not very heavy, he replied, 'Oh, no! for I begin by putting into the waste-paper basket all letters addressed to B. Latham, Esq.' One most characteristic anecdote has not found its way even into Leslie Stephen's *Life of Fawcett* or into Mr Thorneley's gleanings. It was told me in 1885 by an old Hertfordshire parson who had been present on the occasion. Latham had taken his degree from Trinity; but he applied for a vacant Fellowship at 'The Hall'. He asked the great Whewell for a testimonial, which arrived at the moment when he was entertaining some friends (my parson included) at breakfast. Whewell's certificate rehearsed, in characteristically stately style, how Mr Latham was primarily a mathematician, but was also 'capable of grappling with the most difficult passages in the Greek and Latin Classics'. 'Ben' put the paper down with 'Yes, I could *grapple* with the Tipton Slasher, but what would be the result?' (The Tipton Slasher died somewhere about 1880; I well remember his obituary in *Bell's Life in London*. He was, like so many prize-fighters of the day, a collier; neglect in infancy had made him grow up awkward and knock-kneed; but he had the torso of a Hercules.)

Latham was a bachelor don of the best sort; his pupils were his children. He was a friend of Leslie Stephen, and a muscular Christian of the Kingsley school. If he had been a parish parson his sermons would often have been on the text which Disraeli popularized at some public occasion in the seventies: *Sanitas sanitatum, omnia sanitas*; 'Look to the parish drains: cleanliness is next to godliness'. He took great pains to try us candidates out. I think all—certainly the majority—were entertained one night in Hall and Combination Room: it was encouraging to see how the two or three dons treated each other familiarly like schoolboys.[1] Henn, the Mathematical Tutor, came in for most chaff, probably because his brother Henry was a candidate. On the third day, Latham had us in, one by one, for a brief 'oral'. Nowadays, whenever I come home to my College rooms, I make a point of taking the alternative route through Trinity

---

[1] Since writing this, I have come across a similar record in the *Long Retrospect* of T. Anstey Guthrie, author of *Vice Versa*. An admirable portrait of Latham is to be found in T. Thorneley's *Cambridge Memories*.

Hall, for the sake of looking again at that window where the Senior Tutor sat and gave me a second, third and fourth guess at the word κύβος, which had occurred in our 'Unseen' from Plato and in which I entirely failed to recognize *dice*, the ancestor of our modern *cube*. Incidentally, I wonder even now why the ύ has not there followed the usual rule, of transliteration, and thus made *Kybe*. I was prepared for the final result: the Classical Scholarship went to Henry Henn, and I can say with Gibbon that I fell by no ignoble hand; for, after years of fruitful college work as a Fellow, he became Bishop of Burnley. I went back to Felsted resolved to do better next time.

Through those beautiful months of April, May and June I worked hard and happily under Hardy's encouragement, watching the grass and corn grow and feeling that I too was growing with them. One special quarter of an hour I remember, between midday school and midday dinner, lying in a deep flowering meadow just to the north of Colborne's and my study, and fully conscious for the first time in my life of the beauty of common grass at its moment of midsummer perfection.

In late May or early June I started again for Cambridge, and sat in the Hall of St Catharine's College with some thirty men who were also at their last attempt: for this was practically the end of the academic year. But here I remember no feeling that this was a forlorn hope. I knew that Hardy had brought me on rapidly in the past five months; moreover, I was growing physically also, after three or four years of very slow development. It did not now seem so incredible that the world might become my oyster. The papers suited me; in Latin verse, especially, I fancied I had ended up with a couplet as good as my examiner could do. On the way home, I filled in the change of trains at Bishop's Stortford by getting the church keys and climbing the tower. Looking backwards thence across the sunny land, I had a conviction, none the less overpowering because it was so tinged with wishful thinking, that this was my Pisgah-sight, and that Cambridge, out there to the north, was my Land of Promise. Two or three days after, came the letter offering me the first Classical Scholarship, and I felt as though all this had been fore-ordained from the beginning of time.

This was the last year in which, at Felsted, the old-fashioned

division into two Halves still held out against the modern arrangement of three Terms. Break-up and Speech Day, therefore, came
towards the end of June, a few days after Midsummer. In the
chapel garden, under the old elms, we had masses of white syringa
and roses, which grew magnificently in that clay soil. The scent of
syringa, to the present moment, brings back Felsted as inevitably
as toasted orange peel revives St-Omer. For the last few Sundays
of Term, evening service sent the sun to rest in peculiar splendour.
The beams stole in behind through the north windows, flooding
the southern wall with glowing arabesques, and mingling with the
last hymn in a fusion which brought home even to my unmusical
mind the natural and inevitable sisterhood of sight and sound. Not
that we analysed those things at the time; but they come back with
'the glory and the freshness of a dream'.

> Lingua mortal non dice
> Quel ch' io sentiva in seno.[1]

The last Sunday of this final Term I enjoyed in even deeper peace,
with my great-aunts at Chipping Hill, the two surviving sisters of
that Richard Calthrop whose head had been shot off at the bombardment of Algiers in 1816. (*Chipping*, which we find in other place
names as Chipping Ongar and Chipping Campden, Cheapside and
Copenhagen, means 'market': compare our *chapman* for *pedlar*, and
the German *kaufen*.) It is a crooked little street crowning the rising
ground above Witham, with a fine church of its own, and the
mouldering remains of a splendid old manor house; moss-grown
walls of deep red brick. My aunts' house and garden were as old-
fashioned as themselves, and so was their hospitality. They could
boast of their home-made brawn that it had held unshaken primacy
in Lincolnshire and Norfolk and Essex from the time when the
memory of man runneth not to the contrary; and they assumed,
rightly enough, that I had infinite capacity for brawn with vinegar
and sugar. They had been among the original subscribers to *The
Churches of Lincolnshire*, with other good illustrated books; and
within about a mile was Faulkbourn Hall, one of the best fifteenth-
century brick houses in the kingdom. The little bedroom smelt of

[1] Leopardi, *A Silvia*.

lavender, and had a text on the wall to which one woke in the morning:

> A Sunday well spent
> Brings a week of content
>   And health for the work of the morrow.
> But a Sabbath profaned,
> Whatsoe'er may be gained,
>   Is a certain forerunner of sorrow.
>
> SIR MATTHEW HALE

Under its window grew the first row of tomatoes I had ever seen; they were introduced to us by aunt Louisa under the old-fashioned Pickwickian name of love-apple. Aunt Louisa, the blue-stocking of the family, who wrote a brief memoir of her brother Richard and his death at Algiers, sometimes quoted to us an epigram of her girlhood:

> Men have many faults, women only two:
> Nothing right they say, nothing right they do.

The visit meant always a walk to Braintree and back, six miles each way; and once, at any rate, my brother Edmund and I tramped the further six miles to Chipping Hill. On that occasion I saw, for the only time in my life, three cuckoos together, so near that one might almost have caught all three with one scoop of a great butterfly net. The wild roses in the hedgerows of rural Essex are more luxuriant, in mass, than even their garden and churchyard sisters; and in colour they are even more tenderly bewitching during their short life. All this, on my last schoolboy visit, was sadly discounted by the fact that my shoes, already at their last gasp, began to gape on the way back from Braintree; and the morrow was Speech Day; and all our boxes were already packed on their way for the station! I could only hope, as I went up to the platform for my prizes, that my toes were not so nakedly prominent as they felt. Those prizes included the First Senior Exhibition, of £60 a year, which, with the £60 from St Catharine's, removed all uncertainty as to my matriculation at Cambridge.

CHAPTER XI

CAMBRIDGE IN 1877

IT is borne in upon me now that a sixty-four years' membership amounts to rather more than one-twelfth of the whole existence of Cambridge University, and indeed to a pretty exact twelfth of all University life in Europe. It would be strange, therefore, if this did not show considerable changes, roughly parallel with the general trend of society within that period.

There is a moral behind that slender monument which stands on a triangle of green, exactly opposite the Chapel of Trinity College. This commemorates the church of All Saints, which had become inconvenient and almost useless: for its tower projected into the street, while its parish had practically faded away, leaving it stranded among College buildings. By a healthy move, therefore, funds were raised for pulling the dilapidated edifice down, and building a new church in the poorest part of the parish opposite Jesus College. This was begun by one vicar, and finished by his successor. The latter appealed to the generosity, among others, of W. H. Thompson, then Master of Trinity, whose handsome sardonic face looks down upon us from the walls of that Hall. Thompson was famous for his command of sarcasm; and the vicar approached him with deferential circumlocution. It seemed unbecoming (he said) to leave the old church to complete oblivion; therefore the committee hoped to erect some modest monument on the old site: something, in its less pretentious way, like the Martyrs' Memorial at Oxford. Thompson, in his politest tones, gave his sympathy and the promise of a cheque, and continued, 'But, Mr X, may I ask you who are the martyrs you propose to commemorate? Your own congregation, or your predecessor's?' I had this, as one of the less known Thompsonian stories, from the late Master but one, Dr Montagu Butler; and, if Ovid might be moralized in the Middle Ages, this event may perhaps be moralized to-day. Seventy years ago there were still a good many medieval encumbrances left at Cambridge: things which had their use until the tide of time left them high and dry. They have not been removed without sarcastic comment, sometimes from the highest quarters. Respectability has always been lynx-eyed for 'the thin end of the wedge'. This, as a witty modern University politician has pointed out, means in plain English, 'Beware of doing an obvious justice now, or you may be confronted presently with another, equally obvious, which you do not feel yourself brave enough to face'. Again, even the salutary change has its attendant disadvantages. St John's College Chapel, a stone's throw from that All Saints' memorial, was very dilapidated just at that same time; so the Fellows committed it to Sir Gilbert Scott, who obeyed their wishes in pulling it down and building one of his own white elephants in its place. The modern All Saints, opposite Jesus, is indeed far more graceful and less pretentious than this; but present-day authorities, dressed in a little brief authority to play with bricks and mortar at the public expense, are gradually learning more conservatism in the face of what they may see around them on the way to their daily work. A lady is said to have asked an architect blandly and persuasively, 'Do you see your own creations distinctly in your own mind when you draw up your plans and perspectives?' 'Oh yes, Madam.' 'You visualize them clearly from every side?' 'Oh indeed, yes.' 'Then why do you do it?' Very necessary things have been done from generation to generation, but not always in the right way.

The late W. E. Heitland, who was perhaps second only to Henry Jackson in his command of Victorian tradition, was always emphatic in his insistence that the Cambridge of George V was better than that of Victoria. He would have maintained also that this improvement had gone *pari passu* with the diminishing influence of clericalism: not indeed of religion, but of particular organized religions. The medieval Universities, growing out of one of the finest efflorescences of the human intellect, suffered gradually, and were finally almost smothered by the strict monopoly of clerical discipline and the Latin language.[1] The Reformation did indeed make an enormous change; and University graduations, falling naturally enough during the revolutionary years, went up rapidly under Elizabeth to numbers unapproached in the Middle Ages.[2] But the Church monopoly was maintained, though now in an institution no longer totalitarian but national, and with the elasticity and the frequent compromises which marked the Tudor monarchy and the Elizabethan Settlement in par-

[1] I have tried to bring this out in two little volumes lately published by Messrs Nelson: *Studies in Medieval Thought* and *Europe's Apprenticeship*.
[2] See *Cambridge Modern History*, vol. II, p. 214.

ticular. From (roughly) 1580 to 1620 Oxford and Cambridge represented serious thought in England more exactly, perhaps, than at any time before or since. But the vicious principle of religious monopoly was still there, with its attendant limitation of professional celibacy. In the generation before 1642, and thence to 1688 and beyond, much of the ferment of living thought worked outside the Universities. These settled more and more into a backwater; Gibbon's description of 'the monks of Magdalen' in his Autobiography is as true a page of history as any in his *Decline and Fall*. The general idleness was equalled only by the pettiness of this celibate life in cloistered communities. A Belgian Professor of Economics, refugee at Cambridge during the War of 1914–18, had lived some time in a model monastery, as tutor to a rich young man whose father desired special care for him, and therefore boarded them both among the monks. With all his personal respect for them, he told me that their jealousies and little bickerings were almost unbelievable. 'So much depends upon being in favour with the Abbot; so many are the occasions for little slights or encroachments; so much friction between a score or two of characters, sometimes very different, cloistered together within a narrow precinct for every day of their lives.' That experience showed him clearly how much of that there must have been in our Colleges until successive Government Commissions let in fresh air. Within the memory of many men whom I have known, here was the state of things at one of the greatest and best. *A*, preaching one Sunday in Chapel, complained of lawlessness in the Anglican Church: 'When I look around, and see almost Popery on one side, and Latitudinarianism on the other'—and so on, turning in each case to *B* the Papophil, and *C* the Modernist, in their several stalls. Next Sunday *C* was on to preach: and he began: 'You have heard last Sunday, from the lips of one who should have known better...', continuing in such a strain that sermons were dropped altogether at that College until the vendetta had cooled.

Gunning's *Reminiscences* portray a Cambridge half-way, perhaps, between Gibbon and the seventies of last century. For conditions in the University a century later, those who are curious about social life should read Leslie Stephen's pungent little book, *Sketches from Cambridge, by a Don*, first published in 1865, and reprinted by Professor G. M. Trevelyan in 1932. It took three Royal Commissions to sweep the main medievalisms away. In 1869,

Henry Sidgwick and a few other stalwarts, including Leslie Stephen, renounced their clerical Orders, resigning where necessary their Fellowships. In consequence, Parliament passed a Clerical Disabilities Act, enabling men to make legal renunciation of clerical privileges on the one hand, and, on the other, of such a disability as that which debarred all clerics from a Parliamentary career. In 1882, all marriage disabilities were swept away. The result is well described in Sir J. J. Thomson's book.[1] At Trinity, in 1920–4 inclusive, only 24 out of 909 members had taken Holy Orders. In 1886, the new statutes of Trinity for the first time permitted the election of a lay Master. 'At this time there were only two laymen who were Heads of Colleges: now [1936] there are only two clerical Heads.' In 1882 all Colleges removed the bar on marriage. 'Until then the only university families resident in Cambridge were those of the Heads of Houses, Professors, the Registrary and a few clergymen, doctors or lawyers who happened to be members of the University. I doubt whether there were more than 60 families all told. . . . My wife, who was born in Cambridge, and who has lived there all her life, says that there were certainly not more than ten young women among them in her girlhood.' In 1882 the stampede was remarkable; for a good many dons were already engaged in anticipation. There is no actually incredible exaggeration in the story that, at one College, a whole High Table of bachelors went down for the Easter Vacation, and the summer High Table consisted only of married men. That was a year after I had taken my B.A.

In 1877, living in St Catharine's and looking across the street to Corpus, I was in a world of strange survivals. On the façade of Corpus, and the south side of the main gate, pedestrians may still read the half-effaced inscription, in great capitals,

[HEN]SLOW

[COM]MON INFORMER[2]

which goes back to the great mid-Victorian quarrel. A Royal Commission was impending for reform of the most crying abuses. Conservatives[3] were in considerable perturbation, and with good reason,

---

[1] *Recollections and Reflections* (1936), pp. 74, 90, 274.

[2] I seem vaguely to remember that it was even more legible, in 1877, on the north side. But I could never find anyone to verify my impression.

[3] I use this word here only in the University sense: generally a political Conservative is also a University Conservative, but by no means always. I have

as to the evidence which might be given upon oath when the Commission sat in earnest. Among the staunchest Liberals was Henslow, Professor of Botany. When the time came, Henslow was the only, or chief, witness who spoke up against certain notorious abuses. It was not that he was a censorious person—very much the contrary—but that he had a conscience which compelled him to testify, when the point came, against many of his brethren. The Conservative revenge is thus recorded on Corpus walls *in perpetuam rei memoriam*. Not only, I think, because the smooth Bath stone of that College was then in a virgin whiteness which tempted the inscriber, but also by reason of its political colour, and especially of the man who, as Tutor in my time and Master soon afterwards, partly led and partly followed (as is the habit of successful leaders) the unrepentant oldworldliness of his brethren. This was E. H. Perowne.

As Proctor, he and his 'bulldogs' were reputed merciless, and some Classical wit quoted from the *Agamemnon* of Aeschylus: Περῶν κυναγετεῖ—'Perowne goes a-hunting with his hounds.' Thompson, Master of Trinity and Arch-Sarcast of the University, was reported to have said, 'I presume God created Perowne in order to keep Senior Classics humble'. Undergraduates—and specially those who had been 'progged'[1]—had their own ribald rhyme:

> Teddy Perowne
> Has gone to his own,
>   He's gone in a flaming chariot.
> And he sits there in state
> On a fizzing-hot plate
>   Between Satan and Judas Iscariot.

My Grammar School contemporary, Greenland, got a Scholarship at Corpus in 1877. It was, nominally, £60. But it was reckoned on a weekly basis of the nominal University Term, whereof 'Full Term' (the time of actual University work) constitutes only two-thirds, and the College paid nothing for the non-resident weeks.

heard a Professor say to an equally distinguished scholar, 'My dear X, you call yourself a Liberal and I call myself a Conservative. I only know that, whenever I go down to the Senate House to vote for some change in the *status quo*, I always seem to see you voting on the other side.'

[1] Short for 'proctorized', caught by the official with his 'bulldogs', and fined 6s. 8d. or 13s. 4d., as the case might be. The apparent queerness of those sums is a characteristic survival: they are the medieval *noble* and *mark* respectively.

I was told that one Scholar of Corpus had once tried to get his full pay by staying up the full time. Of course this was not a business proposition, but he was one of those pertinacious persons who, even though it be to their own hindrance, assert their sense of justice. The College met his protest by sending him home, to receive a fresh 30s. only when he reappeared next Term.

So, again, with the letters. It was a year or two before my time that this matter came before the lawyers, though not, I believe, actually into court. All letters passed through the hands of the College porter, who claimed and took a penny on each missive which he delivered within the precincts. It was part of his perquisites, i.e. of the wages at which the Fellows secured his services. This, of course, was flatly opposed to the Crown monopoly, which forbids rival postal organizations. The undergraduates, we were told, had obtained Counsel's opinion to that effect; but the Fellows had sufficient advantage, with their general constitutional supremacy over the students, to maintain a good deal of their ground. Greenland, for instance, had to pay something for his letters: I do not remember what, but something which was in effect an illegal exaction. But of course postal missives were much rarer then; perhaps hardly more than one-tenth of the present.

If I emphasize these 'monks of Corpus', as Gibbon would have called them, it is not that the College was so much more conservative than the rest. Here and there I shall have to give other similar instances. But more conservative than most it certainly was; and at St Catharine's, just across the street with nothing but open-work iron palings to divide us, we saw and heard a good deal of what went on. The famous Fellows' Garden War at Corpus was not within our direct experience; but it became sufficiently well known for me to risk a brief description here. The Master had not that rare quality of a despot, to maintain unity among his subordinates. Later, in Public School life, I learned to test a Head's real greatness by this, almost first among his qualities: 'Do his subordinates work well and happily together?' It was agreed at Corpus to lay out the Fellows' Garden afresh: but this at once divided Big-endians and Little-endians. Should it be laid out in terraces, as some suggested, or not? The terraces finally won, after setting the College by the ears, and the non-terrace party had no refuge but to sneer at the 'moule-hills', Charles Moule having been a keen champion of the winning side.[1] The losing leader was Fanshawe, one of the three best-known free-lance Classical 'coaches'. He never set foot into the Garden again. In 1912 or thereabout, he was lunching with Miss Alice Gardner of Newnham. As they waited for the viands to come in, he drifted to one of the windows and remarked on the charming view. She answered with some surprise, 'Why, it's your own College Garden!' He turned away, without a word, to the other corner of the room. Fanshawe took two other vows which he kept to his death: not so very distant, after all. First, never to use a telephone; and, secondly, never to ride in a motor vehicle. With all this, he was charming in his old-fashioned courtesy, and a scholar of real refinement.

The Cambridge Fellows and undergraduates were far less numerous than now. One of the smallest Colleges was St Catharine's, where I believe there were only 52 students in my first year, and 50 in my third. Downing was, perhaps, even smaller; and the numbers were scarcely more at Magdalene, Peterhouse, Sidney, Queens', or even at King's, which had quite recently grown out of the medieval restrictions limiting students to 48, all Eton scholars, and all entitled to claim their degree without any University examination. St Catharine's will be dealt with in detail in Chapter XIII. Magdalene had a dubious reputation for generous laxity; sportsmen or aristocrats who had kicked over the traces at stricter Colleges seemed to find easier acceptance there than at any other at which they would have deigned to apply. The aristocratic character was partly due, no doubt, to the fact that the Head of Magdalene is not elective, but appointed at the free will of Lord Braybrooke's family, as Founder's representatives. Thompson of Trinity once characterized it as 'that transpontine refuge for fallen undergraduates'. The Master of Magdalene (it is said) could do no better than to retort upon 'that overgrown establishment opposite Mr Matthew's shop'.

Sanitas sanitatum, omnia sanitas: let us go back a few decades on that path. Professor G. D. Liveing of St John's, who lived to ninety-seven, until he collided with a woman cyclist on his way to Hall, was the yearly guest of honour at the Fellows' Dinner on his birthday, December 21. The Master always made a short speech.

[1] C. W. Moule, Senior Classic in 1857. His teaching on Propertius was among the few benefits I got from the nascent inter-collegiate system of lectures.

Somewhere about 1922 he reminded us how the Professor had witnessed the introduction of railways, electric telegraph, motors, aero-
planes, etc., etc.: a formidable list. He added, drily, 'and we hope
he will live to see baths at St John's'. These had been begun some
years earlier, but immobilized during the war of 1914–1918. College
baths had been suggested as early as the seventies, but one objection
raised at the Council meeting proved decisive—that no Term lasts
longer than eight weeks. The saucer bath of those prehistoric times
was far from negligible: but few folk took anything like the modern
attitude towards the hot bath. My schoolfellow, Ernest Owen, was
son of a Lincolnshire rector. His father noticed that a full-length
zinc bath was to be sold among the furniture of a great house not
far off, and sent his coachman to bid for it up to 25s. The man came
back empty-handed. He confessed to having stopped short at 15s.:
'I didn't think the Master could really want to go further with a
thing that, you may say, one wants only half a dozen times in a
life-time.'

The least dignified of the Colleges in those days was the youngest,
Downing. It owed this reputation, in great part at least, to one most
eccentric Fellow whose tastes were rather of the squire or the farmer
than of the model academic. It was to him that we attributed a story
which (I am now told) dates at least as far back as the seventeenth
century. A man was found at midnight in the tiny runnel which
flows down the side of St Andrew's Street. He was striking out
lustily, and cried to his would-be rescuers, 'Never mind me, I can
swim: look after the other man'. The Fellow in question was a die-
hard Tory, and sat once in the chair at a political meeting. Levin,
a blind man who lectured in philosophy at St Catharine's, sat in the
front row. The first speaker began with an awkward variation on the
usual phrase, saying, 'Mr Chairman—and Gentlemen!' Levin called
out audibly, 'A very proper distinction, Sir!' Levin examined in the
Moral Sciences Tripos; and, as blind men sometimes do, insisted that
there should be no exception made for him: he would sit and
invigilate the candidates. F. W. Maitland sat in that Tripos; and,
as he went away down the Senate House steps, he heard a fellow-
candidate say, 'Just like those sneaks of Dons! they put up a man to
sham blind, and so catch somebody cribbing!' I had this from
Archdeacon W. Cunningham, who also sat for the same Tripos.

CHAPTER XII

COLLEGE SMALL-BEER

I NOW see clearly that time and space would fail me to round off with any completeness the subjects suggested in the last chapter. Yet I am reluctant to omit many small things which occur to me, trivial in themselves but sometimes exalted into significance by the whirligig of time, after the actors are all gone and the scenery has been shifted. While revising this book for the press, I have had the great good fortune of getting access to Mr D. A. Winstanley's *Early Victorian Cambridge*, which gives a most illuminating history and description of the University 'during the first sixty years of the nineteenth century'. These dates force me to reflect that my own date of 1877 comes nearly half-way between 1800 and 1942, and may therefore have, here and there, the usefulness of a landmark; except that I am often obliged to rely upon memory for facts not easily verifiable in war time beyond the Atlantic.

First, then, for the change in undergraduate manners and conventions. I write this last word advisedly; for, at that time of life, men are as much influenced by convention nowadays as they were sixty years ago—creatures of convention whether in compliance or in revolt. Durkheim, in his *Division du Travail Social*, explodes the idea that modern civilization is destructive of individuality. He points out how there is more sameness, less individuality, in the minds of a hundred aborigines taken at random than in a hundred factory hands. So it is, I think, with men just emerged from their teens, in comparison with their elders. The quiet tyranny of custom is often more repressive than the law and the police, and even more operative in reaction upon the rebel's mind than in action upon the conformist's. Thoughtful Agnostics are sometimes ready to admit that, among undergraduates at all present-day universities, Agnosticism is, on the whole, a line of less intellectual resistance. Thus it has to a great extent changed places, during my lifetime, with Orthodoxy. But more of this in another place: meanwhile, I turn to smaller matters.

One of the most interesting things in Sir J. J. Thomson's book is the photograph facing page 56, showing a group of sixteen brilliant Cambridge mathematicians on the eve of their Tripos in 1880. One of the most engaging faces is that of which the author writes truly on page 41: 'He was one of the clearest-headed men I ever met, but remarkably absent-minded.' A scholar of his year, still happily with us, has reminded me of the motto with which this man was ticketed by irreverent contemporaries: 'No God, no Soap, no Stick.' The clauses were supposed to be in ascending order of indecency. Everybody had a walking-stick, cleaving to it with a fidelity which to-day would be ludicrous. One of my first purchases on King's Parade was a Malacca cane with silver-gilt band, for which I paid only 7s. 6d. because it had a blemish on its polished surface. What modern undergraduate can realize Pope's 'nice conduct of a clouded cane'? Yet in our lives there was definite reason for its value. When Caius gave a complimentary dinner to the late Dr Henry Venn for his eightieth birthday, he looked back upon Cambridge sports somewhat in these words: 'And now, how shall I describe our most usual exercise in those undergraduate days? Picture to yourselves a bicycle without handles, without wheels, without pedals and without frame. Imagine the exercise of riding that round by Trumpington and Grantchester. We called it "walking".' As Sir J. J. Thomson says, even men who rowed or played football often walked in the intervals, especially along the 'Grantchester Grind' by Trumpington and round by Chaucer's Mill.

But upon this there was one abominable restriction. The cap-and-gown rule was enforced in much of its medieval severity. After dark always, of course, but also on Sundays for the whole twenty-four hours. At the end of my second year, half a dozen of us got leave from our Tutor to cut Chapel and go to Sunday-morning service at Great Shelford. Every one of us, by way of precaution, took his academicals with him. It depended on the Proctor: some would wink at wayfarers three or four miles outside the town, but others took every advantage of the law. There was one particularly gross case. We had two hard winters in succession: 1879–80 and 1880–1; I think this occurrence was in December 1880. There was first-rate skating in flooded meadows at Grantchester, and one Sunday it was at its best. The Proctors fell upon Grantchester like an eagle hasting after his prey, and caught ninety undergraduates: that, at least, was the current calculation. For Sundays the fine was double: thus the University Chest benefited by 90 marks, or £60; but immense weight was thus added to the too common contrast between loyalty to one's College and antagonism to an impersonal tyrant called University. Here, incidentally, is an illustrative instance, from about twenty years ago. A very wealthy young man was dying, practically without relations. He told a friend that he scarcely knew how to dispose of his money. The friend suggested the University. 'Why, what has the University ever done for me? The College, now, if you like!' And so, I believe, a great College was enriched by some £250,000.

To return to our Proctors—*revenons à nos loups*. I was told in 1880 that an undergraduate insurance society had just made a generous contribution to Lady Margaret Boat Club. The society was formed by Johnian old Salopians: there was then almost such a bond between Shrewsbury and that College as between Eton and King's. The associates paid 2s. 6d. each time they went for a Sunday walk, and the society underwrote their possible 13s. 4d. fine.

Peter Mason, of St John's, a great Hebraist and great disciplinarian, had consuming zeal for the Lord's house in this matter. He would prowl along the river to rebuke men who basked on the sunny Sabbath banks 'tobacconing', as our Puritan forefathers phrased it: for academical costume and the weed were incompatible under University law. One custom which was increasing in my time excited his special indignation: men would carry their gowns jauntily on the arm and not over the shoulders.[1] On one occasion, as a man loafed thus through the Johnian courts, Peter managed to hobble down and intercept him. 'My boy, do you think the gentleman whose gown you are bringing into College would like to see you wearing his cap?'

A prominent Cambridge citizen, my predecessor in our house beside Parker's Piece, told me that his father was at the Perse, the local Grammar School, when Peter Mason's father and namesake ruled it as Headmaster. He saw Peter and his usher fight each other with canes in full class. At the end of that Term Peter left. The usher, incidentally, had shown crushing superiority in this cane duel.

---

[1] In 1862, the Trinity authorities had tried to put this down by a fine of 2s. 6d. (Winstanley, p. 421).

Let me linger a little longer round St John's: a College which in earlier days contributed several Masters even to Trinity, including Bentley, perhaps the most famous of all.

Liveing, who lived to ninety-seven, was half a dozen years older than Bonney, alpinist and geologist, who died at ninety. They used to dine in Hall at the head of the table, facing each other. Bonney, in whom much kindness and merit underlay a somewhat hasty temper, was deferential not only to Liveing's words but even to his silent glance. It was a lesson in University psychology to watch that fiery temper subside in face of the long white beard which could claim six years of College seniority:

> Hi motus animorum et haec certamina tanta
> Pulveris exigui jactu compressa quiescunt.[1]

When Bonney lay on what proved his death-bed, his ninetieth birthday came. Professor G. C. Moore-Smith of Sheffield, who was spending part of the Long Vacation in College, got up a round robin congratulating him on the event, and hoping to see him soon in Hall again. It was brought in due course to the next oldest resident Fellow, who, as he signed it, remarked meditatively: 'Poor Bonney: but what can you expect? When he was young, he was always about in the mountains, climbing in the heat and sleeping in the cold: and I doubt that will have shortened his life!' He himself was guiltless of mountaineering, and had crept in and out of the same set of College rooms with cat-like tenacity for at least half a century; yet he finally fell short of Bonney's age. When the College Library developed destructive beetles in its magnificent oak ceiling, and we had to spend £6000 for mending the past and insuring the future, a satirical question came from outside the College: 'Is it true that poor X has got the death-watch beetle in his head?' Yet I caught once from him a startling flicker in the socket. Somebody in Hall had told a story of undergraduate ebullience, and X suddenly woke up, as from a stupor, to cap this. Routh (he said) or some other great mathematical teacher, met a candidate in the College Court, just after the Tripos. 'That was a d—— good answer of yours, A,

---

[1] Virgil, *Georg.* IV, 86, concerning civil wars in the beehive: 'Yet, if you sprinkle a handful of dust over them, all that excitement and all those battles are reduced to quiet.'

to the sixteenth question.' 'Yes, Sir, but it was a b—— good question, wasn't it?'

The close interdependence of Shrewsbury School and St John's College had been mainly due to Benjamin Hall Kennedy, chess-playing, gin-and-water-drinking Headmaster of Samuel Butler's *Way of All Flesh*. Two remarkable representatives in this twentieth century were W. E. Heitland and H. M. Gwatkin.

Heitland was small of stature, but nimble and elfish in body and mind. He had been Senior Classic in 1871. In my undergraduate days it was a great privilege to be admitted to his Long Vacation reading parties. My inferiority to H. Henn in the Trinity Hall Scholarship examination was emphasized by his admission to that select society, while the letter was rejected in which I introduced myself to Heitland and pleaded for a like privilege. It was in 1879, I think, that *Punch* recorded an incident at Fishguard in South Wales, which Heitland had chosen for his reading party in that year. The whole village had an ancient and a fishlike smell, and Heitland suggested to his landlady that her drains might be at fault. 'Oh no Sir! inteet to goodness, we haf no drains!' This was published not by any of the party, but by someone to whom it had been passed on.

Heitland was an inimitable raconteur. His manner was almost as effective as his matter; but I will try to reproduce as nearly as possible the story of Bishop Colenso which I have twice heard from his lips. Colenso, hitherto known mainly as Second Wrangler and author of a standard arithmetic for schools, was a Fellow of St John's who leapt suddenly into embarrassing fame throughout the English-speaking world. As Bishop of Natal, he was brought into intimate association with a Zulu chief who at last put it bluntly to him: Did he believe the literal truth of the first chapters of Genesis? Colenso was a bold and straightforward man. (Let me confess here my private grievance that his portrait has been removed by an Amenities Committee, together with those of such other Johnian worthies as the great Strafford and Palmerston and Titus Oates, from the Smaller Combination Room. Any College, for a few pounds, could furnish a comfortable room in impeccable modern boudoir-taste; but not all can hang it with portraits that rehearse four centuries of English history.) Colenso, then, was a man of leonine courage, and he has a leonine head in that portrait, wherever it may now be stored. He honestly confessed his incredulity, and was naturally hounded down by his brethren of the Bench. This quarrel reached its height in 1869, when 600 years of history had been successfully obliterated by tearing the old Chapel down, and bleeding the College and its benefactors for Sir Gilbert Scott's new erection. The solemn dedication festival, naturally, attracted old Johnians from every walk of life, and especially clergy from the remotest country cures. This was two years before Heitland took his degree; and I will try to give the rest in his words.

Selwyn was a big man with a big black head; he had rowed for Cambridge against Oxford, and had been Bishop of New Zealand. He used often to preach from the University pulpit; he seemed always to say: 'This is what I believe; and, if you believe differently, take off your coat and come round the corner with me.' That was the sort of sermon he gave us for this Commemoration in the new Chapel, and he ended with a flare-up: bidding us recall to mind all the great prelates and divines who had rendered this College illustrious, and repudiate the 'recreant Bishop' who had lately besmirched its good name. In the evening, as I went through the screens, there was a Babel of talk and laughter in the Hall. I couldn't help peeping in; it was crammed full; and as I stood there they took compassion on this undergraduate, and made me get up on a table, and passed me up and up until I was close to the dais, and heard every word of Bateson's speech. He said a lot, of course, about the great men of the College, past and present, and then he ended by demanding our sympathy, whether we agreed or not, with the Bishop who had had the courage to make an unpopular confession. The old parsons felt that this, after all, was the right note, and they cheered him heartily.

Bateson was in every way a remarkable figure; follow him up in the index to any memoirs of the time, and you will find admiration even from those who disagreed with him. Two of his children have left their mark in the annals of learning: William, the anthropologist, and Mary, the historian.

Gwatkin, Heitland's contemporary, was a very different figure. His father, a Senior Wrangler, had married late in life: Gwatkin told me in 1914 that this was the centenary of the paternal B.A.

degree. At Shrewsbury he was a strange unboyish figure, growing a beard before he left. At Cambridge he took four Triposes, obtaining a First Class in each. In History, which was in the end perhaps his strongest subject, the Tripos had not yet been instituted. His sight was extremely defective; yet with glasses, through the extreme corner of one eye, he had a small radius of very acute vision for anything held up to his face. One of his main interests was in the palates of snails, which, cut into thin sections, reveal under the microscope the most marvellous prismatic patterns. He could cut finer sections than most professionals, and had collected innumerable specimens. In his last years, when he confessed to the impossibility of doing more than twenty consecutive minutes of real work, he would leave his table and refresh himself with his snails. He had a private vocabulary of his own: tobacco, for instance, was 'filth', and when he characterized a colleague as 'a very filthy fellow', no more was intended than 'inveterate smoker'. Women, again, were 'vanities'; and when, in process of time, he married, it was quoted against him that 'the creature was made subject to vanity, not willingly'. He taught mainly Theology and Church History, to a very few pupils in College or at his own house. Bishop Henry Knight, who coached with him in 1881, described to me the regular routine. Gwatkin always had a cold in the head, and sat over the fire. Behind him sat two or three pupils, at a table, scribbling at full speed the words which fell from his golden mouth. He had the whole subject at his finger-ends, and was independent of notes. His bad sight made him rely upon memory: and he dealt these things out just as he had arranged and crystallized them in his head: this made him an ideal coach. Later on, he became an equally remarkable lecturer. For in 1884 a brilliant Oxonian, Mandell Creighton, was imported to fill the newly created Professorship in Ecclesiastical History at Cambridge, and Gwatkin greeted his successful rival with a letter of monumental dignity. He wrote:

For twelve years I have taught Ecclesiastical History, I may say almost alone in Cambridge. I have worked faithfully and to the utmost of my power hitherto, and I trust not without success; and now that my work is taken up by stronger hands than mine, I pray the Lord of all History before whom we both are standing, to give you health and strength and

heated correspondence. One or two letters were signed 'Veritas', or by some such name; and one of these tried to explain at some length how the whole thing might have come about. Jackson believed that this 'Veritas' was Myers himself. He did not dogmatize on the psychology of the affair, but remarked that Myers had his queer side, and reminded us of his enthusiasm for Psychical Research. He was willing to accept the suggestion of kleptomania: of a clever man fascinated like a jackdaw by brilliant verses, and swept away in a moment of instability. Lee-Warner was my neighbour in Norfolk; when I once asked him, he spoke without undue bitterness, but added, 'He was always a queer fellow. Once, when I came into my room, I found him reading my letters.'

Another of Jackson's stories concerned his own rooms in Nevile's Court. These, like all first-rate sets, consisted of three chambers; a large room, a smaller room, and lastly a bedroom. Blakesley, Dean of Durham, when he came back for some feast, looked in upon these, which had once been his own, and told Jackson of a dream that he had once visited him there. He had been reading Defoe's *Plague* till the small hours, and this haunted him in sleep. He dreamed that he was himself plague-stricken, and heard the cart come rumbling down the street, and the bellman calling out as he went, 'Any corpses here?' He paused and knocked at Blakesley's door: the patient struggled to rise and cry out, but in vain. The cart went rumbling away, and the bellman's cries faded out; and so he lay for twenty-four hours. Next morning, the same story, the knock at the door, and the same helplessness. The third day, at last, he burst the bonds that had paralysed him, and started up to cry for help. There stood his bedmaker who, as usual, had knocked successively at all three doors. Between each knock, Blakesley's dream had recorded twenty-four hours of suspense. After this Jackson told us a similar story from another friend. He dreamed of the Highlands, and found himself standing on a hillside at the entrance of a great stone-walled field, into which a gillie was driving, one by one, a splendid herd of cattle. When the last had gone in, the gillie turned to the dreamer and said, pointing to the herd, 'Your cattle, Sir!' He woke, to find his bedmaker holding the hot kettle for his bath: she had said, 'Your kettle, Sir!' This would seem an even more brilliant brain play with time.

Somewhere about 1880, on the 'Grantchester Grind', I saw a man slouching along, of whom my companion said, 'That's Hardy of Sidney: he used to be a great Alpine climber'. Those who have read the first series of *Peaks, Passes and Glaciers* will remember how Kennedy and Hardy were caught by night near the summit of the Bristenstock in flannel shirt and trousers, on a ledge so narrow that they were in constant danger of rolling over, and at a temperature which compelled them to embrace each other till dawn for escape from actual frost. They will not have forgotten how, in the middle of the night, Hardy told Kennedy of his aunt's parting words. He had suffered from bad rheumatic fever; and she had warned him, whatever he did, to keep himself warm among those dangerous Swiss mountains. 'Since this experience of ours,' writes Kennedy, 'Hardy has never felt the least twinge of rheumatism.' There, then, is one of the actors in Jackson's tale: the next is A. A. Vansittart, whose name I used to pass almost daily on the lintel of a staircase in Nevile's Court. He had a beautiful pet donkey, Egyptian, I believe. Hardy, a great *bon-vivant*, preached to him by report the exquisite qualities of donkey-flesh, and at last persuaded him to sacrifice the poor animal on the altar of Brillat-Savarin. It was a famous dinner, and Jackson was among the guests. He told us:

It was delicious; it was like venison, better than English: it was like Tyrolese venison, *Rehbraten*. The waiters noticed how we were appreciating it. Whereas, at the start, they had gone round asking, 'Saddle of mutton or Mr 'Ardy's dish, Sir?', in the second round it was, 'Saddle of mutton or donkey, Sir?' This was shortly after the Siege of Paris; and Hardy got up another dinner, this time on rats. Large numbers were fed for a few weeks on cereals, and then cooked in elaborate sequence—rat soup, fricassee of rat, etc., etc. But that was not a success.

A last gastronomic story of Jackson's. An undergraduate complained to the cook that his chickens always came up without liver. It was explained that this was inevitable, since Mr Blank, a Senior Fellow, always demanded three livers per chicken.[1]

---

[1] This reminds me of one of the happiest translations ever made. The old *Punch* jest: 'Is life worth living?' 'That depends on the liver', has been rendered into French as 'La vie vaut-elle la peine?' 'Question de foie.'

One famous retort was made not by Henry Jackson, but upon him: he was wont to repeat it with glee. It was at an *Ad Eundem* dinner. Another Cambridge man, after a fairly long series, had just been elected to a Professorship at Oxford. This tempted Jackson to rally the great Homeric scholar W. W. Merry: 'You will have to put a tariff on Cambridge men'. 'No, no, Jackson: not even Joey Chamberlain would put a tariff on the raw article.'

CHAPTER XIII

ST CATHARINE'S

As I have said, the College had in my time only from 50 to 52 undergraduates. A notable proportion had begun as non-collegiate students, whom our Tutors had admitted for their last year to jump off from the College. One happy result of our modest numbers was a very strong *camaraderie*. There was very little distinction of years: two of my closest friends were third-year men. Again, nearly all took some share in the sports, especially on the river, where we were sometimes in the First Division, a distinction which no other small College enjoyed except Sidney. I can imagine even Marcus Aurelius, in his list of gratitudes for good fortune in early youth, enumerating 'the fanatical enthusiasm of the towing-path'.[1] In cricket, St Catharine's had H. v. E. Scott, who was not many places outside one of the finest elevens the University ever had: and he also stroked the boat and played three-quarter at Rugger. It was only very occasionally that a football team could be raised. I never attempted Rugger myself until I had gone down: but I remember vividly the story of a College match against Christ's. C. R. Haines, who was a plucky player of slight build, expatiated that evening in Hall upon the enormity of one of their forwards: 'You couldn't get your arms round the man!' He was, in fact, a phenomenon of undergraduate obesity. 'Fowler of Christ's' became a byword in the University, and I was one of a crowd which watched him once getting into a scratch eight for the May Races; the boat dipped almost to the gunwale as he stepped in. I sketched him once as he sat opposite me at Henry Jackson's Plato lectures; later on, I found he was brother to H. W. Fowler, of *The King's English*.

The other classical scholars of 1877 were C. C. S. Bland, afterwards Headmaster of Ripon School, and two Christ's Hospital men, J. Woolcott and J. M. A. Stewart. This pair stuck very much together all through our time; school traditions united them, but they con-

---

[1] F. W. Maitland, *Life of Leslie Stephen*, p. 49. Again: 'Now this is the real glory of rowing; it is a temporary fanaticism of the most intense kind; while it lasts, it is less a mere game than a religion.'

trasted sharply in appearance. Woolcott looked as if he had creole blood, with dark almond eyes and hair only slightly waved; Stewart

FOWLER OF CHRIST'S

J. M. A. STEWART

was an almost exaggerated type of the shaggy ginger-haired Scot. Both had two marked Bluecoat characteristics. First, the hair of men who had never worn a hat except in the holidays. Next, a passion for conspicuous dress, in reaction from the monotonous Bluecoat uniform. Stewart, especially, took full advantage of the prevalent fashion for loud checks. I remember none louder in Cambridge except another Christ's Hospital contemporary at King's. That man had one unforgettable suit, exaggeratedly shaggy in texture, and of that luscious green shade which is called *merde d'oie* in French. It did not last long: he found that the burden of notoriety grew too heavy even for his shoulders.

Woolcott and Stewart both inherited Housman's blessing (if blessing it be) upon 'the lads that will never be old'. But there was no such melancholy streak of Housmanic romance in the Governing Body. It occurs to me to calculate their average span of life, taking Robinson, Carr, Spratt, Lumby, Southward and Browne. Browne heads the list with ninety-six years; Lumby comes last with fifty-nine; the average is (unless I am mistaken) very nearly seventy-nine. The Master, dying at eighty-five, in 1909, had held office for forty-eight years. The main events of his long reign are given now, far more fully than ever before, in Dr Jones' *History of St Catharine's College*. The fact that concerned us in 1877 was that, whether justly or unjustly, he was ostracized by nearly all the senior members of the University. To us he was an ineffectual and pathetic figure. Still more pathetic, but in a different way, was Mrs Robinson, a dignified and refined lady, standing up proudly against troubles which had certainly come through no fault of her own; she and her fair-haired children were always at their places in Chapel.

The Senior Tutor was Edwin Trevor Septimus Carr, who had been 8th Classic. He was short, round and thickset, with a rubicund face over his clerical white tie. He had on one cheek a large mulberry-mark, the size of an elongated half-crown. In any tense interview, one's eyes fixed instinctively upon that mark, and naturally he saw this, and became tenser. There was a legend, which we only half believed even in those days, that he had once won a lady's heart, nearly always keeping one side of his face towards her, and thus giving full advantage to his other features, impressive in their rugged way: in the intimacy of her engagement, however, the mark asserted its natural prominence, and she broke it off. He had rowed as a boy at Durham, and then in the Christ's eight, where he had been a very useful bow: the beak of the boat, duly emblazoned, stood out conspicuously from his wall among a series of enormous classical

Italian engravings by Rafael Morghen, very recherchés and expensive a century ago, but never seen nowadays.

There was another legend of a wild Irishman, La Touche, who had taken into his head to climb out of his dormer window in his nightshirt, and whom Carr, also in nightshirt, chased intrepidly along the roofs until he ran him to earth. Long afterwards, I met La Touche (then a Headmaster) and verified what may be called the kernel of this story, though the shell of it had been much embellished in the intervening years. Carr was easy going, yet highly critical. He had a pathetic tremor in his voice, most effective when he read the service in Chapel but less opportune for his ordinary dealings with us. He was hopelessly unbusinesslike, not to say negligent. I remember his coming into the Hall to give out classical papers for the May Examination, either in my second or in my third year. Coming to Bland, the second Classical Scholar of the year, and the most regular of all attendants at lectures, he said, 'Mr Bland, the *mathematical* examination is in the Lecture Room'. Poor Bland looked hopelessly bewildered, and Carr repeated the notice in more emphatic tones. Only then did Carr pause to remember that, after all, Bland was a Classic. But, even in those days, one could not seriously quarrel with him: he was a gentleman, however sadly out of place as Senior Tutor, and he had much humour and ready repartee. His tricycle was one of the last survivals of its species in Cambridge. He must have been seventy or thereabouts when he turned too suddenly on a downhill run, and found himself grovelling in the dust with the machine on top. He told me, 'I picked it up and was just going to curse it, when I thought of Balaam and feared it might turn round and expostulate: "Am not I thy tricycle, upon which thou hast ridden ever since I was thine unto this day? was I ever wont to do so unto thee?"' The doctor pulled a long face over his bruises, and prescribed bandages and medicaments. Carr's account was, 'I put them very carefully by my bedside at night, and found myself wonderfully better in the morning'. 'Septimus' is a tell-tale name: there were nine brothers and sisters of whom he was the only one to reach eighty, though most of the others came very near. I called with C. R. Haines at his rectory of Little Shelford, to congratulate him on this birthday. Haines, who was always somewhat hypochondriacal, said, 'I shall never get to eighty, Mr Carr.

My father died young, and *Fortes creantur fortibus*, Mr Carr'. 'Yes, Haines, and eighties creantur eightibus.' It was, I think the quickest and most natural repartee of the kind that I ever heard. But by this time he was conscious also of his limitations, and I remember the words in which he declined the Commemoration Feast of that year. He quoted from II Samuel xix, 35, where Barzillai declines David's royal invitation: 'I am this day fourscore years old: and can I discern between good and evil? can thy servant taste what I eat or what I drink? can I hear any more the voice of singing men and singing women? wherefore then should thy servant be yet a burden unto my lord the king?' Under polite pressure, he would probably have acknowledged that the decay was less in his palate than in his legs. It was pleasant to see him with the robin in his garden, which he had tamed to come and take cheese from between his lips. One felt that there was here a natural affinity: he himself had gone through life like a care-free redbreast. He had, of course, been a good scholar, but his indolence made him an uninspiring teacher, though as Senior Tutor he was responsible for all the work in Greek and Latin composition. The natural escape from his composition lectures was to coach with somebody; in those days, classical coaches were almost as necessary as mathematical for anyone who aspired to a high place.

Among the half-dozen men at Cambridge who were always ready to take pupils from any College at 8 guineas for the Term and 10 for the Long, Spratt was perhaps the most popular and efficient. Thus it came to pass that I frequently paid my own Junior Tutor in order to escape from my Senior Tutor. Spratt's whole appearance bespoke force of mind and will. He dressed like a gamekeeper, in a well-worn bob-tailed coat, loose enough to hold a hare in either of the two inner pockets. His broad face was tanned, all except the forehead, which had been sheltered by his sporting cap, and therefore stood out as conspicuously in complexion as it did in breadth. He was the best scholar in the College, and contemplated all his life an edition of Thucydides which never came off. Coaching bored him, though he did it efficiently; he would say, 'If I had gone to the Bar, I should have made much more money with no harder work'. That was true only of Term-time; Spratt enjoyed such vacations as no barrister knows. He would perhaps have been happier as gamekeeper or poacher than he was at Cambridge; though here also he managed to get a great deal out of life. As a Norwich man who had worked his way up, he possessed the Norfolk dialect in perfection, whenever he chose to use it in telling a story. His keen literary sense gave further point to his words: in accent and vocabulary at such times, he spoke essentially Chaucer's language. Between him and

A. W. SPRATT

his pupils, in coaching hours, there was no formality—on his side at any rate. He once gave me for Latin verse a copy from *In Memoriam*. Glancing at it as I left the room, I saw that I didn't understand it:

> And but for fancies, which aver
>   That all thy motions gently pass
>   Athwart a plane of molten glass,
> I scarce could brook the strain and stir
>
> That makes the barren branches loud:
>   And but for fear it is not so,
>   The wild unrest that lives in woe
> Would dote and pore on yonder cloud....

So I came back to Spratt's table and asked what Tennyson was driving at. He dismissed me with a level volley, 'D— you! it's

my business to teach you Latin, not English'. At what was almost
our next meeting, thirty years after, I reminded him of this; and
he suggested frankly the explanation which had always been in my
mind: 'No doubt I didn't know myself.'

Once at least, however, he met his match. A frequent visitant, in
those days, was one whom we will call Kaufmann, traveller for a
firm of wine-merchants in Frankfort. He called one summer morning
when Spratt was busy, hot, and irritated. But no ill-humour ever
disturbed Kaufmann's professional persistence. After a few minutes,
Spratt ordered him out of the room in the plainest language. Yet
still, as he moved to the door, he tried one last insinuating plea:
'You will take just a leetle of my special Moselle, Sair...just six
dozenn?' 'If I took six dozen of your stuff, it would only be to
wash my feet in.' 'Ah, sair, if it is your feet you would wash, you
must take twelve dozenn!' Such at least was Kaufmann's report
of the interview to other customers. W. E. Heitland, who told me
this story, added that even his great intimacy with Spratt never
emboldened him to ask for an authorized version from that side.

I remember one occasion only on which Spratt showed embarrass-
ment. He was praelector in 1881, so that I took my B.A. under his
wing. As we all stood on the floor of the Senate House waiting for
the ceremony the men in the gallery shouted 'Caps off, caps off' to
the praelectors. Most of them, if not all, gave way except Spratt.
Then there was a cry of, 'Oh let him keep it on, he hasn't got any
hair'. Spratt could have refuted this libel in a moment; but he could
afford to scorn it. Then, however, they began to throw pennies at
him, and this drove him, in spite of his assumed air of indifference,
to give himself a countenance by coming and talking in a fidgety
way to me. Having myself no cap to protect me from the coins,
I heartily wished that he had had sufficient indifference to keep
him in his original place.

Another fine Classical scholar on the Governing Body was Alfred
Pretor, who was one place above Spratt in the Tripos of 1864. He
had been a favourite pupil of Vaughan at Harrow, not much junior
to Calverley and H. M. Butler and Sir G. O. Trevelyan. But, in
my days, Pretor drew his dividend practically as sleeping partner.
He had a special reputation for skill in composition; but I never
heard of his teaching anybody in those days. I think he resided only

two or three Terms at most, out of my ten. But there his rooms stood opposite to Spratt's, with a beautiful many-branched porcelain chandelier always on the inner window-ledge, advertising to passers-by that the College possessed a man of refined taste who condescended at rare intervals to show his attractive face and select dress at the High Table.

The Rev. Joseph Rawson Lumby, D.D., was in his own way as masterful as Spratt, and of equally exuberant vitality. He probably helped the men in Divinity; he became Norrisian Professor in 1879 and Lady Margaret Professor in 1892. I don't think there were serious College quarrels; but in one sense there was no room for two such men in a very small society. Spratt is the reputed author of the epigram: 'Lumby is omniscient and omnipotent, but (thank Heaven!) not omnipresent.' We undergraduates had not heard this then, nor Spratt's parody which Heitland recited to me many years afterwards:

I heard the voice of Lumby say
'My height is six foot one;
I'm forty inches round the chest,
My weight is twenty stun'.

I heard the voice of Lumby say
'I know six hundred creeds;
I don't believe in one of them
(We never did at Leeds)'.

I heard the voice of Lumby say
'Sense I postpone to sound;
Let others argue to the point,
I argue round and round'.

He had been Vice-Principal of Leeds Theological College under the famous Dean Hook, author of that classical repartee to a Roman Catholic controversialist, who asked, 'Where was *your* Church of England before the Reformation? . . . ' 'Where were *you*, Sir, before you washed your face this morning?' Lumby, originally a Fellow of Magdalene, had vacated this by marriage, and was elected later to St Catharine's. His physical proportions were, practically, as described in Spratt's hymn. His voice was as ultra-manly and as pompous as his gait; he could bend pokers on his arm like reeds. Being short-sighted, he tripped badly one night over the chains in front, and his fall upon the cobbles is said to have shaken the College to its foundations. Certainly he was laid up for some time; and malicious tongues whispered that the real trouble was in the bottle.

J. R. LUMBY

I need hardly say that this was a most unjustifiable libel: but, as Dean, he was not popular. What had been said of Whewell was repeated concerning Lumby in a smaller way: 'Omniscience was his foible.' Before getting his Divinity Professorship, he stood for the Chair of Anglo-Saxon against Skeat. An oft-repeated story of the wooden leg I believe to be indubitably true in the main: here is the variation current in my time, which may be corrected by Dr Jones' more classic version.[1] The High Table, weary of his omniscience, conspired to pose him with an out-of-the-way question. 'I say, Lumby, what does a wooden leg cost?' The reply came with un- hesitating precision: 'Ten shillings.' 'Would it surprise you to know that I happened to enquire of the maker this afternoon, and was told 7s. 6d.?' 'Not at all, if the leg you asked after was not shod with brass. Enquire to-morrow and you will find the brass tip adds an extra 2s. 6d.'

[1] *History of St Catharine's College*, p. 188.

We knew that Lumby was not conspicuous for humour; but it was not until six years after I went down that he produced a work upon which Spratt's private comments must have been worth hearing. In *The Cambridge Bible for Schools and Colleges* he undertook I and II Kings. In the latter (p. 20) he had to deal with those irreverent children who greeted Elisha with ' Go up, thou bald head,' and forty-two of whom were consequently torn in pieces by two she bears. 'It may be' (commented Lumby solemnly) 'that he was wearing Elijah's mantle. Elijah, the hairy man, had probably long shaggy locks, and so the contrast between the two would be marked at once.... Such a man would be thought fit sport for the Baal-worshippers of Beth-el, and they were most probably set on and encouraged in their mockery by their parents. Their home education and all the associations of the place would have given them a contempt for the true servants of God.' And Lumby ends with a quotation from Bishop Hall: ' God and His seer looked through these children at the parents, at all Israel. He would punish the parents' misnurturing their children, with the death of those children which they had mistaught.'

Another widower rescued by St Catharine's from his sorrow was Turnbull, who had vacated a Trinity Fellowship and was elected in May 1879. When I went down in March 1881, I had never set eyes on him, nor had anyone else that I knew of. He was a Board of Education Inspector, and there can have been no decent excuse for adding this Cambridge sinecure to that whole-time job. The offence was all the more flagrant, because Hubbersty and Haines, in 1880, did quite well enough to deserve Fellowships according to the College standard, and Henry Knight did distinctly better, with a decent First in Classics in 1882 and Senior of the Theological Tripos in 1884. It can only have been a deliberate resolve to keep younger blood out of the Governing Body, and to guarantee the Old Gang against uncomfortable criticism.

Another absentee Fellow of those days was Southward, by far the youngest of the body. He, however, had every excuse; with Carr, Spratt and Pretor here to look after the fifteen or twenty classical men there was no room for him. We only knew his name on the door of his vacant room. He was busy all those years teaching the Sixth Form at Dulwich College.

I have left G. F. Browne to the last; but he was by far the most important person of all from any real University point of view. His story may be read in his own *The Recollections of a Bishop* and in Dr Jones' *History*. As Secretary to the Examination Syndicate, and helper in the newly invented Extension Lectures, he laid the most solid foundations for the present Extra-Mural Teaching Syndicate. He was the inventor of the *University Reporter*. He was not a member of the Governing Body at St Catharine's in my time. His face was clean-shaven except for broad dark whiskers; he had the keen and alert look of a hawk, never aggressive, but with a quiet resolute dignity which rendered the least liberty unthinkable. His portrait in the Hall loses much by the absence of those whiskers which gave so much character to the face in its prime. In addition to his great University activities, he taught mathematics in the College. When H. v. E. Scott, coming up to take the M.A., had the usual business interview with Carr and handed in his cheque, he explained with his usual frankness that few of us had got our money's worth out of the College, only adding an exception for Browne, who by this time was Canon of St Paul's. Carr was as imperturbable as ever, with his pathetic half-lisp: 'Oh yes, Scott, you were a mathematician, and that part of the College work was specially under his supervision. We all felt the better for Canon Browne's genial and manly influence.' But when, after Robinson's death, there was a serious question of electing Browne to the Mastership, Carr's objection was characteristic: 'I don't want to spend the rest of my life "disputing in the school of one Tyrannus".'

Among the freshmen of 1878 were several model reading men. Moffatt, I believe, never went to a lecture on any author, and troubled himself comparatively little about annotated editions, but read steadily through Tauchnitz texts and mastered them for himself, somewhat as Housman, a year his senior, was doing then at Oxford. Thornton came out Fourth Wrangler in 1882, better than any St Catharine's man had done for half a century past. But the best student of that year was Henry Knight, who rivalled the heroism of Scottish students like Peter Giles and James Adam. His father was an impecunious parson in North London, with three boys and two girls. His mother was from an artistic family. One of her brothers was Fred Walker, whose 'Harvest Moon' is to be seen in the National Gallery, unless it has been superannuated lately; another was an organ-builder. When one of Knight's sisters died, about 1911, he said to me, 'She, and my Caius brother who was killed at football soon after his degree, were the only two of us who inherited my father's imperturbable optimism. In all our difficulties, I never saw him depressed; his spirits were always buoyant.' Boys and girls alike had to make their beds, black their boots, wash up plates and knives daily before they could trudge off to a rather distant day school. The second son became Bishop of Rangoon and Principal of St Augustine's, Canterbury. Henry, the eldest, was an enthusiastic cricketer, but never touched bat or ball at Cambridge: he couldn't afford it. He slept in an attic on the Library staircase, without a fire except in the coldest winter weather; and nothing ever kept him for an hour from his allotted time of daily reading. In later life, he found that even music took him too much from his work, and seldom indulged in a concert. The majority of us, the unregenerate, looked upon his perfection as rather discouraging: it was obviously impossible to live up to Knight's standard, yet of course nothing short of that was the right and proper thing to be done for one's parents' and for one's own credit. I used to watch him come in from the 'Grantchester Grind' and climb up to that garret with something of the same feelings with which, almost daily after breakfast, I used to walk through Queens' to the Backs, and look in for a moment at Erasmus' portrait in the Hall. Knight in one way, and Erasmus in another, were too distant stars. But regret is not amendment: and I have never disguised from myself that the three idlest years of my life were spent at Cambridge. One at least of my closest friends was always ready to confess the same.

The main fault, of course, was in ourselves. In those days there were no 'Parts' of Triposes: you swallowed all at one gulp ten terms after you had come up as a freshman. The May Examinations in College were not always very strict. A good many were too fresh—in plainer words, too childish—to look forward steadily for all that while, and to discipline themselves into necessary self-control. Spratt once abandoned his homespun English to put it to me in Horatian Latin: 'You are too fond of *desipere in loco*', adding with an only half-repentant confession, 'And so was I, at your age.' Moreover, like so many others, I could repeat of my own freshman's

experience what Mark Pattison writes of his: 'My first consciousness
is that of stupidity. A very feeble germ of intellect was struggling
with a crushing mass of facts and ideas which it could not master,
and with the tyrannical force of more powerful intelligence in the
persons around me.' [1] Therefore, the difference between one College
and another was far more important then than it is now. Inter-
collegiate lectures were only in their infancy. Henry Jackson, at
Trinity, had a class in Plato's *Republic* open to the whole University,
and practically all Classical men attended it. J. S. Reid, again,
lectured at Caius on Cicero's *Academica*, and out-College men might
attend and pay their fees. But for the two Aristotle subjects we were
dependent on lectures from Spratt which thoroughly deserved that
medieval technical term, 'cursory'. He made no pretence of interest
in the subject, but brought in the recently published edition of the
Rhetoric by Cope, which I had bought for myself, and from which
I got but little extra information by hearing Spratt read from it with
occasional amplifications. At the end of my third year the results
came out only towards the end of July, and then only in a bald
notice on the screens to the effect that Bland and I had been bracketed
for the prize. Yet all that Long Vacation Term I was coaching
again with Spratt, and might have asked two or three times a week
when we should get a chance of hearing what had happened. Of
course I abstained from any such question. I should only have been
met with the sort of reply that Kaufmann got; and I had nothing
like Kaufmann's retort up my sleeve.

That Long Vacation Term of 1880 swims to me now in a golden
haze. I got leave to keep it informally, lodging for myself at Grantchester and tramping in to coach with Spratt. It was an ideal little
lodging on the main road, Audley Cottage, still existent, with only
a meadow between me and the river, whence I came back after each
morning's swim with the heroic irrecoverable appetite of twenty-
one. My landlady was as ideal as the cottage, and the whole village
was a mass of roses in that perfect weather. On my tramps to and
fro along the footpath to Cambridge I often met a gaunt woman,
with a haggard face like coffee-coloured parchment and fixed eyes
that saw nothing but the end of her journey. I found out later that
she was an opium-eater, who did a man's work at the coprolite pits

[1] *Memories*, p. 325.

of Grantchester, now disused. She had to come in one day a week
for laudanum, since the chemist could not sell her more than a
limited dose at a time. This was fairly common then in the Fens;
farmers and labourers took it against the malaria that still haunted
those half-drained marshes. A Lynn doctor with a scattered country
practice told me once how he remembered in his youth, a curiously
exact boundary between his northward and southward patients.
Northward, in the Fens, ague was prevalent; southward, on the chalk,
hard water bred stone in the bladder.

All that Long, and during the Autumn Term, I tried convulsively
and ineffectually to make up for past omissions. Whether I really
overworked, or whether the vegetarianism which succeeded so admirably with 'Johnny' Mayor was not suited to my viler body and
brain, or from whatever other cause, I felt something more than
mere exam.-fever in February, with the Tripos a few days ahead.
Boils and pimples plagued me; one came on my lip; and, in those
days when the Pasteurian-Listerian gospel was but imperfectly understood, it was not so rash of me to operate with a penknife as it
would be nowadays. The result was that, a week before my Tripos,
my head was swelled like a football, and the doctor was keeping
my cheek on ice until he could risk using his own lancet. Spratt
advised me to take an *aegrotat*, promising a testimonial which would,
at least, do more for me than the sorry place which was sure to result
from papers written in my room when I ought to be in hospital.
I am inclined to think his judgment erred there, however naturally;
but of course, if the choice was mistaken, the main fault was in my
own pusillanimity. In those days, an *aegrotat* candidate had not even
the poor consolation of seeing his name at the bottom of the Tripos
list in the *Calendar*. Moreover, it was rather notorious as a refuge
of the destitute. This will be best understood if I conclude with an
unedited anecdote which, in its naked details, I can tell only under
unrecognizable pseudonyms. Tyke of St Ambrose's was, I have
always understood, a Yorkshireman; certainly he had some definite
Yorkshire characteristics. His forte was light-weight pugilism, with
an all-consuming passion for sport; classics were his foible. He had
brains enough to get an exhibition; but, once over that hurdle, he
left the Tripos more or less to chance. Towards the end of his career,
going as usual to Newmarket, he won a very heavy bet, but found

the bookie bankrupt, and could only relieve his feelings by taking pugilistic revenge. He came back, naturally, by the last train. On Cambridge platform he was accosted by the repentant bookie, who was now ready to pay in full; being a Christian gentleman himself, he was ready to forgive and forget what had been a natural hastiness on Tyke's part. All this while he was fumbling in his pocket, and drifting northwards down the platform. When they had got well into the darkness—and the less inhabited parts of that platform were very dark in those days—Tyke suddenly found himself confronted not only by the bookie himself, but by half a dozen of his pals, who reduced him to a jelly, and disappeared before any help could come. He was pointed out to me in the street a few days after, with every colour of the rainbow on his face. Less than a week later the hour struck for his Tripos, and Tyke of St Ambrose's managed to get a medical certificate which legitimated his claim for an *aegrotat* degree. It has always been a sobering reflection to me that, though in a different year, my class was the same as his.

I write all this just as I remember it, but doubtless with a certain lack of perspective. In later days, when Spratt became Senior Tutor, I believe he took things more seriously. And, in any case, I cannot claim to represent the real Carr and Spratt any more truly than Carr and Spratt, if they had ever taken the trouble, would have represented us in print. Especially would I warn readers against the idea, which these rough notes might too easily give, that St Catharine's was a Vale of Tears, either objectively or subjectively, in the late seventies. 'What I saw there once, what I see there now,' is, I think, what most of my contemporaries saw. We knew the 'Grove' as a group of true 'immemorial elms', not too obviously decaying, which lent singular charm to the College as seen from the street. The trees were alive, if not with 'the moan of doves', at least with busy rooks, upon which we looked with the same sort of distant curiosity from our higher human angle as we did upon the Dons from our subordinate *status pupillaris*. To the present day, whenever I open Malory, I find myself at Scott's window one sun-flooded Sunday morning, almost on the level of those rooks' nests, reading and smoking alternately with him, and heartily convinced that Tennyson's *Idylls* were negligible in comparison. With all the buoyancy of youth, we didn't want the College better, ourselves better, or the

Dons better, except as that might subserve our selfish interests. Better Dons (from the ideal point of view) would have been a standing rebuke to us.

There was strong patriotism in the College, where we all knew each other. Lord Birkenhead, who was our guest of honour at the first Commemoration after the War, struck that note with great depth of feeling. He himself had been at Wadham, one of the smallest and ordinarily least conspicuous of Oxford Colleges, at the same time as Sir John Simon, F. W. Hirst, and C. B. Fry. He said truly that a very small College has advantages often unsuspected by outsiders. We of the seventies may echo that, without for a moment forgetting the almost incredible success with which a younger generation, led by F. M. Rushmore and W. H. S. Jones, has multiplied not only the numbers at St Catharine's, but what is far more, its Firsts and University Prize-winners and Blues. Yet, to a survivor from the old years, the familiars of those days are the lads that will never be old.

> Was ich besitze, seh' ich wie im Weiten,
> Und, was verschwand, wird mir zu Wirklichkeiten.[1]

[1] Goethe, *Faust*: 'The things that I possess, I see as from afar, and those which have disappeared are my realities.'

CHAPTER XIV

MALVERN WELLS

DEAN VAUGHAN, who at Harrow had shown himself one of the most successful Headmasters of the century, and had retired in full vigour of mind and body, dropped once in my hearing a casual reference to 'the healthy little humiliations of a schoolmaster's life'. That phrase has the felicitous accuracy characteristic of all his sayings. An ideal educational scheme might well consider the advisability of requiring from every University student, before matriculation, a year's work as teacher at some school not his own. If, again, it could be ensured that he should do another school year after his degree, before appointment to any University post, so much the better. We should then, if nothing else, go far to eliminate the sort of examiner who prides himself upon 'brilliant' or 'original' questions.

The last weeks of Lent Term, 1881, I passed at Hunstanton in good east coast air, and came in good health and spirits to my bread work. The *aegrotat* was depressing, and I had to depend mainly now upon the French of St-Omer: that is, so much as was left of it from the Grammar School and Felsted, or picked up again from Balzac and George Sand at Cambridge.

The Wells House at Malvern Wells, some two miles south of Great Malvern, is a large white building high up on the slope of the hills: so high and so big that it can be seen with the naked eye from Severn bank at Worcester, ten miles distant. The Rev. William Wilberforce Gedge had taken a lease of this house and founded there a solid and well-respected Preparatory School, of some thirty boys. Normally, he had four Assistant Masters. At this moment we were a most harmonious group—Ernest Owen and I were old Felstedians; E. W. Elliott and H. E. Huntington were old Malvernians—moreover, there was this strong cross-bond, that Elliott and I had been fellow-collegians for three years at Cambridge, while Owen and Huntington had for a year been colleagues under Gedge.

Gedge himself was an excellent man for his job. His father, an ex-Fellow of St Catharine's, had been for many years Second Master at King Edward's School, Birmingham, under that Prince Lee, after-

wards Bishop of Manchester, who had worked under Thomas Arnold
at Rugby and, as Headmaster, at Birmingham, had taught the future
Archbishop Benson, with Bishops Lightfoot and Westcott. Wilberforce Gedge himself was vigorous, upright, broad-shouldered,
looking in his frock-coat the very type of that prosperous Victorian
figure which Max Beerbohm has drawn for his inimitable triptych
in the Fitzwilliam Museum. He always came down to breakfast
with a vigour which contrasted, though not too crudely, with our
less exuberant energies, damped by an hour of class work. For of
course the Head, even of a preparatory school, may be called, in
classical phrase, the master of sixty legions. Or, perhaps I should
have written, *especially* of a preparatory school. My old colleague,
A. V. Jones, left Sherborne to become 'Headmaster' of one of the
largest and oldest established of these. He wrote to me: 'This
doesn't for a moment mean that I am the Boss. That is the "Warden":
his duties are to read prayers twice a day and flush the drains once
a fortnight: but then the school is his own personal property.'
Gedge, then, came down to us exuding vitality from every pore, and,
before attacking breakfast proper, he always needed a glass of cold
Malvern water, purest in Britain as it gushes from the hard volcanic
syenite. Often he would blow off something from his morning
letters. Once: 'Here's the sort of business letter I get from women.
My terms are £x for under twelve, and £x plus ten for over twelve.
This mother writes to ask, since her son turned twelve only six
months ago, will I count him as under twelve.' Or, again: 'The
funniest things are the things written unsuspiciously by people who
have no sense of humour. Here is an old lady of sixty-five who writes
to announce her engagement to marry. She says, "I had thought
to have spent all my days in quiet solitude at Little Mudbury, but
man proposes, and God disposes".'

On the other hand, he was a very able teacher, both for the boys
and for us masters. A few of the tenderer boys he overawed and
sometimes paralysed; but from all he exacted hard work, and to
most he gave excellent guidance. His handwriting was beautiful:
almost copperplate in regularity and clearness, but with much individuality and self-assertion. His up-strokes did not tail off to a
point, but ended with a slight thickening, almost a dot, which
seemed to say, 'See how I keep control of my pen to the very end'.

The boys—as their habit is—imitated this: in later years I have seen one or two startling instances of Wells House handwriting, constant amid the changes and chances of this mortal life. At a very early stage, he taught me a very valuable lesson. I was doing 'perfects' and 'supines' with my class: '*pasco, pascere, pavi, pastum*', etc. He said, 'You are teaching those boys to go wrong. You set so many for evening prep. that only the very best can memorize them exactly. The majority go wrong, this their first time, and they start thus with a confusion from which perhaps they will never completely recover.' In that and similar ways he kept us in rein; and I have always been grateful for such a healthy send-off. Some years after, I acknowledged to him what he had taught me. Perhaps my manner was too off-hand; for he said, 'Yes, you were very young'. Schools like his did very sound work for English education; and no doubt there were others better still. On the other hand, some were far inferior; and those were not always the least 'classy'. The day-school system, if it becomes supreme in England, will have the advantage of combining elementary and secondary teaching, if not in the same school, at least under the same direction. Yet, if the Old School Tie disappears, it will leave a real gap to be filled. Gedge's boys, I feel sure, started life under better auspices than their French, German, or Italian brethren. I speak here, of course, of the nineteenth century without reference to later events and conditions.

The real social centre of the school was Hal Huntington's room on the third storey. My own classroom, a storey below, had a magnificent view, and his sanctum was still better. Just at our feet, the village and its two hotels. First, the 'Hornyold Arms', called after the ancient Roman Catholic family (Hornigolds in old time) who owned the whole estate and had their ancestral hall some three miles off down the plain. Then, the Essington Hotel, with an enormous whiteheart cherry tree, glorious alike in spring and summer and autumn. In good years, all through June, a gipsy family encamped under the tree with their antique shot-guns, hired to keep off the birds by some fruiterer who had contracted to buy the whole crop. It was parent, perhaps, of the many self-sown cherries which splash all the hill-woods of Malvern Wells with orange and crimson in the autumn. Far beyond this tree, in the middle distance, rose Bredon, a hill that starts up, in its smaller way, almost as lonely and abrupt as those of Malvern. Then came distant glimpses of the Severn, with a great red cliff in one place, and Worcester Cathedral just in face of us, and Gloucester far away to the right, and Tewkesbury, just off the main stream, in the middle. Southwards, the Cotswold Hills stood all along the horizon, with Cheltenham in a hot corner at their foot, while we at Malvern enjoyed the free hill air. Directly eastwards, where the Cotswolds break away, we saw Edgehill and its battlefield in clear weather; and, beyond, where eyesight melts into imagination, all the Eastern Counties came in under the Virgilian *aut videt aut vidisse putat*.[1]

Hal Huntington, like Ernest Owen, was a born schoolmaster; and they exactly complemented each other. Owen was solid, leisurely, the soul of method, and British to the core; Huntington brilliant, elastic even in his step across a room, and Italian even in his features, though he had no Italian blood, and only a little, remotely, from Greek merchant stock. His sallow complexion had elicited from an unsympathetic Malvern College schoolfellow (so he told us) the unfeeling question, 'Hullo, you new boy, do you ever wash?' His father was a Continental Chaplain, first at Livorno (Leghorn) and later at Malaga. At Malaga, when the newly arrived family were looking out for suitable lodgings, Mrs Huntington exercised her right of search in one bed, and found a bed bug squatting imperturbably in the middle. She summoned the landlady, who could not at first understand. Then, when the cause of all this fuss dawned upon her, she answered contemptuously, 'Now, if it had been a bull!'—*Si fuese un toro!* At Leghorn, though Huntington père had been there many years, he never learned to speak the language respectably: Italian, by the bye, is one of the easiest languages to understand, but one of the hardest to speak correctly. He had a Dachshund called Schnaps; and he would often say delightedly, 'Listen to those Italian servants; they turn that monosyllable into five: they call to the dog "O! Genapese!"' But Hal had made use of his Italian opportunities, and this stood him in good stead at Oxford later on; he was bracketed for the Taylorian Scholarship in that language. He was *anima naturaliter Franciscana*. Very

---

[1] *Aen.* VI, 454. In Hades, Aeneas catches sight of Dido's pale shade, 'as he who, on the first evening of the month, either sees or thinks he has seen the moon rising through the clouds'.

early in our friendship he gave me his *Fioretti di San Francesco* and Dante's *Vita Nuova*; and with him I read much of Leopardi. He had also a little twopenny-halfpenny paper-covered collection of songs for the mandolin, old and new, which he sang delightfully side by side with negro melodies. Italy was the home of his child-hood, and sometimes of his dreams; but in this prep.-master's exile he never refused to sing us the songs of Zion. Whenever I hear 'Nellie Gray', I see him on the platform at a little school concert, singing that to his mandolin, with his future fiancée and wife, Nellie Gedge, sitting below. The most important piece of furniture in his eyrie was 'the deal box'. It was an ancient packing-case, which had transported his few belongings from his study at Malvern, and into which everything now went which could not be left on the table or the chairs or the floor. 'Look in the deal box' might have been inscribed over Huntington's door. He had come straight from Malvern College to pick up money for future expenses at Oxford; and, meanwhile, he lived among us as the most gracious of migrants. No nightingale did ever chant more welcome notes.

He went up to Keble, where he soon attracted the attention of the Warden, Talbot, afterwards Bishop of Rochester. In due time, Talbot passed him on to his brother-in-law Wickham, Headmaster of Wellington. Here he soon made his mark, and was given, after a few years, a House Mastership at his own Malvern College. With a young family, he was always working up to or above his strength, either for himself or for others. In great schools, there is often at least one master who, like Nelson, expects every man to do his duty. When I went to see Huntington in December 1890, he was so tired that his wife gladly backed me up in a proposal for three weeks in Italy, which we could pay for by publishing a book of select French 'unseens' for Army candidates. In Paris we spent half of our day on the Quais, picking up cheap volumes which were to be gutted for our work. For three or four francs, we had each bought as many as we could carry in a corded parcel. Next day, in the train, we had reduced each volume to a dozen pages or so, for further winnowing, at leisure. The rest we cast out periodically from the window. It was difficult to make our fellow-passengers understand that there was any method in this madness. We had the proper luck on Mt Cenis: mist on the northern side, and brilliant sunshine

to greet us as we emerged upon the southern slope. We visited
Pisa, Florence, San Gimignano, Siena, Perugia and Assisi, ending
up with two or three days as guests of Huntington's sister, at Lerici
on the Bay of Spezia. From her windows we could look down upon
the little seaside villa from which Shelley would run across the road
in puris naturalibus to plunge into the sea, and from whence he
started on his last fatal cruise. It was a fine holiday for both of us.
The school book, in process of time, paid for it with a few pounds
over: moreover, we had missed, at home, one of the worst modern
epidemics of influenza. But, even so, Huntington came home in
carpet slippers with a festering foot, the result of a blister acquired
on our long climb up from Assisi to the summit of Monte Subasio.
Two years later, in 1892, there was another great plague of influenza
at Malvern. The sick house was full to overflowing. Huntington,
after a full hard day's work, undertook the evening visit to the
infirmary which some colleague had been unable or unwilling to
make in his own turn. After an hour or two, he came home
shivering, and was put to bed with ice-cold feet. Double pneumonia
set in at once; and a few hours later he was dead.

Twenty or thirty years ago, I dreamed vividly of a convivial
gathering which broke up at midnight. Huntington put his arm in
mine, and said, 'Come home with me'. I said, 'Why! I had
thought you were dead!' 'Never mind; come home with me': and
so we went out together into the London streets. The dream was
overpoweringly solid and convincing; but it quietly faded into the
light of common day, leaving behind it an abiding sense of reality.
It was Wordsworth's

> Surprised by joy—impatient as the Wind
> I turned to share the transport—Oh, with whom
> But Thee, deep buried in the silent tomb,
> That spot which no vicissitude can find?

The Wells House looked out due east, but one had only to climb
the steep slope on which it stood, and there was a western prospect
no less enchanting in its own way. Two of us could boast of climbing
the gully behind Bath Cottage in two minutes by the watch. On
that side was only one cathedral, Hereford; and the Wye at that
distance does not, like the Severn, show silver fragments here and

there. But there were the hills of Wales and the Welsh Marches; the Wrekin and Titterstone Clee in Shropshire, with the Abergavenny Sugar-Loaf and the almost more remarkable Skirryd. Behind, the Black Mountains, as imposing as their sonorous names would suggest: Pen-y-Cader Fawr, Pen-Allt-Mawr, and Pen-y-Cerrig Calch—Mount of the Great Chair of Arthur, Mount of the Great Forest, Mount of the Limestone Cliff. Behind, in imagination, was all Snowdonia, just as the East Anglian Fens were imagined on the other side. Later on, as I learned to know the country better, fancy recalled Tintern, Chepstow, Raglan, Ludlow, Llanthony Priory and Abbey-Dore and the Golden Valley. One half-Term, I had spent the three days canoeing down from Ross to Chepstow, where the owner's partner received my bark and sent it back by rail. Another week-end was spent at Ludlow; another at Abergavenny and Llanthony. A football match took me to A. E. Housman's old school of Bromsgrove. Malvern, of course, is inseparably connected with the poem of *Piers Plowman*: it was from those hills that Langland saw his vision of the Field Full of Folk. This western view shows us, under the Hereford Beacon, those trees which conceal the ruins of Bronsil Castle, Langland's 'Dungeon in a Dale'; while on Eastnor, conspicuous enough, stands the 'Castle on a Toft'. Moreover, modern research has made it quite possible that William Langland, 'Long Will', was the same man as William, *clericus*, of Colwall; and this Colwall church stands here under our feet; well worth a visit for the beauty of its carved capitals, and the grand old half-timber manor house just opposite, built by a Bishop of Hereford, distant successor to that bishop who marked the division between his own lands and those of the Earls of Clare at Tewkesbury by a ditch which is still plain all along the ridge of the hills.

Here I may recount my friend Alfred Stable's ghost story; for I remember that Mr John Masefield listened attentively when I told it, as a recent occurrence, at the table of Thomas Seccombe who had been with me and Stable at Felsted. Here, again, I will try to reproduce the narrator's words:

I had been to Coddington, and on the way back, not long after passing through Colwall, where the road goes gently a fair way down and then up again, I found a little haze in that hollow. I was alone in my pony trap, thinking of nothing in particular. Suddenly I saw a white figure, almost between the pony's ears; before I could even slow down, we had run over it and were a dozen yards beyond. I looked round, and it was following us; not stepping up and down, but just gliding after us with even motion. That was so uncanny that I whipped up hard, and never looked round again until we had passed the Neck under Camp Hill and were coming down to Malvern Wells. When I gave the pony to the groom, he noticed what a sweat he was in. I told him what I'd seen; and he said: 'Why, that's the Colwall Ghost; but that hasn't been seen since Parson Custance and the rest of the parsons took and laid him four or five years ago.'

Custance was the vicar, who had held a retreat in his house, attended by a dozen or so of the neighbouring Anglo-Catholics. Stable never quite made up his mind on the matter; the nearest rationalistic explanation that he could suggest was that, in that hollow, the gathering mist might collect in wisps; that he had driven through an eddy of that kind; and that it had been sucked along after him.

It was about this time that Stable's dog, Lob, an affectionate and intelligent mongrel, was run over in Great Malvern by a furiously driving butcher. The dog was nursed back to health by Stable's landlady, who loved him as her child. Some months later, Lob saw the butcher standing in the street; he came up behind and took a piece out of his calf. The landlady could not conceal her satisfaction: 'You see, Sir, that dog remembered it all, just as if he'd been a Christian!'

Stable told me another story fresh from its happening. Contemporary at Keble with him and Huntington was John Dawber (afterwards, Dauber, Colonel R.A.M.C.), who came home very late one night and wanted to mend his fire. Keble is built on the hostel system: at the end of each corridor is a communal coalhole and wood store. Dauber went down the dimly lighted passage, into this dark-room, and began groping about for some wood. He stumbled, and fell very heavily. After pitying himself for a minute or two, he rose again, scraped enough wood together, and went back the five doors to his own room. When he opened the door, behold! there was another man sitting by a lighted fire, and nothing of his own was to be seen! He had in fact fallen a whole floor. Each coal room had a trapdoor, and a pulley at the top of all for hoisting sacks.

MALVERN WELLS

Someone had carelessly left one trap open: luckily not all. It was a fine example of the truth that the safest way of falling is to know nothing about it.

Behind Colwall rises the hill of Hope End, with its meadows and groves and the stately house where Mrs Robert Browning lived all through her girlhood. Then, a little farther behind, to the right, the little spire of Coddington, to which I owe many of my most pleasant and profitable memories. For, to pay off Cambridge debts, I looked out for a Tutorship in that summer of 1881. What presented itself was ideal. One of our Wells House boys, Reginald Curtis, was destined for the Navy. Nowadays, candidates are mainly selected by personal interview and examination. But in those days, unluckily for him and luckily for me, it was a written examination, and the age limit was twelve or thirteen. He was solid but not brilliant; and his parents did all they could to make sure. At Owen's advice, I asked for what was fairly common, though on my own initiative I should not have ventured so far: five guineas a week, with board and lodging, for the required month.

The father was of good Shropshire family, in the Church Stretton and Ludlow neighbourhood. He was erect, square-shouldered and handsome, with the shaven mouth and short grey whiskers which were somewhat characteristic of Evangelical piety. His look and manner were rather those of a naval officer, precise and determined under his quiet courtesy. Mrs Curtis was of a great family of spinners in Derbyshire. In face and figure she was rather heavy, but with remarkable black eyes which in excitement or thought lit up her whole face. Her autobiography, printed at Ledbury in aid of a local charity when she was in advanced age and unceasing pain, is a book of great sociological value. For, all her life through, she had been interested in visiting the poor; and she marks very exactly the contrasts and similarities between wage earners in a highly industrialized district or, again, in one of the most stagnant corners of agricultural England. They had one daughter and three sons, of whom Reginald was the eldest. The youngest was Lionel, later Fellow of All Souls, and eminent for his connection with *The Round Table* and the Institute of International Affairs.

My afternoons were generally at my own device, but I sometimes took my pupil out and, more often, walked till tea time with Mr and

Mrs Curtis among those delightful fields and orchards and woods: for there was no such preserving in that corner of Herefordshire as I had been used to in Norfolk. Lionel, who cannot then have been more than eight, commonly took his lunch and wandered alone till tea time, lying motionless for hours among the trees, and proud to report that a squirrel had actually walked over him.

For a village parson's, the family was very well off, for both parents had private resources; and, to a certain extent, they retained 'county' manners among this most primitive village folk. We dressed regularly for dinner, except on Sundays; at tea, the porcelain and the heavy silver were on a par with the strength of the beverage. For myself I know, and of Mrs Curtis I suspect, that we approached it daily with twinges of conscience; but daily I took it freely in full strength, and saw a happier world until it came to getting sleep at night. In short, common life at Coddington Rectory was on the scale of festal life on rare occasions at Pentney; yet in all this there was no sense of sin; for I saw from the first how much of this generosity overflowed into the parish. It was a model household of the kind which is doubtless far rarer now, and will be rarefied, perhaps, until it disappears.

Of the country parson we may say even more emphatically than of the Old School Tie, that nothing will really replace it in the march of civilization until men can manage to revive, among the newer conditions which they are creating, much of its peculiar virtues. The Scribes and the Pharisees can be justly superseded not by any mere negation, but only by something which exceeds them in righteousness. Havelock Ellis, whom no man will accuse of clericalism, has subjected the *Dictionary of National Biography* to an analysis which is of great scientific value.[1] Taking those men, 30,000 or more, from many different angles, he studies what may be called the pedigree of talent. What parts of Britain have been most fertile in this field? Have different counties, again, showed different propensities? and so on. Finally, what professions have produced the finest crop of famous children? and his last enquiry, worked out in cold blood, came to a very remarkable result. He writes:

The proportion of distinguished men and women contributed from among the families of the clergy can only be described as enormous. In

[1] *A Study of British Genius*, pp. 68 ff.

mere number the clergy can seldom have equalled the butchers or bakers in their parishes, yet only two butchers and four bakers are definitely ascertained to have produced eminent children, as against 139 parsons. Even if we compare the Church with the other professions with which it is most usually classed, we find that the eminent children of the clergy considerably outnumber those of lawyers, doctors and army officers put together. This preponderance is the more remarkable when we remember that (although I have certainly included eminent illegitimate children of priests) it is only within the last three and a half centuries that the clergy have been free to compete in this field. It is of interest to note that genius is not the only form of mental anomaly which is produced more frequently by the clergy than by any other social class. The clerical profession, as Langdon Brown pointed out many years ago, also produces more idiots than any other class.

After all, the word 'clergy' meant originally 'élite'; and, when all deductions have been made, those of the Anglican and Free Churches of the Roman Church are picked men. After knocking about the world for many years, I am confirmed in my belief that the men who profess greater seriousness than the multitude, and who live by shouldering the responsibilities of that profession, are in fact better men on the whole, by any impartial standard, than the average of that multitude from whom they have separated themselves. Here, as in our view of medieval society, we need to beware of penalizing men for conceiving a high ideal.

From the first, therefore, Coddington was a kind of home to me: but I reaped far more from it in later years. Sometimes alone, sometimes with a friend, I went over to tea or dinner. Of the whole five miles, scarcely two were along any actual road; and the levels were as varied as the turnings. First, straight up to the ridge, some 500 feet, and then some 700 feet straight down, to Colwall station. Thence mainly footpath to Colwall church; after that, perhaps a mile and a half of road; then orchard paths almost to the rectory gate of Coddington. In late autumn, coming home from dinner, we trod among the fruit, red and juicy as cider apples sometimes are, and silvered with hoar frost when we picked them up. This was the first house I had ever known which possessed all Browning's works: for Mrs Curtis was a passionate Browningite. In my four tutorial weeks she read me *Christmas Eve and Easter Day*, *Luria*, *A Soul's Tragedy*, and many of the smaller pieces. This, of course, modified greatly her traditional Evangelicalism; but not consciously; whenever she was aware of an irreconcilable conflict, one found a watertight compartment. Her inexpugnable refuge was Luther's *Commentary on the Galatians*, with its overwhelming emphasis on Justification by Faith. Yet she was conscious of a natural tendency to scepticism which could never be entirely suppressed. All this was very valuable in waking me out of undergraduate thoughtlessness. As Gedge said, I was very young; but I was growing up.

One of the books which at that time most attracted me, like the majority of my generation, was Shorthouse's *John Inglesant*. It was brought down to us from Oxford by Huntington and his new friend Henry (afterwards Sir Henry) Hadow. In this, one of the most famous of problem novels, a candid young Englishman of good position, in the seventeenth century, is shuttled backwards and forwards between Roman Catholicism and Protestantism. Plausible arguments are plausibly stated on both sides; Hobbes comes in on one side, and Jesuits on the other; the background and scenery are delicately and attractively painted. Nicholas Ferrar's Anglo-Catholic community of Little Gidding is brought in very prominently and with great art: everywhere the play of abstract thought is lightened here and there by striking scenes. But I saw how closely the Plague pictures were imitated from Manzoni's *Promessi Sposi*, to which Huntington had introduced me, and a good deal more seemed to smell of the lamp. Thus, though I greatly enjoyed the book, and the mere sight of the two volumes in their quiet binding thrills me mildly to the present day, I have never been tempted to turn back to what was a sort of classic for a few months of my half-fledged spiritual life. It was only a quarter of a century later that I came across Lord Acton's letters to Mary Gladstone. Here I learned for certain that some of my Protestant misgivings had been historically correct, and that Shorthouse's apparent impartiality grants points to the 'under dog' of Rome which our greatest of Roman Catholic historians cannot find it in his conscience to accept. Meanwhile, however, it took me into a land of spiritual romance and brought me into grateful contact with that Oxford from which the flaming sword had driven me.

Hadow brought to us from Oxford the suggestion that Shorthouse's description of the most attractive Roman Catholic household was modelled upon Little Malvern Court, just beyond the village, and almost under the shadow of that Priory which shares with Great Malvern the probability of having been that cloister school where William Langland found that 'all is buxomness and books, and great love and liking; for each loveth other'. Whether that were so or not, certainly this Court, where the Beringtons have kept their ancestral faith for generations, like the Hornyolds of a dozen miles off, was most attractive. Moreover, there was an equal attraction nearer still, in the handsome stone house by the roadside which the Beringtons had built for their chaplain priest. Many a day, coming home in the afterglow, I saw the priest in his study, through the great mullioned windows, reading or writing by the light of wax candles at an oaken table in his oak-furnished room. It may possibly have been a consciously studied effect: but certainly it was most impressive: it made me ache with envy of this man who, my fancy told me, lived a life of buxomness and of books worthy of *John Inglesant*. Incidentally, either that man or his successor was an enthusiastic musician, but of the old school. Criticizing Wagner to my friend E. P. Frederick, he remarked once, 'He always seems to say: "Here is the *air*, come let us kill him!"'

Meanwhile, my talks with Owen crystallized more and more into a resolution to take Holy Orders. The motives were certainly mixed: I thought then, as I do still, that I should have more chance of a Rectory than of a House Mastership, and should find preaching more congenial than class work. But that side was not all: the resolve was, on the whole, a step upwards rather than downwards. I read over the Thirty-nine Articles with Owen. Some I found very difficult to swallow: impossible, indeed, in their strict sense. But in those days most bishops were already willing to accept *assent* rather than *consent*: the question was: Could one pledge oneself to agreement with the spirit, apart from the letter? Therefore, in December 1882, I left Malvern Wells and began at Pentney to read for my examination.

Here, at Pentney, I found other work also. My brother Jim, who for some time had been officer in the Royal Mail Steamship service, had by this time become impatient of slow promotion, and resolved to turn over to medicine. In those days, the Medical Preliminary demanded compulsory Latin, and he had forgotten every word that

he learnt at school before twelve. In that, and in a little else, I had
to coach him; and the first steps were certainly difficult. He had
even to begin with the parts of speech; and I shall never forget the
sailor-like bluntness with which he saluted them. 'What's that little
———?' 'Oh! that's a ——— adverb, is it?' Again, the two set Latin
books were the *De Senectute* and the *De Amicitia*, and I almost shud-
dered at the grisly curses he invoked on the 'silly old man' who had
written these. But we both varied our studies with a ten-days' cruise.
Jim, who was a typical sailor and could do anything with his hands,
taught me to make a canvas canoe while he made a little canvas
row boat for himself. Rick hired a canoe in Lynn, and joined us
when we had navigated the Nar. Thence we all went up the Ouse,
and turned up the Little Ouse (or Brandon River). This we followed
so nearly to its very source, that six miles with a hired cart brought
us across to the tiny ditch which represents the new-born Waveney.
Down this we paddled in easy stages, but with one awkward drawback. Rick, our nominal steward, had neglected to lay in bread
enough, and the whole of our last day we had nothing to eat but
bully beef and raw oatmeal. That night we reached Breydon Water,
a wide salt-water 'Broad', just before sunset, and meditated a hasty
push for Yarmouth. But our tent, heavy with rain, weighed us
down so deep that a very little extra wind would have swamped
us, and we encamped on the foreshore under the ruined Roman walls
of Burgh Castle. The day's crude diet had upset Rick; he dreamed
that the tide had risen and was swamping us; he claimed such merit
for saving Jim's tobacco-pouch just as it floated away, that for a
minute or two we also were hypnotized into belief. Next morning
at daybreak we put forth upon Breydon, and nine o'clock saw us
seated in Lord Nelson's room at the 'Star' in Yarmouth, with our
canoes registered homewards by luggage train. We began with four
bloaters apiece, and the breakfast finally degenerated into lunch.

CHAPTER XV

LLANDAFF

A few weeks later, Alfred Stable and I were sent as examiners to the cathedral school at Llandaff. Owen had recently been appointed to the Headmastership of this school, which was Dean Vaughan's favourite child. Here was a renewal of old Felsted and Malvern days: for Stable had taken my place at the Wells House. Under my bedroom window ran a little stream to join the Taff; and this lingers in my memory, side by side with a similar streamlet under my bedroom at Poligny in Burgundy, among the sweetest lullabies of my life. While I was there it was arranged, at Owen's mediation, that Dean Vaughan would find room for me next Term among his 'doves'— as those who lived with him were called. C. J. Vaughan, Dean of Llandaff and Master of the Temple, was, with his contemporary, A. P. Stanley, one of Thomas Arnold's favourite pupils at Rugby, and was bracketed with Lord Lyttelton at the top of the Classical Tripos on proceeding to Cambridge. He became a Fellow of Trinity, and shortly after this was elected as Headmaster of Harrow at the early age of twenty-five. On his resignation from Harrow, he was presented to the important living of Doncaster where he began his system of preparing young ordinands—his 'doves'—without a fee. The *Church Times*, some twenty years ago, noticed this retrospectively, and remarked that, with all Vaughan's care, there was no clear distinguishing characteristic in the men who had passed through his hands. That is quite true: in fact, he much disliked the nickname which outsiders fastened upon his pupils. Their only characteristic was the fact that they could not be labelled, except in jest. The one thing in common was the influence of a man who was a born teacher: who set himself not to mould the youth but to teach him moral and intellectual self-reliance. He would not solve a personal difficulty, but only turn the man inside out, and make him see what he himself really felt upon close examination of the actual factors. One of his first pupils was Randall Davidson, afterwards Archbishop of Canterbury and, by special creation, finally Peer in his own right. Among his last was Father R. H. Benson, one of the most brilliant and noisiest Roman Catholic converts of our time.

He was soon promoted from Doncaster to become Master of the Temple in London, and Dean of Llandaff. It was said that he refused three bishoprics. Certainly he categorically refused one. There were several stories about this; but I had the actual facts from his favourite pupil and successor at Harrow, the Master of Trinity, H. M. Butler. He was offered the See of Rochester. In his own mind he definitely accepted, so much so that, since this would give him the right of appointment to the vacant Chancellorship of the See, he wrote offering this to a friend. But he was conscious of his own temptations to ambition: and that night, in prayer, he asked himself whether he coveted the See for the Church's sake or for his own. The fruit of that examination of conscience, rightly or wrongly, was in two letters next morning; one of refusal to the Prime Minister, and another of apology to his friend. It was those two sides of Vaughan that made senior Fellows of Trinity fear lest this 'ecclesiarstic' should be set over them by the Crown after Whewell's death. Henry Jackson, for instance, used to speak of the contingency with horror.

Gwatkin once spoke to me very frankly about his old Shrewsbury Headmaster, Kennedy, the figure so prominent in Samuel Butler's *Way of All Flesh*. 'Kennedy', he said, 'had every fault a Headmaster can have, except idleness and ignorance. But, all the same, he was a great Headmaster: for he knew his own faults, and he wove them into his system. He was like Queen Elizabeth. She also knew her own faults, indecision, etc., and she deliberately wove them into her system.' Vaughan also, with a wonderful insight into characters around him, was keenly self-conscious. He knew that he had peculiar gifts of irony and sarcasm, bound up with his literary sensitiveness and command of language. Some of us saw an instance of this in 1883. There was a large dinner party at the Deanery, perhaps twenty guests, with the Mayor of Cardiff at the Dean's side. It was a time of bitter political agitation, especially over Home Rule for Ireland. The Mayor tactlessly asked in rather a loud tone: 'What are your politics, Mr Dean?' Vaughan, with tactful dissimulation, appealed to Mrs Vaughan at the other end: 'My dear! what are our politics at the present moment? I can't quite remember."

Mrs Vaughan, always ready, played up to him from her end; there was a witty interchange, and the poor Mayor realized uncomfortably that this was not a time for serious discussion on the Home Rule question.

For Mrs Vaughan, sister of his old school friend A. P. Stanley, was a hostess of inexhaustible resource. Her afternoon and evening gatherings at the Temple were often crowded to suffocation. Once, she noticed in a corner, Sir Willoughby Jones, an old friend, for he was a Norfolk squire and she daughter to the Bishop of Norwich. He looked bored: so she worked her way to him on behalf of a similarly silent lady in another corner who 'was dying to know him'. When they had worked their way back, she introduced him to his own wife, recently married and therefore unfamiliar to Mrs Vaughan.

Our work was mainly Greek Testament, text and exposition, with a weekly sermon to write. Vaughan was a specialist in Greek scholarship as understood in his youth: he 'properly based *Oun*', and would not pass on until he had squeezed out every drop of sense or suggestion. This was, no doubt, too microscopic: but nothing could have been sounder in its own way. It did not tempt us to believe that we were scientific theologians in the scholastic sense. Vaughan, consciously or not, was following an even greater Dean, John Colet of St Paul's, who for the first time in English history lectured straightforwardly upon what St Paul had actually intended to convey to the readers of his own time, and not upon what hundreds of later commentators had deduced from Pauline texts. As to his sermon teaching, it was just perfect common-sense, of which one prime factor lies in the preacher's recognition of his own limitations. Once the text was 'For we walk by faith, not by sight'. His criticism fixed first upon the fact that only two had seen the logical necessity of reversing this order: the rest, therefore, had spent nearly all their time upon elaborating the *not* clause.

It was noteworthy how simply and curtly he would refuse to answer, even what 'every schoolboy knows', unless he were fairly certain. Only those who have often heard him answer in three unvarnished words, 'I don't know', can read behind the lines of Matthew Arnold's judgment as reported in the second volume of G. W. E. Russell's *Collections and Recollections*: 'Vaughan, a dear fellow, but brutally ignorant.' They had been at Rugby together; and the character Vaughan once gave me of his schoolfellow needs the same epigrammatic discount: 'Poor Matt! What his father was, he just was not, and what his father was not, he just was!' Russell's book brings out also his partial estrangement from Stanley, his *fidus Achates* at school and afterwards his brother-in-law. Stanley was as brilliant and versatile as Vaughan was solid. He, at Oxford, had absorbed everything knowable, while Vaughan had followed Greek particles, with a considerable dose of compulsory mathematics, to the exclusion of much wider reading. Stanley, again, was from one of our oldest families, the Stanleys of Alderley; and, at his deanery at Westminster, London society combined fashion and intellect as, probably, nowhere else. Moreover, while Vaughan kept as much of his hereditary rough-hewn Evangelicalism as a man of his intellect and originality was likely to retain, his younger brother David had joined with another Trinity Fellow, Llewelyn Davies, in a translation of Plato's *Republic*, and both had thrown in their lot with the definite Broad Church. Davies was the author of a well-known answer to an enquiring friend, 'I would much rather men should ask: *Why isn't Davies a bishop*, than *Why is he?*' Meanwhile Stanley was moving faster still, and his growing latitudinarianism scandalized some of his oldest friends. One speech recorded by Russell bears the clearest marks of authenticity. Calling upon Vaughan, he mentioned that he had just come from the Deanery at Westminster. 'Whom did you meet there?' He gave the names. 'Ah! elderly unbelievers of rank—the Dean's favourite associates!'

While at Llandaff we had a certain amount of district-visiting assigned to us in the poorer parts of Cardiff. In my street was one peculiarly painful case: a drunken wife and children neglected, practically abandoned. Nothing I had seen in the poorest Norfolk cottages approached this sordid story. The woman, they told me, was niece to a Free Church Minister at Pontypridd, some twenty miles distant; so I went off by train to see him. His story was that the husband, a miner, had driven her to drink by his ill-treatment. After a long talk, he insisted on my sharing the family tea, reinforced (I think on my account) with a Welsh rabbit of formidable proportions and leathery consistence. I pleaded in vain; his politeness even

From a drawing by the author

Plate VI.   Moonlight at Pentney (see pp. 56 ff.)

Plate VII.
Rothenburg.
From an
etching by
the author

assigned to me a Benjamin's mess. The tea was almost black, well stewed on the hob: and that night, with the morrow, stand out in my memory among my worst indigestions.

Ordinarily, however, we had our afternoon exercise as freely as at Cambridge: to me, indeed, it was a real Indian Summer. We were, roughly, contemporaries, and mostly Cantabs, though I remember two Oxford men. The schoolboy spirit was far from dead. *L*, who later on clung resolutely to a tweed coat and red tie all through a laborious clerical career in London, was our most original spirit. *R*, a first-rate cricketer but an extremely shy man, was once bound for London with *L*. They had to walk the three miles by footpath into Cardiff: and *L*, on a hot afternoon, was provokingly slow. *R*, in the hope of quickening him, finally walked on at what seemed a necessary pace. The result was, that *L* loitered even more. *R*, stopping a Cardiff citizen on his way out, begged him to tell that gentleman they would lose the train if he did not hurry. *L* received the message with a smile, and explained that he was a keeper, and no notice should be taken of his delusion. For the rest of *R*'s time at Llandaff, he was haunted with the fear of meeting that citizen again on the path to Cardiff. .

But the most irresponsible schoolboy prank was that which happened shortly after our ordination, when we were all dispersed to our different curacies. *A* and *B* were from rival schools and rival universities. Each, with a fund of real good nature, was inclined to be argumentative. During all their months with the Dean, they had had many discussions, never finished by mutual agreement. When each was settled in, *A* came up from thirty miles south of London to spend a friendly day with *B*, thirty miles north, and to compare notes. The day passed happily as of old, mainly in agreements to differ. As *A*, son of a bishop and future bishop himself, rose at last to go in the evening, he said, 'Give me some silver; I've got nothing but my return ticket'. *B*, as of old, met this with 'I haven't got anything'. 'If I find anything in your rooms, may I take it?' 'Yes', replied *B*, seeing *A*'s gaze fixed upon his mantel-piece. *A* pounced at once upon what had every appearance of a gold sovereign, but was in fact a token from the 'Inventories', a London exhibition at which (among other mechanical marvels) one could throw silver into a little tank of water and receive it back duly gilded.[1] *B*, in a momentary impulse of mischief which he regretted afterwards, let *A* hurry off to the train under that illusion. Next day, *A* got special leave of absence from his parish to retrace those 120 miles and tell *B* what he thought of him. 'I gave the thing to the booking-clerk on the Underground, and demanded my change. He threatened to call a Bobby. Then I saw what it was, and said, "Don't you see I'm a clergyman?" "Oh yes! they mostly are, that try this trick."'

Llandaff, though its cathedral makes it a 'city', is little more than a pleasant village, dotted around with charming houses and gardens of Cardiff merchants. There is a medieval bishop's palace in ruins, a substantial modern palace in its park, and a still more modern deanery on the steep ground that rises from the west front of the cathedral. That façade is admirable work of the turn of the twelfth century, with one tower restored and another rebuilt, the whole in excellent taste. Indeed the carved capitals are of that peculiarly subtle lily-like curve which seems characteristically Celtic, meeting us also at Abbey-Dore, Llanidloes and elsewhere. Over the altar is a triptych by Rossetti, one of his finest achievements in colour. The quiet charm of the whole place makes it far more seductive than many better known cathedrals; and the country round, when we avoid the intensely industrialized areas, is charming also. The Marquis of Bute (the young hero of Disraeli's *Lothair*) had spent freely of his wealth for the restoration and beautification of his two castles, the great one at Cardiff and the smaller but more picturesque Castle Coch, up the valley. A fine hill, the Garth, rises straight behind Llandaff, with beech woods which in autumn are magnificent.

Vaughan's choir school was perhaps unique of its kind: the boys' education came first, and their public services, however important, were secondary. Holidays were almost on the ordinary preparatory school scale; and residents sometimes murmured that cathedral services were least musical in the best summer weather, when visitors were most frequent and most expectant. A full half of the

[1] Incidentally, this idea led to a revolution at Her Majesty's mint. When, in 1887, Jubilee sixpences were coined on the principle that any statement of values is base and inartistic, there was no difference but of metal between these and half-sovereigns. The result may easily be imagined, and the hasty withdrawal of these dangerous sixpences.

boys, probably, went on to good public schools; and for this, apart
from the lower aim of scholarship-winning, my old schoolfellow
Owen sent them out as well prepared as any in the country. At daily
Matins and Evensong, the 'doves' formed more than half of the
congregation. The choir had a peculiarly plaintive chant which I have
never heard elsewhere, in Gregorian plain-song, for Psalm 137:
'By the waters of Babylon we sat down and wept: when we remembered thee, O Sion.' The melody almost carried one away from the
savage vendetta of the last three verses. To me, it struck the same
chord as the dreaming evening light on the south wall at Felsted,
and the 'Through the day thy love hath spared us' at Malvern Wells:
the fullness of present peace, and yet something of the hierophant's
thrill on the threshold of the mysteries: something which evaporates
here as I try to describe it, and makes me wonder whether I have not
now cracked the glass of pure memory for ever.

In November, I advertised on my own account for a curacy, and
accepted one at £100 a year under Vaughan's old Harrow pupil
A. E. Northey, at Offley in Hertfordshire. The appeal to me was
not only in the vicar's attractive personality, but also in the quiet
country life, with as much time as I could fairly expect anywhere
for that reading of which Llandaff had made me feel the need.
Vaughan was pained at this, and, as I at once saw, justly: he had
thought of placing me with some specially energetic incumbent in
a large parish.

Meanwhile there appeared one of the most remarkable books of
the century: Renan's *Souvenirs d'Enfance et de Jeunesse*.[1] For its
literary fascination I was full ripe; but of its deeper significance I saw
clearly, as yet, only one half. He shows most cogently his own reasons
for leaving the Church of Rome—significantly, in the very same
year in which Newman entered it.[2] These I hailed with satisfaction,
blinking the extent to which many of those same reasons tell against
Anglicanism also. I emphasize this qualifying word *many*, because
it seems to me almost as necessary now as it did then. Anglicanism
does not stand or fall with Roman Christianity. The Roman creed

[1] I have written at length on this in the introduction to an English translation
reprinted by Messrs Routledge some twenty-five years ago.
[2] Mr Belloc characteristically puts an interval of 'a lifetime' between these
two well-known dates (*The Universe*, Oct. 22, 1926).

is a steel chain, no stronger than its weakest link. Anglicanism is a
rope, far more composite and less imposing to look at, but capable
of holding fast at the core even after half of the strands may have
frayed away. There was nothing, therefore, to trouble seriously the
peace of my last weeks at Llandaff. The tramp in me drank in those
days to the full. Here we were on the borderland of Celtic romance:
here, as at Malvern, was all Snowdonia in imagination behind each
nearest mountain: here, indeed, within a single day's walk, was true
Wild Wales.[1] The great beech woods half-way up Garth, just
behind us, seemed, and perhaps were, more glorious in their autumn
colours than any other beech woods I have seen. And those last
weeks of 1883, with the first of 1884, were lit up by the famous
Krakatoa sunsets. One of the greatest eruptions of our time was
caused by that volcano, in the Sunda Straits between Java and
Sumatra—Mr Korthals, Dutch Consul in Java, whom I met four
years later in Heidelberg, told me how the air in the streets was like
midnight, and his own study table was some two inches deep in
volcanic dust before clearance could begin. And even to us, all those
thousands of miles from the spot, the sun went down again and again
through that dust in matchless splendour. The afterglow often
lingered, even in the eastern sky, for hours. In the brightest west,
emerald green was not occasional but almost normal. We seldom
see it except as a background to the sunset; strips of sky come out
green in contrast to the vivid crimson or vermilion of the clouds
which form the main pattern. But in those Krakatoa skies, the green
was often in the forefront and more striking than anything else.
The nearest approach in art to these skies is in a few of Turner's
watercolours dashed off at lightning speed, especially the Petworth
series, which used to be in the National Gallery, and are now, I believe, at Millbank. In those sunset glories, which once made us drop
a game of football and watch for an hour, nature gave us a splendid
send-off from Llandaff.

Another farewell scene is as fresh in memory, and has far deeper

[1] See Taliesin's prophecy,
> 'Their Lord they shall praise,
> Their tongue they shall keep,
> Their land they shall lose,
> Except Wild Wales.'

significance. The bishop held an ordination for Llandaff diocese
shortly before Christmas: I believe this was our last Sunday there.
Vaughan had been asked to preach. He was a most impressive
preacher and reader. I have never heard his equal with the Pauline
Epistles: he rendered them with the slow measured diction of a man
who was recording his own personal convictions on some occasion
no less vital than Baxter's

> 'I preach'd, as never sure to preach again,
> And as a dying man to dying men.'

The thoughts seemed to come straight from the well, with no suggestion of a personal intermediary. I could not, if I would, get away
from his words in Galatians, 'From henceforth let no man trouble
me: for I bear in my body the marks of the Lord Jesus.' His sermons
were much of the same character when delivered, though naturally
much evaporated in print. They were scholarly, weighty, unadorned
but nearly perfect in their union of plain Bible English with classical
rhetoric in the best sense of that much-abused word. In this particular sermon, the last of his that I ever heard, he ended with the
inevitable exhortation: 'Young men, remember your profession;
you have dedicated yourselves and are no longer your own, in the
sense of yesterday.' He clinched it all with the last stanza of Keble's
poem for the second Sunday in Advent:

> Think not of rest: though dreams be sweet
> Start up, and ply your heavenward feet.
> Is not God's oath upon your head,
> Ne'er to sink back on slothful bed,
> Never again your loins untie
> Nor let your torches waste and die,
> Till, when the shadows thickest fall,
> Ye hear your Master's midnight-call?

In some later chapter, I must come to my drift away from Llandaff.
But the cathedral deanery will always have for me the sweet scent
that those days at the Petit Séminaire d'Issy had for Renan. We, as
he, were intimate pupils to a childless man who had dedicated himself to our youth in the highest spirit of disinterestedness. He, like
Renan's masters, was in many ways an ancient rough-hewn Druidic

figure whom we must needs outgrow some day, if we were to grow at all. But if, as I believe, I have been able to realize the feelings of Langland in old age towards the monastic teachers of his youth, I owe that to Vaughan. It was an immense advantage to us that, our turn to teach being now come, we started with the conviction that we had known religion in the flesh; that what we should now be struggling to convey would be (with due reverence) 'That which we have seen with our eyes, which we have looked upon, and our hands have handled, of the Word of life.' Our last sun went down over the Welsh hills with the promise of healthy rest, and vigour for whatever work the morrow might bring in the great world, the world of all sorts and conditions of men, to which we were now to step out.

CHAPTER XVI

PARISH WORK

ON DECEMBER 21, 1883, I was ordained Deacon by Bishop Claughton of St Albans. Henry Rogers, one of my Llandaff companions, was in the same batch, as curate to the dean's elder brother, E. T. Vaughan of Harpenden. It is part of the Anglican ceremony to hand each ordinand a Bible, in token that he is now commissioned to preach in church. To each of us, the bishop increased this formula of *traditio* with a clause of his own: 'in these difficult and dangerous times'. It was the day of St Thomas, the doubting Apostle. But my own reaction was less of anxiety than of Luther's trust in the liberty wherewith Christ hath made us free: *Plus profuit nobis dubitatio Thomae quam citissima fides Mariae.*[1] The bishop was a dignified and scholarly old man; his palace of Danbury Hall, on a hill above Chelmsford, was an abode of squirearchy for centuries, utilized now at last for this recently created See. Most people, I suppose, look back to at least half a dozen occasions, almost as fresh as yesterday, when they brushed deeply through fallen autumn leaves. Two stand out with me in clearest relief: the daily trudge to early chapel all along Trumpington Street to St Catharine's; and the long walk with Rogers round and round Danbury Park, looking back to Llandaff and forward to our Hertfordshire work: the leaves seemed to share our feelings as we walked.

Offley is a pleasant village on high ground, part of the same ridge as the forest of the Chilterns. Eastwards, it looks down upon Hitchin, three miles off; and at the same distance to the west is Luton, a busy industrial town. The parish itself is wide and scattered, with outlying settlements of the kind so common in Essex and Hertfordshire, 'Ends' or 'Greens' or 'Hoos'.[2] Charles Lamb's Mackery End is a classical example. Offley has Cockernhoe at its southern edge, and

---

[1] Augustine, *Serm.* LXI: 'More helpful to us has been the doubt of Thomas than the most ready faith of Mary.'

[2] *Hoo* or *Hoe* I take to be the Scottish *Heugh*, *Hough*, and the German *Höhe*.

Offley Hoo to the north-west. Cockernhoe had a little supplementary schoolhouse for the needs of the clump of cottages which served the needs of the squire and his park. The two young mistresses, sisters, did admirable civilizing work, if only by their mere presence, among these labourers' families, who were cut off otherwise from almost all civilization: for the park wall meant social even more than physical separation, and the village itself was a good mile off, even by footpath. I remember one occasion on which a mother, usually up in arms against school discipline, appealed to the two girls to come and whip her boy for some family misdemeanour. This little settlement was to be my special province, with frequent visits to the school and a service in the schoolroom on Sunday evenings. The vicarage was nearly a mile away from the village in the other direction. The arrangement in general was reminiscent of Church life in Trollope's novels. But our squire at Offley Hall was a public-spirited man, son to that George Hughes who stroked the 'Glorious Seven' of Oxford in their victory over Cambridge at Henley, and whom his brother, the author of *Tom Brown's School Days*, commemorated in a little volume called *Memoirs of a Brother*.

It was a great sporting neighbourhood. The squire of Cockernhoe paid for this with his life. He reared up a stag from infancy; it followed him like a dog. One day, the squire took a sudden fancy to photograph the stag. He brought his apparatus down, set it up, and put his head underneath the black velvet cloth in order to get the focus. The beast, seeing this strange and ominous business, took that fright which is inseparable from anger, saw red, and charged straight at the camera, the velvet, and the squire. The sequel bore out the ancient proverb: 'The wound of a boar a barber can cure, but the wound of a hart brings a man to his bier.'

But the great centre of sport was Hitchin Priory, with its park outside the town. The Delmé-Radcliffe of a generation earlier had been, we heard, a typical fox-hunter of the Jorrocks school: and his successor carried on the family tradition. He had begun in the navy, and had many naval friends, especially a certain Admiral X. His nephew once described to me a Homeric meal at the Priory. Towards midday, when justice had been done to all the courses on the table, the squire reminded his guest of the spiced beef on the sideboard. 'No, thank you.' 'Just one slice?' 'I couldn't do it.' 'You won't get anything more until lunch.' Under such pressure, how could the admiral resist further?

One Sunday, the two came down, as usual, to morning Church. The parson was on his holiday: and his *locum tenens* appeared in a hood of strange pattern. 'Durham!' said the squire, and 'Dublin!' replied the admiral. 'What'll you lay?' 'A tenner.' They went straight up to the Priory, consulted *Crockford's Clerical Directory*, settled the bet, and came back to Church. Yet both of them, in case of need, would cheerfully have carried a rifle in defence of the Anglican Establishment.

At one distant ball, the Priory guests were so many that all the home vehicles were filled with ladies, and for the men a bus was hired from Hitchin, to be driven by the squire. It snowed hard all night; and in the small hours, when the bus started homewards, the ground was so freshly covered and the air so thick with driving flakes, that even the squire lost his way over ground where he had hunted for years. They came at last to a lonely farmhouse, and the squire threw gravel up to the window until a sleepy head appeared. 'What's the way to Hitchin?' 'Where d'yer come from?' 'What the devil is that to you?' 'Nawthin', nor where ye're goin' to nayther!' and the window slammed down. The squire sat down on the doorstep to laugh it out, and made a point of finding the farm afterwards and sending a brace of pheasants.

A friend once capped this to me with a similar dialogue. 'My good man, which is the way to Mildenhall?' 'How d'yer know I'm a good man?' 'Oh, I guessed it.' 'Then yer may guess yer way to Mildenhall!'

My vicar's father was of a county family in Kent, who had been at Eton, then Queen's Page at Windsor, and finally Colonel in the Guards. Northey himself was an old Harrovian: thus, without neglecting his work, he did see something of the magnates. At least three other of the neighbouring village clergy were of county families. Naturally, I saw only the fringe of all this: no more than was good for me. Indeed, looking back over all these years, I see myself very much in the light of the curate in *The Private Secretary*, one of the most popular farces of the eighties. All the London stations were plastered with bills of this man, bearing a carpet-bag and clad in a long Inverness cape, and saying 'I don't like London!'

On my infrequent London visits, with similar cloak and bag, I always instinctively edged away from this poster.

Offley village, like most of the neighbourhood, was deeply affected by the straw-plaiting industry, which fed the Luton hat factories. Girls learned this at an early age, and became so deft that they could do their plaiting at every spare moment, walking about the roads or sitting to gossip together. In those days, however, Japanese competition was revolutionizing the market: the foreign plait was inferior, but it came in by the ton. Compulsory schooling was scarcely a dozen years old in practice. The chief farmer in the parish had a bailiff who could neither read nor write. The man would go down to Hitchin market, transact the most complicated business throughout the day, and come back to dictate it all in the evening—things bought and things sold, offers accepted and offers rejected—as though it were all written before him. Comparing Offley and Cockernhoe schooling with what I had known at Pentney, I was able to measure the extent to which the Education Act bade fair to civilize village life.

Visiting went on conscientiously, but it was a difficult job. In some cottages it was difficult to say anything which did not seem a mockery of the poor folks' actual condition. In others there was downright ill-will; and when, after several attempts, the friction rather increased than diminished, I struck them from my list. In other cases, I was naturally looked on as a sort of relieving officer; and the parish funds often justified this, especially as Northey gave generously from his own private means. When he went for his summer holiday, I was of course in charge of the school, and had to collect the fees: for the law, while it prescribed compulsory attendance, demanded also compulsory payment: the fees looked small to us, but not to the cottagers. My harvest during Northey's absence amounted to over £40, which I locked in my desk. A month or two after his return, I suddenly remembered this bag of coin, and brought it to the vicarage, with many apologies. Northey, strangely enough, looked far more embarrassed than grateful. Mrs Northey exclaimed, 'Why, Alfred, and you've balanced the school accounts without it!' So in fact he had, being no great arithmetician, and dealing with auditors who did not look closely into details.

All this visiting seemed to bring out a contrast which others have

noted to me: between the many small acts of kindness between
cottage and cottage, and the many contrary cases of envy and petty
spite. Many years later, I found this noted in, and have often quoted
it from, one of the greatest of all mission preachers, the Franciscan
Berthold of Regensburg, who was roughly contemporary with
Saints Bonaventura and Thomas Aquinas. He says, in one of his
sermons: 'Because the fishes are poor and naked, therefore they
devour each other. . . . None are so false as the country-folk among
each other: for these are so untrue that for envy and hatred they can
scarce look upon one another.'

The most unpleasant cases were very few here, though a little
more frequent when I went on to the little town of Rickmansworth.
I mean, those where the cottager has picked up a religious phraseology, and brings it out for the sake of loaves and fishes. At Offley,
we had in one case the exact opposite. The man was employed on
a windmill: he showed me once round all the machinery in the top
storey: very little iron, but great wooden wheels with wooden cogs,
probably as old as the century. The cogs, he explained, were made
of crab-apple wood, harder than oak and even than hornbeam.
Polished by all these years of friction, and mellowed by time, they
were as beautiful as amber, and gave a similar impression of trans-
lucency. That man told me once how another had acted towards
him with malice aforethought. He said to me slowly and deliberately,
'I can never forgive that man. I'm not an unbeliever: I know what
Christ said: but I shall never forgive him.' In another cottage, there
was a cricket behind the stove; and in front an apple-cheeked old
lady in her chair: worthy of Dickens, I thought. Therefore the cue
for conversation seemed obvious: 'What a cheerful noise that is!'
'Well, Sir, that insec do set there and holler, holler, holler till I don't
know what to do with myself!' 'The heart knoweth his own bitterness, and a stranger doth not intermeddle with his joy!'

It was a healthy, quiet introduction; and I got much time, if not
all I had hoped, for reading. Now at last I was to some extent like
the Roman priest I had envied at Malvern Wells; if not outwardly,
at least in what I supposed to be his inward comfort: here at last
the square peg was finding a square hole. Already at Malvern Wells,
working at Plato with Huntington, I had found that Cambridge had
given me a fair key to Greek and Latin; and now I could read as

I desired, without constraint of examination. Here, at O'ffley, I began reading medieval Latin more seriously. During that Oxford attempt in 1876, I had found in the Union Library the Camden volume of Goliardic songs, and enjoyed the spirit of *Mihi est propositum in taberna mori*. In Antwerp, I had bought a charming old copy of *De Imitatione Christi*. The night before Ordination, in the bishop's palace at Danbury, I had found on his shelves a volume of selected letters by St Jerome, including that in which he enlarges upon the ascetic achievements of one among the most unwashen and most unkempt of all recorded saints. But now I was to make the acquaintance of a very different religious hero, St Bernard. On the morrow of Ordination, or perhaps on that very evening, walking across London from Liverpool Street to King's Cross for Hitchin, I saw in a dirty little junk-shop a single volume of the unusual octavo Benedictine edition of St Bernard: the volume containing his *Letters*. It was in excellent condition: print, paper and calf binding in the best traditions of French work at the turn of the seventeenth century. The junk-man demanded 6*d.*, and we parted from a bargain after the ideal of St Thomas Aquinas: gain and satisfaction on both sides.

I was destined to board and lodge at Offley in the hall butler's cottage: but his wife was dangerously ill, and during her tedious convalescence the Northeys gave me most hospitable quarters at the vicarage. I slept in the vacant nursery—they were as yet childless—with an old-fashioned open grate, and a high protective fender upon which I could rest my feet. I could thus come some real way towards Macaulay's definition of a scholar: I could read, if not Plato, at least St Bernard, with my feet on the fender while the household was in bed. Here was a fresh stage of my pilgrimage, more decisive in the long run than Trevelyan's *Macaulay* itself. Even now, I wonder whether we can find, within that number of pages, any better guide over the threshold of medieval life. For if we reckon not merely the text itself with its Benedictine notes, but also the categories those letters supply and the questions they raise for every serious reader, the Saint takes us through Hell and Purgatory; and he does not quit us at the gates of Paradise. Those letters led naturally on to St Augustine's *Confessions*. Northey had inherited from his father an excellent library, in which I remember with special gratitude a fine Italian edition of Vasari's *Lives of the Painters*, the two curious volumes of Old French Proverbs by Le Roux de Lincy, and a set of the *Fortnightly Review* almost up to date.

When at last my landlady could take me into her cottage, the sitting-room was just high enough to allow me to move without bending. I painted on the whitewashed beam, from Martial,

> Liber eris, coenare foris si, Maxime, nolis,
> Si tua non rectus tecta subire potes.[1]

In my bedroom, I had a whole blank wall of whitewash by the side of my dormer window. Here I painted a rising sun, and, between the rays, in Greek script from Ephesians v, 14: 'Awake thou that sleepest, and arise from the dead, and Christ shall give thee light.' Just about thirty years later, when my wife and I cycled through Offley, we found ideal week-end comfort at the little house of Miss Gertie Foster, whose father had been the village carpenter in my time. She told me these inscriptions were still there, charitably spared through subsequent whitewashings: so we got leave to see them. A few years later, they had gone the way of a thousand more valuable inscriptions in our parish churches.

Hitchin is a great Quaker centre: the banker family of Lucas, with Seebohm, one of our best amateur historians, and Tuke, a well-known name in art. This last family had just begun to invite me, and I had revelled in one pleasant evening in their valuable illustrated art books, when Northey told me that he had accepted from the bishop a much more important parish, that of Rickmans-worth, not far from Harrow. He asked me to go with him: and I had little hesitation in accepting. For, though I had already grown very fond of Offley, it was pretty certain that no vicar there would keep a curate unless he had private means. As it turned out, the living went to a man with four children and little money of his own.

---

[1] 'You will be a freeman, Maximus, if you don't care to dine abroad, and if you can't get into your house without bending your head' (II, 53).

CHAPTER XVII

FRESH WOODS

RICKMANSWORTH, in 1884, was a small town to which the Metropolitan Railway had not yet quite extended: it stopped three miles short, at Northwood. In these succeeding years, it has gone much farther, and the little place is almost a London suburb. Like Offley, it had its outliers: but three of these, Croxley Green for instance, had grown into parochial independence, each with its own church and benefice in the gift of the Rickmansworth vicar. It had two fine mansions: Rickmansworth Park rising up the hill near the church, with an avenue of ancient Spanish chestnuts, and Moor Park, of much wider fame, with a very striking classical façade and portico. This last belonged to Lord Ebury, one of that Grosvenor family which, like the Wellesleys, was distinguished by having five brothers at a time in the House of Peers. Lord Ebury was then an old man: he bore his dignity with great courtesy, and was a sincere Evangelical churchman. For the first and last time in my life, I dined at the ancestral board of an English peer, and heard the once fashionable pronunciation of *goold* for *gold*, and *laylock* for *lilac*. Mr Birch, at the other Park, was a governor of the Bank of England, and a great figure in the City. His brother, Canon Birch, had been tutor and director to the Prince of Wales (i.e. Edward VII) on his journey to Palestine. His return was celebrated by a congratulatory dinner from some select coterie; I think, of *Saturday Review* men. That was the undisputed weekly of those days: Leslie Stephen was one of its pillars; J. R. Green made his début there, and its style was to a great extent fixed by Venables, who had broken Thackeray's nose in the famous fight at Charterhouse. Venables, when it came to speeches, formally proposed the toast of 'Canon Birch—and the Rest of the Royal Family'. His brother was freely hospitable, and I met most interesting guests at his table. One night it was Mr Childers, one of Gladstone's most devoted henchmen, who told us an incident which had occurred a few days earlier, on the first of April 1885. European affairs were sufficiently ticklish to give some anxiety to the Foreign Secretary, Lord Granville. He was dining out that night, and one of the guests casually mentioned some sensational report in the evening papers. The minister sent round at once to the Foreign Office for all the papers that had come since he left. A large box arrived in the middle of dinner, and he begged leave to rise from table for it. With trembling hands he broke the seal, and found inside another box. Inside this was a third, and so on *ad infinitum*. The inmost contained nothing—all that had arrived since he left the office. The clerk (said Childers) who played that April prank was an old Etonian; and in his time he had served as Royal Page. Once, in sheer boredom, as he held Victoria's train, he 'put his thumb unto his nose and spread his fingers out'. The room was a mass of mirrors: the Queen saw him, and he was expelled in disgrace. I have constantly regretted that I did not ask his name and keep it in memory. It would be interesting to know what became of this eccentric character. Childers went on to relate, quite frankly, the difficulties of working under Gladstone in those later days. 'When we want him badly, he can't be found: and then at last we find him in the library, perched on a ladder and reading in some theologian.' A few weeks after this came the rejection of Gladstone's budget (on the beer clause?), and the collapse of that ministry.

Most interesting of all was the companionship of A. E. Garrett. He was of the well-known Ipswich family, cousin to Mrs Fawcett whose daughter beat the Senior Wrangler at Cambridge, and Mrs Garrett-Anderson, our first woman doctor, and Miss Rhoda Garrett the architect. He himself was junior partner in the best practice of the neighbourhood. His senior partner, on principle, avoided all after-dinner work: consequently Garrett had all the night cases, and averaged scarcely more than four hours of sleep. Some years later, he read before the Obstetrical Society in London a paper based upon 3000 births recorded in his books. He attributed his almost universal success to the fact that he never left the house, for any reason whatever, until he had been able to assure himself that things were going well, or at least to diagnose any difficulty and take definite steps to meet it. The work broke him down: when, at nearly fifty, he had retired with a competence to Eastbourne, he enjoyed his leisure for only a few years. He very often took me round in his dog-cart: my own parish visits fitted with his, or I took my day's relaxation that way, holding his horse meanwhile. On his return to the reins, he had often something of human experience to say: e.g. 'The man in that house has a constitution which some men would buy at an enormous price: he gets drunk twice a day, first in the morning and then in the evening.'

I had less time for reading than at Offley, but one priceless advantage. It was easy to go for an hour or two to London, and this is when I first began research in the British Museum Reading Room. Unless my memory betrays me, 1885 is the date of my little green ticket, very dilapidated by this time, in virtue of which I have life-long access to that sacred chamber, and which lies in a drawer at St John's College, Cambridge, waiting for some better day. Regulations, since then, have come and gone: but none can act retrospectively and deprive me of that perpetual privilege. It stood me once in very good stead, when there had been some scandal, and a stricter watch was put upon the door, and I produced my own Open Sesame in face of Rashdall and Tout, neither of whom had troubled to bring his ticket. Tout passed from explanation to command, and from command to commination; but the ex-sergeant-major at the door was adamant. It was a duplicate to the legendary dialogue at the gate of Portsmouth Dockyard: 'Why, sentinel, I'm the Admiral's lady!' 'Sorry, Ma'am, but I couldn't let yer through without a ticket, not if yer was the Admiral's wife!' So I passed in to fetch the Reading-Room Superintendent and unlock this Purgatory. Not long afterwards, I lost my little green ticket, and had thenceforward either to take my chance or to waste twenty minutes in procuring an emergency permit. Then, ten years later or more, an attendant brought it up to me, and said, 'Isn't this yours?' Somebody had picked it up when I dropped it, and used it furtively all those years: 'The priest that slays the slayer, and shall himself be slain.' Incidentally, I am reminded here that the Museum itself was one of the many jobs I applied for in early life. But in those days there was one necessary gateway to all Civil Service employment: a Preliminary Examination in elementary subjects. I failed hopelessly in the arithmetical test, in which one had to add up several long columns of L.S.D. figures. Later, I compared notes with Professor Rapson, who on his first try for the Museum was ploughed in geography. But, as another friend in the eighties put it to me,

'Whenever I am specially depressed, I take out my printed testimonials and read them over again'.

After all, whatever I lost at Rickmansworth in bare leisure time,
as compared with Offley, was more than counterbalanced by wider
practical experience. We were tinged, so to speak, with something
of Metropolitan life. Close by, at Northwood, is the Metropolitan
Railway, and a good many Rickmansworth residents were London
workers. Dickinson's paper mills, in the parish itself, send their
fine products all over the world. Three miles off, at Watford, is
one of the biggest breweries in the kingdom. The Autotype Company had started their fine-art studios and factories within an easy
walk. Even nearer was that last infirmity of urban mind, the golf-
links of Chorley Wood, where A. J. Balfour might often be seen
working off the cares of State and the problems of philosophy. At
garden parties one might meet a Harrow Master, such as the great
Bowen, or a Professor at London University, or W. S. Gilbert,
partner with Sir Arthur Sullivan.

I took a daily lesson with the upper class of the Elementary
School. The cottages offered a variety of experience quite strange
to unsophisticated villages. Here, for instance, was a young married
couple from North Scotland. The husband was a carpenter: the wife
told me her childhood story. Her mother was a widow with six
children, this the youngest. The mother had no resource but washing.
Two nights a week she worked literally from dark to dawn: for
the other four she lay a few hours in bed. She was sorely tempted to
shirk the school fees in the case of this youngest; but she said, 'I'll
give her schooling if I can't give her butter to her bread'. The child
herself began to help in the washing before she could reach to the
table: she had to stand on an inverted tub. A Sheffield master-cutler
once said to me, 'I told Fisher, when he was made Minister of
Education: "You have here the chance of your life. If you can
find out what it is that makes the Scotsman regard education in
such a different light from the Englishman, you'll have made a most
valuable discovery in sociology."' Pending the chance of continuing this in a later chapter, let me give here the answer of two
Scots, Professors at Cambridge, to his question. One said off-hand,
as one would expect, 'John Knox'. The other considered rather
longer, and suggested, 'The Shorter Catechism: a most remarkable

and philosophical first stage for the young scholar'. Others may suggest that the Catechism is rather a symptom than a cause.

My landlady herself, Mrs Odell, read me many lessons in simple human kindness. She was a widow, and sheltered her brother's widow in the house. The latter was always querulous and extremely deaf, and the little rooms had thin walls; sometimes therefore, after supper, I heard not dialogues but semi-dialogues of the kind that we get nowadays on the telephone. 'You don't know why God ever made you, don't you? . . . Think you'll go some day an' make a hole in the water? . . . That's wicked, an' you'll be sorry for that.'

The house was in a little side street, quite inconspicuous; yet tramps came to it by the sort of freemasonry by which wasps find out a picnic party. Therefore I formalized my charities. First, I assured the tramp of bread, butter and tea from Mrs Odell at any time. But that would not do: 'A kind lady up the street' had already done that for them. The real need was that of fourpence for a night's lodging. I arranged, therefore, with the nearest public house that it should give a bed to any tramp who produced my visiting card; and charge it to me. Only two tramps ever accepted that card, and neither of them presented it at the inn.

But, during these weeks and months when I was getting a firmer grip upon my practical work, and making new and very pleasant friends, my speculative foundation was slipping away.

The first clear stage came with my examination for the priesthood. Three of the set subjects were Pusey's *Commentary on the Book of Daniel*, Liddon's *Bampton Lectures*, and Bishop Pearson *On the Creed*. Pusey's puerile want of logic and common-sense horrified me, and reflected upon the bishop and chaplains who could employ such a Mrs Partington with her mop against the Atlantic of free-thought which was so plainly beating upon us. I understood then the contemptuous pity with which Renan recounts Pusey's visit to him, and his senile warning to the younger scholar against the newer standard books of Oriental philology. As Mark Pattison was writing at that very moment, if German scholarship in England had been pursued not by the learned and purblind Pusey but by the keen-sighted Newman, the whole fortunes of Anglicanism in that generation might have been different.

Liddon, again, harped incessantly upon one point: If Christ was not God in the fullest sense, then He was not even a good man. In the face of Liddon's inconclusive arguments for the first part, this was a dangerous and almost fatal position. Pearson I tried to avoid, pleading with the bishop that my move from Offley had made me lose a good deal of time. He, however, insisted, and very rightly from his point of view: for here was a book upon which our Church had relied for centuries as upon a classic. I had then only a week to the examination, but I set to at once and, confronted by the examiners with good straightforward questions, answered them with more confidence and actual success, I think, than in any other examination of my life. For, in one sense, the book fully deserves its reputation: it is careful and logical in argument, and in style fully worthy of its subject. But the stress laid upon the spurious text of the three Heavenly Witnesses (I John v, 7) was enough in itself, if there had been nothing else of the kind, to perplex any serious student in the years when Froude and Thomas Huxley and Buckle's *History of Civilization* were books read even by upper-class artisans. It was, in fact, just such an artisan who pushed me another inch towards the precipice. We were in the train between Birmingham and Worcester. He had engaged in a theological dispute with another passenger; and, observing my cloth, he turned to me. Did I believe that I had special power to remit sins? I did not, and never had done, observing that both at the ordinary services and at the Communion the priest does not forgive, but prays God to forgive. I might, of course, have relied upon the similar formula in the Roman Mass, if I had known it well enough. But the other, gravely and politely, said, 'You're in a false position, young man', and I knew how my 'Roman collar', in conjunction with what was asserted or implied by the majority of my colleagues, seemed to implicate me in a doctrine which I never expected to believe. I was increasingly uneasy, also, about the Thirty-nine Articles. It seemed more and more obvious that I must either spend my life in misleading conformity, or proclaim nonconformity, perhaps with increasing emphasis, and take the consequences. In other words, my position made me feel in an aggravated form the eternal difficulty: we must make people think we believe either less than is the fact, or more. Less, if we speak out quite freely: more, if we take refuge in silence. About the same time, at our ruridecanal study meetings, we were reading a chapter from a Pauline Epistle. A knotty point turned up: the chairman asked opinions all round, in turn. One curate pointed out that some highly respectable commentary deprecated one particular explanation as leading to heresy—let us say, to Sabellianism. I protested that it was our business to study the context more carefully: that we must not allow even the most respectable names to deny what might seem the Apostle's plain meaning. This raised an outcry which seemed a plain denial of the principles I had learned at Llandaff. I told Northey a good deal of this: but he was no serious theologian. I spoke to Reginald Stuart Poole of the British Museum, who was spending a week-end with the Birches, and who took me a walk round the Park. He pointed out, what I feel still as strongly after nearly sixty years as I did then, the enormous superiority in authority of tone, in philosophical force and in psychological truth, of nearly every chapter of the Canonical Scriptures over even the earliest and most respected Fathers. I read eagerly, also, in the *Life and Sermons* of F. W. Robertson, and his translation of Lessing's *Education of the Human Race*. All these helped to greater serenity of outlook, but not much to conformity with my position as an Anglican priest. It was the converse of Francis Thompson's *Hound of Heaven*. Something dogged my steps until I halted and faced and recognized it, and knew then that my soul was escaped from the snare of the fowler. Whichever way I turned,

Experience, like a sea, soaked all-effacing in.

I wanted to read one of the greatest of all apologists, Origen, in his *Contra Celsum*. Ernst Abraham in Berlin, whom as yet I knew only by correspondence, heard of this, and generously watched the auctions until he had got me, as a Christmas present, the great Benedictine Origen in four folios. But, when I got to work, I found as J. A. Froude and others had found before me, that the pagan philosopher's objections were often strikingly modern, because they were based, so far as I could see, upon plain human common-sense. Renan's *Vie de Jésus*, at the other pole from Origen, led me quietly in the same direction, in spite of its obvious appeal, here and there, to sentiment as against serious thought. I felt myself on shifting ground where every movement, whether for progression or for retrogression, had the same effect of sinking me deeper. Such, at least, was my feeling for some time. Slowly, however, my feet seemed to feel more definitely, at every movement, the firm rock beneath. I think I may claim to have grown, during those days, not so much in the belief that others were wrong, but in the conviction that my own contrary beliefs could not be wrong, for myself at least, so long as I kept watch over their truth and growth. Years afterwards, reading the *Discours de la Méthode* of Descartes, I seemed to see there the Gospel of Common-sense which I had less consciously followed in the past. The first requisite (he says) for arriving at such truth as our nature makes us capable of comprehending, is the real wish to grasp that truth.[1] And for the reality of such wish he supplies a test: 'I resolved to notice more what men did than what they said, . . . since we are so constituted that the process by which we believe a thing is not the same as that by which we know that we believe.' Therefore the serious truth-seeker will, among other things, narrowly scrutinize his own intellectual limitations. He will be compelled to take much at second-hand: he will give to tradition, both in Religion and in Science, the honour that is their due: our ancestors were not all fools, nor always fools. Only he must beware of accepting such second-hand ideas as sacrosanct dogmas. His attitude should be: 'I can't focus my own mind more exactly than this, for the present at least: therefore I think and act and speak in conformity, pending clearer comprehension to the contrary.' Above all, he must not out-Loyolalize Loyola in his acquiescence to authority. That great founder of the Jesuits does indeed insist that a man must believe apparent black to be really white, if the Church says so. But even he gives no justification for believing that we believe, when in fact we do not. That which seems black may be white; but that which seems black must still so seem, unless or until the thinker's mind undergoes a conscious change. To insist otherwise would result in the supreme mechanization of a world which many religious writers condemn already for being inhumanly mechanical.

This inward struggle lasted long: and, after a while, I ceased to pray against it as a temptation. It was not my fault if the bishop

[1] It is as Chesterfield wrote to his son in another field: 'The first secret of pleasing is the wish to please.'

pinned his faith to three books which would not bear the light of modern scholarship. Pride was not the dominant motive here; for I saw that, to put it mildly, my companions were almost as much tempted to party pride as their adversaries were to personal conceit. I could conceive it as a duty to believe with men whose moral and intellectual superiority I recognized; but not to believe I believed where calm reflection assured me more firmly that I did not. My doubts were not dogmatic and self-asserting; but, on the other hand, I could not see dogma as clearly victorious over doubt. In short, I was really on the threshold, here, of my theological education. I felt by this time, and have felt all the more strongly since, that no body claiming supernatural authority should venture to set such a seal upon the forehead of any officer below the age of forty. But, in the meantime, here I definitely was, and what must I definitely do? This, at least, I must do—I must leave the question of priestly powers in abeyance until I could recover certainty in my own mind. If, for all my efforts, I could not believe those things, and could mark no advance towards such belief, then clearly those things were not for me to build upon. I must quit parish work, where death-bed ministration and the consecration of the bread and wine compelled assertion, if only tacit assertion, of two of the most hotly debated matters in human thought: I must quit this and go back to school-mastering, if only for freedom to debate all this dispassionately in my own mind, apart from the question of loaves and fishes. For Northey had three livings in his presentation; and of course a small living was the first goal of my ambition. The breach with old friends might be softened by discretion; but not this business question of L.S.D. and the parson's freehold. And I have never ceased to be grateful that the choice came upon me as a bachelor of twenty-seven, instead of upon a man of forty with wife and family. At this moment, in 1885, the renunciation was fairly easy. My father and mother, who had many other things to think of, regarded it as little more than a mere change of employment. They trusted me, and were willing to accept my choice as serious and reasonable. Vaughan was distressed, as he had just reason to be; and he naturally tried to dissuade me, but with no violence of persuasion: that was not in his nature or in his system. Mrs Curtis took it more passionately, and her husband treated it as a moral offence. But I cannot

claim to have passed through any agony of mind. I had never risen
high enough to claim Clough's pathetic contrast:

> Ah, well-a-day, for we are souls bereaved:
>   Of all the creatures under God's wide cope
>   We are most hopeless that had once most hope,
>   And most beliefless, that had most believed!

I had not lost any Heavenly Paradise: of that I was becoming more
and more convinced. On the contrary, though each step had been
taken unwillingly, yet, once taken, it gave me a sense of standing
on more real and firmer ground. Much more truly could I have
quoted Milton's final and consoling words on those who had tasted
the Tree of the Knowledge of Good and Evil:

> Some natural tears they dropped, but wiped them soon.
> The world was all before them, where to choose
> Their place of rest, and Providence their guide.

CHAPTER XVIII

WALES (1)

GARRETT kindly allowed me to store my Origen in his attic, together with an even bulkier Bayle's *Dictionnaire* which I had bought in Oxford Street, and a few other volumes. These seemed to have something of the mystic significance of Matthew Arnold's Signal Elm: so long as they were there, the Scholar-Gipsy might at any moment return again. It was only seven years later that I burned my boats, and sold these monumental tomes—*tombstones*, as that class was called by the vendors on Farringdon Street barrows—for a few shillings.

I think I must have stayed at Rickmansworth to the end of July: but in August I was private tutor at Llandaff, in the house of Sir Edward Hill. Two of his sons, Wykehamists, were all that could be desired at cricket, but somewhat backward in class, despite fair natural abilities. I had to coach them mainly in Bradley's *Latin Prose Composition*, which I had not opened for ten years or more. Fairly soon, they caught me ignoring one of the rarer niceties of diction to which Bradley sometimes devotes a whole exercise. Thenceforward, they studied to pick out such anomalies and catch me again: a very healthy exercise for us all. It consoled me much, some forty years later, to hear a Senior Classic like W. E. Heitland confessing: 'My latest years of Latin study are being spent largely on the discovery that a Latin Classic might permit himself the things that I used to mark heavily against my pupils.' I spent a fortnight of the month alone with them in a shooting-box on the Mendip Hills. The engagement ended on a Saturday, and on Sunday I tramped over the hills to Wells, with a volume of Uhland in my pocket: for I was now beginning seriously to learn German. It was a brilliant day, of a kind much rarer with us than in continental climates: the sky one vault of real blue: not our usual tender grey, but almost aggressive azure. It came perhaps after a good deal of wet; for I remember an equally aggressive feeling of self-assertive life as I went over the springy turf somewhere near the highest point, and sat down to read Uhland's 'Shepherd's Sabbath Hymn':

> Es ist der Tag des Herrn!
> Ich steh' allein auf weiter Flur:
> Noch eine Morgenglocke nur,
> Nun Stille, nah' und fern!
>
> Anbetend knie' ich hier.
> O süsses Grau'n, geheimes Weh'n,
> Als knieten viele ungeseh'n
> Und beteten mit mir!
>
> Der Himmel, nah' und fern,
> Er ist so klar und feierlich,
> So ganz, als wollt' er öffnen sich:
> Es ist der Tag des Herrn![1]

To me, that poem recalls the day as inevitably as such days recall the poem. The highest poetry, no doubt, is independent of time and place and circumstance. But whenever a few simple words fall in exact harmony with the outer world and the inward mood, that is what poetry exists for; just then, and just for us, the cup is full. Uhland and Heine, it may be, are not so widely read as once they were in Germany; but I am not restrained from quoting the 'Shepherd's Sabbath Hymn' by the fear that my children will say 'That dates you'. I could wish them no better keynote than this for their first view of Wells Cathedral façade, and the stained glass of the choir, and the Vicar's Close.

This brief contact with Llandaff in 1885 was deeply significant in another way. A layman used to frequent the cathedral services whom one of us nicknamed The Serpent. This was, I suppose, because he used often to lean against the oaken pilaster of his stall, winding one long arm round it. He wore a monocle and a slightly cynical expression, and was brother to a well-known Agnostic University Professor. Dining or lunching at the deanery, I once

[1] It is the Lord's Day. I stand alone on the broad plain: just one single morning bell, and then silence, far and near. Here I kneel in worship: O! sweet thrill and onward yearning, as though many knelt unseen and prayed with me! The sky, near and afar, is so clear and solemn, so unbroken, as though it would open [to me]: it is the Lord's Day.

heard him remark, 'I am sick in mind, body and estate'. There, at any rate, was not cynicism; and something led me to tell him a little of my own plans, or planlessness. Then he unbosomed himself very fully and frankly. At about my age, he had completely lost his early faith, and was ready to label himself as anti-clerical. But he did not break off his social work that he was doing in London. More and more, however, he began to criticize his present state as he had criticized the former. 'Why am I putting myself out to do all this work?' On analysis, he found his present principles substantially identical with the old, under new names and with new implications. Love of man, duty to fellow-man, seemed to lead up irresistibly to love of, duty to, something higher than me or my fellow-man; something which certainly must exist, however we may doubt about the how and the when and the where. He had printed a long semi-dramatic poem to that effect, which he gave me. My old master E. G. Hardy, from his Oxford Greats point of view, condemned it as a vain attempt to galvanize dead beliefs. But, for me, certainly it helped to keep me then from 'throwing out the baby with the bath': and, to the present day, the substance of it seems unassailable.

But, for the moment, bread work was a pressing question; and I was ready to take almost any teaching job rather than slide into unemployment. School-work is, or at least was then, a great lottery for those who had not definite Old Tie or similar connections. Paradoxically, much depends on being out of work at the right moment: once, for instance, I could have got work at Rugby if I had not recently taken a job at a less-known school. I dare say this is a difficulty inherent everywhere in the employment question. Here, in 1885, I was much disappointed by failure at Lampeter School, in spite of a very generous testimonial from Dean Vaughan. Two or three weeks later, however, I had an offer from a much better school. John Owen, who, as one of the Lampeter staff, had read my testimonials, was now appointed to the Headship of Llandovery, vacant through the promotion of A. G. Edwards to the See of St Asaph. Owen afterwards became Bishop of St David's, and might have been Archbishop if he had not studiously stood aside in deference to his old friend Edwards.

He had one quality which swallows up a host of minor deficiencies:

deep, natural generosity. His father was of peasant and Nonconformist stock in North Wales. He told me a characteristic story of
the village school. It was bilingual: Welsh was the native tongue
of the great majority in these Snowdonian districts, and therefore
English needed protective legislation. At certain lessons it was
penal to drop into Welsh; but the sanction was of a kind more
practical than moral. The teacher had on his desk a piece of wood
five or six inches long. The moment he heard a word of Welsh, this
ceremonial talisman was handed to the transgressor. He, in his
turn, was now on the watch for the next offence; at which he immediately held up his hand and passed the wood to the culprit:
and so on. At the lesson's end, the boy in whose possession it was
now found must take a scapegoat's punishment for the whole lot.
John Owen's speech, to the very last, was more natural in Welsh
than in English. At Oxford, one of his cherished ideals was that he
should never lose this; and (as Lord Sankey remarked on recalling
this many years later) that prayer was abundantly fulfilled. He was
master of the 'hwyl', that cadence into which the true Cymric
preacher falls—or rather, soars—as he warms to the subject, and
which bears him along in a crescendo of enthusiasm to an ecstatic
peroration. One Sunday evening when the Abergwili party had
gone, as usual, to the English service in Carmarthen parish church,
the bishop preached a Welsh sermon at a district chapel. Our
wagonette waited for him while, through the west window, we could
see his gesticulations and, presently, hear the rising tide of the hwyl.
As my sister put it to me irreverently, it was like her dear Welsh
collie, Griffie, baying the moon at Pentney. In English he had far
less facility, and gave me an instance from one of his first extempore
adventures: 'Suddenly, in the middle, I lost myself altogether, and
could not find another word. I clung on with both hands to the edge
of the marble pulpit. I don't know how long: I only know that
I said mentally to myself, "This marble is *very* cold!"' He might
very likely have added, as another did once in similar circumstances:
'After that, I was mercifully enabled to go on for another hour.'
For in those days some parts of Wales, as of rural Scotland, still
retained a tradition of almost unending preaching: for instance, two
formal sermons from the same man at the same service. When, in
my first Term, I had to preach the Harvest sermon at Carmarthen,

it was hinted as something of a concession to me (and to the congregation) that I should preach only once.

Owen had not that narrow patriotism which is perhaps the greatest weakness of Wales, and which too often springs from an inferiority complex. He was no more in sympathy with the violent reaction at Llanelly, when an Englishman was appointed Chief Postmaster there, than the Birmingham newspapers would have been if a Welshman had been similarly imposed upon them. Therefore, much as he loved his native tongue, he favoured no violent efforts to revive it. He had begun with his own family. For the first two or three children, he made a point of bringing nursemaids down who spoke the Cymric pure and undefiled of Snowdonia. This had one curious and unexpected reaction. His eldest boy was only four or five when, one fine summer day, Owen told me of a dialogue in the garden before breakfast. 'It 's a fine morning, Father.' 'Yes, my boy.' 'Trees growing fine.' 'Yes, my boy.' 'Jesus Christ makes them grow.' 'Well . . . yes, my boy.' '*I* know what he makes them grow for . . . He wants them to burn people with.' The nursemaid from Snowdonia was, probably, a Calvinistic Methodist whose own rudimentary eschatology had been absorbed in a still cruder form by the child. Moreover, these importations from Snowdonia failed even from the utilitarian standpoint. For no sooner had these girls learned enough English for their purpose, than they dropped Welsh altogether except in his presence. Thenceforward he resigned himself to the attraction inevitable, and generally healthy, which a civilization reaching from the Far East to the Antipodes exercises upon a neighbour hampered by narrow geographical limitations. He saw that the best friends of Wales are not the Anti-Saxons, but those who strive to rise from a foundation of ancient Cymric traditions to something which can compete with or outvie Saxondom. Like others whom I have known, he wrote English better than the average Englishman, going back unconsciously to the Bible, the old divines, and such modern masters of straightforward prose as Newman and J. A. Froude. He outplayed Lloyd George in the long and bitter fight for Disestablishment, and got better terms at last than most churchmen had dared to hope, because he was fundamentally no less patriotic, and kept his temper better. A story published soon after his death is, I believe, genuine, but I regret never having asked his confirmation while it was possible. There was a great Disestablishment meeting, with Lloyd George as orator, and a local Nonconformist minister, naturally, in the chair. The chairman began: 'Everybody knows that the greatest ly-yar[1] in the Principality is the Bishop of St David's. But, thank God! he will find his match here to-night!'

When he came to Llandovery, bringing two other new masters besides myself, I found immediate encouragement in work under this laborious and determined man. In those first days, he took practically no exercise, and paid nature for this by a bilious headache once a month; a whole day spent on the sofa, and then again *da capo*. Later, he played lawn tennis energetically, but remained a very hard worker until his death. H. S. Bennett, who in later days stayed with me at the palace, was by that experience converted from his youthful belief that Anglican bishops passed an idle life.

Llandovery was my first introduction to first-rate Welsh scenery at my very door. The Malvern Beacon and the Abergavenny Sugar-loaf had supplied Pisgah sights, but here it was part of our daily life. I approached it by one of the most romantic of our railway routes. First, the cathedrals and orchards of Worcester and Hereford, with whole acres, here and there, of crimson Worcester Pearmain apples ripening in the autumn sun. Then the castles of Ludlow and Stokesay, and the wild stretches of Radnor Forest; and finally the Carmarthen Vans[2] suddenly raising their formidable cliffs as the train crosses the viaduct of Llanwrtyd. On this first journey I slept at Shrewsbury, and caught that Llanwrtyd view in the earliest morning light. At Llandovery I found my lodging, interviewed the Head, and learned that I was free thenceforth until a Masters' meeting in the evening. Just outside the town, at the meeting of three main valleys, rises the little isolated hill of Blaenos. Hither I took my German book of the moment: that curious autobiography of Jung-Stilling of which Goethe gives a glimpse in his own *Dichtung und Wahrheit* and which fascinated the author of *John Inglesant*. Here I lay in the sun until lunch, and again in the afternoon: and this book also has become part of my life. It means to me, quite

[1] Only thus can the Welsh stress on this first syllable be represented.
[2] The word *Van*, applied also to the Brecon Beacons and to Trifan in Snowdonia, is etymologically identical with the Scottish *Ben*.

apart from all that the author ever dreamed of, a sense of more definite settlement in life, and a feeling of congeniality in this new sphere.

We were five Assistant Masters then, increasing soon to seven; for Owen, wisely adventurous, made a point of over-staffing rather than under-staffing; with the result that the boys increased very rapidly in numbers, for his enthusiasm was contagious, and nothing succeeds like success. The school owed its existence to a Welsh haberdasher who had made a fortune in London, and employed much of it for public utility in his native town somewhere about 1840, I believe. The foundation provided for only four Masters apart from the Head, and the buildings were on that same narrow scale. The main entrance bore a noble motto: GWELL DYSG NA GOLUD—*Better Learning than Gold*. But the good haberdasher's ambitions had outrun his resources, and a disproportionate amount of the building-money itself had been spent upon mere façade. The Library was specially significant. It was a capacious room, and the shelves were about half-full. But nearly all of the volumes had been bought, from time to time, in job lots at London auctions, and sent down at random to enrich this seat of learning. One very conspicuous item was the great Kehl edition of Voltaire's works, in seventy volumes. There were about eighty boarders in 1885; so the buildings were narrow for these boys and the necessary classrooms. Only one Master, Winter, had rooms in the place; the rest of us lodged in the town, on the market square. One fair-day a bullet went astray from the shooting-gallery, and drilled a hole through one of my colleagues' windows.

The want of a Common Room for the Masters was serious; for we had no refuge in the School House but Winter's room, where we had breakfast and tea; and this laid great stress upon general clubbability. Memory compels me to confess that I must have been the least clubbable, by the hard test of practical results; for to me alone, at any time, did Winter formally forbid his room. He was rather argumentative, and perhaps I was even more so. Ancient discussions had an awkward way of turning up again, and lasting longer each time: and that was not wise in either of us. Three or four times during those two years, I received formal notice to quit, and spent a week or so in exile except for breakfast and tea. Later, in speaking of Sherborne, I shall have occasion to note even greater harm from the absence of a Common Room.

As Class Master, I had the lowest but one, with French, English and History for the higher boys, until an Oxford man joined the staff, who had gone through the History mill. He was an enthusiastic and very successful teacher; his first success was with Frank Morgan, who finally became History Lecturer at Keble. For everything of that kind, he knew four times as much as I did; and I do not think I ever pretended to the contrary. Not only was his knowledge uniform over the whole examinable field, but he had treasured maxims and epigrams which always sounded plausible, and were sometimes indisputably true. His great guide, philosopher and friend was Warren, afterwards Sir Herbert and President of Magdalen. For one thing I am most grateful to him: Warren had said, 'Read Michelet; he is often inaccurate in fact, but always most stimulating'. That became to me as valuable as Coleridge's advice which Mrs Curtis had passed on to me long before, 'Read Jeremy Taylor: his very faults are valuable to a young man who is thoughtful enough to mark and correct them'.

My junior, Walters of Keble, and his successor, F. E. Chapman of Sidney, taught with me in the Big Schoolroom. In winter, the draught which came down from the open ceiling went far to stultify the two stoves, even when we heated them red-hot. But irrespective of season, though we kept our little flocks as far apart as possible, each often found himself remonstrating with the other in Winter's room for aggressive loudness and emphasis of voice. A few years ago, I gave six talks on the wireless. Suddenly a postcard came from Chapman, whom I had not seen for a dozen years past: 'I switched on at random in the middle of something; and there was your voice forcing itself upon my ear just as it used to do almost half a century ago!'

These Welsh boys had, naturally, less general background than their opposite numbers in England. As Owen used frankly to confess: if you pick up a book of information in the Welsh tongue—history, geography, science—it is fifty years behind the latest English. But not more than twenty-five per cent, at most, came from homes where Welsh was the really predominant language. Frank Morgan's father, for instance, was editor of a Carmarthen newspaper: and we had a fair sprinkling from clergy of all denominations. And, for French, all started with an enormous advantage over the English schoolboy. They knew that there is more than one language in the world, and that it may be worth while to learn another language, and that such knowledge can come only by close attention and imitation. The witty Frenchman who wrote under the name of Max O'Rell from his classroom at St Paul's School puts the whole thing in a nutshell—I quote from memory: 'French Master to Form Master: "Your boy X has quite a remarkable accent in French." "I can well imagine it; the fellow is a mass of affectation!"'

In many ways it is far better practice to teach a low form than a higher; and I have always been grateful for my two years at Llandovery. We did our work honestly, and yet found a little time for reading even in term time. I pursued my German greedily, *pari passu* with another beginner on the staff, G. Hartwell Jones, afterwards for a short while Professor of Latin at Cardiff.

Here I tasted first the real pleasures of Rugby football. Having grown slowly, I was far more active and stronger at twenty-seven than at seventeen. In 1883, I had played in the Lynn Association team which beat Norwich for the County Cup, thanks to a most energetic secretary who managed to recruit two Internationals and a Cambridge Blue: A. T. B. Dunn, C. P. Wilson, and his brother K. P. The Norwich goalkeeper was the long-armed, long-legged H. P. Hansell, afterwards tutor to the then Prince of Wales (Duke of Windsor) and his three brothers: perhaps an example unique in European history of a single Tutor to two successive kings. The conscientious vigilance of that Tutorship inspired a current epigram, that the royal princes saw more of Hansell than of Gretel. It was one of the thrills of my life when, on that Easter Monday, I got in a hard slanting shot which passed a couple of inches beyond Hansell's desperate fingers, struck the post, and rebounded quietly into the net. This earned me later an invitation to play for the County against Surrey: but by that time I had passed on to Llandaff; and in any case I was too clumsy and too dependent upon erratic impulses for anything like first-class Association football. In Wales, I found myself far more in my element; for in mere energy and absence of unnecessary flesh I could beat most of the boys. The school always recruited from its staff for all matches except against their great

rival, Brecon. In the season 1885–6 each school was captained by
a future International, and the game was drawn. Next season,
Llandovery had two future Internationals and one Oxford Blue:
and in both seasons there were one or two others, who, if they had
gone up to Oxford or Cambridge, would have earned their Blue.
It was fine work to play side by side with these boys against teams
which always held them, and perhaps beat them more often than
not: Swansea (A), Llanelly (A), Lampeter and so forth; teams which
always contained a sprinkling of Old Llandoverians, and sometimes
an ex-International. The one drawback was, for out-matches, that
I was in charge to stop smoking: and, during those two years at
least, I was too new myself to wink at minor infringements. But
the home journey, when not by train, was always worthy of musical
Wales, and our wagonette could probably have been heard for a
mile along the road. A special favourite was one song originating
as a satire upon an enterprising Scotsman who had founded great
engine works in South Wales:

> Crawshay-Bailey had an engine,
> And his engine wouldn't go
> So he pulled it with a string
> All the way to Nantyglo:
>
> *Chorus* Was you ever see
> Was you ever see
> Was you ever see
> Such a funny thing before?

To this tune the singer fitted innumerable quatrains, often extem-
porized. I can remember only one other fragment: he characterizes
his future fiancée, and ends:

> She can darn and mend a stocking,
> But her cooking's something shocking:
>
> Was you ever see, etc.

It excellently exemplified the truth which underlies the epigrammatic exaggeration of Grimm's theory as to the communal origin
of the medieval ballad: 'The People poetizes'—*Das Volk dichtet*.
Moreover, there was always a soloist who would give us 'Men of

Harlech', or 'Land of my Fathers', or 'The Ash Grove'. Culley, a man of remarkable musical gifts who was Mathematical Professor at Lampeter, used to rank the communal singing of those parts, side by side with that of the West Riding of Yorkshire, as the best that he had ever heard.

We had also, on the Staff itself, a tenor whose sweetness was equalled only by his unembarrassed willingness: F. E. Chapman, father in later life to A. P. F. Chapman, a name memorable among amateur cricketers. When I first read Salimbene's *Chronicle*, with the good friar's list of musical friends, I recognized my Chapman at once in the thirteenth-century Brother Vita, who, 'unlike the singers satirized by Horace, disdained to heighten his value by pleading a cold in the throat'.

CHAPTER XIX

WALES (2)

BEST of all, however—far beyond even the happiest of games—was the exhilaration of that Welsh countryside. Passing the Castle ruins and crossing the smaller river, one came in a quarter of an hour to the crest of a ridge which commands the valley half-way down to the Castle of Dynevor; beyond which again lies Jeremy Taylor's famous Golden Grove, and then that Grongar Hill which inspired a whole pastoral poem by Dyer, well worth reading even to-day. In winter the beauty is diminished, even as it is in the Dart valley near Totnes, by the prevalence of deciduous larch timber on the jutting promontories; but in spring and summer the balance is rather the other way. Thence we may turn west and east and north to see far wilder valleys, leading to the sources of the Towy and its affluents. Most of these streams, at different times, I explored almost or quite to their sources; for, in process of time, I earned by seniority three extra hours of free time in the week. In company with Richards, I went up the Carmarthen Vans on St David's Day (March 1), 1886. We slept at Llanddeusant, the last village facing the cliffs, and climbed up next morning by one of the 'chimneys', quite easy in fact, but impressive to us novices who had never before faced anything so lofty and precipitous. We came down by the two lakes, upper and lower, from the latter of which came the fairy princess who taught the medieval Physicians of Myddfai their hereditary art.[1] I remember how, impressed by the story of Kennedy and Hardy in *Peaks, Passes and Glaciers*, I put a big ship's biscuit as emergency ration in my pocket, and persuaded Richards to accept another. About a fortnight afterwards, on our usual after-tea constitutional, he suddenly fished something from his pocket with an incongruous 'Thank God! and damn you!' and threw this biscuit over the hedge. Every day, in class, he had felt it in his pocket, but had always forgotten to rid himself at the proper moment.

Nearly always I took these long walks alone; but once, to Towy source, I went with Aneurin Rees. His father, Rees of Ton, had

---

[1] I have given the whole story, in brief, in *Medieval Panorama*, p. 453.

bequeathed to him one of the finest existing libraries of Welsh manuscripts and rare books; but he himself was far more sportsman than scholar. We took advantage of a Saturday whole-holiday and its Sunday. On Friday night we got up as far as the Rock of Twm Sion Catti, called after a famous seventeenth-century outlaw who lived there in a cave; George Borrow has a good deal to say about him in his *Wild Wales*. It forms a striking pyramid where two arms of the river join; and there, under a precipitous cliff to the left, stands the lonely farm from which, later on, my sister bought a very charming grey collie. I had already been there several times and made friends with the family. Welsh mountain hospitality is kindly in any case; but, by an old campaigner's advice, I always took care to carry a newspaper or two, and sometimes a toy for the children. This farm of Troed-y-Rhiw ('Foot-of-the-Rock') was typical of its kind. The owner, Mr Jones, scarcely ever left it, year in, year out, but to go down to Llandovery fair; and sometimes also to the ordinary weekly market. There he would not fail to turn in at the public house; for at home he drank nothing but milk from his own cows. Ordinarily, other farmers would not drink more—or at least, not much—than they could easily carry: but naturally the temptations were great, and they might sometimes stay a week or more. My particular Jones of Troed-y-Rhiw was a straightforward temperate man, and his wife was a woman of some little education; her cousin was a doctor at Tregaron whose son was in the sixth form at Llandovery. They took Rees and me up to a loft, boarded off from the rest of the upper storey, and containing one bed. We agreed to sleep as we stood, and tossed up for sides in the bed. He won, and chose to lie next to the partition. I envied him at the time; but, next morning, he had nothing but curses for his luck. There was, it appeared, a knot-hole in the board exactly against his ear; and, however he shifted, he could never get quite away from a piercing draught. However, we were up long before daybreak, and pushed up the main branch of the river, often making our own path; the banks precipitous at first, and very grand in the sunshine: then merging into a high tableland, more and more boggy, until there was little to be seen on any side but green slime and marsh plants—especially the beautiful starry asphodel, and sundew, and butterwort, which the Welsh call 'cuckoo's slipper'. Here we recognized the morass

to which Jayne, Principal of Lampeter and Bishop of Chester, had
led a picnic party some years ago and embogged himself to the very
waist. The search for any more visible 'source' of the Towy seemed
hopeless; so we took a bee-line across the hills to Llanwrtyd, where
the reddening evening light showed the Vans at their best and most
impressive, and thence by the next train home.

From among scores of splendid wild walks I must record one
more, though I have forgotten the name of the village. There was
a landlady whom Phillimore, Secretary of the Cymmrodorion Society,
lauded as a repository of country traditions. It did not detract
from her virtues that she had always cream in the dairy, and red-
currant jam in the cupboard, and home-made bread with bubbly
crust. Not a mile from her inn was a haunted pool in the little
stream; such a spot as is adumbrated in that poem of W. H. Davies
which expresses the magical fascination of a South Welsh village:

> Can I forget the sweet days I have seen,
> Where poetry first began to warm my blood?
> When from the hills of Gwent I saw the earth
> Burned into two by Severn's silver flood? . . .
> . . . Ah, when I see a leafy village now,
> I sigh, and ask it for Llantarnam's green,
> I ask each river where is Ebbw's voice
> In memory of the sweet days that have been.

To that pool, at the edge of a meadow, peasants still brought sometimes their sick cattle, and left bread and cheese on a sacred stone
in acknowledgement of the healing they expected from the spirit
of the waters. The landlady told me how her brother-in-law had
owned to this: 'all except the bread and cheese: but *I think he did.*'
It was just possible, by running a good deal of the way, to visit this
pool and sup at the inn on an ordinary half-holiday, and be back
before midnight. Years afterward, I attempted a novel about it,
but fortunately never got beyond a chapter or two.

The country clergy were definitely behind their English brethren
in culture, and even in theological knowledge. They were mostly
Lampeter men, who had seldom been able to burst the bonds of
parochialism. One, I remember, pleaded at an archidiaconal meeting
under the bishop's chairmanship, for frequent exchanges of curses

as in the modern Methodist and the ancient Franciscan policy. For there, up in the mountains, a man might perhaps have only a score of Anglican parishioners, and seldom set his own foot in any town. For the following story I can only plead that it was told me by the bishop, who gave it at least the sanction of *ben trovato*. In one 'uplandish' parish the parson once gave out: 'My brethren, next Sunday will be Good Friday. Indeed, last Sunday should have been, only I did forget.' Side by side with this, let me put two cases at which I just missed being present, but heard them from first-hand witnesses soon after the event.

Llandovery had two ancient churches, Llandingat in the level land and Llanfair on the hill; both were united into a single vicarage. Service was in English at Llandingat in the morning, Llanfair in the evening. The vicar generally preached at this morning service. He was a rather grotesque person in every way; his wife was far cleverer, but somewhat eccentric: they were childless, and had grown into all sorts of mental knots and excrescences. The boys were parked in a gallery at the west end, and the vicar never showed the least condescension towards them in his sermons. One discourse was devoted solely to marriage; and it concluded with a peroration of five words which rang out like a pistol-shot: 'In short, it's a panācĕa!'

The term before Owen came, considerable scandal was caused by a bad case of cheating in the Government Certificate Examination. One candidate, a son of a chemist, knew a good deal more of that subject than the rest. He complaisantly passed on his answers to three or four others, who copied not wisely but too well. An inspector was sent down from South Kensington to investigate. The Headmaster passed him on to the vicar, who had invigilated at that paper. The vicar's protest ran to the following effect: 'Indeed to goodness! I am sure there was no copying. For I said to myself, "You must be careful here. This is not like an examination for Holy Orders. These are schoolboys, who may fail and come again another time; it is not like an examination for Holy Orders, where to fail may ruin a man's whole life." So I looked very carefully, indeed I do assure you!'

Llandovery leads on naturally to Lampeter, the main college for Welsh Higher Education until the foundation of Cardiff, Aberystwyth and Bangor University Colleges in 1883. Lampeter had had its difficult days. The Vice-principal, Rowland Williams, who had been one of the authors of the famous *Essays and Reviews*, left a bequest to the Town Crier to proclaim yearly, through the streets, that he, Williams, had nothing whatever to do with the election of a certain scholar by influence of the Principal, Dean Llewelyn. But in the eighties Lampeter had at least three young men who were already making their mark: T. F. Tout, Hastings Rashdall, and E. H. Culley. This last, who died of consumption early in his Headmastership of the newly reconstituted school at Monmouth, had overlapped Tout at Balliol, while Rashdall was from New College. Culley, following the fashion of Balliol epigrams, had written thus of his senior:

> From behind his tinted glasses
> Peer the lurid orbs of Tout.
> 'Most men I consider asses:
> You are one, without a doubt.'

For this last verdict there was naturally more justification at Lampeter than there would have been at Oxford. Tout's forceful character found vent in politics also; and we were told that, in fairness, he should have been Mayor of Lampeter in 1887. But a wealthy citizen, scenting the hope that all mayors would be knighted in that Jubilee year, presented to the town a gorgeous set of mayoral insignia; and this blinded the eyes of Justice. So, at least, was what we heard at the time. It was a great pleasure to meet Tout and Culley when our team played at Lampeter; and Rashdall, to my abiding profit, came and examined at Llandovery from his newly won Tutorship at Durham University. His *Universities of Europe*, a few years later, became one of the books to which I have owed most.

The Jubilee year, 1887, began badly. Frosts and floods in the mountains wrought havoc among the flocks, and dead sheep drifted down past Llandovery to Carmarthen Bay. But with April and May came real summer; and men already began to speak of 'the Queen's weather': for Victoria, proverbially, had it almost always fine. June was sheer sunshine and good temper. A few neighbouring gentry had begun to recognize the rising value of the school, and we had charming picnics or excursions here and there; one, in especial, to the magnificent crag castle of Cerrig-Cennen, which Turner enshrined in his *Liber Studiorum* under the false identification of Okehampton. For the Jubilee night itself, our college staff joined with a few friends in a drive to Llanddeusant and the Vans. It was deliciously warm, and we lay among the heather and fern on the upper slopes until it became time to climb the summit. From that we watched the beacons kindle one by one: fifty-seven we counted in all; one, over the sea, was evidently on Lundy Island. Then, after we had gazed our fill and sat down to supper, came the most picturesque sight of all. A party of miners had come up from Cwmamman; and now, in the small hours, they began to dribble down, taking each a burning brand to light his footsteps. We could thus watch the whole trail down into the distant valley.

Certainly that year was one of optimism and hearty enjoyment, especially when the daily sunshine had begun to give solid promise of 'Queen's weather'. The Towy valley is fairly rich in 'county families'; and all neighbours were beginning to take notice of the school's success under John Owen. Among the first were Sir James Hills-Johnes, who had been Lord Roberts' intimate friend and partner in India, and Lady Hills-Johnes, of the family of the well-known translator of Froissart and editor of much other valuable matter from his private press at Hafod. She was learned herself, and the letters she received from Bishop Thirlwall of St David's, who for learning had no rival on the bench if we except Stubbs at Oxford, are still worth reading. Besides their generous parties at Dolau Cothi, we had quite as many others in the Vale of Towy as we deserved: or, by Hamlet's famous computation, something more. Ruskin confesses his habit, in early life especially, of regarding all the people round him as pictures, and of losing interest in them if they did not seem well painted. In this long perspective of time, I am conscious now of some such abstraction in my own case. The hosts and hostesses of those days, the fellow-guests, flit across my memory as vague translucent figures, like those of Dante's *Paradiso*. I see there one retired officer, always jovial and cheery, and never to be seen about the countryside without a gigantic pair of field glasses slung over his shoulder: that case, if report said true, harboured a generous flask of whisky. Again, I see a very little girl who possessed what Ruskin describes in his Rose Latouche, the most unearthly and innocent intuition of her own fascinations, even with those who took greatest pains to keep a face of marble.[1]

[1] *Praeterita*, vol. III, § 56.

Calculating here (as I have a right to do with one so strictly anonymous) I see that this small enchantress must now be just about the age of my own wife. There was a third at the end of her teens, so delicate in feature and complexion, so self-possessed, so quiet and cool in her muslins under the hottest sun, that I never ventured to speak to her at either of the two parties where she appeared. Chapman did, and I heartily enjoyed his social success. He had preserved some of the best of the English boy, and had less sex consciousness, perhaps, than anyone I have ever known. He treated girls as though they were fellow-boys, but without the least undue liberty: and, through my own vapours of self-consciousness, I watched him always with boundless admiration.

Next Term, when we all came back in mid-September, it was again a fine autumn. But before a week of Term had passed, I received a sudden passport to another world. A letter came from my old college chum H. v. E. Scott: would I accept a job at Heidelberg? A man was wanted to do chaplaining and scholastic work: but he must come immediately. The details Scott gave offered solid guarantees; and I put the matter at once before the Headmaster. He made the most generous allowances; and it was soon agreed that I should be free from the moment when he could find a successor. This took only a matter of a few days. Berryman came to fill the vacancy, and proved a most popular member of the staff.

On my last evening I climbed the hills above Llanwrda and watched a glorious sunset. Coming down, I fell in with a lively procession: the young squire had just come into his inheritance, and the tenantry had harnessed themselves to his carriage. The dusk came on as we walked home, and Chapman sang his best song from Moore's *Irish Melodies*, the song which his mother had taught him as her own favourite:

> Farewell! but whenever you welcome the hour,
> That awakens the night-song of mirth in your bower,
> Then think on the friend who once welcomed it too,
> And forgot his own griefs to be happy with you. . . .
> Long, long be my heart with such memories filled,
> Like the vase, in which roses have once been distilled—
> You may break, you may shatter the vase if you will,
> But the scent of the roses will hang round it still.

CHAPTER XX

HEIDELBERG

HERE then, at last, I was to swim with my little bladders in a sea of glory. I was to be paid for going and living at a place for which I had once paid to the utmost limits of my slender purse, at a city that was a very Mecca of my dreams. Longfellow's *Hyperion* had long since kindled my desires. With all its weaknesses, it is a book of hearty enthusiasm; he had grasped what was best in Germany, and his freshness, even where he becomes almost childish, is contagious. Moreover, I had already reinforced this with some personal experience. In 1885, I had gone for the Christmas holidays to a Berlin Jewish family, the Abrahams, with whom my elder sister Etta had begun as governess and ended as family friend. Next summer, Etta and I spent another month in Germany: from Rotterdam to Mannheim by Rhine boat; thence to the famous little medieval city of Rothenburg; thence to Nürnberg, and home by Würzburg. On that journey we got just one tantalizing glimpse of the Castle and the spire of the Heidelberg Heiliggeistkirche, and vowed to return some day. Next Easter, 1887, this was fulfilled for me though not for her. My eyes had troubled me; I bought myself off from the last week of Term in order to see an oculist and get a month of holiday. This enabled me to get a week at Strassburg, and tramp to Sesenheim, in memory of Goethe's love romance. An artist at Rothenburg had already taught me to look onward from his *Faust* and his better known lyrics to the reflective poems such as *Ilmenau*. From Strassburg I carried off one lasting regret. On a barrow in the market lay a copy of the *Nürnberg Chronicle*, minus its binding and two or three leaves at either end. I could have had it for five marks; but the weight of the book for a tramping expedition, and the lightness of my purse, decided me against it. Crossing to the Black Forest, I walked from end to end of the southern portion. I made my headquarters at Todtnau; one day I climbed the Feldberg in the morning and the Belchen in the afternoon, over hard snow and under a brilliant sun. Here I had my first view of the Bernese Oberland, microscopically small on the distant horizon but as clear as crystal. I spent some days at Heidelberg on the way home; mostly in wandering round the Castle and sitting on the seat where, as the inscription records, Goethe was wont to reflect and write his poetry. Meanwhile I had been reading German assiduously; and on this journey I was encouraged to find that I could get on fairly in railway-carriage talk, and exchange thoughts with my neighbours at the hotels. I was at the stage where the folk songs, and Uhland's poetry, and the present-day survivals from medieval life in town and village, made their strongest appeal.

And, in a certain sense, most just and abiding appeal. After my childhood, my journeys abroad had been tentative and progressive, as travel should be. When I could scrape together £5, in 1880, I went with Rick and Edmund to Rotterdam and Antwerp. Thence, next year, we had a sort of family expedition to Bruges and Brussels for a few days. Here we saw in perfection what may be called the homely side of Gothic art. Now the Rhine cities, with Strassburg, Nürnberg and Rothenburg, extended and heightened that experience. I had been one day in Amiens and a week in Rouen, and had seen the obvious differences between those cathedrals on the one hand, and Cologne and Strassburg on the other. But there was nothing to put me out of conceit with what I saw in Germany: and, as I look back, it still seems the most logical and helpful order of travel to extend one's tentacles thus, and leave France and Italy to the last.

Here, then, was the fulfilment of my dreams. In April, 1887, looking down from the Castle terrace upon the town at my feet, and the cherry orchards that clothe the hills as far as eye can see along the Bergstrasse, I had yearned to call this place my spiritual home some day; and here in fact the day had come.

I reached Heidelberg before September was out, just in time to see the last days of the vintage: there was not a week's interval between the 'joyeuse entrée' of that Welsh squire into his hall at Llanwrda, and the rustic mirth of Neckarthal peasants outlined against the afterglow as they brought home their barrels of freshly pressed grapes. That was the sight of my first evening. Next day, Alan Armitage took me for a walk to Neckargemünd, through the Castle grounds and the miles of riverside forest; a walk such as Burton praises in his *Anatomy of Melancholy*, 'betwixt wood and water'. We had a gentle haze of rain all the time: but the valley was all the more beautiful in its way: and I felt I had entered upon the medieval charm of Rothenburg without losing the hills of Wales.

The town itself, ancient capital of the Counts Palatine, is shaped by strict geographical limitations. It is built on the left (south) bank, just where the Neckar debouches from its hills into the plain. Those hills left so little room for the old town that it consisted, practically, of two long parallel streets, the High Street and the Ploeck (an old word meaning *suburb*). But the modern town, naturally, has spread far into the plain; again, a whole populous suburb has grown up along the northern bank, with the village of Neuenheim behind it where the hills leave room.

My work was at Neuenheim in a private school which had been founded by a certain Dr Klose for boys mostly from abroad. Like many others of its class, it lived by supplying what was too seldom taught at our Public Schools: but to that I must come in a later chapter. The school was bought over by F. A. Armitage, a retired Clifton master who had been Head of the Modern Side under Percival. I once asked an Old Cliftonian from the Classical Side what he remembered of Armitage. 'Oh, yes, I remember him: he once stopped School Roll Call until the fellows would keep quiet; and we thought that was awful cheek for a Modern Sider.' Neuenheim College was thriving enough to support two departments. The elder son, Alan, governed the smaller Army House, and the bulk, thirty or more, were under 'the Old Man' and Lionel in the original College a hundred yards down the road. Armitage himself was a keen but desultory student. Dissatisfied with his degree from Worcester, Oxford, where he had been idle, he went up as a married man to St John's, Cambridge, and thence took a First in Classics. His speciality was Old French; he had been admitted to a certain amount of collaboration with Gaston Paris. His interests were wide, but his specialities were philological. One or two French novels in his library were a jest and a scandal in the family, especially to the two daughters. He had gone through the books from end to end, blue-pencilling every subjunctive, in order to familiarize himself with those rules, so familiar and instinctive to even the Parisian chauffeur that he never gets them wrong, yet as difficult for the outsider as our English *shall* and *will*. He was tall and handsome; so also was Mrs Armitage, of good Irish county family, whose brother had rowed in the Oxford boat. The school had become a regular jumping-off ground for young British schoolmasters who wanted to work at the University. I came only a few terms after the departure of Joseph Wright, that most remarkable man who, without ever spending a single full day at any school whatever, became finally Professor at Oxford, and, by sheer courage and hard work, compiled that *English Dialect Dictionary* which is a model for the world. His memory was still green there in 1887; and one or two boys treasured caricatures of him on the flyleaves of their books by John Hassall, the poster artist, who had left the College only a few weeks before my time. But commercial success had bred here, as often, commercial disputes. Three of Armitage's masters, dissatisfied with his terms, had recently broken off and founded a rival 'Heidelberg College' on the northern bank of the Neckar itself, in a most conspicuous position for the public. These men prospered rapidly, and were patronized by the official Chaplain of the English Church. Therefore the College must needs have a chaplain of its own and a chapel of its own; and I was to be the man. I was to do a certain amount of class-work, with two services on Sunday and one sermon. Almost at once I bought myself off from the class-work, and contracted to do the rest for £50 a year with board and lodging. On those terms, the scheme worked smoothly, and I was soon on very pleasant and enduring terms with the family. It took me a day to write my sermon: I liked preaching to the boys here, as at Rickmansworth earlier and Sherborne later on. The rest of the week I was free to follow lectures, read in the University Library, or wander about the country, by day and night. The school was within a couple of hundred yards of the vineyards and cherry orchards which clothe all those hills. There I learned, what few Britons realize, the significance of Bacon's love for the flower of the vine: 'it is a little dust, like the dust of a Bent, which growes upon the Cluster, in the First comming forth'; words which are now inseparable in my memory from Gray's 'breezy call of incense-breathing morn'. Even after all that has happened since, I know nothing more enchanting than the peasant mirth of that old folk-song, 'Drunten im Neckarthal'.

Those sixteen months, from September 1887 to Christmas 1888, gave me all that I had dreamed, and more. Nothing has been to me since, and nothing ever can be now, quite the same as those days of wandering feet and wandering brain, among people whose sense of discipline had not yet been so fatally poisoned from above. Police and military might sometimes be absurdly strict: but that, to us, was only laughable, not in any real sense oppressive. Moreover, therein lay a lesson for us which we too often neglected. The later mortal conflict of 1914 rested, to a by no means negligible extent, upon British shortcomings, exaggerated to the German eye by contrast, just as the real parochialism which lay at the bottom of their national pride was exaggerated in our eyes. Mrs Armitage warned me at the very beginning: 'You will find Germans unending in their little kindnesses to you if they like you, and unending in the pettiest pin-pricks if they don't.' Both those clauses are true; but I found that the choice between them depended mainly on myself.

During this Heidelberg time I picked up enough German for my main purpose of getting a Public School job at home, but not enough for getting high up the educational ladder, as some others did. I attended no philological lectures; formal philology, the gospel of Grimm's Law, had been the only subject that really bored me in my Cambridge Tripos. I read just as fancy dictated, sometimes in the eighteenth century with Goethe and Herder and Lessing, but more often in medieval poetry and chronicle. I had a perennial coffee-pot on the little iron stove in my room at the College— perpetual *a parte ante* and *a parte post*, as De Quincey says of his own tea-pot—and there, from my third-storey room, I could drop my book and go to the window and watch the lights of the city through the frosty night. Once again, in summer, I saw, soon after sunset, the most majestic thunderstorm of my life. It marched over from the Hardt like a black wall, gradually invaded the whole Rhine Plain, and broke upon us with a fury which made it possible to read a book, so continuous was the lightning. Later, from autumn 1888 onwards, family arrangements led Armitage to transfer me to his villa to Farnleyberg, among the vineyards in the southern suburb. There I occupied his study lined on every wall with French books, sometimes two deep, and sometimes also hiding a ripe cigar, which by his law became always the perquisite of the discoverer. He loved a particular Manila brand, loose-rolled and herring-gutted like a roach, which he bought by the chest and sorted out to ripen behind the volumes. I found a dozen such or more, which in some cases had lain two or three years maturing.

My obligations to the school proper were loose: little more than to take notice of such cases of discipline as came directly in my way. The boys were of that miscellaneous character which always marked the 'crammer's shop', but with a small sprinkling of day-boys. There were always three or four Germans on the staff. Two, at least, were working more or less steadily at University lectures, in view of a Ph.D. degree. With Müller, however, there was no such pretence. He once appealed to me as the person finally responsible for discipline on Wednesday half-holidays. 'Gascoigne Minor must have broken bounds; for he has just been sick in the playground, and brought up tarts which are to be bought only in the City.' He was the most picturesque, though not the most interesting, of our German colleagues, and was, we heard, son of a Bavarian peasant girl and an aristocratic father, who had finally grown tired of him and cut down or cut off his allowance. His figure was remarkable in height, breadth, and symmetry. As Lionel Armitage once said to me, 'It's splendid to watch that man walk, straight from the hips, as though he were on parade before the Kaiser'. His broad, red face and fair hair would have suggested Nietzsche's 'Blonde Beast' to us if we English had known Nietzsche in those days. Being lowest in the Neuenheim hierarchy, he necessarily suffered many shocks to his immense pride. As a Roman Catholic with aristocratic connections, he had once enjoyed months, or perhaps years, of favour in good English and Scottish society. Once, in indignation at some real or fancied slight from the Armitages, he complained to me with unconscious want of humour, 'Duchesses have shown me the door in England!' But the heat of the dog days, in the Heidelberg of 1888, became unendurable to his ultra-sanguine temperament. Beer was the natural resort; but, as he complained, beer was poison to a liver like his. 'I doss and I doss on my bed and I can get no sleep.' He went off at a week's notice; and no doubt he joined the ranks of those who, not entirely without reason, looked upon England as decadent and effete in comparison with the 'Vaterland'. A man of that name was shot as a spy in Scotland during the first world war: my old colleague Pressland, who was then in Edinburgh, made some inquiries, but decided against the identity. Next to Schmidt, Müller is perhaps the commonest name in Germany.

Normally, as I have said, my position was privileged; outside Sunday services and sometimes charge of the house on that day, I was free. Our Church, rival to the pre-existing S.P.G. Church, was the original Sankt Anna Kapelle, part of a superannuated seventeenth-century hospital in the Ploeck. It was characteristic of medieval survivals that in this street, only a door or two from us, almost in the middle of the city, there was a farmhouse and yard with every rural feature, including a muckheap of gigantic proportions, such as Mark Twain satirizes in his *Tramp Abroad* as constituting the chief wealth of a German agriculturalist. The typhoid-rate of Heidelberg was enormously higher than in any British town of that size. The Kapelle had been, and still was very occasionally, used by the Old Catholic community, i.e. the few who in 1870 had refused to accept that Infallibility Decree which they regarded as false and unhistorical, and who therefore had formed their own Church under Bishop Reinkens. They included some of the best scholars; but no minority of that kind can long hold out against the immense attraction of a crushing majority. We whitewashed the chapel afresh, and I was commissioned to make stencils for decorating the choir with a sort of Morris pattern. I admired this myself, but if I were to record here that the congregation agreed with me the reader might be tempted to put in Archbishop Temple's query: 'Did she?'

It was very interesting to be brought into contact, however vague and occasional, with the Old Catholic priest, Pastor Stubenvoll. This man had published a small volume concerning the heathen beliefs which lingered and were even encouraged among the uneducated orthodox: it was little more than a summary of Trede's four volumes on *Paganism in the Christian Church*. But it fascinated me then, and has helped me ever since, to hear one who had been an orthodox Roman priest, yet could now speak out freely, though without much bitterness. It warned me, at that early stage, against more than one of those pitfalls which await the Protestant controversialist, and give force to Father Tyrrell's famous epigram.[1]

[1] See *Autobiography and Letters*, ed. M. Petre, vol. II, p. 294. 'They [the Jesuits] live on the blunders of their critics. Instead of saying "They have

Two stories from the Sankt Anna Kapelle, not long after my time, I may give here as told me by my colleague A. J. Pressland, who was afterwards master at the Edinburgh Academy. There I found him living in Carlyle's first married house at Comely Bank, and he retired finally to Cambridge, where he bequeathed generously to his old college of St John's. He told me how, one Saturday afternoon, 'the Old Man' said: 'Alan, my boy, you will have to preach to-morrow: I have just been cabled to London to fetch a pupil.' 'But I haven't got a sermon.' 'Oh, you will find plenty in the drawer in the vestry.' Alan, therefore, came down to the Kapelle at eleven on Sunday, not too punctually, perhaps; caught at a sermon whose text suggested good ordinary doctrine; and in due course mounted the pulpit. But this unfortunate discourse turned out to be a sermon preached during the American Civil War, when his father was curate at Rochdale or some other Lancashire cotton town. Alan presently found himself alluding to the present fratricidal strife, beyond the Atlantic, between blood-brethren. He tried to skip; but that became too evidently impossible. There was nothing but to wade stolidly through to the end; to describe the pallid faces of these unemployed and starving operatives whom his hearers saw every day about the streets; and (so Pressland assured me) even to finish with an appeal for charitable subscriptions.

The only lectures I attended with any regularity were those of Kuno Fischer on German Literature. He was a survival from the period when Heidelberg had been perhaps at its peak of fame in modern times. He, like Bunsen, the great chemist, had refused invitations to far richer Universities, such as Berlin and Leipzig. He was youngest, perhaps, of that group, for he was still in full vigour and full pugnacity. His lectures were admirable: learned, and yet as clear as a Frenchman's. As philosopher, he had carried on a bitter pamphleteering feud with Trendelenburg. A few days after Fischer's final pamphlet, he heard the sudden news of his adversary's apoplexy and death. His only comment was 'I didn't mean that much!—'*Das hatte ich nicht gewollt!*' When Warren, afterwards President of Magdalen, came to Heidelberg during one Oxford vacation, Armitage did him honour as to an Old Cliftonian,

killed three men", [the critics] say "three men and a dog." The Jesuits produce the dog alive, and win a repute as calumniated innocents.'

and introduced him to Fischer. Warren, anxious to be polite, assured the philosopher with great emphasis that his writings were considered 'gemein' at Oxford. But the German *gemein*, 'common', is an epithet which often denotes the extreme of common vulgarity; and Fischer's face was a study for a moment until he realized that the word was intended to assure him of widespread respect.

But certainly my greatest stimulus, on the whole, came from the friendship of Baron C. R. von der Osten-Sacken, with whom I enjoyed weekly walks during the latter half of these Heidelberg days. He was a Russian from the Baltic Provinces, a diplomat by profession but by choice a scientist. As dipterologist, he was in the first rank, and his monograph on *The Oxen-born Bees of the Ancients* is a fascinating little chapter in historical research.[1] The University finally gave him an honorary doctorate, a very rare honour from Heidelberg. As Kuno Fischer said to him, in somewhat patronizing congratulation, 'Numberless people besiege us for the honour, covertly or openly, but they all come to grief'—*aber sie fallen alle durch*. The Baron's cousin and namesake, a few years later, was Foreign Minister in Russia. He himself had begun in the Embassy at Rome, and thence had been transferred to Washington, where he spent twenty years until his retirement. Then he hesitated for a time between London and Heidelberg, choosing the latter at last on account of his friends there. He was the most genuine philosopher, in the ancient sense, whom I have ever known. I think his wife was dead: at any rate, they had lived apart even before the end of the Roman days. He studied books and men with much of the detachment with which he studied his insects; yet he had a warm heart and a strong sense of social responsibility. He made a point of reading the latest book of mark, especially in French: it was through him that I came upon the *Journal des Goncourt*, Marie Baschkirtseff, and Anatole France in his *La Reine Pédauque*. I offered to translate the Baschkirtseff book for a London publisher: he wanted me to put down £80 and bear all the risk. A year or so later it was translated; Gladstone got hold of it; and then, like all others which enjoyed such luck, it sold like hot cakes. *Reine Pédauque* entertained the Baron; but he commented with a shrug of his shoulders: 'How

[1] It forms the main subject of Sir Arthur Shipley's later paper in *Journal of Philology*, vol. XXXIV, pp. 98–105.

impossible it seems for a French moralist to get rid of sexual obses-
sions!'[1] Again, at another time: 'The ordinary Russian is always
very fond of the Frenchman's company, but he seldom takes him
seriously.'

When he dined at Neuenheim, he always praised Mrs Armitage's
Steinwein, in those little pot-bellied flasks which the Germans call
'Bocksbeutel'. He would put forth polite feelers as to its origin;
and she took a feminine delight in outplaying this diplomat. For,
in fact, it came from the ordinary stock of the ordinary railway
station; and she knew better than to reveal this. Not, however,
that she or the Baron were ignorant of the fact that the railway
buffets, especially in vintage districts, make it a point of honour
to supply the best they can procure, and often outdo all other
restaurants in the town. There was a relevant incident at Heidelberg
just before my arrival. The railway buffet was so seductive that
deboshed students got into the habit of drinking there from dusk
to dawn. Therefore, in the interests of discipline both for university
and for city, the stationmaster closed the buffet for half an hour at
midnight. This caused a serious riot, since the actual drinkers were
reinforced by comrades who resented this trespass upon immemorial
student liberties. One midnight a pitched battle was fought up and
down the platforms between the rioters and the whole posse of
station officials, joined presently by police. But the rioters were just
sober enough to take one necessary precaution. They had three or
four Great Danes with them: those hounds without which no
ambitious student swaggerer felt himself complete. These, before
the fray began, they tied up to the railings; otherwise there would
have been carnage in the most literal sense. I was told that the
yelling of these great beasts, all through the tumult of the fight,
created an unforgettable pandemonium. The students, of course,
were finally beaten; and the half-hour rule remained, for all my time
at least, to the inconvenience sometimes of orderly passengers.

[1] Compare Leslie Stephen's letter to a friend in 1867 (*Life*, by F. W. Maitland, p. 267): 'Of course it is true that English writers—Thackeray conspicuously
so—are injured by being cramped as to love in its various manifestations. Still
I doubt whether the French gain much by the opposite system. . . . They are
always hankering and sniffing after sensual motives, and I consider them far
inferior to English writers in colour—in description of character especially.'

Like a true scientist, Osten-Sacken had almost a mania for collecting. He was inspired by, or perhaps had done something to inspire, those millionaire benefactions which were beginning to be fashionable in America. One scheme, the products of which filled nearly all his rooms at Heidelberg, was to endow some middle-western town, not yet a dozen years old, with the rudiments of culture in the shape of photographs of Italian art. All were strongly mounted, sorted into appropriate cases, and catalogued. Another of his collections was far less bulky, yet, as history has turned out, of far greater immediate utility. The nearest equivalent to our *Manchester Guardian* in the German Press was the *Frankfurter Zeitung*, which now, of course, no longer exists. That journal used to make a point of recording, in plain terms, every case it could find of anti-social militarism or of *Bismarcksbeleidigung*.[1] This collection had swelled to a considerable size; more words, probably, than in this present volume. When I last saw him, in 1904, he was still in doubt as to its final destination. I pleaded for the British Museum, and he allowed me to approach the authorities. But I failed to arouse their interest: even a good librarian is too readily tempted to look upon a scrapbook as junk, without further enquiry. It was doubtless remiss of me not to trade here upon my saving vice of pertinacity, and knock at door after door until I could get attention from somebody. But there, in fact, the matter was left; and within two or three years the baron was dead. His heiress was a niece at Handschuchs-heim, five miles off, married to a Junker of sorts. If the meaning of the book was recognized at all, it was doubtless burned. As things have turned out in Europe, it would now be worth its weight in diamonds. Even if any complete run of the *Frankfurter* exists in Germany, nobody could exploit it fully for Osten-Sacken's purposes without finding himself in a concentration camp.

This scientist, then, studied his fellow-men as he studied his diptera. He was obsessed by the follies in Anglo-Franco-Russian relations. He said: 'My brother, who was in the Foreign Office at the time of the Crimean War, and therefore saw the official figures, tells me that far more men died between the moment of their enlist-

[1] *High treason* in German is *Staatsbeleidigung*: in the days of Bismarck's greatest power, it was almost as dangerous to criticize him freely as to revile the Emperor.

ment and their arrival in the Crimea, than all those who perished in the actual campaign.' Again: 'Why are all these Europeans preying upon China, and irritating her like so many insects? Her resources are enormous: if once she wakes up fully under all these provocations, she will shake us all off like flies.' But most interesting were his judgments upon Germany. He saw the good, of course: otherwise why should he live at Heidelberg when he had the whole world for choice? He appreciated all that was solid in German character, and especially the serious pursuit of learning. But he deplored the *Zunftwesen*—the Gild-spirit—which, in its exaggerated form, did so much to mechanize the Universities at the expense of free initiative. A man was nobody if he was not Professor, or at least *Privat-Dozent*. He saw how easily that spirit allied itself with militarism, each helping to feed the other. And, more than once, he would generalize to me about the national spirit as a whole. 'The average German, whatever be his nominal religious category, is at bottom Roman rather than Protestant in mind. He wants to be told what to do. He enjoys arguing with strict logic from premises which he has not really tested. Therefore he is far more sensitive to mass emotion than the American or Englishman.' I find confirmation of this judgment here, in Canada, from a colleague who, like myself, studied at a German University. As he puts it to me, the German is essentially a Romantic, with the weaknesses as well as the enthusiasms of Romanticism.

For America, Osten-Sacken had hearty, though far from indiscriminate, admiration. A propos of the scandal of Boss Tweed, and that man's final ruin, he said to me: 'One thing always encourages me about the American people, when any abuse has become intolerable, they seem to have the power of rising up against it and putting an end to it.' Those words, only the other day, I found corroborated in a brilliant epigram by the late Lord Tweedsmuir: 'If America's historic apparatus of government is cranky, she is capable of meeting the "instant need of things" with brilliant improvisations.'[1]

One very remarkable sidelight upon professorial mentality at that

[1] *Memory hold-the-door*, by John Buchan (published in America as *Pilgrim's Way*), 1940, p. 259. The whole of that chapter ('My America)' is of special value.

time was supplied to me by Lionel Armitage, who was afterwards
Taylorian Reader in German at Oxford. Having been some years
at the Gotha Gymnasium, he spoke German fluently, and his pleasant
manners recommended him everywhere. He used often to dine at
the mid-day table of the Hotel Victoria. There, at the head of the
table, was R. W. v. Bunsen, greatest of living chemists, with half a
dozen almost equally venerable colleagues. Bunsen was nearly
eighty: he had enjoyed his doctorate for all those years, for he was
born during his father's rectorate of the University, and a complimentary doctor's diploma had been laid in his cradle. He was a
Liberal in politics, anti-Bismarckian, and as little of a militarist,
probably, as any of his class. One day in 1888, shortly after the death
of the Anglophil Frederick III and the accession of that sabre-
rattling Wilhelm II who died in exile at Doorn in 1941, Armitage
said to me at tea, 'They nearly took my breath away at the "Victoria" to-day. They were all discussing the new Kaiser so freely
that, like a fool, I must put my oar in. I said, "Er soll doch etwas
kriegerisch gesinnt sein". Bunsen came down on me like a knife,
and said, "Warum denn nicht, wenn er nur den Schneid hat?"'[1]
'This' (continued Armitage) 'reminded me of a few years ago at
the Anglo-American Club.[2] They put me up to propose the toast
of *The German Army*. I said what seemed proper: "A few years
ago your army covered itself with imperishable laurels on the fields
of France: let us now hope that Germany will enjoy many years of
peace and prosperity." But there was an immediate outcry from all
the lieutenants in uniform—"Nein, Krieg, Krieg!" and the civilians
only looked down their noses.' There was no country in the then
world, except Germany, in which those two things could have
happened.

Another hint came to me from my friend Ernst Abraham in Berlin.
On one of our walks he said to me, apropos of I don't know what,
'In the nature of things, we can hardly expect that our two nations

[1] 'But he is said to be rather bellicose in his disposition.'—'Why on earth
shouldn't he be, so long as he has the grit for it?'

[2] This club held an annual dinner, to which a large number of guests were
always invited. It was at such a dinner that Mark Twain made his famous speech
on German Genders, printed in his *Tramp Abroad*. Armitage told me, 'There
wasn't a dry eye in the assembly; the few who couldn't follow caught the
contagion of laughter from the rest.'

will get on indefinitely without any serious quarrel. What, then, will happen to you, who have not one soldier to our ten?' This took me aback; I realized instantaneously the absurdity of my patronizing mental attitude towards Germany; the suggestion hit me full in the face. It added to the significance of those bare words that Ernst, seeing how he had shocked me, politely changed the subject at once.

To that I must return more fully in a later chapter. This, however, I may add here. Alan Armitage, even after the direct connection with Neuenheim had been severed, had to go backwards and forwards twice or thrice a year to look after his father's house, Farnley-berg. I met him somewhere about the year 1911. He said then, 'The English barometer goes down steadily: I see this every time. They think we are sluggards or cowards, and they mean to fight us.'

I cannot pretend that these things impressed me so deeply at the time as they came to do afterwards. Revising this present chapter on Christmas Day, 1941, with Handel's *Messiah* fresh in my ears, I see Germany fifty years ago as an Arcadian wander-ground; river and valley in the day time, and evening rest at the little inn outside the town gate, as in Schubert's 'Lindenbaum'. Terrible potentialities were visible enough under the surface. I knew well, when I cared to reflect, that in twenty-four hours every peasant might turn his ploughshare into a sword, and that the tailor and barber and inn waiter were better specialists in soldiery than many of our own red-coats. Indeed, I once put this plainly to a National Service League audience at Caxton Hall; and a lively *Westminster Review* paragraph of that evening pointed out that I might have quoted from Milton, 'They also serve who only stand and wait'. But life would be impossible if we treated all potentialities as actualities. Often, of course, they spice our present enjoyment, 'Let us eat and drink; for to-morrow we die'. Several of my Heidelberg companions used to discuss frankly the scholastic and social conditions of Britain and Germany; and we all felt that things might well be worse at home before they could be permanently better.

CHAPTER XXI

SHERBORNE

BEFORE the Conquest, this little Dorsetshire town was the site of a bishopric. All through the Middle Ages it had a fine abbey; and it supplied to Europe one of the most remarkable saints, Stephen Harding. Like most large monasteries, it had a small Choir School in the Middle Ages: perhaps even a small open Grammar School. The scanty records suggest that here, as usually elsewhere, the schoolmaster was not a monk but a hired cleric. Whether this school survived the dissolution of the monasteries, we cannot tell.[1] It is possible that, when Edward VI set up a Grammar School here, this was not entirely new, but a confirmation and extension and secure endowment of the old. Certainly he adopted part of the Abbey buildings: but not necessarily any part which had in the past formed a regular schoolhouse. The boys, under the new foundation, were taught in a hall built from the Abbey ruins, and the Master had lodgings patched up from portions of the church itself. One chapel was divided by a new floor into two sitting-rooms, while the Lady Chapel furnished a bedroom above and kitchen or offices below.

The school lived on with varying fortunes until early Victorian times. It was then for a short time decadent, like many others of its class; but a fresh epoch began with the appointment of a Headmaster who had already made his mark in the small Welsh school of Cowbridge. This Dr Harper, side by side with the thirty-eight day-boys, found two boarders at the school, and expelled them in his first term: so I heard, and have reason to believe it substantially correct. He soon made it, for its size, one of the most conspicuous schools in the country. His most famous pupil is still alive, Professor A. N. Whitehead, of Cambridge, London, and Harvard. After twenty-seven years of uninterrupted success, Harper resigned for the Principalship of Jesus College, Oxford. One characteristic incident of his Headmastership may be recorded here. The celebrated actor Macready took a house at Sherborne (Dickens often stayed

[1] Wildman's *History of Sherborne* seems to suppose a more definite organization than can really be proved in the case of these medieval monastic schools.

with him, and there picked up the names of Minifie and Guppy for
his novels). The School Charter provided for the gratuitous instruction of the sons of townsfolk: and Macready determined to vindicate
that clause literally: not for his own sake (for he was a very generous
man) but in the public interest. He therefore announced his intention
of acting strictly upon that word 'gratuitous'. After some heated
correspondence, it came to open war. One morning, after prayers,
Harper gave out, 'The boys will now go to their classrooms—all
but the two Macready boys. I am bound by the Charter to teach
them for nothing: but I am bound only to teach them Latin Grammar. You Macready boys, sit in this corner of the schoolroom with
your Latin grammars, and go on learning until someone comes to
hear you.' Against this, Macready had no appeal: and, as I have
heard, he presently quitted the town. The difficulty was finally settled,
as at Rugby and elsewhere, by diverting some of the revenues to a
smaller school for townsfolk who preferred a cheaper non-Classical
education.

Harper was succeeded by E. M. Young, an old Etonian and Fellow
of Trinity, Cambridge, who had been Sixth-Form Master under
Butler at Harrow. When I left Heidelberg, Young had been eleven
years at Sherborne, but there was serious trouble brewing; all the
more serious because it was not fully recognized. E. G. Hardy, who
examined the school about this time, told me afterwards how, in
connection with an affair which brought another well-known school
into invidious prominence for a time, Young had said to him, 'We
don't have that kind of thing here at Sherborne'. Suddenly, at
Christmas 1888, he dismissed three masters at one stroke, including
the Senior Master of the Army Class. It was for one of the vacancies
so caused that I applied and was asked to go down and see him.
He wanted both French and German, but especially French, and
naturally tested my accent. He picked up a Baedeker's *France* from
the table and asked me to read at random. By a real or calculated
mistake, this was the English edition and, where he seemed to be
testing only my pronunciation, it actually put me through my paces
for translation. I stuck for a moment here and there. Then he
apologized for his mistake, and gave me his approval. He took my
German for granted, in consideration of my eighteen months at
Heidelberg. Thus these romantic days had justified themselves from

the most strictly business point of view, for four terms more at
Llandovery would have done next to nothing to help me to this
post into which I had now fallen at once.

Edward Young started with many advantages. At Eton, Lady
Young's house had become a natural refuge for some unusual boys
(among them Swinburne and Lord Avebury) to whom that royal
foundation made imperfect appeal. Thus the Youngs had a wider
acquaintance among their contemporaries than would have come
from a bare boyhood at Eton and Junior Mastership at Harrow.
Edward, again, had a handsome face and figure, rode gracefully,
and was courtly in manner, apart from a certain air of condescension.
Furthermore, he had learnt much as Sixth-Form teacher when he
was understudy to B. F. Westcott, one of the most elegant and
meticulous of Classical scholars. He collaborated with Bowen in a
once-famous Latin Eclogue, when the Headmastership of Haileybury
was disputed between two colleagues, Bradby (final victor) and
Farrar (beaten then, but afterwards successful at Marlborough).

The best Sixth-Form scholars clearly recognized Young's value
in the Classical field; thus Professors Hort and Bensly at Cambridge
entrusted their sons to his care. Moreover, he had fine opportunities
quite apart from his own scholarship. The agricultural depression
of the seventies and eighties had changed greatly the attitude of
many families for whom, in earlier generations, Eton or Harrow or
Winchester had been natural and instinctive. In Sherborne Schoolhouse, therefore, were probably a score of boys whose fathers,
or even elder brothers, had been at great, dignified and costly
schools. Thus, in the first years of Young's rule, he was widely
regarded as a coming man: one who would out-Harper Harper for
Sherborne, and pass on in due time to govern Eton or Harrow.

The disadvantages, on the other hand, were very serious; and
the more so because Young was often so unconscious of them.
Harper's long reign had allowed the growth of certain anomalies
which he himself had not realized, perhaps, and which at any rate
he had not grappled with. For example, there was no official school
bookseller: the boys might order their books from whom they chose.
Therefore, whenever there came a change of class books (and those
were frequent) a shop might be left with an unsold remainder upon
its shelves. In those circumstances, no shop could afford to allow

discount upon its sales. Young insisted upon discount for the boys, appointed one definite school purveyor, and bought up at a fair estimate the stock of the other. This made one more grumbler in the town. Equally unpopular was his action in the matter of school doctors. The post seemed to be becoming hereditary in a single family: he imported an outsider of his own choice. This worked well from the school point of view: but, here again, it was very unpopular in some quarters. A third cause of offence was, on the whole, less justified. Young was a Liberal in politics, and enjoyed making political speeches in that Tory fox-hunting neighbourhood. Archbishop Temple of Canterbury, it is true, had done the same at Rugby, and Temple was one of the Sherborne Governors: but Young did not sufficiently realize the danger of a very great man's example for more ordinary mortals. Lastly, he had married in middle life, after coming to Sherborne, a widow who had settled in the town for the education of her son. She was of aristocratic military stock: her first husband had been cousin to a distinguished peer. This lady, in spite of real kindness of nature, was by no means always tactful in her present position, or sympathetic to the peculiar nature of the English schoolboy. But perhaps the most fatal disadvantage of all came from the defects inherent in certain qualities. The sudden revival of the school, and personal loyalty to Harper, had raised the cult of the Old School Tie to an unusual pitch. I believe it is still true that the Old Shirburnian Dinners, and the O.S. Society in general, are active and loyal almost beyond any school of equal numbers. Certainly it would have been difficult (even in 1889, when the O.S. Society had not yet been formally constituted) to find any instance where the Old Boys were more attached to their school, and—here comes the snag—were more tempted to forget that a Public School is a growing, changing corporation, governed not by Old Boys, but by the present-day Governors, Headmaster, and Staff, who bear the burden and must assume all the responsibility. The Old Shirburnians came near to wrecking Sherborne School. I write this in spite of my admiration for the persons, and sometimes even the motives, of some who organized resistance to Young.

The trouble had begun very early, I believe, as a sort of dull muttering against this man who was so different from Harper, and

who took so little pains to hide the differences. But it reached a crisis
in the latter part of 1888 in a quarrel between Young and his House
Tutor which ended in a libel action and much publicity. This proved
to be fatal for him and the school. At the Masters' Meeting six
members had shown sympathy with the House Tutor and more or
less definite disagreement with Young; he dismissed three straight
off (it was at this time that I was appointed) and, later, the other
three. The affair was taken up warmly by a London daily, on the
staff of which the malcontents had some influence: so, also, by the
Old Shirburnians, who counted three among the six sufferers.

The libel action was put in the hands of a specialist, Blake Odgers,
afterwards K.C. As time went on, it came practically to this, that
all the forces of discontent in Sherborne, and all private grudges,
were willing to use this expelled House Tutor, himself a prominent
Old Boy, as a battering-ram primarily against Young but finally,
as the quarrel spread wider and deeper, against the school itself.

The libel suit rolled and rolled along, and the whole school knew
of it. For a week at least—I rather think, for more—every House
Master but one was in London, under subpoena as a witness, thus
casting upon us juniors the whole weight of discipline in an almost
mutinous school. And meanwhile the Old Boys—not, of course,
en masse, for they also were divided, but a strong clique among
them—were more or less deliberately striking at Young through the
school. By chance, my brother Jim came down at this time for a few
weeks to the neighbouring town of Yeovil, as *locum tenens* to a
doctor there. That man's son was articled to the firm of Sherborne
lawyers who were running the case. One week-end the son came
home and boasted in my brother's hearing 'We are sure now to
win the case, and there won't be fifty boys in Sherborne School
this time next year'.

The mere fact of getting into the lawcourts is ruinous; and, here,
some of the attendant circumstances were themselves so unpleasant
as to show everybody concerned in his least favourable light. The
plaintiff was shown acting in glaring contrast with his usually
generous nature. One witness, again, was brought forward on his
side who, under cross-examination, broke down so shamefully that
the judge, in full court, went out of his way to congratulate Oxford
and Cambridge on the fact that this boy was not destined for either

University. The attack was pressed home so fully that part of the case had to be heard *in camera*. On the other hand, Young often showed his weakest points. To the very end Young's want of tact impelled him frequently to do the right thing in the wrong way. Walker, the great Headmaster of Manchester, had once dismissed nine Masters for disloyalty at a single stroke: the Manchester press was full of this incident for weeks, but Walker had deigned no reply. Young was far too sensitive to hold his tongue; he could not see that he was talking himself down. Quite towards the end of his reign, he gave a most interesting lecture upon the adventures he had met with, one summer vacation, in a boat down the Volga. The vermin, naturally, had worried him much: 'and their stings, like certain pin-pricks to which I am now subjected, did not conduce to Resignation.' Neat sarcasm of that sort does not impress boys; and they knew by that time that their Headmaster was practically doomed. It was in a few weeks, I think, that even Archbishop Temple was obliged to transmit the Governors' decision that he should be asked to resign.

CHAPTER XXII

SEDBERGH

YOUNG left Sherborne at Easter, 1891, and, with him, three Assistant Masters, A. V. Jones, C. L. Barnes, and myself. This, however, was a mere coincidence: we had different reasons behind the one factor which was common to us all. For we were all 'blacklegs', and had lived as unwilling participants through this painful domestic quarrel. We had seen the Old School Tie on its least edifying side of scholastic parochialism. Sherborne was not, after all, one of the schools with consistently great ancient traditions; its patriotism was partly that of an upstart, and all the more fervid on that account. Therefore, in this particular case, its mischievous working was patent, and even ridiculous, to the impatient outsider's eye. A. V. Jones, as it happened, was an intimate friend of intimate friends of one of the anti-Youngite House Masters' wives. But, as House Tutor at the Schoolhouse, he was to them a pariah: they never called upon him.

Barnes was a Balliol man with a curious history. He was one of Walker's Manchester pupils, and a scientist. Greek was compulsory in those days for an Oxford degree: but Barnes so despised this mere veneer which the scientist had to cram up that, time after time, he risked the narrowest possible margin, and was ploughed time after time. In fact, he scraped through finally at the last possible chance, only a few weeks before his Final in Science Honours. But, all this while, Barnes was resolved to show himself and his friends that, if he failed in compulsory Greek, it was not for want of diligence or literary sense. He therefore learned by heart the whole of *Paradise Lost*; and, in those Sherborne days, he would go on anywhere for hundreds and hundreds of lines. Indeed, somewhere about twenty years ago, in St John's Hall, I suddenly caught the end of the sentence from a guest opposite to me at table, '. . .he knows *Paradise Lost* by heart'. I struck in at once, 'Is that C. L. Barnes of Balliol?' and it was. He had been a master at Bromsgrove, A. E. Housman's school, in the days when Housman was no more than a rather unsuccessful Civil Service clerk: and he was, in fact, of Housman's year at Oxford. He told me a story which Housman had never heard until I passed it on to him at Cambridge. The Bromsgrove masters had a little plot of ground outside the windows of their Common Room; and they resolved to adorn this with a sundial. The Senior Mathematician made all proper calculations: but they hesitated to fix it permanently until the sun itself, at one of the equinoxes, should corroborate their calculated position. As it happened, time after time, the sun absolutely refused to appear for a single minute of the crucial day, When, at last, after two or three years, it deigned to appear and the position was verified and fixed, there came up the question of a motto. It was suggested that, against the figure 12, they should inscribe from *The Ancient Mariner* 'The bloody sun at noon': 'the bloody sun at one', 'at two', and so on, through the whole circle.

. Both of those men left Sherborne without regret. They anticipated that it would long be an uncomfortable place even for the Elect, and still more for us. So in fact it turned out.

My own departure was in no way directly connected with all this disorder. True, it might have been delayed if the social atmosphere had been different. There was, indeed, great attraction in Louis Napoleon Parker, the Music Master, grandson of an American judge, and true citizen of the world. His autobiography goes far to correct the youthful exaggerations of an autobiographical Sherborne novel.[1] Parker's house was a place of great hospitality and resort to others beyond the Staff, on Saturday nights, when he would often read to us from his own dramatic essays, and always entertain us with wit and humour which habitually ended in the merriest laugh I have ever heard from a man's natural heart, for all the world like a blackbird suddenly fluttering off behind the hedge. One night he was beginning his translation from Ibsen's *Rosmersholm*. One hearer asked, 'Are you sitting high enough?' 'Yes; high enough to see the bald spot at the top of Coulton's head.' I date a whole era of self-consciousness from that revelation: it made me feel the pathos of one sentence in Marie Baschkirtseff's diary: 'It is an unspeakable

[1] L. N. Parker, *Several of My Lives*; Alec Waugh, *The Loom of Youth*. Parker's index gives more than eighty dramatic pieces in which he had a hand, and his boyish Continental experiences are most entertaining. He is, fortunately, still alive at 90; see *Who's Who?*

pain when one's hair begins to fall.' Apart from the enjoyment of
Parker's evenings, I had formed a real friendship with James Rhoades,
the poet, and his gracious and warm-hearted wife: so, also, with
G. A. Bieneman and his wife. He was an Oriel man, son of a
Russian from the Baltic Provinces, who for wife's and family's sake
had quitted his post as Surgeon to a Guards' Regiment, and had
made himself a practice in Brighton. Bieneman was a cultivated and
consistently high-minded man, a student of Lotzè, and a passionate
mountaineer. Pretty regularly, we put on flannels and went out for
a run together across country. His wife was a Swiss from Lausanne,
who helped him greatly in his Modern Language work. With the
rest of the staff I was only beginning to reach normal terms of
brotherly familiarity when I left the school. It was nearly seven
years now since I had begun to feel serious misgivings about my
clerical Orders. The sermons to the boys, and the routine Chapel
Services, I had on the whole enjoyed: but I saw now no prospect
of a return to normal orthodoxy. Indeed, the drift was in the opposite direction. Those seven terms at Sherborne were the only period
of my life at which I had found no time whatever for private reading.
In the holidays, something could be done: but, even so, my first
summer holiday was almost entirely taken up by pupils whom I led
to Switzerland for intensive French work. At school, the necessary
day's work was as much as I could get through; for my predecessor
had been Head of the Army Class, which the school was struggling
hard to render efficient; and it was even more vital to us than to
larger and more established schools that we should be able to stem
the alarming leakage to 'crammers'. In these circumstances, I had
done little more than drift, and the current had carried me, if not
towards Agnosticism, at least towards indifferentism. Indeed, I often
caught myself neglecting prayer altogether; and perhaps the least
orthodox times of my life have been these latter Sherborne days.
Therefore I was resolved to put my house in order; and, since there
seemed no prospect of return to full parish work, I would now drop
my clerical dress and retire into lay communion. There was no need
to go beyond that. I have never taken advantage of the Clerical
Disabilities Act of 1870. If I now wanted to deal in general agriculture or commerce, for instance, I believe I could not legally enforce
my claims upon debtors. Once, indeed, I came very near. I wrote

to Crockford's *Clerical Directory*, asking the editor silently to omit
my name. He refused; it was his business to record facts, and he
owed that duty to the public. I replied that this might compel me
to fall back upon the Act. But, for the moment, I did nothing: and,
later, I found that my name had been silently omitted from the
ordinary list.[1]

There was no inward trouble about all this: only the external
trouble that it meant resignation of a job in which I had some real
sense of success and progress, and a certain legitimate ambition: just
this for the moment and, for the future, abandonment of such
seniority as I had already earned towards a House Mastership. If
I had become attached to the school, as such, that would have made
a greater wrench. But, as it was, the decision seemed natural and
inevitable; so I wrote to Westcott as soon as he had been elected.
I told him I must assume that he shared the current feelings on this
subject, so that he would not accept a man whose change of garb
seemed to force his unorthodoxy upon public attention: therefore,
in default of his approval, I must resign. He answered as nine Headmasters out of ten would have done,[2] and thus again the world was
all before me.

This time, I resolved to seek no other work for the Summer
Term. I had in fact a right to make holiday; for I was rather run
down with hard work, more and more exacting as the Great Libel
Case had relaxed discipline everywhere; and my bad ear had begun
to trouble me. A few weeks under a London aurist put that right;
and I spent the spring and summer very happily, partly at Pentney
and partly at Oxford with my old master, E. G. Hardy. This was
specially welcome for the fuller glimpses it gave me of University
society. At Cambridge, to a great extent by my own fault, I had

[1] One of Thomas Hardy's most interesting interviews with Leslie Stephen
was when the latter asked him to sign as witness to his deed of renunciation, in
accordance with this Act of 1870 (F. W. Maitland, *Life of Leslie Stephen*, 1909,
p. 263).
[2] I might probably put this proposition still higher. Gilkes, who was very
broad, accepted me at Dulwich only on condition that I should do nothing to
proclaim my former clerical status. But, just outside the College gates at Dulwich, lived a boy whom I had known very well in my French set at Sherborne.
He remarked to his parents on the change, and thus it became known to the
Staff. Gilkes sent for me and asked whether it was through me that the facts
had spread.

known scarcely any reading men. C. L. Feltoe, soon to be elected Fellow of Clare, by whose side I had sat at a meeting of the Antiquarian Society, did invite me twice to his rooms, and introduced me to Fulford, a junior Fellow four years my senior. Outside those two, I cannot remember ever entertaining or being entertained by any man who, at any time, became a College Fellow. But, by this year 1891, I had grown to know in my wanderings several scholars of about my own age. Albert Clark, afterwards Professor of Latin at Oxford, had examined at Llandovery, where a lively girl, his fellow-guest under the Headmaster's roof, had freely chaffed him for his rather solemn manner, and had sent him off from the railway station with a packet of Albert biscuits. A. E. Cowley, the 'Good Samaritan' of Sherborne, was at Magdalen College School, pursuing the Oriental studies begun in his school days, and destined to take him to the Librarianship of the Bodleian. 'Joey' Wells had examined also at Llandovery: pleasant glimpses of him will be found in the biographies of two famous pupils of his at Wadham.[1] I got a few hours, again, with the future Sir Henry Hadow, in renewal of Malvern days.

To me, by far the most important Oxonian was Hastings Rashdall, who had examined both at Llandovery and at Sherborne, and whom I now saw much more frequently. Once I dined with him at the High Table at Hertford, where Walter Pater was also dining that night. His host asked us after dinner to his own rooms; and the mere sight of him was interesting, with his heavy jaw and military moustache, strangely dissonant from preconceived ideas of the man who had written *Marius the Epicurean*. But that evening he talked like his books: not offensively like, but with a marked flavour of the same style. He discoursed at some length upon *Manon Lescaut*, where I was able to follow him because I had discovered the book through George Sand's *Léone Léoni*. This, of course, dates me: a modern reader of to-day would be far more likely to discover the existence of George Sand through *Manon Lescaut*. Another time, I tramped with Rashdall to Brill, a hill village on the Buckinghamshire Downs. We started after lunch on Saturday, and got there for dinner. Next morning was very hot, and I began to doze very early in the sermon: it was Trinity Sunday and the discourse seemed

[1] *Life* of Lord Birkenhead; Humbert Wolfe, *The Upward Struggle*.

painfully commonplace. But, later on, I gradually began to feel a quite different atmosphere; the change in the preacher's tone had roused me from sleep. For he was concluding with that passage from Newman's Trinity sermon which haunted Matthew Arnold for all his life: 'After the fever of life, after wearinesses and sicknesses, fightings and despondings, languor and fretfulness, struggling and failing, struggling and succeeding; after all the changes and chances of this troubled, unhealthy state,—at length comes death, at length the White Throne of God, at length the Beatific Vision.'[1]

Thus, all that spring and summer, I had the same freedom with books as at Heidelberg, and nearly or quite the same enjoyment in that freedom, as at our old Pentney home. It was not until 1892 that I could afford to make a regular practice of spending a few holiday weeks abroad, mostly in Germany or German Switzerland. But here in 1891, with the help of my brother Rick's copperplate press, I revelled in attempts to follow him with the etching-needle and aquatint.

The Autumn Term drew near, and I began formally to approach the agents for some fresh job. It was healthy for my self-esteem that headmasters did not tumble over each other for me. The Headmaster of Bedford did indeed bite for a moment. But this was only for a temporary vacancy, and I took the liberty of asking civilly what chance there might be of a permanence. He sent word to the agent that this was a young man who must change his attitude if he wished to succeed. Term began, and I was still unemployed. I therefore took volunteer unpaid work for Toynbee Hall, in the East End of London. There, it need hardly be said, were many congenial companions, under the leadership of Canon and Mrs Barnett. My sponsor here was Dr Bradby, formerly Headmaster of Haileybury, whose daughter afterwards married Mr J. L. Hammond, and also collaborated with him in *The Village Labourer* and other books, among the most valuable of our time. I had met Bradby when he came down to Sherborne; and here, at St Katharine's Dock House in the East End, he and his family were showing the way towards reconciliation of rich and poor. To anticipate here by a few months, this Toynbee Hall connection was of immense interest and profit during the fight over the Education Bill for the County Council

[1] *Parochial and Plain Sermons*, vol. VI, Sermon XXV.

election. G. N. Bruce stood for the Progressives on this question
and Cyril Jackson for the Conservatives: two names honourable
in the later history of British Education. The fight was mainly over
the Cowper-Temple clause for undenominational religious education; a cause in most cases of bitterest antagonism. Here, however,
the rival candidates had their headquarters in the same building, and
discussion went on outspokenly at meals, entirely free from undue
heat, so far as I ever saw. Being among the few who could speak
German, I had the Jewish refugees assigned to me for canvassing on
Bruce's side. They were mostly Poles or Russians, but they generally
had a little barbarous German. Their housing conditions, of course,
were such as to make one wonder how any of them could take any
interest in anything whatever. One typical case is clear in my
memory. Five or six cobblers were working in a room perhaps
fifteen feet square; more likely, smaller. Their chief—employer or
foreman—spoke a little broken German. 'Religion', for instance,
he regularly pronounced 'herilyōn' with a powerful initial guttural.
When I tried to interest him in the Progressive cause, as a matter
of religious freedom for his children, he said, 'Look here: I am a
Jew, and my religion bids me cease work for one day in the week.
If I and these others did that, we should all starve: as it is, we work
twelve hours a day, and only just keep ourselves alive. So what is
the good of talking to me about other religions? I have lost my
own and I don't want any other.'

It was about this time that I learned of the death of my school
friend, Hubert Gepp, who had gone from Oxford to be Lector in
English at Upsala. He formed a friendship with Nansen, who taught
him the use of the ski. He became so proficient and adventurous
that he used to aim at the first crossing of lakes in the early frosts,
before others had led the way. One day he started on an expedition
of that kind, recognizing the risks and therefore holding a drawn
clasp-knife, like Monte Cristo, to free himself from the skis in case
of accident. Some days after, his body was found, with the skis still
attached, but his legs pitiably lacerated in his attempts to free himself.

Half the Autumn Term was thus passed at Toynbee Hall, when
a temporary Mastership at Sedbergh came suddenly within my reach.
Chastened by the Bedford experience, I caught at it greedily, the
more so because I had heard so much good of the Headmaster and

his school. It had had very much the same sort of career as Sherborne. Founded in 1525, it was the best Grammar School of the district, but had sunk into very low water about the beginning of the century. From that it was raised by an exceptionally successful Classical teacher, Heppenstall, who had previously made his mark at the Cambridge Perse School. Henry Hart, his successor, was an even more remarkable man.[1] The school motto was *Spartam nactus es, hanc exorna*: 'You have become a citizen of Sparta; adorn her now.' Unsparing of himself, he expected, and often got, the very best from his masters and boys. The school is delightfully situated on the slope of the Yorkshire Fells, close to the borders of Lancashire and Westmorland. Just below what is practically the only street of the little town, stand the old parish church, the old schoolhouse, and the playing fields checkered with modern buildings of fine local stone, in the honest impressive style of North Lancashire masonry. The climate contrasted crudely with that of Sherborne, where Cowley had constantly inveighed, not without justice, against the relaxing climate of that pastoral valley. Here, at Sedbergh, was a sub-mountain climate, often raining and still oftener bracingly cold. A fine hill, Winder, rises up straight behind the town; the view eastward is magnificent, up a long valley ending finally in Baugh Fell, one of the loftiest ridges of the Pennine range. On a spring day, the cloud shadows would chase each other over those slopes, in an atmosphere of pearly greys which is probably almost peculiar to Northern England. Mr Dent, the publisher, whom I had met at Toynbee Hall, and whose family hailed from Dent, not far from Baugh Fell, came by chance into my railway compartment some years later. He had just returned from Italy, where his pilgrimage had been mainly to Assisi. He expressed a certain disappointment: 'It was splendid in many ways; but I did miss the pearly greys of our own Fells.' The little rivers are all romantic, torrential in bad weather, but offering in summer an alternation of cliff and rapid and pool unrivalled, I must think, by any other school neighbourhood.

All those advantages Hart exploited to the utmost. Some of his

[1] After his death, I was commissioned by the old Sedberghian Committee to write a memoir, with a brief history of the school. It was published under the title of *A Victorian Schoolmaster: Henry Hart.*

rules were consciously, I think, modelled upon those of Loretto near Edinburgh, where Almond had made a great reputation for healthy individualism. Loretto, in fact, was Sedbergh's main rival at football; the honours were fairly equally divided, and both schools were nearly up to the exceptional standard of Llandovery.

Every Sedberghian was bound every day, and in all weathers, to be out of doors in flannels between 2.30 and 3.30 except, of course, for a certificate from the school doctor. If not playing in any of the school games, he was to walk or run along the rivers or up the hills. Written punishments were minimized, and one of my predecessors, Grant, a Fellow of Queen's, Oxford, had dealt in them even more sparingly. One of his ingenious devices, where he had to punish at all, was to leave his visiting card on the top of Winder, under some distinguishable stone, and send the offender to fetch it.

Hart was wise enough to resign when he felt his health failing; and it may safely be said that he left to his successor a far better organized school than Harper had done. Some might think it too well organized, with too little of the go-as-you-please way in which we had lived at Felsted, and boys at greater schools and of earlier generations in even greater freedom. His teaching, again, was felt by the cleverest boys to be too formal, though he was a good Classical scholar and keenly interested in social and philosophical questions. A distinguished Cambridge scholar who had been under him at Haileybury had vivid memories of his management of one Platonic dialogue, the *Protagoras*, remembering how he said 'He made us feel that, though Socrates seemed so victorious, he had not always been really fair, and there was something to be said for the defeated Sophist.'

·Where his sincerity and strength of character came out best was, perhaps, in his dealings with the Staff. To begin with, Heppenstall and he had chosen them with such care that anything like the Sherborne mutiny would have been inconceivable. One real malcontent there might have been, or even two; but they would have had no support from the rest. Bernard Wilson was one of the most impeccably devoted assistants I have ever come across. Nothing would have tempted him away from Sedbergh. Bernard Tower, less monumental and more versatile, was a fine musician and devoted teacher and House Master. The Headship of Lancing was more than once pressed upon him; and at last he accepted it, but strictly upon his own conditions. Lancing College was one of the Woodard Schools, founded on a definite Anglo-Catholic basis. One very important feature there was the office of Warden, combined then in fact, if not on principle, with that of Chaplain. Tower was a very sincere Anglo-Catholic layman, fellow-collegian at Oxford with the well-known party figure of Athelstan Riley. To the electors who pressed him to stand, he insisted that this Wardenship should be mended. 'I have no objection to Confession at school: it may be said that I have spent my whole Sedbergh life in hearing confessions. But I will not have a man who, *ex officio*, hears confessions apart from me, and gives sacramental absolution.' His first condition, therefore, was that the Warden-Chaplain should be superseded. Thus came the curious constitutional anomaly that a prominent member of the Governing Body should be, in effect, dismissed by a person who had no nearer connection with the College than that of Old Boy. After the election, Athelstan Riley wrote in friendly congratulation, but with a postscript dictated by his conscience: 'I voted against you, because I have always felt that you were never truly Catholic.' Tower, as he told me, replied: 'I am sorry you find me wanting in Catholicity; but please remember that I suffer from the disadvantage of six years at Lancing College.' I rather think it was *seven*; certainly he had been one of the model scholars for an unusually long time.

Comparable even as a schoolmaster, and far more remarkable in other ways, was H. W. Fowler, author of *Modern English Usage* with other philological and literary work which has now become classical. At the invitation of the Clarendon Press, as one of his few surviving intimates, I wrote a brief memoir of him for the Society for Pure English.[1] One episode of his Sedbergh life must be summarized here, for the sake of the light it throws on scholastic conditions in latter Victorian days.

Hart was a very broad Churchman, but very sincere. Here, as elsewhere, the Rugby tradition of Thomas Arnold was all-powerful with him. Therefore, whenever candidates presented themselves for Confirmation, it was his rule that the boy's House Master should prepare his pupil for it. Fowler, though quite willing to teach

[1] S.P.E. *Tracts*, No. 43.

Scripture in class, did not care to commit himself so far as that. Later, when he retired into literary leisure, he became definitely Agnostic; but at this time it was only that his sincerity forbade his committing himself so far as Hart's rule required. Therefore, when one House became vacant, he waived his claim of seniority and heartily supported its transference to Ainslie, remaining himself a contented House Tutor to Tower, his most intimate friend. Some ten years later, when another vacancy occurred, Hart committed the mistake of taking for granted that Fowler's objections had in no way changed, and offered the House to another man. This complicated the matter, and made it seem a merely personal grievance when Fowler chose that moment to send in his resignation. As a matter of fact, he would again have refused the House, and objected only to the unfairness of not being consulted. The move to Lancing of his old friend Tower, to whom he had acted a dozen years as House Tutor, meant that he would now serve under a man considerably his own junior; he also conscientiously suspected that his own work at Sedbergh was becoming stiff and rusty; therefore, having a patrimony of about £120 a year, he resolved to drop school work and live upon that. But he seized this opportunity of discussing Hart's principle in the abstract, as naturally and unsparingly as his resignation now permitted. That correspondence is fairly fully summarized in my memoir; and I have deposited the actual letters, by permission, in the Library of St John's College, Cambridge; they will be invaluable in the next generation to anyone who tries to describe English education as it really was. At the time, to some of us who were familiar with these and similar facts, the greatest interest was in the behaviour of the two men. It was a conflict of naked principle. Hart maintained the traditional principle; Fowler, what he felt with all his soul. The gradual breach was inevitable; neither yielded one inch of ground; yet their personal friendship remained unbroken. Not, perhaps, that they could ever have renewed one hearty vacation of some years before, when four of them went together to Norway, all ex-Heads of the Schoolhouse at Rugby. But neither ceased to speak with sincere admiration of the other; and there was nothing unedifying about this contest, which in itself might have given better excuse for revolt than anything at Sherborne. Hart had elements of real greatness, and was devoted to his profession. Fowler had by far the harder burden to bear, and accepted it with that stoicism which was the very foundation of his character. Time and experience have only strengthened my conviction that the Staff under Hart had few or no rivals among schools which had no more natural resources than Sedbergh. Their harmony was not less remarkable than their individual values. H. W. Fowler's room was there what Parker's had been at Sherborne, a place of common Saturday-night resort. Our host would come in as soon as he had finished reading to the boys in their dormitory: at that time, Conan Doyle's *White Company* was the book. There was utmost freedom without acrimony. The nearest approach to undue heat that I can remember was once between Gooch, the athlete who rather disclaimed literary pretensions, and Ainslie, an unusually handsome and all-round man. His voice was so fine that Parker had once tried to get him a public trial at a London concert. He was an accomplished amateur artist in water colours, and at Oxford his caricatures had been among the most popular and financially remunerative in Shrimpton's window. He ended as Headmaster of Greenbank School at Liverpool. But there was one fly in his ointment. The world-famed *Oxford English Dictionary*, casting about for an example of the special University use of 'Blue', chose a quotation at random from *The Oxford Magazine*: 'Ainslie, of Oriel, may be successful in winning his blue.' That, alas! is one of the greatest things that he never got. He had rowed in the Trials, and was tried for a while in the University Eight; and it was cruel that his failure should thus go down to fame. He was exceedingly ready and happy in all Shakespearian quotations, and here and there in elegant puns. One night, a lively discussion arose between him and Gooch. Ainslie delivered himself at considerable length, in a somewhat rhetorical speech. Gooch put in a level volley from the Scriptures: 'Go up, thou bald head!' That personality touched almost as sore a point as the Oxford Blue; and Ainslie found no reply.

In the spring of 1892 I was offered a place at Dulwich College. Hart told me I might consider my job at Sedbergh as a permanence; but London was a temptation which outweighed even those healthy hills and that healthier companionship.

CHAPTER XXIII

DULWICH COLLEGE

DULWICH is a great school, founded by Shakespeare's contemporary Alleyn, and in the nineties a great Headmaster was reigning there in the plenitude of his power. He has been commemorated at worthy length in a book which, rightly, treats him and the College as inseparable subjects.[1]

His father was of Quaker stock. His mother, an impressive old lady with plenty of quiet humour, told me of her first introduction to her husband's family. They sat all round the room with religious formality; and her natural attempt to break the ice brought down stern rebuke: 'Sister Gilkes, thou shouldst wait to be spoken to.' He was, I think, a Shropshire lad; certainly Shrewsbury School had done much for him. He was a fine athlete in running, cricket, and football. He stood considerably over six feet, and was well proportioned. When, in middle life, he stood for the Headmastership of Dulwich, though his testimonials earned him a place on the 'short list' of candidates to whom the Governors would give the privilege of personal interview, yet few or none thought seriously of him in comparison with two or three brilliant names. He came up last, and then the very sight of him produced an immediate change of feeling. Doubtless, with all his due respect for the electors, he treated them with that quiet self-possession which was one of his great characteristics; and he was elected by a good majority.

I had admired Gilkes, unseen as yet, from Llandovery days. My colleague, G. H. Jones, told me of his own experience in the Sixth Form at Shrewsbury. Gilkes habitually took a low Form there, but had an hour or two in the week with the Sixth. His subject there was English, or at any rate something not directly concerned with the sacred Latin and Greek of that most classical academy; and his success was very remarkable. On one occasion the lesson had been badly prepared, not by one only but by many. After ten minutes or so, Gilkes rose from his chair and left the room, saying, 'Boys, I am ashamed of you, and I will go no further with this lesson'.

[1] See M. Leake, *Gilkes and Dulwich*.

The class, instead of unregenerate joy at their riddance from 'Old' Gilkes, were really chastened, and Jones looked back upon this as one of the outstanding memories of his school days. John Shearman quoted to me what an Old Alleynian friend had once said to him, 'Gilkes never hustled us'. There was a monumental tranquility about him which suggested his exceptional strength. One Australian boy, it is true, fresh from the democratic ease of the Antipodes, met him one morning in the cloisters and greeted him with, 'You're just the man I've been trying to find. What about that Scripture lesson, now?' But this afforded us infinite jest for a whole term. Again, one particular Master was often of different opinion from the Head, and sometimes impertinent: but that was X, who boasted Eton as his School, and King's as his College. X's classical ὕβρις once provoked Wade (who was Head of the Modern Side in so far as Gilkes recognized any organized Head for anything so unclassical) into perhaps the only epigram he ever committed: 'They sent X to Eton to make a gentleman of him, and they made a scholar of him by mistake.' Gilkes, moreover, did not like X's independence.. With many of the qualities which made Walpole a great Minister, he had something of Walpole's preference for yes-men around him. Sanderson, for instance, got on badly with him until he went off to Oundle, where he became an educational pioneer; and I sometimes heard, from an able scientist and mathematician on our Staff, words that might almost be called mutinous. To X, Gilkes finally pronounced the true and melancholy words, 'No man is irreplaceable'. X was a good scholar and a remarkable teacher; but, when he went off to try his fortunes as 'coach' at a south-coast resort, Gilkes found two successors no less efficient for teaching, and one of even higher scholarship—Pearson, who ended as Greek Professor at Cambridge.

The Dulwich rule of salaries rested mainly upon a flat rate, in addition to which the House Masters made what they could by boarding fees. New-comers were docked of £30—or it may have been even £50—for their first year; and Gilkes treated me on such beginners' terms. But it was not so much he, as the system, which made no allowance for the fact that at least half of the younger masters were my juniors in age, and had far less varied experience. After a term or two, he promoted me to run the Army Class, as

at Sherborne. For Dulwich had then begun to follow the example
of half a dozen other schools, and to stem the exodus of good pupils
by giving them special teaching for Army Entrance Examinations.
At first, I had to make bricks without straw. An able young mathematician was to help me on that side as at Sherborne: but I had to
do all the rest. At Sherborne, I had never had the older and the
younger together in the same class. Here at Dulwich, there were
from twenty-five to thirty, some almost illiterate while others were
already good enough to pass straight through into Woolwich or
Sandhurst, with any luck. I was compelled, therefore, frequently
to take two classes at once. This meant that one must be writing
while I taught the other. That again meant that I carried home a
cruel amount to correct, often before next morning's lessons. True,
on my way home I frequently met women teachers from the High
School staggering under the weight of copybooks in their net bags;
but the weakest of all defences for an abuse is in the existence of
worse abuses next door. For one term at least, and I think two,
nearly all my waking hours were spent in this drudgery. Yet, for
a Classical Master, Gilkes was not narrow. His own lessons here,
even more than at Shrewsbury, since he now had full control, were
full of wider and deeper suggestion for the boys. But he had a
profound distrust of mere intellect. Matthew Arnold, in his exaggeration, might almost have said of him as of C. J. Vaughan, 'brutally
ignorant'. When once I had to plead at a Masters' Meeting that
our large and richly endowed School Library—which, by the way,
possesses a First Folio of Shakespeare—ought for shame to possess
Alfred de Musset, if only in the cheap one-volume edition, he showed
no sympathy down from his throne. Personally, I have never
doubted the supremacy of character over pure intellect, often in
what may seem purely intellectual matters. But, in a later chapter,
I shall try to explain the weakness of his tacit assumption that
character can be moulded only, or almost only, through the Greek
and Latin classics.

When my work had settled down, it was possible to enjoy the
company of several pleasant colleagues and, especially, the proximity
of London. Dulwich, though its charming village character has been
wonderfully guarded by the Trustees of Alleyn's wealthy Charity,
is only four miles and a half from Charing Cross. For half-holidays,

the British Museum was easily accessible, and for Sundays the art collections, or Westminster Abbey, or other less orthodox conventicles. One incident at Essex Hall is very clear in my memory. Leslie Stephen gave the evening lecture in that home of free thought; his subject was the English Philosophers of the Eighteenth Century. The chairman noted the presence of Bernard Bosanquet, and invited him to move the vote of thanks. Bosanquet began: 'If Mr Stephen had been a philosopher...' and went on to criticize him freely in the same strain. Stephen pulled a wry face and stroked his long beard all the time; but it was pleasant to see his manner when he shook hands with the younger man.

Gilkes had one characteristic which different readers may judge differently. In every case of conflict between boy and master, his instinct was on the boy's side. Rightly or wrongly, there was a fairly widespread feeling that he was more loyal to the school than to his colleagues. It was the same feeling which made him divert part of the Governors' yearly grant for the Library, and use it for the increase of boys' scholarships in needy cases. Again, I feel that he bore responsibility, after myself, for perhaps the biggest blunder I ever made in Public School work. X was, on the whole, the ablest boy I have ever had in my class, and one of the most interesting in every way. Our Army Class work naturally, if not necessarily, offered a dull routine in comparison with the Classical Lower Fifth under Griffin, who afterwards became Headmaster of Birkenhead School. I could see that X, who had come from the Lower Fifth, was growing weary of the damnable iteration which it was next to impossible to avoid in a class where the average boy had only about half his intellect. Then came one question of discipline, small at first, but rapidly magnifying under disagreement. I put the case to Gilkes: he not only agreed with me that a principle was at stake, but felt even more strongly than I that I must not give way to the boy. There, as I saw afterwards clearly enough, we were both wrong. I ought to have talked it over quietly with X, waived any disciplinary regrets for the moment, and appealed to his generosity (which was great) not to make this into a precedent which might affect the class. Instead, I followed Gilkes' advice, and pressed my point even when the quarrel had become bitter. His father, a very distinguished and influential man, wrote plainly that the quarrel was warping his son's life, and he must be withdrawn if the disagreement could not be made up. Gilkes then transferred him to his original Lower Fifth; a definite blow to my prestige and discipline. For forty years this incident remained one of my most painful memories, until a fortunate chance gave me the opportunity of exchanging mutual confessions and regrets with my pupil-antagonist.

My last two years at Dulwich are those which have left the deepest impression. The winter of 1894–5 stands out as the longest in living memory, and one of the most severe. Spring was proportionately welcome; and it came with a rush. Silver and gold seethed up from the sod: daisies and buttercups and cow-parsley outdid the garden flowers not only in God-given directness, but even in mass of colour. Many spots in Dulwich were rural enough to do justice to this. The great country house and park which stretched from the College to Herne Hill had indeed been recently cut up into building lots, and a single tenant's rent of £600 a year had been replaced by ten times that amount from whole streets of suburban villas. But still, almost within a stone's throw of the College gates, were at least two houses that were wealthy enough to possess each its grove of trees and its small attendant farm. One of them, in these latter days, has been converted into a spacious hotel for tired Londoners: giving sufficient evidence for its former comfort for a single family. Dulwich folk were sociable and hospitable; and, when two of my sisters in succession came to keep house for me and my pupil (for I was three times allowed to house the son of some friend for a few terms) we had pleasant calls and invitations. Thus the spring and summer of 1895 were comparable to those of Jubilee Year in the Towy Valley, or of Heidelberg. In some ways, it was even more idyllic. It did not bring greater devotion into my school work. That did indeed prosper, and I had far abler pupils, on the whole, than ever before, but I no longer tried to persuade myself that this was most at my heart. One of our hospitable neighbours, a London barrister and old Trinity (Cambridge) man, discoursed once in my hearing upon the disadvantages of a schoolmaster's life. One of his College friends, of a County Grammar School, had just been superannuated without pension (such was the common custom of those days): and I realized that his comments were painfully, even brutally true. It reminded me how, at Sedbergh, one House Master's wife had enlarged outspokenly upon the unequal distribution of salaries which made it almost impossible in those days for an assistant to marry until well on in middle life. London, too, was unsettling with its British Museum Library, and its Art Galleries at a short hour's journey from my door; and I was beginning seriously to think of a livelihood by literature. Thus, those early days of 1895 bred in me—and, I dare say, in some of my colleagues, if we could frankly compare notes— something of the headlong medieval spring passion. The hawthorns were magnificent, among those untidy patches of unbuilt ground which I had to cross on my way to and from school; they outdid even the garden lilacs and laburnums. Presently, also, I discovered the delights of rambling at dawn on Sundays among the railway cuttings and banks; for there, as in the waste fields that awaited the jerry-builder, I found magnificent natural blossom. The railway prospector had broken the ground, and wild meadow flowers grew thus, within a few miles of Charing Cross, more plentifully than in many of the quietest country places. The great ox-eye daisy almost smothered the rest, and it was superb until the smoke and dust had begun to dim it. Moreover, it is from the railway that many suburban rose gardens show their best face to any leisurely tramp while the world is asleep. In front, they are often concerned to defend themselves from the public, but they dream of no such enemy from the line. This close juxtaposition of mechanical civilization and weekday work, so far from spoiling those Sunday wanderings, often gave them added zest. The Mighty Suburb might have its cruel and sordid side; but here the Mighty Suburb was asleep, and on these railway banks I brewed my coffee at dawn with something, at least, of that free soul with which I had boiled that very same tin over that same lamp while the morning mists were lifting from the Rhine. After all, Hamlet was not wholly unjustified in surmising, with Boethius, that 'there is nothing either good or bad, but thinking makes it so'. Something there was that lent to springtime in those London suburbs the glory of mountain, grove, and stream:

> Bright columns of vapour through Lothbury glide,
> And a river flows on through the vale of Cheapside.

I can never regret that long winter, wearisome and sordid as the ice and slush were, with the ensuing dirt and discomfort of thaw over those irregular spaces that had ceased to be honest fields, but were not yet arrived at the comparative decency of bricks and mortar. The Sunday mornings before dawn, in that steady summer weather, with not a few equally pleasant afternoons, more than made up for all that. Even if I had had other grudges against Dulwich, yet the April, May and June of 1895 would have wiped them out. In the last days of term, however, a certain weariness had set in: Nature's Priest was travelling farther and farther from the East. Again, during the summer holidays, I rashly undertook a certain amount of tuition with the youngest brother of my dead friend Huntington, who was struggling to get to Oxford. During the next year, I became absorbed in reading. Rashdall's *Universities of Europe* had come out, and given me an even greater impetus than Trevelyan's *Macaulay*, of twenty years before; St Bernard's letters had laid a medieval foundation; again, I had read Sabatier's *St Francis* at its first appearance, and noted his unscientific use of the Stigmata evidence.[1] 'Nature, grove and stream' were certainly possessing me less, and I was learning 'the stormy note of men contention-tost, of men who groan'. Modern politics and social questions threw me more and more back upon the past, and Rashdall's masterly book brought conviction, in directions where hitherto I had done no more than feel my way with increasing certainty. I feel that our modern problems can often be studied best in the Middle Ages, not as a golden Reign of Saturn but as a period during which men like ourselves were struggling for objects of which many have nowadays been attained through inspired and honest work, while perhaps the greater part awaits our efforts as it awaited our forefathers. Thus, then, I went on—let me say, drifted—until an overmastering and decisive impulse came. Though it was at Dulwich that the spring worship of 1895 came on, this was not accompanied by any proportionate attachment to the place as my domicile for the rest of my life.

The first days of Autumn Term found me there in full health, and bearing easily enough, at 37, the physical strain of Rugby football. Yet, before Christmas, I found myself a convalescent at Eastbourne under the roof of my old College friend, H. v. E. Scott. I know by experience, from that time forward, what change of

[1] I have treated this at length in *The Hibbert Journal* for January, 1926.

thoughts may come to a man under the stress of fever. My first coherent recollection would fit into Donne's words: 'For me, if there be such a thing as I', life and death are indifferent. Next, I can see a hired nurse at my bedside, in the attitude of a corpulent Buddha-image, immense in the smooth spread of white linen over her lap. She ministered periodically, by doctor's prescription, what she called 'Fishy Water', and betrayed persistent anxiety to get the key of my cupboard: Rick irreverently christened her 'the Belly-god'. Then, with growing strength, a strange gulf opened between Past and Future. Behind me, lay a sea which had nearly beaten out the swimmer's life: but upon which he can look back as irrelevant and impotent, now that he lies upon the shore.[1] In front, a new land, long glimpsed in imagination, but now at last touched and recognized as his own. In proportion as physical forces returned, I seemed to see for the first time a clear and consistent plan for the conduct of life. The uncertainties of future years seemed only to open fresh possibilities. Wherever I was alive, I lived now in reaction to the past. Not always in contradiction, but ever in reaction; here repudiating the old, and there chafing the old to greater heat. Mr H. G. Wells has emphasized his own difficulty in believing that the Wells of fifty years ago was the same creature as the Wells of to-day. For myself, without any weakening sense of personal identity, I have been obsessed since 1896 with a sense of two different lives in one person; 'Old things have passed away; behold, all things are become new.' The new life may perhaps run as definitely in a rut as the old, for no man can 'jump away from his own shadow'. But at least it is a different rut. For nearly half a century I have possessed my soul more truly than in the first thirty-eight years of my life. At a much earlier date, I had picked up the little twopenny-halfpenny edition of Descartes' *Discourse on Method*, and read where he writes: 'My third maxim was that I would strive always to conquer myself rather than fortune, and to change my own desires rather than alter the World Order' (section III). This maxim, which I had long accepted with passive acquiescence, I tried henceforward to adopt consciously and deliberately as my own.

[1] Dante, *Inferno*, canto I, l. 22.

CHAPTER XXIV

LAUSANNE AND NAPLES

I HAD made up my mind to begin my new freedom with a few months in Italy: so I sold my life-insurance policy and took the plunge. Scott came cycling with me for as long a time as he could spare. We crossed to Dieppe, and arrived there in the small hours of a cold December night. Next day we rode in frosty, but kindly weather by the coast road to Eu, and thence by late evening train to Abbeville, unvisited hitherto, but familiar in distant imagination through Ruskin's *Praeterita*. The next days were fine and bracing still, and we pushed up the Somme valley in the mood of escaped schoolboys. Rapid convalescence is a bliss: but to enjoy it with an old College chum is very heaven. He had lost most of his hair in the past eighteen years, but none of his spirits. I tried at the wayside inns to pose as his son; but no Frenchman could be thus hoodwinked for a moment. Our ride through Amiens, Courcy-le-château, Laon, and finally by train to Reims, was such a renewal of the best old Cambridge days as formed a fitting prelude for Italy. At Reims we parted; he for Eastbourne and I for Dijon and Lausanne.

Lausanne became to me a second Heidelberg, but with even greater freedom. The University Library was open and generous. I could not take books out; but there was a good, cheap, lending library; Payot had an excellent second-hand stock, and the barrows in the market place were a hunting-ground comparable even to the quays of Paris. I hired a little bed-sitting-room on the south side beyond the Grand Pont, hard by a tower of the medieval fortifications which has probably disappeared by now. My little stove, without extravagance in wood, gave me that comfort which surprised Montaigne so much in Switzerland: the warmth which rendered bonnet and fur cloak superfluous, and left him to put them on only when he went out into the cold air. It was in just such a room that

Descartes hit upon his famous 'I think, and therefore I am'.[1] In this
way I began my first conscious and systematic study of medieval
life. I ferreted out from an old bookshop a copy of C. Meiners'
antiquated but suggestive *Historische Vergleichung*, a comparison of
medieval and modern manners. The market-place barrows groaned
under old numbers of the *Revue des Deux Mondes*, at two sous each,
from which it was possible to make a fine collection of Renan's and
Taine's historical essays: and these filled in my hours when the
library was shut. Here and there I went on lone excursions. One
foggy, depressing morning, I took the tramway to Montreux and
the funiculaire to Caux; thence I climbed to the Col de Jaman,
through snow sometimes knee-deep, in a grey silent mist that was
almost oppressive. Suddenly there was a flapping of wings, and a
great raven flew almost into my face; then wheeled off into the mist
with a hoarse cry and a violent wing effort which made his feathers
look like a hundred outspread fingers. Five minutes later, my head
came suddenly into the sun while my feet were still in the mist,
and there stood the Dent de Jaman almost toppling over me, and
all the great mountains from the Dent du Midi to the Grand Combin
and Velan.

Another time I took a week-end, hired a little toboggan, and went
by train to Martigny. Thence I climbed to the Col de la Forclaz,
hoping for a spin down; but there was too little snow that day.
Instead, I resolved to try the next pass, the Col de Balme, which
affords one of the most famous of all Mont Blanc panoramas.
I borrowed from the little post-office hotel a pair of native Swiss
snow leggings, mere bags of stout cloth, tightly tied at ankle and
at knee. Then, leaving my toboggan and disregarding my host's
warning, I plunged straight down after lunch into the Trient valley
and began to climb that great trough, which looked so short in the
bright air and was really so long, towards the summit of the pass.
I argued, to my own satisfaction, that the whole thing was straightforward: there was no chance of losing one's way so long as one
kept to this hollow trough; the difficulties might finally prove insuperable, but they would come gradually and leave retreat always

[1] Montaigne, *Voyage*. In French, as in German, the same word was used for
'stove' and 'room warmed by a stove'—*Stube, poële*. Descartes' own words
were (2me partie) 'je demeurais tout ce jour enfermé seul dans un poële.'

easy. It was only in later days, when I did that climb in the summer, that I realized the frightful traps hidden at the bottom of the ravine under that smooth snow, some of which I may, in fact, have unsuspiciously crossed without breaking through the fragile bridges. I kept to the sunny side, where the alternation of heat and cold had rendered the snow hardest. Yet, even so, after about an hour every step went in up to the knee; then deeper and deeper as progress became slower; then breast high, and I was as yet scarcely half-way to the top, and the sun's rim was slipping behind the mountain on my left. The game was evidently up, so I turned and hastened down. There was still light enough to show the bridge over the Trient, and the rest appeared easy, for it seemed that so long as I climbed straight up the hill face, I must strike the road which slants upwards towards the Forclaz. Evidently, however, I began the climb too early, to the right of the spot where the zigzag begins. The climb was stiff in any case; I slipped constantly into holes under the snow, or fell over fallen trees in this thick forest: and, as there seemed no end to this, I gave up after an hour or so and made for the few twinkling lights at the little village of Trient. The big summer hotel there was in its natural winter state: no guests but the family and servants hibernating in a kitchen and a little parlour with its iron stove. With them were the travelling cobbler and the travelling tailor, welcomed during the dead months to repair the ravages of summer wear. I was ready to do full justice to all the eatables and drinkables they produced, and listened complacently to their exposition of my folly, not half realized even then. Presently they started the subject of the Diamond Jubilee due in that year, 1897. It was pleasant to find how genuinely they were interested, and anxious to hear all I could tell them about my own country. All the negative side had fallen away here; all the money-grabbing and mistrust which does so much to poison relations between host and guest in these crowded summer resorts. We were all hibernating in the same hole and talking as from man to man; seldom in my life have I had a more enjoyable evening than this. Next day, at the Forclaz, I could apologize for the anxiety I had caused my host, and I bought from him a rather less primitive specimen of native Swiss snow leggings, which will reappear later on.

Every now and then while at Lausanne, I went and watched the

sunset from the terrace of the Hôtel Gibbon, which now no longer
exists. In those days, that terrace was directly reminiscent of the
historian; for here, as he tells us himself, in June, 1787, between
eleven and twelve at night, he wrote the last sentence of his *History*
at the table of his summer-house, and then paced the terrace in full
enjoyment of the silent moonlight on the lake, yet reflecting that
'whatever might be the future date of the *History*, the lifetime of
the historian must be precarious'. Those words, I think I may
honestly say, appealed far less to any literary ambition in me than
to the enthusiastic student. Self-deception is, perhaps, most dangerous when we think we have overcome it. Yet I believe that,
in the famous dilemma formulated by Lessing, I should have taken
Lessing's choice.[1] Not even Gibbon's fame, if that had been possible,
would have outweighed that which I distantly hoped for at Lausanne,
and which in fact I have since enjoyed: namely, forty-five years more
of free browsing among such books as Gibbon would have given
both his ears to possess.

Moreover, all this enjoyment of Lausanne was heightened by the
hopes of more and more in Italy. I knew already enough of that
land to feel what I might justly expect from a whole springtime
there. I did not want to be Italianate; but I did reckon upon adding
to what was English in me certain things which I believed then, and
still believe, can scarcely be picked up except in Italy. Chaucer
found in his Italian journeys all that the modern Englishman finds
in America, with all that the American finds in England. The Englishman, across the Atlantic, sees a busier material civilization than his
own, and democracy on a larger scale: so did Chaucer find in such
Italian cities as Milan and Genoa and Florence. On the other hand,
the American in England sees something far more mature than
anything at home, and something more powerful, when he comes
to study it in its roots, than the first hasty experience would have
led him to expect. So must Chaucer have felt with that ancient Latin
civilization and those 'rivers gliding under ancient walls' which,

[1] 'If God held all truth in His right hand, and in His left nothing but the
ever-restless instinct for truth, though with the condition of forever and ever
erring, and should say to me "Choose!", I should bow humbly to His left
hand, and say "Father, give! Pure truth is for Thee alone".' Carlyle was
perhaps the first to quote these significant words in his *Essay on the State of
German Literature*.

even in Virgil's time, were counted among the glories of Italy. So the Italy of my present hopes was now the Italy which Walter Savage Landor held up for inspiration to his young friend and beginner, Robert Browning:

> Warmer climes
> Give brighter plumage, stronger wing; the breeze
> Of Alpine heights thou playest with, borne on
> Beyond Sorrento and Amalfi, where
> The siren waits thee, singing song for song.

I entered Italy this time as one ought always to enter. On that January day of 1897 there was cold mist and drizzle as the train panted up to Mont Cenis; but from the tunnel we came out into dazzling sun and snow.

At Florence, I stayed some weeks with two aunts of my friend Huntington, but not long enough to wait for the scarlet tulips that come up among the young wheat. I wandered farther south; and, by a lucky impulse, I determined to go to Naples by sea from Livorno. At Pisa, on the way, I was lucky enough to pick up Salimbene's *Chronicle*; it was almost unprocurable in those days, but this and several other good medieval books had just come into the market by a scholar's death. At Livorno, my finds were almost more numerous, probably from the same scholar. In those two days I collected more volumes, of the exact kind that I specially wanted, than I could have got from the London market in a year at four times the expense. One, Thomas Wright's *Anecdota Literaria*, a tiny volume but desperately rare, is now in the Bryn Mawr University Library with many others which I sold in 1911 to defray my settlement at Cambridge. There must have been nearly a hundredweight of these, which I left with a very honest shipping agent to forward by sea to England. More honest, it occurs to me as I write this sentence, than I was myself. For I seized what seemed an excellent occasion to add a score of Tauchnitz or American pirated volumes— Ruskin, Swinburne, and so forth. The medieval books turned up at Eastbourne before me, safe and sound; but of the pirated there was no trace; doubtless H.M. Customs had seized upon their lawful prey.

The next morning at Livorno was delicious, considering that we

were still in January. The blue waves raced steadily up the sands
and burst upon the walls of the parade. Where the sands were wide
enough, I enjoyed an ideal bathe; nor did it specially disturb me
that the wind was obviously freshening after noon. The ship sailed
soon after sunset, in what promised no more than half a gale, and
I got at once into my berth in a fair-sized single cabin. An hour
or two later there came a storm upon us which took even the ship-
folk by surprise. The steward's crockery and glass began to fly
about; he ceased struggling with it, and simply locked up his pantry
to let the whole stock grind itself to pieces as the ship pitched and
tossed. The can of water in the corner of my floor was built so as
to look perfectly safe, broad-bottomed and tapering to the neck;
but it was soon rolling about the cabin; I had to fish out the loose
clothes, and leave the locked valise to its fate. Sleep was impossible:
I should have fallen out of the berth if I had relaxed my hold. A little
before dawn the tempest subsided almost as suddenly as it had
arisen: we had probably passed through the vortex of a sort of
cyclone. The shore looked very cold and inhospitable as we skirted
it at a distance of some twenty miles. Yet, by about nine o'clock,
the sun struggled out, and an hour later we came within sight of
those islands which guard the Bay of Naples and have music in their
very names—Ischia, Nisida, Procida. As we approached the bay
itself, there was a very striking and unusual effect. We were steaming
through a troubled sea, churned by the storm into the colour of
pea-soup. It was to be expected that the bay would be more tranquil;
but there the different colour of water was almost too spectacular
to be credible. In the distance, it was as though a great cloud threw
an indigo shadow upon just that part of the landscape. As we drew
nearer, in proportion as the true cause of this contrast became
apparent, it became even more striking. The bay was so definitely
sheltered from the general current, that the line of demarcation
between pea-soup and indigo was unnaturally harsh. I believe that,
without exaggeration, our bow was in the pure bay water before
the stern had well left the muddy Mediterranean.

Then came the full view of Naples itself, with those fantastically
graceful islands on our left. Yet, on the whole, the sight impressed
me less deeply than that of the Firth of Clyde, into which I had
steamed from Liverpool six months before. It may have been that

I was more seasick now; but certainly even that combination of romantic scenery and ancient walls and splendid colour spoke to me less effectively than the still small voice of a voyage where everything had seemed so exactly in its place. From the first sunrise over the coast of Galloway we had had the dappled sky which so often shows Britain at her best; so that the shadows chasing each other in and out of the glens of Arran, and the lonely majesty of Ailsa Craig, come to me far clearer than Naples and Vesuvius when I shut my eyes to look back.

Naples city, again, did not detain me more than a week or two, for my hopes still turned southwards. Bathing was heavily handicapped by the accumulation of civic detritus upon that tideless shore. I walked once to Virgil's Avernus, and another time to Pozzuoli (Puteoli) for St Paul's sake. I saw Virgil's Tomb, and that succession of villas on the road to Posilipo where the Bersaglieri rest on their morning marches. Later, a pupil told me how his father owned one of those villas, with its green lawn sloping gently to the road, at just the spot for a halt in that six-mile-an-hour pace which is compulsory for those select troops. After ten minutes or so in the shade, the lieutenant would always ask, 'Siete pronti?'—'Are you ready to go on?' Invariably, a chorus of 'No! No!' from the soldiers sprawling about the grass, and five minutes more before the actual start.

One of the greatest curiosities of Naples I discovered only on my return journey. A half-pay German officer from the war of 1870 had told me what to look for in the obscure church of St Agostino alla Zecca; and I found it plain enough. In front of one of the altars stands a very remarkable realistic figure, life-size, in glazed and coloured terra-cotta. I seem to remember that they told me it represented Sta Agata. She raises her outspread hands and is about to stagger backwards, while a dagger sticks to the hilt under her collar-bone and pierces to the heart. This realism comes home to the population of Naples, where stabbing affrays are far more frequent than in any other European city of similar population. This little church, therefore, has become consecrated in the popular mind to what we may call Our Lady of the Stiletto. The man who has a vendetta on hand vows it to this altar in case of success, just as the mother has vowed a head of wax (or silver, if she is rich enough) for her child's life, or the lover a heart for success in his love. Thus the altar is hung with dozens of triumphant stiletti; moreover, the boards erected to receive them show also a considerable number of empty nails, which tell an even more gruesome tale. For, here and there, some other man has vowed his own particular vendetta, and has reinforced the religious force of that vow by borrowing one of the consecrated stiletti to do the job with. He has never come back to replace it; and each empty nail stands for two murders at least. The objects speak plainly enough for themselves; but I took care to get full corroboration. The sacristan, questioned on the subject, admitted reluctantly that each of these daggers stood for a *mala morte*. Thence I drifted across the street to get my hair cut, and the barber told the same tale in plainer language.[1] I may add that later on, when I visited the Cathedral of Salerno, I found half a dozen stiletti there at one of the side altars. That sight often came back to me when the course of lectures brought me to the death-bed of Gregory VII at Salerno, with his cry of 'I have loved righteousness and hated iniquity, and therefore I perish in exile'. Comparing that utterance with the passage from which Gregory parodied it (the word is scarcely too crude, in the face of Hebrews i, 9) then I could not forget that they were gasped out within a few yards of where I had seen that irreligious altar.[2] It must be added, however, that some ten years ago, when a Cambridge colleague went to Naples, I told him to go to St Agostino and report. Unfortunately he could not speak Italian, and his evidence was confused. He thought he had found the right church, but he had seen no such votive offerings there, nor met anyone who could enlighten him. It is likely enough that the clergy of 1930 had managed to get rid, at last, of offerings which are shocking to the modern conscience.

For, only a few months before my visit to Naples, there had been a very striking infusion of the modern spirit. One of the street-corner Madonnas suddenly worked a miracle. There were hundreds of such images in the city, possibly even thousands, both great and

---

[1] A part of this curious collection is figured in my *Art and the Reformation*, p. 278, where I deal with the similar case of the 'Toothache Capital' in Wells Cathedral.

[2] For the paganism still flourishing in Naples at the end of last century, see Trede's four volumes, *Heidentum in der Christlichen Kirche*, or the brief summary by Pastor Stubenvoll of Heidelberg.

small, conspicuous and inconspicuous; often only a foot or eighteen inches high, and half smothered in neglect, yet none the less Madonnas. What this miracle exactly was, I am not sure that the papers clearly specified at the time. But certainly it was one of the obscurest images, at the corner of two of the narrowest and poorest streets. Not much was ever needed to raise a sudden commotion among a population of whom the majority were illiterate, and thousands, literally, awoke every morning without knowing when or where or what would be their next meal. They flocked to the spot; and, in proportion as the crowd grew, the Madonna multiplied her miracles. The press at that street corner rapidly swelled to amazing, and then actually to dangerous, proportions. Neighbouring streets were blocked also; pickpockets had begun to scent their prey; quarrels arose; the few police were powerless; and a major commotion in the city seemed almost unavoidable. The Prefect called upon the archbishop; and fortunately both were reasonable men. The prelate gave out: *haec est mutatio dexterae Excelsi*—'This is the change of the right hand of the Most High: here we have an image far too sacred to be left to the chances of a crowded and tumultuous street corner. We ourselves will step in now and give Our Lady all the honour She deserves.' He sent a dozen of his canons down from the cathedral, with all the banners and solemn ceremonies befitting such a procession. They removed the Madonna from her corner with ostentatious reverence, and bore her to the cathedral at the head of an immense crowd. There they put her into an out-of-the-way corner of this building which, as everywhere else in Italy, leaves the populace cold: a wilderness of great pillars and arches and lofty roofs and expensive marbles: a place where the ordinary poor of Naples would feel themselves as little at home as a London costermonger in the National Gallery. Many of the procession did indeed remain in prayer that day. Next day, there was again an edifying concourse. But, by the end of the week, a stranger would have noticed nothing very remarkable; and at last this Madonna enjoyed no congregation beyond the few enthusiasts who can always be found to follow the latest religious fashion.

At Pompeii I saw the recently discovered House of the Vetii; intensely interesting, but too far out of my main road to detain me for more than a single day. For my thoughts still turned southwards,

to places which, I scarcely know why, I had grown to associate
with what seemed most Italian in Italy. For instance, it was quieter
and more idyllic regions than Naples which had always presented
themselves to my imagination in connection with that poem which
Aleardo Aleardi entitled 'Yearning', and in which, from his Austrian
dungeon in 1859, he voiced the mood of passive patriotism under
generations of leaden tyranny.

> Poesie Volanti
> Sehnsucht
> S' io potessi portar meco sottera
>   L' amor mio, la mia casa e la mia terra,
> Lunghe dai ceppi, lunghe da gli affanni,
>   Lunghe da questa plebe di tiranni:
> Oh, come volentieri oggi morrei,
>   Quantunque chiuso, qui, lontan dai miei!
> E là nell' aurea region dei morti,
>   Ove non son nè schiavi, nè risorti,
> Mi comporrei del mio terrestre eliso
>   Un paradiso in mezzo al paradiso.[1]

[1] 'If I could bear with me below the earth my love, my house and my small
domain, afar from prisoner's chains, afar from miseries, afar from this rabble of
tyrants: oh, how gladly would I die to-day, despite my imprisonment here far
away from mine own! And there, in the golden realm of the dead, where there
are neither slaves (on the one hand) nor rebels (or the other), I would compose,
from this earthly Elysium of mine, a paradise in the midst of Paradise.'

CHAPTER XXV

SORRENTO AND AMALFI

SORRENTO was the true goal of my pilgrimage: to me, as for many others, it had more romance than Naples. I had heard of it as a fit land for Goethe's *Tasso* and for the real Tasso; and, though I do not believe I ever read the *Gerusalemme Liberata* all through, I had long known and hung upon that stanza to which Spenser paid the compliment of barefaced robbery:

> So passeth, in the passing of a day,
> Of mortall life the leafe, the bud, the flowre.[1]

Moreover, I had more definite reasons; for here two of my sisters had recently stayed with a cousin at the Cocumella, one of those many Italian hostelries which are housed in a dissolved monastery. This was, and still is, I believe, a favourite resort for artistic or literary folk. Well out of the town, on a lofty cliff, it looks straight across the bay to Ischia with its attendant islands, and to Vesuvius. The garden is full of orange trees, and there for the first time I realized the luxury of picking up the fallen fruit and eating them warm from the sun. The water, cool even in the dogdays, is drawn from an enormous cistern cut deep into the solid rock for some wealthy Roman who had lived there before monks were known. A staircase, hewn no less uncompromisingly through the rock, led the Roman, and now leads the degenerate modern tourist, down to a tiny bay where he may dive in from the rock or creep in from the sand. My room—indeed, I think nearly all the rooms—had its own little terrace outside the window, with a pergola upon which the

[1] *Faerie Queene*, XII, 75; TASSO, XVI, 15.

> Così trapassa al trapassar d'un giorno
> Della vita mortale il fiore e 'l verde:
> Nè, perchè faccia indietro april ritorno,
> Si rinfiora ella mai, nè si rinverde.
> Cogliam la rosa in sul mattino adorno
> Dì questo dì, che tosto il seren perde;
> Cogliam d' amor la rosa: amiam or, quando
> Esser si puote riamato amando.

vines were just beginning to show their tender shoots. From other
higher points of view, the sun went down into the sea with a directness which made one almost expect the hissing of steam. One
evening we had an effect nearly as magnificent as that sunshine after
storm at La Riccia which Ruskin has immortalized in one of his
most famous word-pictures. The rain had drenched us half an hour
earlier; and now it was falling in sheets, far away, between us and
the sunset. Through that heavy veil of raindrops the sun burst out,
and flooded all the East with crimson light. There, in that view
behind us, were orange groves and cypresses and white houses; the
combination which is so fascinating always and everywhere in Italy.
All this, for the space of almost a quarter of an hour, was transfigured
in a fashion which, I found, could be clumsily imitated by first
sketching the scene in its native green and white, and then washing
the whole with a full brush of alizarine crimson. To steal Ruskin's
words: 'I cannot call it colour, it was conflagration.'[1]

That was but one of many experiences such as no Florentine
picture gallery could have given me, or any book. Of books I might
perhaps have gathered a great harvest here thirty years earlier, when
the monasteries were dissolved and so many of their libraries dispersed. Osten-Sacken, in those days when he was attaché in Rome,
had picked up many valuable books from the barrows in the market.
At Sorrento itself, I found the grocer wrapping up his stuff in the
stout folio leaves of Baronius' *Annales*; but there was not enough
left, among the two or three remaining volumes, to be worth bar-
gaining for. But one literary experience was unexpected, though
gratifying enough. I had come to Italy for medieval atmosphere,
yet it was Virgil whom I met everywhere, even more than Dante.
Here, at Sorrento, the *Eclogues* and *Georgics* were alive and up to
date. His little peasant-farmer was still to be found here and there;
the thin runlet of water drawn from the stream to refresh the
meadows; the shepherd and his flock; the goat nibbling at cytisus
and willow leaves over our head as we bask under the rock. One
glorious surprise, again, came quite early in my visit. Monte Sant'
Angelo rises some fifteen hundred feet above the Plain of Sorrento:
masses of green pasture, fold above fold, with crags and snow at
the summit, and a sanctuary to which the priest comes for Mass

[1] *Modern Painters*, I, pt. II, sec. ii, ch. ii, § 2.

once a year. I climbed this succession of slopes with a growing disappointment at their monotony; when suddenly, a few hundred feet below the top, I came to the edge of a great hollow, perhaps a quarter of a mile across, as full of yellow crocuses as Wordsworth's bay ever was of daffodils. Nowadays, even in face of our yearly miracle of flowers in the lawns of Cambridge, I cannot quite repress the ungrateful murmur, 'But you are not my crocuses of Monte Sant' Angelo!'

The inmates of the Cocumella were always interesting. The great majority were Germans, though it was not so completely Germanized as Capri, where shop windows were filled with water-colours in those hard and overladen blues and yellows which the Teutonic artist loved to produce, and the Teutonic public could be trusted to buy. Gerhart Hauptmann, already at the height of fame, occupied one secluded suite of apartments at the Cocumella; we sometimes saw him under the orange trees with his lady companion of those days; and her masterly violin-playing was often audible from the inner rooms. One conspicuous group, again, was evidently Jewish. All of those were well travelled and agreeable; the most interesting to me was Diercks, a German orientalist who had finally settled into a professorship in Spain. He said once, 'The Spaniards are the cleverest people I have ever met—and the laziest'. Those of this group were generally in close confabulation with each other; and it gradually became pretty plain that they had political business on foot. This was the time, in fact, when the Kaiser's spectacular visit to Jerusalem was impending; and the rest of us had little doubt that these Orientalists were commissioned to prepare the way for him.

Another guest was a Prussian Inspector of Forests, a State employment which ranked almost next to the military in dignity. He was remarkably cultured and courteous, with a dignified consciousness of knowing his job a good deal better than it was commonly known in Britain, but without the least tinge of vulgar pride. Equally interesting, in a very different way, was a retired clerk from a business house in Manchester. He was the model of Calverley's

> worn-out city clerk,
> Who'd toiled and known no holiday
> For forty years from dawn to dark.

Pacifist, idealist in every direction, he was quietly enjoying what he knew for a very brief epilogue to a very laborious life. He had come to rejoin his kinsfolk in Germany; but he made no secret of his strong preference for the freedom of English life. On the other hand, his diametrical opposite was the half-pay major from Heidelberg, a typical military bore. In matters of ordinary gossip he was sometimes interesting; but whenever he harked back to the Franco-German War he repeated mercilessly the same tale of how he once had an interview with Wilhelm I, and how the Kaiser dismissed him with a studied 'Knall-Effect': 'Ja! ich weiss es, all' unsere Leutnants sind Helden.'[1]

The spring flowers were just coming out on the Plain of Sorrento when questions of time and money compelled me to move on. I sent my baggage by rail to Naples; packed my rucksack for a few weeks; and then 'afoot and light-hearted, I took to the Open Road'. The way across the 'Peninsula of Sorrento' to the port of Amalfi is one of the most famous of its kind in Italy; and I had magnificent weather. An ascent of four miles or so brings us to the ridge of the peninsula, with views of the Gulf of Naples and the island of Capri to the west, and of the Gulf of Salerno to the east, with its legendary Isles of the Sirens. The road then drops even more steeply than it had mounted, and thenceforward it winds twelve or fifteen miles from cliff to cliff, from bay to bay, in a crescendo of beauty until we come to Amalfi. At Positano, about midday, I stopped at a wayside inn for lunch. Half a dozen natives were sitting at cards in the room; and all looked up to stare at the stranger with his rucksack. One, however, took advantage of this to shift furtively one of the cards on the table. Another saw him and cried out; the rest turned; and for a fraction of a second the culprit stood, as it were, in the dock. But only for a fraction; then there was a lightning change which would have made the fortune of any actor. The furtive manipulator became a magnificent figure raising his hand in indignant protest: 'What! I cheat at cards? To hell with you and your lies!' Then, with one commanding sweep of his hand, he mingled the whole tableful of cards in inextricable confusion, and struck again the Coriolanus attitude. Some, apparently, took his part; at any rate there arose such a pandemonium that I feared stiletti would be

[1] 'Yes, I know; all our lieutenants are heroes!'

drawn. I was appealed to as a stranger, presumably impartial; but my Italian reached no further than to disclaim any knowledge of that particular game. Soon, however, in characteristically Mediterranean fashion, the tumult subsided almost as suddenly as it had arisen: but there was no question of returning to cards. They were more concerned to learn, first, what particular wares I was hawking (for this is a great district for hawkers), and, next, when undeceived, why I should choose to tramp thus from place to place, being presumably a wealthy Englishman.

Amalfi stands on, or rather climbs up, step by step, the two opposite sides of a narrow and precipitous ravine. From the Sorrento road there is no access to the city but by a tunnel pierced through a great rock that rises straight up from the seashore. Just short of that rock, to the left, stands an almost perpendicular cliff, broken at the height of two hundred and thirty feet by a long narrow ledge behind which the mountain rises steeply again. That airy ledge contained the buildings and gardens of a Capucin monastery, transmuted now into one of the most celebrated hotels on the Continent of Europe. Just below, by the roadside, stood the much smaller hotel of Sta Caterina, kept by a local doctor. This suited my purse far better, since one can always climb the one hundred and ninety-three steps to the Cappuccini and see their garden freely as a visitor. Mine host of the 'Caterina' had a room to spare; so I unpacked, washed and changed after my hot walk, and strolled up the ravine to look for early cyclamens among the rocks. But, coming back for supper, I found that all was changed. Two other travellers had come in the meantime; mine host saw that he could persuade them to sleep in my room; therefore he had turned me out into a little closet with no bedstead, but only a couch: moreover, even this couch was not straightforward: it was S-shaped, for the convenience of two talkers leaning over to each other. Into this closet my effects had been bundled just as the manservant found them: my sponge, for instance, was to be found inside my shirt. I called for the doctor and expostulated: he merely shrugged his shoulders: *Vae victis!* he had done a good piece of business for himself. This inspired me, for the only time of my life, with immense volubility in Italian, and (I hoped) with corresponding fire. I remember calling him *Medico a due soldi*, by which I meant 'twopenny-halfpenny Doctor', and his manner suggested that he understood me. Then I packed hastily, marched through the tunnel into Amalfi market place, and tumbled at once, by good luck, into one of the most attractive billets I ever found in my tramping career. To borrow from Rousseau: 'Of all the dwellings I have ever had (and some have been charming) few have given me such true happiness, or bequeathed such tender regrets' as the little Albergo Sirena at Amalfi. Its seductions stole from me nine out of the ten days which I had planned to spend in Rome Immortal; but for this I have never felt even a twinge of regret. Rome is, no doubt, unique; there can never be another. But whereas that Sirena was in its day unique, it is now

> gone away from earth,
> And place with those doth claim,
> The children of the second birth,
> Whom the world could not tame.[1]

As an idea, no doubt, it exists still and always has existed in the Mind of Plato's God. But in actuality, on this planet, there lives perhaps nobody now, except my unworthy self, who has enjoyed the privilege of familiar converse with that old host: moreover, I myself have now lost his name.

In that dark corner of the market place, under the southern rock, a door opened into this extraordinary hostelry. Once inside, one found it to be a sort of rabbit warren, with rooms at all sorts of height from the ground, sometimes opening out of each other, and sometimes approached only by tortuous passages of stairs. Outside, from the sea, it resembled a series of swallows' nests built into crevices or upon ledges of the great cliff. My own bedroom was lowest of all; the window stood perpendicularly, or even perhaps projecting, some twenty feet above the sand; and the sea itself was so close that, at the least agitation, I slept to the drowsy thud of waves against the foot of my unshakable rock.

There was room for only about a dozen guests, or perhaps a score. They came and went rapidly: most of them stayed only one night, as wayfarers pressed for time and for money. Many were all the more interesting on that account. Our host slept on a mattress in

[1] M. Arnold, *Obermann*.

the kitchen, being indeed host-of-all-work to an extent which I have never met before or since. He was not Padrone: the Padrona was his married daughter, who apparently had supplied the capital to float this modest concern. Signor Gaetani—I must invent, since I have forgotten his actual name—was up as late, and down as early, as anybody ever required him. He took his daughter's orders, which were frequently in the categorical imperative, with the most un-ruffled good temper. He was an impeccable cook, within his own considerable range of traditional Italian dishes. If garlic was a little more prominent there than in our own homes, that was a fault easily forgiven by unpretentious guests who, moreover, were all in the same box. More than one of his dishes suggested that which Dumas has immortalized in the episode of his famishing banker: 'Those dreadful vulgar onions recalled to Danglars certain sauces and side-dishes which his cook [in Paris] prepared in a very superior manner whenever he said "Monsieur Deniseau, let me have a nice disreputable fricassée to-day".' When I had become a sort of habitué, he set himself to educate me in dishes which smacked, so to speak, of the soil. There was brown macaroni, such as the peasants ate, made not from bolted white flour but from fine-ground whole-meal. That dish, I confess, did utilize more garlic than I should have chosen of my own accord. His greatest triumph was a fish savoury which he described at first as almost unprocurable, but managed finally to secure one day when we were alone; for the population of this Sirena fluctuated as rapidly as it passed on. This dish looked, at first sight, like two large poached eggs. The white was represented by a sort of creamy mess. The place of yolk was taken by a brownish grey mass which, on close inspection, turned out to consist of hundreds—I might almost say thousands—of embryo fishes. Cer-tainly their size, compared with whitebait, was as whitebait itself compared with herrings. Certainly, again, they pleased the palate; but I was not a sufficiently hardened gastronome to forget this massacre of the innocents. Gaetani's own comments, also, gave me furiously to think. For he told me of the immense trouble he had taken to secure this small dish, and how seldom these microscopic fish came into the market nowadays. And his conclusion was not 'That is what comes of tapping our fisheries at the very source!' but 'The very fish of the sea began to fail us as soon as the Bourbons were driven out!' Here, then, was a man invaluable to the inquisitive

English traveller; a Loyalist of the Ancien Régime. Little by little, he told me his whole life history.

The original hotel patronized by aristocratic travellers of the Grand Tour lay just outside the city to the north, 'Luna' by name. That, like the Cappuccini, was a dissolved monastery. Byron's signature had stood in the travellers' register there, until some marauding globetrotter cut it out and carried it off. Gaetani's father had been host of that prosperous hostelry, and had bequeathed it to his eldest son. That man had used Gaetani himself (and, I believe, other younger brothers) simply for his own convenience and pleasure.

He treated me from the first as a menial [said Gaetani], and, after some years, worse and worse. For he never married himself, but persuaded me to take a wife, and then tried to seduce her. When she told me this, I took her straight away, and we lived with our children as best we could. For some years I went as a sailor. But most of the time I lived by hawking, as so many of us do in these parts, because there are so many little hamlets and scattered farms. Most of that work was in the Maremma, between Salerno and Pesto. I used to take the things they make here at Amalfi, macaroni and paper and soap: coming back, I collected rabbit skins, and old linen rags for the paper mills. All that Maremma reeks of malaria, and there's only one way of keeping fairly safe; you mustn't sleep there. So I used to drive my little cart all through the night from Salerno to Pesto, and hawk from house to house through the daylight, and then back to Salerno: thirty-six hours at a stretch. Over and over again I have fallen asleep over my reins for sheer weariness; and then, if it was winter, I would suddenly wake up with a start, and there was a wolf, perhaps, trotting by the side of the cart and waiting for his chance. So, in one way or another, I managed to bring up my five children. At first, I had wicked feelings towards my brother. I went once to my room, resolved to put a knife into him. But there hung the little print of the Madonna, and Quella Graciosa seemed to say to me: 'Will you do such a wicked thing as that?' and I threw the knife away. But the land has gone from bad to worse, ever since they turned the monks out. I won't say that the monks were all good; but what are the men who have taken their places? Look at the Cappuccini, over there! That place was not sold in the open market to the highest bidder; it went to one of the gang for a price that I would willingly have given for the mere garden, let alone all those fine buildings! And so things went everywhere; there are many of us who would be glad to see the Bourbons back again.

16-2

There was a murder there during my few weeks, semi-social and semi-political, connected with the Camorra, a sort of Tammany organization. Heated discussion broke out in a café; one of the disputants burst out into the market place and appealed to the public like an ancient orator: 'O Amalfitani! we are all being robbed by these villains of the Camorra.' A partisan of the other side promptly put a stiletto into him. Gaetani shook his head ominously: not that one man mattered so much, but 'we shall now get a whole series of vendettas, each of them repaying the other.'

The parochialism of this cathedral city is, to a foreigner who takes the trouble to look into it, almost beyond belief. The nearest other cathedral, Ravello, is one and a half miles off as the crow flies, and about two hours to walk. Those tiny episcopal sees make one understand how it was not impossible for a medieval Italian bishop to keep a list of all householders in his diocese;[1] or again, how there were three hundred and twenty Italian bishops at the Vatican Council which voted Papal Infallibility, thus outnumbering by forty-four those from all the rest of the world.

The active portion of Amalfi is higher up the ravine, where a succession of waterfalls drives the paper mills and macaroni factories, and the rocks are gay with crimson cyclamens. The main body of the city rises from the sea, tier upon tier, round a little oval market place. The higher houses can be reached only through the lower: sometimes we must pass through three or four before reaching the topmost. The focus of social life is, of course, this market place. There the housewives bargain and chatter through the first half of the morning, while the men look on from their numerous cafés. Nothing can be bought, of course, without an eternity of chaffering. *Prezzi Fissi* ('fixed prices') is a maxim which the buyer would not willingly adopt even if the seller proclaimed it. One day Gaetani pointed out to me a fat, middle-aged man loafing at the door of a café. 'That man's nickname is *Ceci*.[2] He is a spoiled old bachelor, the only son of a widow who lives here on the left, in the top house of all. One morning, he was so impatient for his dinner that he called out to

---

[1] Salimbene records this of one particularly zealous bishop in his day, about A.D. 1250.

[2] 'Chick-peas': Latin *ciceres*. The prominent germ of this little grain resembles a caricature of a nose, and may possibly suggest the origin of Cicero.

his mother who was still gossiping down in the square: *Mamma! Mam . . . ma! I ceci sono pronti*—"the chick-peas are ready cooked". The whole city heard him, and laughed, so that's the only name they have for him now.' The common prison, again, is practically part of the cathedral, and occupies a great part of the north side. As we mounted the great broad steps to the west door, haggard men's or women's faces sometimes glared at us from behind the bars.

St Andrew is the patron saint, and he had much ado to protect his city during those centuries when Moorish pirates infested the Mediterranean. All along the coast are picturesque watch towers, each on its own rock, fulfilling the office of those martello towers which were built during the Napoleonic wars along the south coast of England. Stories of great victories at sea, and great defeats, are still very living among the people. When I went off by carriage to Salerno, I pitched upon a driver who turned out almost as interesting as Gaetani himself. He pointed his whip at those decayed castles, expatiated on the cruelties of the Saracen marauders, and recounted the miraculous sea victory which had put an end to all such horrors. The infidels came in irresistible numbers: the whole bay was black with their ships. But they had not reckoned with St Andrew. He came riding upon a tempest which crushed the ships against each other like eggshells, or dashed them upon the rocks. Out of all that infidel multitude, one man alone survived. For he had the presence of mind to fall upon his knees and pray: 'O, St Andrew, your victory will not be complete if none is left to tell of it. Save my life, and it shall be spent in proclaiming your virtues and your might!' The saint saw obvious propagandist advantages there, and thus the whole story was published to the world. The same driver told me, incidentally, that cats were very commonly eaten in those parts. 'But not the head', he added: 'he who eats a cat's head goes mad.'

Side by side with all this folklore were the delicious walks in early spring weather, whether along the coast or up the ravines, and especially the climb to Ravello, where the beauty of the site is enhanced by rare specimens of medieval art in bronze and in marble. There was no bewildering multitude of interests, whether in nature or in art: but there was God's plenty for me during all those days, and for many more if time and money had served me better.

CHAPTER XXVI

HOMEWARD BOUND

But in fact time pressed: my purse was dwindling, and my sands ran out rapidly. I was due on a fixed day to pay a short visit to the Huntingtons on the Bay of Spezia; and even one day more at Amalfi would have cost me all my prospective twenty-four hours in Rome. So I turned northwards: *satur ut conviva recessi*, in a mood where natural regret was swallowed up in deep inward satisfaction. All this Italian journey had been as fresh and helpful for manhood as Yarmouth had been for our childhood; a chapter in the eternal lesson that each of us is not the only pebble on the beach. By the side of that Norfolk sea, we had sought and sorted everything that came under our eyes. We had treasured each our own little harvest, ranging from real amber or cornelians or agates, worthy the labours of 'the only working lapidary', down to those wave-worn fragments of brick which, when glazed with sea water, shone for the moment as most imposing of all. Here and now at Amalfi, I had fallen upon a little lump of amber from the Mediterranean, enshrining the most curious of little insects. I brought it home in my memory fresh from its own blue waters, and have treasured it throughout this long succession of years that have worn off all merely adventitious gloss.

At Naples I queued up early for the Rome express, and secured a right-hand corner seat, to make sure of seeing Aquino on the way for St Thomas' sake. But presently a fellow-countryman came down the train; he was in difficulties with the booking-clerk about his money, and could neither explain himself nor understand the other. I deposited my bag carefully on the seat; but, on returning, I found this and the three adjacent places occupied by a gentleman and three ladies. They turned out to be American; and I fear that any too detailed report of the ensuing conversation would not make for international amenities. I mildly claimed my own seat, and was asked how I dared to speak like that to a lady. I pointed to my bag, now on the rack above, and argued that nobody would have been rash enough to vacate a seat, in that crowd, without such visible pledge as this. The gentleman asked whether I took him for a liar. No, indeed; yet the porter who brought their baggage had evidently bundled my bag away in order to secure a better tip. At any rate, there was the bag as a mute witness in my favour; and so far as the ladies were concerned, I could plead *ad misericordiam* my very special wish to see an historic place for which this was probably the one and only chance of my life. But all four were always speaking at once; and (my too pronounced English accent standing in the way) it is quite possible that not one of them ever realized what I had to say for myself.

In Rome I made up my mind to do half a dozen things as quietly and unhastingly as though I had months to stay. I found time that evening to hear the nuns' singing at the Church of Trinità del Monte; and, as advised by my sister, I went tó see the great mosaic at SS Cosma e Damiano, where Christ and His Apostles stand out against the golden and crimson and azure hues of dawn, while the quiet flock feeds below; a flock of sheep only; no crude division here between sheep and goats, as in later medieval scenes of the Second Coming. I went to St Peter's, of course, and the Colosseum, and the Pantheon, and the Capitol. Yellow Tiber, again, I crossed once or twice, not as a stranger tantalized to see so little, but as one thankful for seeing so much. Those dozen daylight hours were a time of enjoyment as solid, if not as enthusiastic, as almost any other of my life. They were like the medieval *traditio*, that scrap of a thing which served as token and earnest of the whole great gift. We may treat it as childish that a lord should have laid on the altar a sod from his land or a twig from his forest: indeed, a story of that sort is one of the most venerable of classical Joe Millers: but there may be worse ways than such *traditio* for bringing realities home to men.

I took the night train from Rome, and was reminded once again that we were in the Annus Mirabilis of Diamond Jubilee. The Pullman coach contained one of the greatest Indian grandees, the Rajah of Kapurthala, with his suite. The Ranee, charming in any case to look at, was still more attractive in her childlike enjoyment of one penny-in-the-slot machine at the corridor end. This contained eau-de-Cologne; she washed her hands in it, and called on her courier for more pennies, and more again, till she exhausted his wallet. From the sight of that grand company I stole back to seek my straw in the secluded grange of a second-class compartment, facing an Italian lady of fifty or sixty, her head draped in the black lace veil of Genoa. At dawn I woke to find her awaking also, and performing her toilet. She produced a handkerchief, which, by the way, had not been called to her aid during a sneezing fit overnight. She moistened a corner with her tongue, and went carefully over one square inch of her face; so again with another corner and another inch; and so on to the end. It was exactly a pussy-cat's toilet, excepting only the peculiarly feline gesture of turning the head and rubbing with the wrist behind the ear. At Sarzana station I was met by Pietro, the Huntingtonian valet who might have posed for Jeeves; and once again from the terraces of Barcola I could look down upon the villa from which Shelley was drowned, and the drawing-room with its French window from which he used to run across the road and plunge into the sea. At Geneva, I was most hospitably entertained by Alfred Stable's cousins. Together with one of them, now Professor J. J. Stable of the University of Brisbane, I ploughed up the winter snows of the Môle for the sake of a splendid view. From Geneva I booked straight back to Newhaven.

Even this train journey, the mere tag end of my Grand Tour, brought one most living and unfading experience, equally memorable from the picturesque and the business point of view. My literary plans had been crystallizing all this time; and I was now resolved to begin work with the intensive study of two medieval books which, I still think, have not received from social and religious historians the attention that they deserve. One of these was Salimbene's *Chronicle*, buried for the present in my case of books from Livorno. The other was the *Autobiography* of Abbot Guibert de Nogent. This, in Migne's edition, had been purchasable in Switzerland, with all his other writings.[1] Prices had gone up a little since 1853, when my own Guibert had been printed; but I paid only ten francs for this volume which became a bridge between one life and another. For a few months, in Dante's Italy, I had enjoyed Dante's imperial and pontifical control over myself: twenty-four hours of freedom per diem. Now the years were at hand when again, as of old, each day's bread must be earned in the morning before I could enter into my freehold for the rest of the day. I began upon my own

[1] See Appendix, p. 352.

Guibert in this express train which was to bring me back to homely
Eastbourne, but which, meanwhile, still trailed clouds of glory from
the Alps and the Mediterranean. That road through Burgundy to
Paris, among its innumerable other delights, shows yearly for a few
brief hours a peculiar beauty of springtide leafage. The commonest
colour contrast in nature is, of course, that of red and green: those
two complementaries are familiar to us. Far rarer, and proportionately more fascinating, are the supplementary colours orange
and blue. Cotman looked for that contrast everywhere; he sometimes brings it almost by main force into his water-colours. Once
I saw it almost exaggerated in nature herself. That was in the Black
Forest: a vast and splendid wheatfield rose on our right; with its
ocean of corn surging up to the top of the hill, and kindled from
yellow to orange in the evening light. Behind, over the crest of this
foreground, the next visible object was a vast pine forest, twenty miles
away, in deep indigo blue. That was on the grand scale; but in more
subdued beauty one may catch the same among the poplars of Italy
and France. That tree has a passing stage, scarcely more than a day,
at which it shows like bronze touched with gold. My homeward
journey in 1897 came, for my good fortune, just at that magic
moment. Whenever I raised my eyes from the book, there was this
foreground of delicate colour; and behind, bluer or less blue according to the distance and the incidence of sunlight, those coteaux
which are not more beautiful than our own hillsides, but more un-
questionably French and therefore (if the word may be coined) more
travelleresque. Again, there is a chapel—'a single Church that I have
looked upon'—which sums up for me all the associations of that
journey. It stands a little south of Sens; on the outward journey,
it comes a quarter of an hour after the river has turned aside, and
the cathedral tower has disappeared behind the trees. The hillside
rises bare and steep, on our right, with the old town of St-Julien-
du-Sault at its foot; where, by the way, few travellers suspect the
existence of some of the most picturesque half-timber houses, and
finest medieval glass, to be found anywhere. This lonely chapel
stands out like a gaunt tower half-way up the incline, as the single
surviving fragment of the archbishop's once magnificent castle. In
bulk it is but a speck; yet it dominates the landscape. The essence
of romance is surprise; and those rough forsaken walls, rising

abruptly from the smooth slope, far above us, have all the unexpected-
ness of Wordsworth's *Highland Reaper*, with the same challenge of
'far-off things, and battles long ago'.[1] For those who have once
learned to look for it, it looms in fancy from the first snort of our
engine starting south-eastward; and when at last we catch sight of
this fundamentally un-English scene, we may sink back with the
assurance that we are indeed in the pleasant land of Burgundy—
'l'aimable et vineuse Bourgogne'.[2] Memoirs are essentially ego-
tistical, and personal associations are more so than anything else.
But, if ever I cross the Channel again, no matter where my holiday
may first have begun, I shall not feel it fully crowned and anointed
until it has brought that momentary glimpse of St-Julien-du-Sault.

One more feature, inseparable from that journey, recalls Thackeray's
remark that we all like to read of good eating and drinking. I had
laid in a fresh Camembert, a half-bottle of Chablis, and three
'brioches' to dip in my wine for dessert. That sort of lunch I had
learnt from Rousseau; and in its way it cannot be bettered. There
are, doubtless, many superior lunches conceivable; but for then and
for there and for me this meal was far more satisfying and unforgettable than when, for the only time of my life, I had the honour of
dining with a famous peer of the realm. I fed on the book, the
landscape and the cheese in the quiet conviction that this was the
best of possible worlds. (Here, of course, as always, we must under-
line that word *possible* which is too often forgotten.)

---

[1] Compare the mathematician-poet Sully-Prud'homme's conception of
eternal bliss, in the poem he calls 'Renaissance':

> Si pour nous il existe un monde
> Où s'enchaînent de meilleurs jours,
> Que sa face ne soit pas ronde,
> Mais s'étende toujours, toujours.
>
> Et que la beauté, désapprise
> Par un continuel oubli,
> Par une incessante surprise
> Nous passe un bonheur accompli.

[2] J. Michelet, *Hist. de France*, L. III. A few miles westward from St-Julien
are several villages named officially 'la vineuse', just as our Saffron Walden
proclaims its ancient culture. Compare Will Rothenstein's picture of his Bur-
gundian experiences under William Morris' inspiration: 'Here, it seemed, was
La vieille France, a land of big-bearded, genial men and sturdy, efficient, kindly
women' (*Men and Memories*, vol. I, p. 279).

Let me end with Rousseau's own words, since no abridgement could do justice to them.[1] He is speaking of a certain 'petit vin d'Arbois', of which he had 'conveyed' a number of bottles from the cellar of his host, Monsieur de Mably, and which he used to drink in his own room with the accompaniment of a 'brioche', untranslatable word, and fully comprehensible only by those who have tasted the thing: 'Mais aussi quand j'avois une fois ma chère petite brioche, et que bien enfermé dans ma chambre j'allois trouver ma bouteille au fond d'une armoire, quelles bonnes petites buvettes je faisois là tout seul, en lisant quelques pages de roman. Car lire en mangeant fut toujours ma fantaisie au défaut d'un tête-à tête; c'est le supplément de la société qui me manque. Je dévore alternativement une page et un morceau: c'est comme si mon livre dînoit avec moi.'[2]

Within little more than twenty-four hours after looking down upon Arbois and its vineyards, at the foot of the Jura, I had entered upon my thirteen years of work with Scott at Eastbourne, under the Sussex Downs.

[1] *Confessions*, conclusion of partie I, livre VI.
[2] 'When once I had secured my dear little cake, and, shutting myself up carefully in my room, fetched my bottle of wine from the bottom of a cupboard, what delightful little drinking-bouts I enjoyed all by myself, while reading a few pages of a novel; for I have always had a fancy for reading while eating, if I am alone; it supplies the want of society—I devour alternately a page and a morsel. It seems as if my book were dining with me.' Arbois, incidentally, is the little town at the foot of the Jura, as compact and picturesque and antiquated as a museum piece, of which the train affords two or three tantalizing glimpses far below. It lies within an afternoon's walk of Poligny, that other old-world Jura town so dear to the Ruskin family on the old Geneva road. Its wine is of the Chablis type.

CHAPTER XXVII

SOUTH LYNN

SCOTT had given the name South Lynn to his Eastbourne home in memory of old Mrs Brown's lodgings, in which he once slept with our fellow-collegian, F. P. Nichols, after a row down from Cambridge to Lynn. His Eastbourne house was an outstanding advertisement: a large semi-castellated brick building on the very crest of the hill, almost the first conspicuous sight of all Eastbourne as one comes in by rail. No healthier spot on that coast could have been chosen, and few more charming views than that from the tower. His pupils, almost without exception, were Public School failures: either the boy had failed with his school, or the school had failed with the boy. Therefore, this Eastbourne experience of mine showed me more plainly under the dissecting-knife and the microscope things which I had been aware of all along, and had striven against with such emphasis as was possible for a mere Modern Sider in face of the conservatism of the Greater Schools. Yet that experience has not blinded me, whether in those first days of violent reaction or later on, to the true merits of what is nicknamed nowadays the Old School Tie. If and when Eton and Harrow are superseded, it can only be by a system which succeeds in teaching many of the good things that they have taught. But, in the nineties, their sins of omission in class-teaching were rank, and the best that can be said was that they had improved considerably during the preceding half-century, as they have since improved considerably again. That improvement can best be marked, perhaps, by two small pictures from Eton life a generation earlier.

In 1883, much attention was attracted by *Seven Years at Eton*, by James Brinsley Richards. Some reviewers scouted it as exaggerated and unreliable: but E. M. Young assured me that the general picture was photographically correct. Only one thing puzzled him: How could the author have seen or heard things which covered so great a space of time? Later, he discovered the secret: two brothers had pooled their respective recollections under one name. To show how true the strangest of those stories might be, Young gave me this story from his own experience. Two (or three) classes were always taught together in one long room, divided nominally by ragged and ineffectual curtains. Two Praepostors marched up and down along the rooms: senior boys taken from their own work to act as 'pions', a sort of disciplinary sergeants-major under the Form Masters. One of the masters was an unpopular figure, 'Stiggins' James. Next to him was Thackeray, of the novelist's kin, a fine scholar, but helpless as a disciplinarian. At one moment, James called out 'Praepostor! give that boy 200 lines for pulling Mr Thackeray's hair'. 'Luckily not to me,' said Young, 'but to the other Praepostor'. He looked James in the face for a moment, and then turned on his heel and walked the other way. The double ὕβρις of that would be hard to beat: first, the pulling of poor Thackeray's hair, and next the contemptuous disobedience of the other Praepostor.

I once found myself at a Swiss table d'hôte next to a relative of this Mr James. She told me how she herself was once at tea with Mrs Thackeray, whose drawing-room had a second door leading upstairs to the boys' bedrooms. There came a sudden and portentous bumping from stair to stair, and then a great saucer bath burst through the door and trundled half-way across the room. A tale about 'Stiggins', probably somewhat magnified by legend, was told me by Lowry, boy and master at Eton, and finally Headmaster of Tonbridge. A severe and unpopular master was Snow, afterwards Kynaston, and Headmaster of Cheltenham. He had rowed in the Cambridge Eight, and was a robust person. A gang of desperadoes among the boys lay in wait behind the trees to duck him in the Thames on his way to or from school. Fortunately for Snow, 'Stiggins' came by first; a still more unpopular figure and an easier prey. He was immersed in the twinkling of an eye, and was struggling out when Snow began to heave in sight. The criminals dispersed, all but Chamier, son of an admiral, who lurked behind a tree. Snow, who had a rasping voice (I can testify personally to that), pointed a finger and snarled through his nose, 'I see ye, I see ye, Chamier, Chamier!' The culprit came out, and copied the gesture and the voice with 'Oh, ye do, do ye? damyer, damyer!'

We had an unusually large proportion of Old Etonians at South Lynn, mainly through Scott's cricket-field relations with Edward

Lyttelton, the Headmaster, and his brother Alfred. Undergraduate ties of that kind are enduring, and rightly so. Moreover, the Lytteltons had always been conspicuous for a breezy grown-up boyishness which is one of the best Public School characteristics. Much later, when Alfred came down with an M.C.C. team to Eastbourne, he had to recruit a few local gentry, including Boger, the secretary of the golf club. The bowling was being severely punished, and a change was obviously needed. Lyttelton therefore accosted this recruit: 'Bodger, they tell me you are a bowler. Go on next over at the Pavilion end.' 'I do bowl a bit, sir, but my name isn't Bodger, it's Bow-ger.' 'Rot, my dear fellow! R-o-g-e-r, Rodger. B-o-g-e-r, Bodger: go on at the Pavilion end!'

That kind of thing was thoroughly typical of Scott himself, and gave no offence because it was so obviously part of the natural man. He was one of the few crammers of any note who tried hard to give his pupils more real discipline, if not so strictly conventional, than they had had at school. Wren, king of crammers, did in all probability answer a querulous parent in the words that were currently reported of him: 'My dear sir, you pay me to send your son's body into the Indian Civil Service, not to send his soul to heaven.' A. V. Jones, who had worked for another crammer almost equally famous, told me one of his own experiences. Half a dozen of the pupils got into a serious scrape, ending in the police court. The crammer sent for them: 'You fellows are a disgrace to my establishment. If this story gets into the papers, I will fire you all. Manage it your own way, but those are my terms.' He was known for a man of his word, and the boys bled themselves white before they could pool a sum sufficient to bribe the reporters to silence.[1]

Another case occurred in a town where I happened to be at the time. Mr Blank had a dozen pupils in a private house. One was a Rugby International, who had asked leave to go out for a Christmas celebration. Permission was given, but on the strict terms of return before midnight. 'I shall lock the door then, whether you are there or not.' In the small hours, Mr Blank was awakened by violent knocks at the door. With much of the quiet pertinacity attributed

---

[1] For a brilliant picture of the crammer at a rather earlier date, see the first chapter of James Payn's *Literary Reminiscences*, dedicated to Leslie Stephen, and bringing in such congenial spirits as C. S. Calverley.

to the Scot, he turned round on his pillow and tried to ignore the call. Presently, however, the knocks were punctuated with a crescendo of vilification. 'Blank, come down! Come down, you old —! Come down, you — — —!' A quarter of an hour more, and the police would have stepped in. Blank came down in his pyjamas, admitted the Prodigal Pupil, and (as I was told) killed the fatted calf for him on Christmas Day. Scott, on the other hand, once played a very different part. In his earlier days, walking up from the station on a rainy day, he overtook two adolescents with their heads together over the 'Pink 'Un' (*Sporting Times*). He smote the paper with his stick into the mud. 'You know I bar your reading that rag!' They turned, and he saw that they were not only not his pupils, but absolute strangers! One of them even stammered out a sort of apology as Scott passed on. The action was, of course, extreme, and other chances might have given the affair a very different turn; but it reveals the man. I have heard him speak to robust and whiskered pupils with a plainness which they tolerated because they knew by experience that it was just his habit to say always exactly what he thought, harbouring no malice, but certain of his ground and determined to have his way. From him and from H. W. Fowler I learned how rare a virtue real courage is, and how successful. In the bishop's study at Abergwili, I once met Mr R. P. Hills, K.C., who had lately won universal applause for his masterly conduct of the Swansea Schools case. The talk turned upon qualities and success at the Bar: how often a man proved *omnium consensu capax, nisi...*—I asked him what, in his opinion, was the most important quality of all, in so far as they could be analysed. After a little reflection, he answered, 'I should say courage'.[1]

The pupils, naturally, were of all sorts. Fees were high: therefore they came preponderantly from the more aristocratic schools. We had a grandson of Nubar Pasha, the Egyptian Premier; a youth who excused himself from carving the ham at his end by pleading that it was too hard work—*une trop forte gymnastique*. Two others,

[1] Compare the following characteristic sentences in a letter from Father Tyrrell to Père Hyacinthe: 'I have slowly learnt by experience that courage is the very rarest of all virtues, and has almost innumerable counterfoils. It all but failed in Christ, and failed entirely in his Apostles, and their successors. In the mass Modernists are cowards; but so are all men in the mass.' (*Letters of G. T.* ed. M. D. Petre, New York, 1920, p. 164.)

at least, were sons of British diplomats. Three brothers belonged to a prominent business family, and showed all the qualities of their race. They used to mount South Lynn tower at dawn, locate scientifically through their glasses the plovers in the marshes below, and get their eggs home for breakfast. The youngest of the three, while still with us, made £250 in one year as a poultry breeder. He began by buying the two latest prize-winning cockerels and hens of some particular breed. Their progeny soon began to win prizes: then he bought other winners until he possessed Britain's best stud. He could now sell his Phoenix eggs to other fanciers at a guinea apiece, through the *Exchange and Mart*, or other specialist papers. If, after a few days, no order came, the egg was pricked to sterilize it and presented to Mrs Scott, who consigned it to the breakfast table among the vulgar herd. The fowls themselves were tended, in term time, by his father's gardener at home. He had printed report forms, as elaborate as we used to have at Malvern Wells for the boys. The fowl's name was filled in at the top. Then a series of queries: 'Has he (or she) a good appetite?' 'Are there signs of Pip? Or Quinsy, or Scarlet Fever, or any of the thousand ills that fowl is heir to?' The moment any unfavourable symptom was reported, prescriptions and commands were sent to the gardener by post or telegram. This same boy, who was (I think) only sixteen, showed the same Napoleonic foresight and thoroughness in his cycling. He persuaded the manager of the Birmingham Small Arms Co., a personal friend, to build him a unique machine, geared (if I remember rightly) up to 148. Certainly its driving cog wheel was almost as large as the other two. It had to be cut by hand: and this alone (to speak again from memory) took three workmen six months to saw out, for it had to be wrought straight from hardest steel. On this machine he would sometimes ride down the steepest hills (and some are very steep in those parts) with two friends at either end to time him. They put his pace on those occasions at 40 miles per hour, and were quite possibly right. Scott once warned his mother: 'If a herd of cows came out of those sheds at the bottom of East Dean Hill, or if one of the wheels of that light racer collapsed, your son would have to be picked up with a shovel!' 'Well, I've often talked to him; but he's determined, and he knows his job, so we don't worry about it.' The risks of that kind, and the rider's trouble, were much increased

by the fact that his whole scheme required 'racing' tyres, no thicker
than a kid glove, upon roads which a friend of mine appositely
described as 'highly puncturesque', since the modern automobile
surface was as yet undreamed of, and Sussex roads were made with
broken flints from the Sussex Downs.

One memory tempts to another: but as they press upon my pen,
so they serve my purpose in explaining the varieties of human nature
in a cramming-shop, and the versatility of the crammer's job. The
establishment had always, of course, its jester. One such was attracted by a notice in the window of Evenden, our premier draper
and haberdasher:

UMBRELLAS RECOVERED
WHILE YOU WAIT

He went in, took the nearest chair, and explained with that wooden
face which was part of his stock-in-trade that he had come to wait
until they recovered his lost gamp, of which he began a detailed
description. The shopwalker's reaction was, 'I suppose you think
you are being funny?'

There was always, of course, something of an awkward squad
among the score or more of patients who had come to this exam.-
doctor. There was the boy whom his father, an old major, frankly
confessed to have thrown upon Scott's hands because he feared
physical violence from him at home, and the mother joined him
in rebellion. Lowest of all, there was the son of an aristocratic and
disreputable father who gave him the worst possible example at
home. It was a sad case, for the boy had inherited also the parent's
physical infirmities. Yet I remember noticing a real improvement
all round in that case. For ours was, on the whole, a fundamentally
healthy life: and, when our jester mentioned above had in due
time taken his Cambridge degree and become Head of a prosperous
Preparatory School, he once gave me an unsolicited testimonial for
South Lynn: 'It did me a lot of good: and it would do most Public
School boys good to have a year of this sort of thing before they
go up to the 'Varsity: they would see their way better and not so
often make fools of themselves.'

But all this depended almost entirely upon Scott's exceptional qualities. I think it was the year before our association, in 1896, that Wisden's *Cricketer's Guide* immortalized him as having made more centuries than anyone else (five, I think) in all the matches recorded in *The Field*. He had been on the fringe of the University Eleven. His short sight kept him out of that magic circle; but against any but first-class bowling he was a very formidable bat. Especially, he had the priceless quality of nerve, and a spirit which rose in proportion to the danger. This came out even better in his golf, to which he took very wholeheartedly when age began to render cricket more difficult. One unforgettable match I once watched, between him and a retired admiral. Scott played badly, and the admiral ran up to dormy five. Scott became very serious, and won the next hole after a close struggle. The next he won a little more easily. The admiral grew nervous: Scott played more and more steadily. Presently, therefore, they were holes all, and everything depended upon the next, which Scott won against a sadly demoralized opponent. I have never seen a grown man more childishly distressed: the great sailor turned away to hide his emotion, and the pill was all the more bitter because he knew that Scott would have accepted the contrary result with the most cheerful philosophy.

This it was which had made his fortune from the first days of school work. He began under a well-known crammer, who by that time was past his best. Boys and parents took to him so rapidly that he was soon able, with the help of Cambridge cricketing friends who were already somebodies in the world, to set up for himself. For a long time, he was able to outplay most of his pupils at their own games. 'I must get a try,' he said to me at half-time in one Rugby game, 'because So-and-so has got one.' When, at over forty, a quick run had snapped a sinew in his calf, he could still make enough boundary hits to atone for his slowness between the wickets. Later still, when golf and the suddenly revived passion for croquet were his main recreations, he kept the respect of one pupil who afterwards won the Amateur Golf Championship. In 1911, I sat at dinner next to Charrington, to whose lavish generosity the Fitz-william Museum owes such a heavy debt. He said, 'I would give almost anything for that man Scott's imperturbable coolness and quick decision at croquet'.

For all this, however, he had to pay, for the crammer's work is

crushing when he bears the whole responsibility and accepts it.[1]
Work before breakfast, and all through the morning: a hasty lunch;
off on a cycle across the town to the golf links; back to tea and
classes; classes again after dinner, till nine or ten, and finally, very
often, a keen hour or two at bridge. He never tired of chaffing me
for my frequent indigestions. But it would have been better for
him if his digestion had given an occasional sharp warning, instead
of serving silently as the slave of his will. As middle age came on,
he suffered much from gout at night, and had to keep his feet outside
the blankets. Then, toward the end of those strenuous days, came
rheumatic fever, after which he was never quite the same. He finally
decided to retire; but, even so, he accepted the biggest and poorest
parish in Eastbourne, promising the bishop that he would do the
work for five years at least. The war of 1914 came, and I believe
he had to resign a few months before the promised date. I stayed
with him several times during that period, and regretted the enormous
strain. It became almost impossible to get satisfactory curates. One
I remember, irreproachable so far as I know in other ways, was so
ignorant or so daft that, hailing himself from Scotland, and preaching
on St Andrew's Day from Matt. iv, 18–20, he left hearers under the
impression that he was saluting the saint as a fellow-countryman.

Scott's brother, long and happily settled in Canada, sent him
periodical packets of food, and he shared these liberally with the
poor. He suffered without protest (one of the heaviest burdens of
a poor town parish) the habit of calling upon a parson at meal times,
when he can be caught without trouble. At odd times, he went on
with the translation which he had undertaken of Caesarius' *Dialogues*.[2]
Warning symptoms were neglected until a London specialist diag-
nosed serious heart trouble, and prescribed rest as the only alternative to complete and immediate breakdown. The sale of South Lynn,
at however heavy a discount, enabled the Scotts to buy a little villa at
Eastbourne which they could let in the winter while they migrated

---

[1] For a thinly disguised picture of the daily labours of Todhunter, the most
famous of Cambridge mathematical coaches, see Leslie Stephen's rare booklet
Sketches from Cambridge. By a Don.

[2] Caesarius of Heisterbach, *Dialogues*, translated by H. v. E. Scott and C. C. S.
Bland (Broadway Translations, Routledge and Co.). There again, was a primary
thirteenth-century source of exceptional interest, almost entirely ignored by our
University medievalists.

to Meran. But it was too late: one paralytic stroke succeeded another; he worked at Caesarius from his bed, his devoted wife writing for him as long as he could intelligibly pronounce the words; thus he fought on practically to the end. South Lynn, in the post-war slump, became first a girls' school, then a derelict semi-ruin, and was finally pulled down and built over.

But those who knew his past work intimately—folk who were less partial than I, though few could be quite impartial who were in constant touch with him—will agree in recognizing the influence of that straightforward, unpretentious life, boyish in many ways to the last; an influence comparable to that of many gifted Public Schoolmasters at that same time. One very striking example is that of Laurence Oates, who must have been with him five or six years. He came quite young, perhaps at fifteen, an Etonian of rough off-hand manners. Gradually he grew into a sort of honest, great Newfoundland puppy. Hence, again, he developed into a grown-up tame Newfoundland, boisterous but kindly. He was a fine middle-weight boxer: the sergeant-instructor at the drill hall earned his bread, so far as Oates was concerned, with the sweat of his brow. On this account, and by reason of sheer seniority, he was in his later time the recognized cock of the walk. One day, a major came to tea at South Lynn, bringing his son as a pupil. He sported a rather conspicuous headgear, i.e. a brown 'bowler' (alias 'billy-cock'). Oates came in from golf and found this, among other hats, on the table in the entrance hall. His reaction was: 'What fellow has gone and been such a silly ass as to set up a brown billycock?' He kicked it round the hall, and finally thrust his fist through the exploded crown, plunging his arm through to the very brim. At that moment the major and his son emerged into the hall from their interview, shaking hands with Scott. After a few moments of hasty explanation and apology, Scott took the major back for another cup of tea, while Oates cycled down St Anne's Hill at his usual break-neck speed into the town, and reappeared with half a dozen brown billycocks at the Major's choice.

It was edifying to watch, finally, the happy mixture of reverence and camaraderie in Oates' relations with 'the Boss'. I use 'edifying' advisedly, for the character had been built up: Scott was a born character-builder. *Si momumentum requiris,* here is Oates' later history. About a year after the hat business, he had forced his way into the

Army through the unbrainy sidegate of the Militia, and was sub-lieutenant in the Inniskilling Dragoons, in South Africa. A few weeks later, he found himself in command of a small detachment in an outlying trench. Probably he exposed himself incautiously: certainly a Boer sniper hit him and broke his thigh bone. Presently there was a parley, and he was summoned to surrender. His answer was, 'I've come out here to fight, and I haven't had any real fighting yet'. A dozen years later, when Captain R. F. Scott enlisted men for his South Polar Expedition, Oates applied for the job of looking after the Iceland ponies, and got it over the heads of some two hundred and fifty other candidates for that unpaid post. On that fatal expedition his tragic end excited world-wide admiration and pity, and I find that his name is often familiar to men who were not born when he died. Captain R. F. Scott, in almost the last words of his *Journal*, before death froze his own hand, wrote: 'He went out into the blizzard, and we have not seen him since. . . . We knew that poor Oates was walking to his death; but though we tried to dissuade him, we knew it was the act of a brave man and an English gentleman. We all hope to meet the end with a similar spirit, and assuredly the end is not very far.'[1]

The summer holidays of 1897 were mostly spent in Diamond Jubilee rejoicings. There was the Naval Review off Portsmouth, and the Royal Procession in London. Next year, 1898, Scott and I took three weeks abroad together, going by boat, rail, and cycle to the source of the Rhine and back. I recorded this in my first book: a modest little volume which was well reviewed, but, not being advertised, remained mostly on the publisher's shelves.[2] In all the other years we did a great deal of cycling together. At first, we fixed a weekly afternoon for this: but Scott had such various engagements and activities that the rides became sporadic, though always fairly frequent. We were thus able to get a fairly intimate acquaintance with the churches for a considerable radius; for he was a keen antiquarian. A generous parent used to make a point of presenting him with every new expensive Ruskin book that came out; and he also collected a fair number of medieval books for himself. In due course, I fell in with four literary men, and walked with them often by the sea and over the Downs. T. Bailey Saunders

[1] R. F. Scott, *Journal of Last Expedition*, vol. I, pp. 298, 408; vol. II, p. 271.
[2] *Father Rhine* (Galloway and Porter, Cambridge; 2s. 6d.).

was a translator from Goethe and Harnack: he was working now at
a life of Melanchthon which was never completed. W. Williams
was an Oxford man who had gone over to Rome; he was intimate
with Tyrrell and Von Hügel, and had written a book on *Pascal,
Newman and Loisy*. Alfred Ollivant, novelist, had written a best
seller, which he never afterwards overtook, in *Owd Bob*. By far
the greatest of the four was C. M. Doughty, whose *Arabia Deserta*
had just been rescued from shameful neglect, and republished in a
shorter form which took the public by storm. His shaggy red hair
and beard, and far-off eyes, were just what one would have expected
from his book, and on his table lay two black-letter folios in which
he steeped himself from time to time—St Thomas More's *English
Works* and Thomas Cooper's *Latin Dictionary* of 1565. He deplored
my politics, being himself somewhere near Sir Roger de Coverley's
stage of Toryism; but here our respective planes were too distant
for any serious clash. I asked him once what had struck him most in
English social life after his thirteen continuous years among Muslims
in the East. He had in an even more marked form Housman's habit
of turning his eyes sideways without moving his head; and his
answer ran: 'People helping each other with their overcoats. When
I left England, men were outraged by any such offer—"Am I
decrepit, then?" and now it is the correct thing.'

Such, then, was my social atmosphere, added to which was the
fact that, in such a well-known resort as Eastbourne, it was often
possible to catch a momentary glimpse of friends from other days
and other places. For physical atmosphere I enjoyed one of the most
bracing airs in Great Britain, with an abundance of healthy exercise.
My head work was certainly monotonous, though less so than an
outsider might imagine, for with very small classes the very eccentricities of pupils have their own flavour, if only that of vinegar
or mustard. Like many another, I have often repeated to myself
Matthew Arnold's

> Tasks, in hours of insight will'd,
> May be in hours of gloom fulfill'd,

and, again,

> Still nursing the unconquerable hope,
> Still clutching the inviolable shade.

Every morning, at five, I made a good cup of milk coffee and, with the nearest approach to a brioche that Eastbourne could supply, got in a solid two hours of work before breakfast. Then, after my two or three hours of teaching, the rest of the daylight and evening were spent in my own work or healthy exercise. In one sense, I had an advantage then which I had never before enjoyed for any length of time, nor have since until my superannuation at Cambridge. In University work, one uses the same mind muscles, so to speak, both in class and in one's own study. At South Lynn, the class was easy routine—though I may claim to have established by experience a routine successful for my pupils—and it was only in my own room that I needed to exercise serious reflection. Moreover, even there I worked with a rapidly increasing sense of mastery over my material. I now had the categories clear in my mind; fresh facts arranged themselves in a more and more definite order; crystallization kept pace with accumulation. To the present day, one of my most peaceful and harmonious alleys of thought starts from the experiences begun in the first days of my New Life, fortified in the earlier years at South Lynn, and crowned when my St John's Fellowship enabled me to go abroad almost every summer. With advancing age, sleeplessness becomes a more persistent, if not more evident, enemy; and most of us, like Wordsworth, have one or more remedies against it. One of mine is a mental combination of study and of travel. I get into my train at Victoria, the morning train for Switzerland. I have my mid-morning thermos flask and my book, some volume monotonously technical and needing no thought beyond the marking down, one by one, of familiar facts, recurrent in almost every monastic chartulary or monograph, for future sorting and synthesis. I look up from the book to catch the old familiar glimpses—Dulwich playing fields, Tonbridge, the Kentish orchards, Dover Castle. Then the boat; then Calais and the reserved seat for Paris; then Ruskin's Abbeville, Chantilly, supper and bed in Paris; the reserved seat in next morning's train; and so on. To adapt Rousseau's metaphor, I travel through the book and on through France in the same breath, imagining the one and recalling the other, with a quiet monotony which induces sleep. Thus the journey scarcely ever reaches Dijon—seldom, indeed, beyond Fontainebleau—much as one's mind might find to continue the game beyond and beyond.

Concurrently with those more and more specialized studies, I began to publish. I made a little money by articles in monthly reviews, especially *The Contemporary*, but lost a good deal more by printing at my own expense *Father Rhine*, *Public Schools and Public Needs*, *Friar's Lantern*, and *A Strong Army in a Free State*. Critics were generally favourable, but commercially that avails little if the book is never advertised. Yet the last of these was on one of the most burning questions of the day, to which I must come in my next chapter.

CHAPTER XXVIII

A BEE IN THE BONNET

EILEEN POWER—would that I could hope ever again to come under her friendly lash—expressed herself once in a review to the following effect: that the public seeking my honey is somewhat disturbed by the bee which buzzes in my bonnet. I knew then, and know still, that in this there must be a fundamental truth, and a warning not to be neglected. From the pen of critics less friendly, who have their reasons for antagonism, it takes the form that I am preaching my views on two important subjects with damnable iteration. The noun in that phrase is indisputable; the adjective I shall here venture to dispute, or at least to modify. In every generation there have been matters which the general public are irresistibly tempted to ignore, partly through actual lack of information, but far more through indolence, or even through active dislike of inconvenient facts. In such cases, Parliament and Press are often under the subtlest temptations of all, and bear the heaviest guilt for their neglect of the common weal. In times of dangerous self-complacency, a nuisance may be most useful: indeed, it may become useful in proportion to its crying insistence. That is the point of view from which, after many years of reflection, I still venture to defend my own two Bees. I am no longer much concerned about the strictly personal side of the matter; there would be nothing outside the ordinary course of nature if, before this volume appears, the author had faced a stricter examination than that of the English-speaking public. But for my two Bees I am indeed concerned; here, therefore, I deal with the first.

In Chapter xx on Heidelberg, I described my first shock of confrontation with possible military disaster for Britain. The solicitude of my Jewish pacifist friend, and the world-renowned scientist's deliberate forecast (for such in effect it was) impressed me all the more deeply because they came from such different angles. Not long afterwards, again, I had an equally impressive object lesson from the Swiss citizen militia. I remember exactly neither the year nor the particular village in which my knapsack pilgrimage gave me an intimate glimpse of these men on their autumn manœuvres. I was equally impressed by their commonness and their efficiency. In shabby uniforms, bearded or clean-shaven, clodhoppers or counter-jumpers, carpenters or smiths, the plebeian character of the mass was rendered all the more conspicuous by the small sprinkling of privates in whom one would surmise some black-coated occupation. Even among the higher officers, some spoke rather patois than the French of France or the German of Germany; and the sergeants were of the rough-hewn type of Alpine guides, or Berlin droschke-drivers. They paraded with the minimum of goose-step formalities; but it was admirable to see them advance and take cover, in alternate stages, over their own rough ground under the imaginary fire of an entrenched enemy. I had been in the Felsted Cadet Corps, and learned very little except from half a dozen afternoons at the butts. My father and Rick were both volunteers for a time, but not for long. At Cambridge, from the rather contemptuous undergraduate stand-point, I had supinely watched and criticized the University Volun-teer Corps, with its superabundance of leather and prunella. Here in Switzerland, at last, I recognized something which was not only what our volunteering professed to be, but a great deal more besides. With us, I had seen a veneer of patriotism with little serious founda-tion: in Switzerland, where the superficial traveller might see only a nation of cringing innkeepers and obsequious waiters, the true foundation was evidently that of a nation in arms.

Then came the Boer War, with its rude awakening, and its revelations of almost incredible stupidity or neglect. This particular war had been threatening for months—even years—yet no serious preparations had been made by the War Office. Things began to go badly, and the Government had to face serious criticism in Parliament. Their excuse was that all British wars, proverbially, have begun badly. There was a deficit of 30,000 men in the militia: this the Secretary for War excused on the plea that 'for many years past' it had never been up to full strength. The Under-Secretary for War comforted the Commons with a tale of how Bermuda was once left with a store of only three cannon balls, so that if the Spaniards had fought us for only five minutes they must have taken that valuable British colony; after which he exclaimed triumphantly, 'That is the way we muddled along in the old days!'[1] We were told to keep calm: the War Office pledged its word that 'the outbreak of war would never again find this country with so small a reserve of stores and munitions of war'. And, worst of all, the nation as a whole accepted those excuses and promises. The people at large were, in fact, almost as responsible as the leaders. The vast majority had not wished to learn the truth. Therefore all the discussions in Parliament degenerated into mere exhibition sparring. How could one guilty party be expected to expose another equally guilty, for the edification of a scarcely less guilty nation?

There was, of course, an immediate call for volunteers, and a fine response. Most of the young men who, under Milner, did afterwards such excellent work for Africa and the Dominions in general, were men who left their fruitful and promising work in Britain to fight for our cause overseas. Lionel Curtis was a type of the best of them: another has left a valuable legacy to the future historian in his little autobiographical volume.[2] Everywhere older men were joining or re-joining the Volunteers at home; and at South Lynn practically the whole community gave in their names. We were made into a squad of Garrison Artillery: for there were one or two hopelessly antiquated forts in the neighbourhood, and an imposing drill hall in the centre of the town.

The inner story of this squad of ours, if each survivor recorded his quota of memories, would be stranger than fiction. The War Office sent us down a 'Woolwich Infant', an obsolete muzzle-loading gun of many tons in weight, which broke through the surface of the road (although the weather was quite fine) as it was being towed with immense efforts to the drill hall. A month or two later, this unmanageable museum-specimen was dragged back to the station and returned to its native Woolwich. Then came a battery of much smaller guns, but still muzzle-loaders. When I told this a few months later to Colonel Camille Favre, military correspondent of the *Journal de Genève*, he replied that no muzzle-loading cannon had been seen in Switzerland, outside the museums, since 1871. With these silly toys we played for a few months, under rapidly growing

[1] The facts I give here were printed in my pamphlet, *A Strong Army in a Free State*, and never to my knowledge contested.
[2] *Religio Militis*, by Austin Hopkinson, M.P.

indifference. No doubt we should not have been a model Garrison Artillery unit in any case; but the authorities fooled us to the top of our bent. They not only excused slackness but encouraged it: it might almost be said that they imposed negligence upon us. Our sergeant-major was a lazy and cynical old veteran, a survival from almost Indian Mutiny days. We had, of course, to put in a certain quota of drills in order to be classed as 'efficient' and earn the Government grant. When we held a Church Parade, which with its accompanying march to and fro occupied the better part of two hours, he seized the opportunity to count this as two drills towards our efficiency. After some months, we were reviewed by the local colonel, side by side with another unit drawn from the townsfolk in general. Those, so far as I remember, did at least acquit themselves tolerably in elementary manœuvres. They had certainly one very enthusiastic and efficient non-commissioned officer, a working cabinet-maker, with whom I often discussed these matters later on. But here were we of South Lynn with our own gun, the most ignorant of novices; and I, to my horror, was appointed 'No. 1', in virtue of seniority in age, to give orders and guide the proceedings. To say that it was the most ghastly failure I can remember from my whole life is scarcely to say enough; I knew that our young lieutenant's outspoken curses were thoroughly deserved; and so did the boys. I cannot remember that we ever played any more with that gun: but we did practise pretty regularly with rifle-shooting at a miniature range in the drill hall.

Scott was as seriously disgusted with all this as I was; and he welcomed my proposal to go and make searching enquiries in Switzerland. I went off for a week, having meanwhile collected introductions to several leading Switzers, who passed me on to others, so that I was able to get considered opinions from many persons of recognized position, including the Leader of the National Radical Party in the National Council, the Labour Secretary, five officers, four clergymen (three of them army chaplains), four University professors, the editors of a Social-Democratic and a Conservative newspaper, two bankers, two other business men, and the Headmaster of a school. They not only gave me freely of their time, but revised my proofs for publication. Representing very various political, and even social, shades, they assured me unanimously that there was practically no dispute in Switzerland concerning either the necessity of compulsory service in the Citizen Militia, or the general efficiency of that body. There was no serious complaint that this compulsion 'militarized' the nation. The only nucleus of any party which would welcome its abolition was among the thorough-going pacifists, resting upon the immorality of war in any form. These were, at most, not more than 1 per cent of the whole population. The Labour Party thoroughly accepted universal compulsion as the only logical principle for true democracy. Employers, on the other hand, welcomed it as rendering workmen more intelligent and efficient in team work. The physical benefit was so great that, if for any conceivable reason the Militia should be abolished, it would be necessary to invent some substitute in the interests of national health. The great majority of parents had no anxieties about the few weeks of barrack life, beyond those inseparable from the recruit's age and his first entry into the world. It engendered a healthy camaraderie and mingling of classes. Monsieur Ami Simond, who had been French Master at King's College School and St Paul's School in London, put this to me most plainly. He said, 'Here at Yverdon there is a railway porter whom I always look out for at the station, and he for me. We shared a tent together in our recruit course. This system does, for our whole population, what your Public Schools do for only a small fraction of yours.' The short period of disciplinary co-operation, so far from weakening independence of character, tends in Switzerland rather to make the individual more resourceful and self-reliant. So far from wearying the citizen, this Militia commands a general popularity which few other national institutions can boast. That point is susceptible of the plainest statistical proof. For there is three times as much *voluntary* rifle practice in Switzerland, in addition to the compulsory minimum, as in Britain—in proportion to population, of course. In the schools, again, there is far more of voluntary drill and gymnastics than with us. Finally, every Swiss officer is practically a volunteer for much harder work than the private's. It is true, no man may legally refuse promotion; but nothing could be easier than to do one's military job in an average perfunctory fashion which would avoid all idea of promotion. Yet the officers in Switzerland, taken alone and apart from the privates, form a larger proportion of the national population than the whole body of our Territorials in Britain. Reckoning a man's whole service up to the age of thirty-three, the private does from 103 to 145 days, the sergeant 206 to 222, the lieutenant 333, and the captain 488; major and colonel proportionately more. All these figures have probably been raised a little in the last quarter of a century, but not enough to affect this argument.

The pamphlet was well reviewed and excited a mild interest among a few people: perhaps I recouped £2 or £3 out of the £40 it had cost me, including my travelling expenses. But the general effect was exactly hit off by the postcard on which my friend H. W. Fowler acknowledged receipt: 'Capital; most convincing; by which of course I don't mean that it will ever convince anybody of anything.'

Then the National Service League was started, under the presidency of Lord Roberts, who devoted the remaining dozen years of his life to this 'stunt', as unfriendly critics called it. I joined it at once, and did a good deal of speaking and writing for it. Nearly all my fellow-Liberals, unfortunately, treated it as a Party question, and the few of us who tried to explain that our proposal had the authority of such epoch-making Liberal thinkers as Adam Smith and J. S. Mill were treated as disguised Tories. Later, when Professor J. A. Cramb died, I wrote articles and speeches for Lord Roberts, putting his points into literary form and receiving his imprimatur. Once I was called up to London on short notice to write half the night at Roberts' article in reply to that of the future Lord Snowden in *The Morning Post*.[1] I was at work upon the 'star' speech which he was advertised to make at Oxford in the summer of 1914; but first the sudden threat of civil war in Ireland diverted him, and next, a few weeks later, the Great War. Then he at once suspended the activities of his League in order to avoid the least competition with voluntary recruiting. Finally, during the War itself, conscription arrived tardily in a far more drastic form.

Meanwhile, in the spring of that fateful year 1914, Mr Asquith consented to receive a deputation headed by Lord Roberts on that matter. There were about a dozen of us, each to spend five minutes on one aspect of the question. My task was to cite Adam Smith and

[1] February 6, 1914, in answer to Snowden's of February 3. I reprinted a couple of pages in *The Case for Compulsory Military Service* (pp. 288 ff.).

J. S. Mill, with the whole mass of contemporary Continental Radicals and Socialists, and to ask what excuse there could be for condemning the belief in democratic compulsion as incompatible with true Liberalism in Britain. Asquith's answer was moderate and encouraging: 'Home defence is a common interest to all parties, and whatever can be proved to be essential to that purpose ought to be universally accepted as being beyond the region of party controversy. . . . The more this matter is discussed, and the more public opinion can be brought to bear upon the aspects which you have put to me to-day, the greater will be the advantage to the community, both from the point of view of safety and of educational and social problems.' Yet the editorials in the *Westminster Gazette* of April 27, 1914 and *The Morning Post* of April 28 ran: 'If ever this question becomes practical politics, the Liberal Party will be as solid for the voluntary principle as it is for Free Trade.' And in the *Nation* (March 11, 1914, p. 286) a correspondent wrote: 'If there was an article in the Liberal creed which was sacrosanct [until this War broke out], it was that which anathematized conscription.' This die-hard attitude, with the similar attitude towards the Free Trade issue, opened my eyes to the fundamental weakness of my own political Party. In 1906, I found it arguing: 'Free Trade versus Protection is an issue which was settled finally forty years ago: we will not even discuss the question now'. A Party which refuses even to consider new arguments in a new generation is doomed as a Party of Progress; therefore open-minded Liberalism has naturally drifted leftwards and become increasingly Labourist. Nobody has better typified this fundamentally illiberal Liberalism than Sir John Simon. He quitted the Government in 1916, when it came to conscripting the whole population; yet, while within that Government, he had been partly responsible for one of the most odious and illiberal forms of compulsion ever suggested: for a Bill to the effect that the painful lack of volunteers should be made good by conscripting boys of eighteen and time-expired Regulars, and by violating the express contract under which the Territorials had enlisted![1]

Mr Asquith, at that interview of April 27, 1914, partly confessed the weakness of our Territorials, upon whom the country relied

[1] See Lord Derby's public account (*Observer*, January 16, 1916).

for Home Defence. They were, nominally, 315,000 volunteers properly drilled and armed, and exercised in a fortnightly camp every year. In fact, 49,000 of this nominal establishment was non-existent. Of the 266,000 existing men, 40 per cent had not passed the absurdly lenient test in rifle practice, and 80,000 had not done their full fortnight in camp. Out of the nominal 4,725,000 days of camp for the whole force, only about 2,237,000 had been actually done. Yet Mr Asquith could find it in his conscience to end his survey with 'That is not bad!' and the British Democracy hypocritically accepted his soporific doses as, in these last years, they have accepted them from Lord Baldwin and Mr Neville Chamberlain.

I had spent my Easter vacation of that year (1914) in France and Belgium, interviewing representative socialists. In France, Jaurès was too busy with election work; but he passed me on to his understudy, Albert Thomas, afterwards Minister of Munitions and, later still, Secretary of the International Labour Bureau at Geneva. In both countries I found hearty sympathy for my propaganda. In Belgium I found the exact opposite of our British conditions; it was the Radicals who insisted upon conscription, while the Conservatives fought tooth and nail against it. In the summer, again, I continued these researches in France and Switzerland. At Geneva, the Socialist leader was Jean Sigg. He had done some months in gaol as a 'réfractaire', for his refusal to turn out with a battalion which had been mobilized in 1898, to keep order in the streets during a great strike confessedly aimed at paralysing the whole commercial life of the city by tumultuous processions.[1] Yet he told me frankly: 'I have nothing to say against our national militia system as such. What is more, I can give you a strong point in its favour. It has practically destroyed illiteracy in Switzerland.' For all recruits are examined mentally as well as physically; this casts the fullest searchlight upon the schools; therefore Switzerland has now no illiterates but the mentally deficient. At Berne the leader was Grimm, who went to Russia during the War, and was the main catspaw through which the Germans worked, leaving him free to invite Lenin and start that Revolution which gave Russia into the Kaiser's hands at Brest-Litovsk. Grimm could not say that he saw

[1] For the full story, see my *Strong Army, &c.* p. 43.

any possibility for his own country except in a People's Army: but
he assured me that I was taking useless pains so far as Britain was
concerned. 'For there are, in the German army, two million
Socialists. If ever Germany attacked your country, except in the
most plainly just cause, those men would refuse to march.' 'Why,
then, did Bebel and Liebknecht, their two main Socialist leaders,
say the exact opposite, that they would do all they could to avoid
war; but, when once it came, they would be found fighting with
the rest?' 'Oh, Bebel and Liebknecht just spoke for themselves:
mark my words; I know how things really are!'

Then came the Great War, which (Mr Lloyd George now be-
latedly tells us) would probably never have happened at all, and
would certainly have been enormously shortened, if Britain had
adopted the Swiss system in the crucial years of friction which preceded it.[1] Yet the Liberal Party as a whole still clung to its old
stale shibboleth. As I first remembered Liberalism, under Gladstone,
nobody could have denied it the vigour of a healthy vertebrate; in
these years since the Great War it has grown more and more
crustacean.

At last, in 1916, I got leave with difficulty to visit Paris on my
own account to persuade the Socialists to tell their Labour brethren
of Britain, publicly, the same plain truths which they had made no
difficulty about telling me. Incidentally, I was arrested as a spy
just outside Kensington High Street station, and compelled my
'arrester' to come to the police station hard by, when ten minutes
settled the affair. In Paris, I saw the editor of *L'Humanité*, and
other socialists. We listened together to the M.P.s Stubbs and
Roberts, who had come over as a Labour Deputation to assure a
large audience of representative Frenchmen that Britain meant business. Stubbs, an honest but thoroughly stupid man, explained how
John Bull was indeed slow, but the most tenacious animal in creation.
The official interpreter translated him sentence by sentence; and
when it came to this metaphor of the bulldog, it was painful to
note men's ridicule and disgust for the boasted tenacity of a hound

[1] Lloyd George, *War Memories*, I, 35–40. Mr Austen Chamberlain agreed
with him in that year 1910 (*Daily Telegraph*, November 12, 1936) and Mr Lloyd
George, recounting the unwillingness of other Ministers to join this 'settlement
of our national problem', brands it as 'the Great Refusal'.

which was inventing every possible excuse for not making adequate use of his teeth.

After Versailles, Britain and America were swept by a wave of pacifism which, under much true idealism, was yet in 'the main no more than war weariness: just the cold fit of our military ague. *Corruptio optimi pessima*: 'lilies that fester smell far worse than weeds': and there has always been a festering mass of unreality underneath the noble ideal of complete peace which allured Britain and the Democracies. That ideal soon became a happy hunting-ground for the preacher, the journalist and the political agitator. All three, doubtless, are indispensable to society, but all alike are tempted to that unbalanced rhetoric which intoxicates not only the audience but the speaker himself, making him think he thinks that which, when the pinch comes, neither he nor they would ever translate into action. Most of us have attended one mass meeting at least, where some perspiring orator worked himself up before a perspiring audience, who finally did nothing but sign some scrap of paper which is now in the wastepaper basket.

Lest I should seem to write uncharitably of those unrealities, here is an experience which I did my best to render decisive. The most characteristic manifestation of such passivism—for it was no true pacifism—was the 'Peace Pledge Union', in which enormous numbers signed a promise never to fight in any war whatever. It claimed to be such a world movement as Christianity had been in its earliest stages, but most absurdly. For the early Christian pledged himself primarily to a life of the strictest morality and personal self-denial. Again, he gloried in the title of Christian among a world in which that mere name might cost him his life, or imprisonment at least. This Union, on the other hand, required nothing more than the cheap promise not to do what scarcely any sane man ever wishes to do except under extreme necessity. It implied no other moral code whatever. So far from endangering the signer's life, it offered the most obvious escape from such suffering or violent death as might fall to the lot of the ordinary unsigning citizen. In short, it was as convenient to the slacker or the coward as to the most lofty idealist. Pacifism thus organized is not, in any true sense, organized at all: it is an easy prey for the militarist, who, with all his faults, does at least organize in earnest and demand the utmost exertion and courage from all his followers. Nothing better deserves the common phrase 'cheap and nasty' than cheap idealism.

I put this to a practical test about four years ago, when war was already on the horizon. I chose the three organs most likely to afford information on this particular question: the London *Times*, the *Manchester Guardian*, and *Time and Tide*, which struggles to rise above party. In each I wrote to the following effect:

There are in Great Britain at least 100,000 educated people who tell us that all war is murder, and therefore, in strict logic, the soldier is a potential murderer. Of that number, at least 10,000 have thought the matter over deliberately, and will maintain their thesis against all comers. Out of those 10,000, how many are there who can fulfil the test of Descartes, 'To get at the truth, we must look rather to men's actions than to their words'? What Pacifist has yet put his theory into practice? Which of them has said: 'My taxes go partly to hire murderers; I will protest by refusing to pay taxes so long as this national iniquity is practised'? It was through 'Quixotic' protests of that kind that early Christianity conquered the world: yet how many Pacifists have ever shown this courage of their opinions?

My letters attracted few answers; and not one of these supplied a single instance of what I sought; moreover two, at least, frankly confessed this weakness in their position. One correspondent did indeed refer me to the International Voluntary Service for Peace. I at once paid my subscription, and found that this was organized to collect and employ volunteers for beneficent peace services, just as the Territorials collect volunteers for National Defence. I asked for statistics as to the number of man hours this Service could claim for the draining of waste land, removal of rubbish, helping aged folk to till their allotments, and similar philanthropic work for which its members were recruited. No such figures were available at the time; and those which were supplied to me after some delay, for the whole of this International Society, were not for a moment comparable with the man-hours of work put in by the Territorials in one of the smallest of our counties. I pointed this out to the Secretary; and he could only plead that his organization struggled at a hopeless disadvantage with any other which had the meretricious attractions of drum, bugle, and uniform! Another gentleman wrote to me privately, describing himself as a Quaker lecturer who for four years had refused to pay taxes to a budget which spent money on the Army. He rehearsed in detail what this refusal had cost him, in cash and in inconvenience: the whole total was insignificant in comparison with what a soldier suffers in the trenches.

'Like master, like man', and I must now write equally frankly about my experiences with some of the most prominent Pacifist leaders, especially since one of them is not only alive, but has the *entrée* of any journal in the English-speaking world. Those who thus intoxicated and demoralized the multitude have too often, in the process, intoxicated and demoralized themselves. I write from forty years' experience of such discussions; and, the other day, I found my personal experience supported by a man who, throughout a lifetime of controversy, remained a pattern of intellectual honesty: viz. Thomas Huxley. A. J. Ashton, Recorder of Bristol, has recalled in his Memoirs a conversation in Jowett's rooms, apparently about 1878. He writes: 'Someone—I think Mr Goschen—had been talking about women's rights, with that pleasant flow of easy platitude which in those days also was not unknown to distinguished statesmen. Huxley listened, and suddenly said: "I have served on two Royal Commissions relating to women, one the disagreeable one", with an apologetic look at Jowett, "and my experience is that no witness is so dishonest as a really good woman with a cause to serve." Jowett blinked as if he didn't quite like it, but at any rate the conversation became animated.'[1]

It is not only that an enthusiast is tempted by the dazzling nobility of his cause to shut his eyes to the actual means—'blind with sight', to quote Browning's phrase. He has also his meaner personal temptations. To confess error is humiliating, and the more popular an orator or journalist, the more easily can he manage to shirk cross-examination. Here, then, are some of the literary dishonesties, on points of great importance, which I have encountered and exposed in these past years. I gave many details in my two main volumes, which, though now out of print, may be found in large libraries: both, for instance, are here in the University Library at Toronto

---

[1] *As I went on my Way* (1924), p. 44.

and one in the City Library.[1] I took care, in every case, to send these exposures to the persons concerned, offering full acknowledgement of any errors of fact which they might prove on my part. On one other case, in some ways most significant of all, I am silent here because the person is dead and I destroyed the relevant letters, with many other papers, on the eve of leaving Cambridge for Toronto. But I must here name—for the more these things are published the more chance we have of creating a higher standard of morality in controversy—Mr Fred Maddison, ex-M.P., Secretary to the International Arbitration League, Dr Starr Jordan, Chancellor of Leland Stanford University, and Sir Norman Angell. I have tried repeatedly, but vainly, to persuade the last of these to discuss with me, either on the platform or in a volume where each could cross-question the other and leave the public to judge, some of the most important of his contentions, and the most glaring of his perverse appeals to books which, evidently, he had not himself read when he called them into court. In *The Nineteenth Century and After* (October, 1914, p. 915), after dealing with those three, and incidentally with the unfairness even of the exceptionally honourable *Manchester Guardian* in matters where pacifism was at stake, I concluded:

I have purposely chosen here the most prominent among these men who do evil that peace may ensue. The root of this war difficulty is not only war itself, but also those thousand injustices upon which war is based, and which make some men rush to war as an actual relief. Let me acknowledge again the great service Mr Angell has done by bringing the man in the street to face the possibility that even successful war may not 'pay'. But how shall he really convince the world, until he has proved equally conclusively that there is no salvation in untruth and injustice, which lie at the root of war? The writings of professional pacifists do not really commend their cause. Religion is a noble thing; but the religious tract has too often made itself a byword. Pacificism is a noble ideal; but the first step towards its realisation must surely be this; that its advocates should consistently manifest at least that moral courage which we expect from men of lower professions. . . . Germans see this very clearly; and

---

[1] *The Case for Compulsory Service* (Macmillan, 1917) and *The Main Illusions of Pacificism* (Bowes and Bowes, 1916). See also *The Nineteenth Century and After* for October, 1914, *The Eugenics Review*, vol. 5, 1913–14, p. 201; vol. 7, 1915–16, p. 287.

that curious medley which disciples call 'Angellism' has been responsible for a good deal of very dangerous German contempt. However illegitimate the deduction may have been, it was only natural that Germany should have suspected cowardice and wilful self-deception in a population which rules its everyday business dealings by strict common-sense, but which will swallow the commonest nonsense rather than face the one root-problem of national defence. In a few months there may be room again for an 'Angellism' under cover of which real peace would be gambled away for false peace; and we shall then need to remember that outspoken word of the great Nonconformist R. W. Dale: 'I believe in peace—true peace—at any price; in peace, even at the price of war.'[1]

This democratic Citizen Militia question is important not only from the military point of view: even more so, perhaps, from the social. It would strongly assist the class fusion which, as so many of us hope, will supplant class war when the Democracies become masters again in their own house. It will, again, do a great deal for the political education of Labour, which hitherto has too often acted in appalling ignorance of Continental democratic conditions, under black-coat leaders who have found their own profit in fostering such ignorance. A nation in which every man had a chance of testing his fellows' qualities on the threshold of manhood and beyond, would be a nation less likely to be duped by mere demagogy. It would anticipate more solid help in Parliament from the man who had earned promotion in practical team work for the Militia, than from one whose words had borne little fruit in action. Again, the Swiss Militia is of immense service for police duty on the railway stations and in similar places; we find there that combination which did so much for the prosperity and the liberties of England in the past, when every man was at the same time his own soldier and his own policeman.

Lastly, it would elicit the healthiest social teaching from what is now almost a social sore. On the one hand, conscientious objectors are often serious and most estimable citizens; but, on the other, present conditions lead them to escape public service to an extent which the best of them must feel regrettable. When the crisis comes, we find that they are only about 10 per cent of the total population.

---

[1] *Life*, by his son A. W. W. Dale, 1898, pp. 162–3 and 266–74.

How are we, then, to prevent one man from sheltering his own life and his own wages at the expense of the other nine who must thus bear an extra share?

Under a law of Compulsory Manhood Service the problem would seem easy enough. No State would wish to put those utterly un-willing men into the field. But the State could very easily enact that all conscientious objectors should register themselves as such in peace time, from the time when their conscience first speaks to them, and that any such plea made less than a year before outbreak of war, or declaration of national emergency, should be as invalid as a gift between living persons is when made within view of death.[1]

All high-minded Objectors ought indeed to welcome such regis-tration. It would put them in a definite moral category, almost as definite as that of Minister of Religion. They would not be deterred by the fact that the State might take advantage of such registration to impose an equitable tax equivalent to the six months of drill which all the rest do in their absence; nor, again, by the civilian social work which would be prescribed to them while others were risking their lives. Least of all would they be deterred by nicknames and social prejudices, any more than the Quakers were. They would welcome all this, as bringing them at least some way towards that parallel of the Early Christians which, at present, some of them so vainly claim. And, to the rest of the world, this could hardly fail to prove an epoch-making experiment. Suppose that, at the present moment, some miraculously gifted psychologist could invent a mechanical test by which the quality of conscientious objection to war could be segregated from other qualities. We should then be able to test, roughly at least, how far it commonly exists in con-nection with superior moral courage, superior truthfulness and

---

[1] A friend objects here: 'Surely this would be unfair? How about perfectly genuine objectors whose conscience has not spoken to them before?' My feeling is, that such an exception is scarcely conceivable in any State in which Compulsory Military Service should be the rule. A lad could not grow up to eighteen without knowing what would then be demanded of him; and he who had never faced that legal obligation and decided in his own mind would be no more worthy of exceptional indulgence than one who had ignored any other notorious law of his country. The thoughtless pacifist, from my point of view, is a real danger to his own cause and to society in general.

common-sense, superior unselfishness and self-sacrifice. In brief, we should see whether, and to what extent, the conscientious objector's class of mind makes for good citizenship in general. Any scientist who could invent laboratory tests of that kind would go down to posterity with Darwin and Pasteur. Pacifists ought to seize such an occasion for showing themselves lifelong professional soldiers of peace, clearly distinguishable in civic virtues from the soldiers of war, by characteristics which the social scientist could tabulate, and even the general public would tacitly recognize.

Let it not be said that we have in this chapter that sort of 'cold controversy' which Huxley so wittily and justly deplored. Whatever faults of manner the reader may find here, the matter itself is almost more vitally important at the present moment than ever. If the Democracies of the world find themselves in their present ditch, that is because they have supinely trusted to blind leaders, and have not insisted upon testing for themselves the unreal plausibilities which flattered their ease. What is worse, these plausibilities are constantly preached still: very few are the pacifists who have confessed so publicly and emphatically as Bertrand Russell their miscalculations of the past twenty years. Taking English-speaking countries as a whole, even at the present moment, scarcely one educated man in ten realizes that, for the last hundred years at least, the European democracies have favoured the principle of Compulsory Service for the whole able-bodied population, and have too often been led to doubt the courage or patriotism of Voluntarist Britain. Quite typical is that sentence from the standard book of reference for cultivated Frenchmen, *La grande Encyclopédie* (article 'Armée', p. 1104): Britain has not adopted the compulsory principle because 'the English, more than any other nation, treat money as the sinew of war; hence their incoherent and anti-democratic system of enlistment'. Again in 1900, when the German Reichstag debated the Navy Bill, the Free Conservative leader 'dissented from Herr Richter's anticipation that Universal Service would be adopted in England. That country was ruled by the Stock Exchange, and so long as this was the case there could be no question of Universal Service.' In the world in which we live, the appearance of weakness is often almost as fatal as weakness or cowardice themselves. When we get at last that Peace for which we hope, our danger for the following generation will be scarcely less subtle and fateful than it has been during the past quarter of a century.

Let me end here as I ended first in 1916, when victory was still uncertain in what we then called 'The Great War'; and again in 1917, when the uncertainty was increasing, and the so-called Union of Democratic Control was exploiting the friction over Conscription as a further lever for its plea of 'Trust the German nation; make terms with them at once, and put an end to all this butchery',[1] I wrote:

Let us be honest with ourselves. How many of us would be willing to expose our personal savings or our means of livelihood to the same risks which the U.D.C. wishes us to face as a nation? or, if we could face the risk for ourselves, who would face it for his wife and children also? Is it not enough, for the next few years at least, to take one solid step in advance? Would not this be thoroughly consonant with our national traditions, and has it not been our main lesson to the world? If, after this war, we could show the first example in modern history of a great nation coveting nothing more, yet fearing for nothing that it possesses—too well defended to encourage any hopes of robbery, yet too self-controlled to fall into temptations of robbery—would not that be a glorious achievement for one generation? Men say now that seventeenth-century Britain, seeking her own salvation, supplied the model of constitutional government for the civilized world. Let them say that Britain of the twentieth century, with the same inspired common-sense, laid the foundations of the United States of Europe by the unaggressive measures which she took to protect herself and her children. Such measures would not discourage idealism; they would, on the contrary, supply a firm practical foundation for all higher ideals of peace; the sort of practical foundation which would save an idealist like Mr Bertrand Russell from imagining that Belgium might have avoided the horrors of war by letting Germany loose upon France.

Reading this passage again after exactly a quarter of a century, I ask myself what single word the march of events can compel me to erase, or even to soften.

[1] *The Main Illusions of Pacificism*, p. 293; *The Case for Compulsory Military Service*, p. 299.

CHAPTER XXIX

WINTER SPORT

UNCLE ROBERT CAMPBELL was a collateral descendant of the poet Thomas Campbell, and his brother Lewis was Professor of Greek at St Andrews. The Professor's edition of *Oedipus Tyrannus* I had read at Felsted with as much appreciation as I was capable of at that age. With the poet I was on more cordial, if not so intimate, terms. For one of the extracts which most impressed me in *The Thousand and One Gems* was his 'Last Man': a poem in which I still find, rightly or wrongly, healthy vigour and inspiring idealism:

> All worldly shapes shall melt in gloom,
>> The Sun himself must die,
> Before this mortal shall assume
>> Its immortality!
> I saw a vision in my sleep
> That gave my spirit strength to sweep
>> Adown the gulf of Time!
> I saw the last of human mould,
> That shall Creation's death behold,
>> As Adam saw her prime!

Later on, when I began to listen more attentively to my father, I heard him more than once quote a stanza from Campbell's *Farewell to Love*, written at the age of fifty-three, in 1830:

> Hail! welcome tide of life, when no tumultuous billows roll,
> How wondrous to myself appears this halcyon calm of soul!
> The wearied bird blown o'er the deep would sooner quit its shore,
> Than I would cross the gulf again that time has brought me o'er.

It seemed to me that he quoted that stanza with the same lingering personal sentiment that he had retained for a few old-fashioned songs.

That, then, was Uncle Robert Campbell's collateral ancestor. Yet here I am premature; for Robert is not my uncle at the beginning of this chapter, though he will be before the end. It is, indeed, one of the most curious chances of my life that I ever met him at all. Even more interesting to me than his ancestry was his Cambridge career. He was exactly contemporary at Trinity Hall with Leslie Stephen, whom he beat by six places in the Mathematical Tripos of 1854. By good fortune, however, there were two vacant Fellowships that year: otherwise the College might have lost one of its brightest ornaments. Campbell himself was a barrister and legal author of note; and he always kept up friendship not only with Stephen, but also with Maitland and Pollock and many other 'Sunday' Tramps'.[1] He always reminded me of Sergeant Lankin in *The Kickleburys on the Rhine*, in so far as Thackeray draws his friend distinctly.

After some years at Eastbourne I had attempted trial flights into University Extension lecturing. Scott's generosity gave me great freedom; I might sometimes absent myself for several successive days, and make up for it by double or treble work on other days at South Lynn. In the autumn of 1902 there came a sudden flood; I was engaged to lecture on 'Chaucer and his England' at three Devonshire towns, with my headquarters at Exeter. This divided my week equally between south and west, for I was lecturing simultaneously at Eastbourne. The journey was always touch and go: a before-breakfast train from Exeter brought me just in time for my three o'clock lecture at Eastbourne. Once, however, my otherwise irreproachable landlady at Exeter omitted to wake me, and as I opened my eyes my watch showed the exact moment of my train's departure! My lodgings were on Haldon Terrace, a good quarter of a mile from the station, but, fortunately, down hill. By equal luck, I had left my things ready packed, and in a kit bag; so there was no need formally to close it; only to grasp the two handles and away. Luckily again, my watch was in fact five minutes *slow*; thus, even as I stepped out of bed, the engine ought to have been uttering its first puff, and the race would have been hopeless had I known the truth; as it was, however, there seemed just a sporting chance. Again, though the train was made up at Exeter itself, which generally means a punctual start, yet on this morning it was a few minutes late. Most fortunate of all, the engine driver was a real sportsman.

[1] For this Society, see F. W. Maitland's *Life of Leslie Stephen*, chapter XVII and p. 500.

He saw me and my bag tumbling down the last precipitous hundred yards of short cut to the station, and held his hand until we were in. I had pulled trousers over my pyjamas; over all was a very long Inverness cape in which alone I might claim to resemble the late Mr G. K. Chesterton. But under such a shelter one can coil up decently in a not too crowded compartment; and opposite Paddington there is a haberdashery establishment ready for any emergency. All's well that ends well; and my main reaction was one of gratitude for the healthy elasticity of our British railway system. For in old days at Mannheim, after an evening at the Opera, the guard of the last night train had seen a lady emerge with us others upon the platform, and run towards him. He raised his eyes to the clock; the fatal hand was at the exact hour; he put the whistle to his lips, and had scarcely finished the blast when we were almost near enough to have boarded the carriage if it had not been already in motion.

The twelve lectures at Exeter, with twelve each at Plymouth (where I stayed with the Chairman of the University Extension Committee, F. H. Colson), and Torquay, and six at Eastbourne, brought in £96, clear of travelling expenses. The engagement was to last through the Spring Term also; so I was in unusual affluence.[1] Then came a letter from Ernest Owen, my old friend of Felsted and Malvern Wells, suggesting a winter holiday. By this time, he had long deserted his vigorous football and become engrossed in the old man's pastime of curling, at which he aspired to high honours. The future Sir Henry Lunn was offering mass excursions at a seductively moderate price: a fortnight, I think, for £20 first class from London to London. His chosen snow fields and ice fields were at Adelboden, near the Lake of Thun. His trains went weekly, and one was to start upon Boxing Day. A week or so before that date, when we both had our tickets, Owen wired that he had influenza, and must call off altogether. My first impulse was to change completely, and take the alternative fortnight in Italy which this Lunn scheme offered. But, on consulting his printed list of the Adelboden company, I saw that it included

[1] By the kindness of Mr G. F. Hickson, Secretary to the Board of Extra-Mural Studies at Cambridge, I am able to give full figures for all my work under that Board: such records are often of value to later generations. In the fourteen years from beginning to end (1902–16), I gave 175 lectures, eight different courses, and received, apart from travelling expenses, an aggregate of £385. 5s.

two of my former pupils. Murray was there, the Sherborne Fifth-Form boy who had delighted me by finding French prose even harder to write well than Latin. He was half-brother to the present Headmaster of Eton: and in the Army, when taken prisoner by the Boers, he had beguiled his captivity at Pretoria by re-writing Tacitus' *Annals* from memory in the best Latin he could muster. Again, there was Alick Lawrence, grandson to Sir Henry of Lucknow fame: 'Here lies Henry Lawrence, who tried to do his duty.' He was at Sedbergh in my day: and, as he was a nephew of Mrs Hart, we had seen a good deal of each other, and even corresponded recently about my *Public Schools* and my pet subject of the Swiss Militia. Those names decided me; these two men were already there; I should see their welcome faces in any case, and, with luck, other congenial visitors.

We had a hearty Pentney Christmas dinner at midday, and I found a modest hotel for the night in Broad Street, at convenient distance from Holborn Viaduct station. In the light of what happened afterwards, I have an unusually clear recollection of minute incidents on that journey. For one thing, never before or since have I started from that particular station for the Continent.

I had the initial comfort of a first-class compartment all to myself; for, after a strenuous combination of lectures and cramming, I was greedy for such rest as could be bought with a little extravagance upon the ticket. Next, I remember that momentary glimpse of St Paul's from Ludgate Viaduct, almost as though one could touch the dome with one's hand. Then, in Southwark, the site of Shakespeare's old playhouse within a stone's throw of the railway. Next, Loughborough Junction, where I had often got out on the way home from the British Museum to Dulwich, in order to sup at a tripery of ancient renown, where the tripe and onions had seethed not for a few hours only, but for weeks or months in an everlasting cauldron for an unending flow of guests. Then Herne Hill, with Ruskin's paternal home almost in sight: Dulwich College and its playing fields; the sudden long tunnel under the Crystal Palace, with its mephitic vapours; then, emergence into something like real country outside; and, a few miles further, pure unmistakable rustic Kent. The rime lay here and there upon the meadows; but we had brilliant sunshine, without a breath of wind. On the boat, we sat sunning ourselves in the sheltered corners. At Calais, my lordly ticket procured me another compartment to myself. As we started, I unpacked my *batterie de campagne* and began to make tea. As I settled down to enjoy it, we were running through St-Omer, with its cathedral white in the slanting sun. When we reached the industrial districts round Lille, darkness grew upon us; at Laon we stopped some time for supper, and I could go out into the road and look towards the cathedral, in memory of that ride with Scott seven years before. With my rucksack for a pillow, I made myself comfortable for sleep; and my next consciousness was that familiar incident of many other happy journeys: coffee and irreproachable breakfast-rolls at Basel. In the next stretch, between Olten and Berne, where the railway runs along a trough of meadows sloping upwards to the pine-crested ridges, the contrast of green in sunlight and frost in shade was delicious. Just beyond Berne, where we caught the first glimpse of the Oberland, Eiger and Mönch and Jungfrau looked their best in the clear chilly air. The Lake of Thun, again, was at its happiest and bluest. Then we turned up the Kander valley, and got out at Frutigen for the diligence ride to Adelboden. The air was still clear, but increasingly cold, and we were glad of all our wraps. In the later stages, where the mountains come nearer to the road and break into outlying castellated crags, twilight settled down, and we were all glad to dismount and unfreeze in the warm Grand Hotel.

Alick Lawrence came to my room as I was dressing, and introduced me to his party. They were about forty, all more or less intimate with each other; by arrangement with Mr Lunn they ate in a glass pavilion at one end of the great dining-room. Alick explained that the lady next to his sister was her school friend, Miss Ilbert, niece to the then Clerk of the House of Commons. This Sir Courtenay Ilbert, a Devon man, was obnoxious to many Tories as responsible for the 'Ilbert Bill', which had marked a great step forward in self-government for India. From the University point of view, he had figured in a very curious incident. He was one of those men who, every ten years or so, sweep the boards of University prizes at Oxford. In the year that he took his degree, 1863, a foolish practical joker hoaxed *The Times*, a day before the official 'Greats' list, with an imaginary 'Greats' list of his own. Ilbert of Balliol was in the first class; that was a matter of course; but, with this single exception (I believe) the untimely jester scattered the other names utterly at random. One man, whose whole career depended on success, found himself in the second or third class, and had rushed away in despair before the truth came out, wandering for days on the verge of suicide. Incidentally, the author of the hoax was soon discovered, but no actual legal proceedings were taken. Sir Courtenay was a close friend of his almost contemporary Fellow of Balliol, James Bryce. The two went off one summer to Iceland for a thorough change and rest from legal work. While they were in the mountains, a quarrel broke out between the steamship officers and the port authorities. The boat then steamed off at once, a fortnight before its advertised date; and this was the last of the season! Fortunately, however, Bryce was already sufficiently important for the Government to send a gunboat to fetch him and his marooned companions.

My Devon connections, and the Lawrence friendship, brought me nearer to Miss Ilbert from the first; our case fitted exactly A. H. Clough's rhapsody on Juxtaposition.[1] I never realized till then how frigid ordinary sociabilities are at home, and how often freedom of intercourse is broken—all the more fatally, perhaps, because almost imperceptibly—by a hundred little conventions of time and place and circumstance: the *tertium quid* breaking into a tête-à-tête, or the pressure of formalities which chill many natural boy-and-girl camaraderies with the reminder that, just here and just now, this is out of place. No doubt there is much less of that nowadays; but under the Great Victoria there was more than many of us realized at the time. All that, however, went to the wind in winter sports. Certainly, among the forty diners in that pavilion, distinctions we esteemed so grave at other times were as nothing in the sight of that winter sun. Not only the young, but the middle aged like myself, and even the aged, accepted deliberately the rôle of Monks of Thelema, 'fais ce que voudras'. Mr Lunn on one occasion made some long and formal speech, spangled with frequent complimentary

[1]   'Juxtaposition, in fine, and what is juxtaposition?
       Look you, we travel along in the railway-carriage, or steamer,
       And, *pour passer le temps*, till the tedious journey be ended,
       Lay aside paper or book to talk with the girl that is next one . . .
       Allah is great, no doubt, the Juxtaposition his prophet.'
                                        Amours de Voyage, Canto III, § 6.

allusions to our live bishop. The prelate's married daughter, sitting next to her father, urged playfully that he should rise and bow in acknowledgement of each recurrent compliment; finally, she actually laid hands on his stiff neck to bend it. A lady was heard to comment, as we went out, 'Did you see that outrageous female take those sickening liberties with the bishop?' At breakfast, again, there was a competition for the appetizing Bernese rolls. The winner, who ate fourteen, was a highly intellectual lady of romantic slender figure. Mr Lunn, among other benevolent devices for our entertainment, had installed in the great dining-room a gramophone with an enormous and stentorian loud-speaker. I will not here specify the exalted and dignified position, at home in England, of the gentleman who one evening crossed the crowded room and stuffed his woollen sweater into the throat of this boisterous foghorn, amid the plaudits of the whole company. I need only say that this was not our Viscount, nor our Bishop, nor either of our two Knights, nor our A.R.A. nor our Greek Professor, nor the two Headmasters, nor our Honourable. But at home, in England, is precisely where we were not; and that was the whole point of our holiday. We had paid our money to forget, for the moment, everything except the ferocious individualism of our dear native land. Thus it was that, on the way home, there was serious trouble with the railway guard, when our winter sportsmen, greedy of fresh air, insisted on re-opening the windows closed for the convenience of ordinary travellers. This I record with shame; but it cannot be ignored; for it is precisely this obtuse insistence upon home ideas which too often gives British and American travellers an unenviable reputation on the Continent. Yet something of this Saturnalian *abandon* it was which, by a happy turn of fortune, changed my whole life.

The mountain exactly opposite us, the Bonderspitz, had a great belt of forest half-way up, above which came smooth slopes of snow, seeming to promise an excellent ski field. Alick Lawrence was semi-officially commissioned to go and explore. He asked me to go with him and X, a distinguished Civil Servant who in after years rose to honours. Yet on this particular occasion it was X, the most responsible of us, who did the most irresponsible thing: a conspicuous example of the wayward impulses which possess your true winter sportsman. Emerging from the forest, we came to a little fold of

VIII.   The author and his wife in 1904

Plate IX. 'Gordanus Shelfordiensis'. From the original cartoon by
G. R. Owst, now in the Library of St John's College, Cambridge

the mountain which sheltered half a dozen châlets, deserted in winter but serving in summer for the whole cheese-making population of the village. We wanted somewhere to sit for lunch, and X noted that it was quite easy to insert a knife blade and slip back the wooden bolt which fastened the door of the nearest châlet. This tickled his ingenuity, and he slid the bolt in spite of our mild protests. It was a charming building, of purple larch timber, carved with mottoes in the old Bernese style, and dated about 1730. We ate our lunch in comfort, admired the huge copper cauldron for seething the milk, and went home to report. It might have been physically possible to slide the bolt back again with the knife, but in fact we did no more than close the door. We arranged for a party of ski folk next day. There was a choosing of skis that night from among Mr Lunn's plentiful store; the gentlemen helped the ladies; and I helped Miss Ilbert.

The morrow was as fine as one could wish, and we mustered in front of the hotel after breakfast. I was carrying, with my own skis, the pair which it was my privilege to choose for my partner. Not without a certain boastfulness, I offered to carry for two other ladies also. I wore my plain old Swiss cloth snow leggings from the Forclaz, and a well-worn Norfolk jacket made from Franciscan cloth which a friar had procured for me at Sorrento. The effect was such that a lady came up to me and complimented me on speaking as good English as a native. In the forest, we lost our way a little, and I heard a certain amount of murmuring behind; for the ladies of 1902 were still under Victorian laws of dress, and the snow was sometimes almost knee-deep. When we emerged upon the plateau, X opened the châlet again, and we all crowded in to sit down, twenty or thirty folk rather clammy about the legs. There was the great open hearth on the floor, with dry faggots and logs at hand; it was inevitable that someone should propose a fire to warm the feet and the coffee we had brought; for the now ubiquitous thermos was rare in those days. Here I protested: it is one thing to burgle a châlet, and something very different to light a fire there. I had few supporters, so I ate my lunch outside in the sun.

The ski slopes were not really first-rate, and we were all very raw novices, so some proposed to climb the Bonderspitz instead. I had been to the top earlier in the week, under the wing of an old

Oberland guide whom one visitor had brought with him, and whom he left to me on a day when he himself was taking a rest. So I volunteered to lead, and half a dozen ladies joined the party. It was a laborious climb, for the snow was far deeper in some parts than on the more circuitous way by which the guide had taken me; but we gained the top in good time, and had a splendid view of the Oberland giants, with the valley of Kandersteg and the Oeschinen See, gem of miniature Alpine lakes, at our feet. Time pressed, so we soon turned downwards; and here we had 1500 feet of steep and perfectly smooth snow down to our châlets. It was an intoxicating glissade; one lady lost balance half-way, and rolled thence to the bottom; her very eyelashes were sprinkled with snow when she emerged. Her brother, from below, had followed the whole expedition with considerable anxiety. He watched us reach the skyline and then disappear over what, from there below, looked like a downward slope but was in fact the flat top: and some alarmist then suggested to him that the Kandersteg side of this mountain was one great precipice. His anxiety was not absolutely allayed until he was combing the snow out of his sister's hair.

Meanwhile nearly all the rest had trickled downwards, for the sun had just sunk. But first the châlet fire must be carefully extinguished; and it was voted, not perhaps without some good-humoured malice, that we two should be deputed to manage this. We did the work most thoroughly, taking great slabs of frozen snow from outside, heaping these first in a wall all round the hearth on the floor, and then covering the embers themselves to a depth of four or five inches. This duty performed, we went downwards under a magnificent afterglow. The Gross-Lohner on our left seemed to rise higher and more threatening as the light faded around us. In front, the snowy waste stretched in gentle undulations to the very head of the valley, where the Wildstrubel stood out against the dark red sky. When we came out of the forest, the deep frosty blue was full of stars; and, finally, a Miltonian moon came out in tender sympathy. It may be that we lingered; certainly we did not overtake the rest; and there was a little ironical applause among the forty when we came in late for dinner. Next morning we found each other by accident on the terrace, saluting the Bonderspitz in the early light; and here again, there was a certain shy, half-confessed self-consciousness. To each, this was now *our* mountain; at the very least we had established a sort of totem kindred. Even before this, we had often instinctively paired; but from this time forward I, for my part, was quite frank with myself. I began to hope for the supreme good fortune of finding a partner in life at a time when I was old enough to weigh fully the responsibilities and risks, yet young enough still to accept the Great Adventure. We soon began to find our elective affinities, and, at the same time, a few of our healthy contrasts: the 'little aversions' of Mrs Malaprop. I could accept, with fair allowances, George Borrow's definition of 'Norfolk, where the people eat the best dumplings in the world, and speak the purest English'. But at Exeter I had begun, and here I was continuing, my lessons in Devon, where the cream surpasses even that of Cornwall, and the lanes are fitter for lingering than for traffic, and old-fashioned good nature outbalances hard-headed modern business. Lady Lawrence, who shared with Uncle Robert the office of chaperon to Miss Ilbert, asked me once, as we sat and watched the skaters, 'I sometimes wonder whether it is fair to try to bring young folk together'. I gave her to understand that this seemed to me one of the most beneficent works of charity for ladies whose own days of romance are on the wane; and she saw I had understood. On the other hand, it was her duty to warn against precipitate decisions. Later on, when it was my fellow-incendiary who sat by her, and I passed by skating with another, she enquired critically, 'Does he *never* stop talking?' *Fellow-incendiary* is there used by anticipation: it was our nickname of a few days later.

Exactly fifty hours after we had quitted that Bonderspitz châlet, as we rose from dinner in the glass pavilion, a lady called out, 'What a splendid sight!' I looked up, and my heart sank within me. A great fire was blazing up at the fringe of the forest. The flames rose sky-high, with a red glow down among the tops of the trees, exactly where we had committed that act of trespass two days ago. I got into jacket and gaiters and went straight up. The sight became more magnificent and more depressing at every step. When I reached the spot, nothing was standing but the stone foundation, four or five feet high, within which was a mass of embers with occasional bursts of flame in the quiet air. A dozen peasants stood shaking their heads: two dozen boys were dancing round in glee. There could be no doubt; this was our châlet and none other. Without quitting the friendly shadow of the forest, I turned precipitately homewards and told my friends. They refused first to credit the fact, and then the cause; for indeed nothing but a miracle could have given that hearth any life after the hundredweight of snow that we had piled upon it. But later, when I had gathered all the evidence, it became as clear as daylight. After we climbers and ski-ers had gone out, a few ladies had sat lingering round the hearth. One or two of these now corroborated what I had already heard after the disaster, telling how they had amused themselves with putting out the sparks that flew up and sometimes settled on the great transverse beam stretching some four or five feet above the hearth to support the hanging milk cauldron. That beam was coeval with the hut itself, 170 years, and I remembered then to have noticed its many wrinkles and fissures. One or more of the sparks must have lodged in those fissures: each would smoulder then like a slow match, and the result was inevitable.

On an earlier evening I had got leave from Mr Lunn and the Entertainments Committee to give a twenty-minutes talk on the Swiss Army. The thing itself had prompted a little good-humoured chaff: to many it seemed a ridiculous stretch of imagination to suggest that Britain, continuing her policy of hiring one man to fight in defence of the quiescent nine, might some day find herself in worse danger than at Waterloo. Now, then, the fun at the Grand Hotel grew fast and furious when a squad of cavalry arrived from Frutigen escorting the Syndic with his officials, to make sure that no guilty guest should slink back to Britain. The Swiss Army, it was now suggested, had come to take me captive and carry me off; for in fact, as the only one who could speak German fluently, and also one of the most direct witnesses, I was the one longest closeted under this guard. I confessed the burgling, of course, and could feel no doubt that our illegal fire was the cause of all. Fortunately, in Sir Henry Lawrence we had a business man who took charge of the whole affair. He telephoned to the British Minister at Berne, who reassured the authorities as to our good faith. Then he proceeded to divide the ski party into groups. The ladies were made collectively responsible for one share, and the rest was divided among the men. This male share finally came to £13 each: so leniently did the Swiss authorities press a very serious matter, and so tactfully did our Berne lawyer avoid provoking the Insurance Company to refuse compensation on the perfectly sound plea that this was no natural fire, but the result of flatly illegal action.

The Berne negotiations took several days; meanwhile the Swiss Army was withdrawn, since the only incendiary who had been plutocrat enough to bring his cheque book, signed on for the necessary caution money, and we were put upon parole. Most of the party moved on to Grindelwald, whence superior sport conditions were reported. But Uncle Robert, as a barrister, good-naturedly stayed on at Adelboden. Miss Ilbert and I were among the few tourists detained at the hotel in view of a possible further enquiry. The final arrangement was that I must interview the Syndic and his officials once more at Frutigen, and thence home. I took the before-breakfast coach to Frutigen; Robert and Miss Ilbert joined me at Berne by midday, we took one last view of the Oberland from the cathedral terrace, and enjoyed the solid old-fashioned comforts and cookery of the 'Bear Hotel', which I had first learned to know in Heidelberg days. Thence by easy night stages to Laon and Calais, spending all day at Laon over the cathedral and ramparts and crooked old streets. After dinner, there was still time to mount again by the thousand steps and see the cathedral at its best, by moonlight. Uncle Robert pleaded age and infirmity, and we did not press him unduly. So again, at Calais, where there was a whole morning to fill in before the boat's departure, and more than a morning-full of things to see. By this time, my small reserve of cash was exhausted, and I borrowed thirty shillings from the lady. With part of this I took her across in a hansom from Charing Cross to Paddington, and saw her into her Oxford train. It was only when I had got home to Pentney that I could sit down and get my settled project off my chest. For I must necessarily explain, as best I could, what sort of a person was addressing her, setting out my worldly prospects in their nakedness—'the short and simple annals of the poor'. I wrote that I would not ask at this moment, but would most certainly later on, unless, after full and frank consideration, a clear negative should come. None such came, and presently I was back at Exeter for work. We corresponded daily; and, a fortnight later, a letter came from Lady Lawrence at the Temple; Miss Ilbert had promised to come on the 31st for the week-end: would I come too?

Both of us kept the appointment; and, after a brief tête-à-tête, we found ourselves pledged for life, on the last day of that month whose first day had found us not far advanced beyond ordinary pleasant acquaintance.

A few weeks later, Lady Lawrence gave an Incendiaries' Dinner at the Temple: and for that evening the Adelboden spirit was again alive, not to say rampant. With an effort I calculate, under the falling leaves at Toronto, that this was thirty-eight years and a few odd months ago, counted by the calendar. But in memory that festival comes back most freshly and inevitably in the words of Thackeray's *Mahogany Tree*, or the too-little-known lines of Landor:

> Come, Kenyon, thou lover of frolic and laughter,
>   We meet at a time when we never were sad.
> Who knows what a destiny waits us hereafter,
>   How many or few of the pleasures we had?
>
> The leaves of perhaps our last autumn are falling,
>   Half spent is the fire that must soon cease to burn,
> How many are absent who heed not our calling?
>   Alas! and how many who cannot return?

CHAPTER XXX

THURLESTONE

MEANWHILE, that spring, I had continued my Exeter and other work under considerable pressure: for these particular lectures were new to me, and it was hard work to write one a week in the interval of travelling and delivering the others. But one of my first thoughts, naturally, was to go down to Thurlestone, the little seaside village where my fiancée's grandfather had been rector for nearly sixty years, sending out into the world five sons: one at Westminster, one in the City, and others in China, New Zealand and Canada. The grandmother, with a maiden aunt, was in Rockhill, the house he had prepared for her widowhood. Converted from an old barn, it was as original and characteristic as the rector's own life had been. He had been intimate with the Froudes of Dartington, and when Exeter College expelled the historian, J. A. Froude, as a heretic, Mr Ilbert had stood between the victim and the orthodox father's archidiaconal wrath. The friendship was cemented by those long years when Froude, successful and wealthy, settled at Salcombe, seven miles along the coast. Old Mr Ilbert had so designed the Rockhill drawing-room that, apart from its bow-window stretching all across the south wall, it had two circular western lights which were wheel-windows in the most literal sense. His mother had doted upon him; and, when he married Rose Owen, old Mrs Ilbert had joined in the honeymoon, as an integral member of the party, from a few days after the wedding. When, after many years, the travelling-coach which had carried them for that journey was broken up, the rector used its two main wheels to form the tracery of these drawing-room windows at Rockhill. The other furniture was equally historic. In one room was what his own father had retained from the Waterloo campaign: a travelling-chest of drawers with bed accommodation at the top. Elsewhere were tables pieced together from ancient ships' timbers cast up upon the rocky coast. The porch was wreathed in roses, honeysuckle, myrtle and old man's beard. The house was honeycombed with unexpected cupboards, crammed with old-world treasures. Two bottles of port, discovered in the remotest recesses of one cupboard when the household finally broke up, were more antediluvian in aspect and taste than even that Waterloo port which I had tasted under the bishop's auspices at Lynn. There was, by family recipe, a certain home-made orange brandy, sovereign against all ills, and proportionately seldom seen. Equally esoteric was a recipe for spiced pears, suitable for any climate. The little garden exactly matched the house. It made the most of its few ancient trees, of its great ragged hedges banked up with earth and stone in Devon fashion, and of its broken inequalities of ground. The house's eastern side abutted straight upon the Buckland lane, with a high foundation of native rock and a little kitchen window from which the maids could deal at point blank with the fish hawker or fruit cart or butcher or grocer from Kingsbridge. That same window was open also to all village necessities: here at Rockhill, as before at the rectory, at any sudden demand for embrocation or cough syrup or other homely remedy, Susan would frequently confess that it was out on loan. For each of those maids had stayed on from old rectory days: and, when Mary married a widowed local farmer and mothered his children, she was succeeded by Susan's niece, Emily, and Emily in her turn married the gardener, grandson to the rectory gardener, an ancient who in 1903 was still to be seen on fine days sunning himself at the door of a still more ancient cottage. In earlier days, he had come to church on Sundays in a clean smock made by his wife, in which he would do his daily work for the rest of the week. The single 'Thurlestone Hotel' had, indeed, already been partly modernized. From the big irregular farmhouse of its origin, it now displayed more than half of modern barrack-building; and a few new villas had sprung up between it and the sea. Moreover, the pastures all along the cliff were laid out as a picturesque golf course. Some of the crusted old inhabitants might grumble at these invasions of their 'ancient solitary reign'; but to most visitors the village seemed as near to a quiet seaside paradise as man could expect, or even desire, in the 'modern' days of Edward VII. It showed the happiest contrasts of wild nature and fertility. The rough grey church tower rose high and uncompromising on the wind-swept slope, a beacon to mariners from as far as Eddystone Rock. There is a local legend that this tower gave the first warning of the approach of the Spanish Armada. Inside, the pillars were granite monoliths, brought down by oxen from the medieval quarries on Dartmoor. Close by, on

ledges of the cliff, hawks and ravens found themselves a nest. Yet behind the churchyard, only a few yards over the ridge, ploughed fields
shelved steep down to the meadows of Bantham; and on summer
Sundays the villagers creeping up to evening service, or downward
for their courtings, seemed no less native to the landscape than those
seagulls which, in spring, had followed the same plough through the
same furrows, and which inspired Lucy Kemp-Welch with one of
her most characteristic pictures. The village itself, with its steep
uneven street, its thatch and rough stone or lime-washed walls,
rarely interrupted by modern brick, and its haphazard trees and
bushes and flowers, seemed rather a natural growth than the work
of man. The inhabitants, gentle or simple, not yet over-diluted with
mere visitors, were worthy of Cranford or Sir Roger de Coverley.
And most Thurlestonian of all were old Mrs Ilbert and Aunt Helen
and Uncle Donald.

Rose Owen had been the daughter of a squire near Tiverton;
the little town for which Lord Palmerston sat in Parliament, and
whose ancient foundation of Blundell's School (A.D. 1604) has long
been famous in the west. In early girlhood, she had stood indignantly
between a big ill-dressed awkward lad and the persecutors who were
hounding him back from school with all the arrogance natural to
boarders in their relations with the outcast day boy.[1] This particular
outcast was the son of a distinguished officer, Major Temple, whose
widow was bringing up eight children on her exiguous pension.
Soon after our engagement, I had a sidelight upon those days from
my Norfolk neighbour Henry Lee-Warner (competitor in that affair
of F. W. H. Myers) who had first been pupil to Temple at Rugby,
then Fellow of St John's, Cambridge, and finally assistant to his old
master at Rugby. When Temple was made Bishop of Exeter, being
a man of great physical vigour, he had taken Lee-Warner with him
on a short walking tour.[2] 'The other day' (said Lee-Warner to me
in 1903) 'I was looking up my old diary of that tour. One passage
will interest you. There was a bit of wild broken ground not far
from Tiverton, and Temple said to me, "We once had a picnic

---

[1] For Archbishop Temple's schooldays see the official *Life* by seven friends
(chapter IV). He boarded in a private house in the town. In earlier years, he
had worked in the fields with his father, who had tried to make his way by
farming, with results only too frequent in the story of retired officers.

[2] For instances of his athletic prowess, and his extraordinary accuracy of
eye and ear, see the *Life*, pp. 159, 207 ff.

at that place . . . Rose sang to us ". (And then, after a pause) "I sometimes think that, if we have no nightingales in Devon, it is because
the girls have such sweet voices".' On the other hand, Rose Ilbert,
when an old woman, used to insist that Frederick Temple, as a young
man, had a very pleasant voice; until, having plunged in to save a
drowning man on a bitter winter day, he caught a cold which
permanently affected his throat. Henceforward, having at his command no modulation beyond that rasping voice which to a younger
generation seemed congenital, he became naturally famous for those
occasional crushing retorts which form the point of such popular
anecdotes as cling round his name. Be that as it may, in the later
days, when Archbishop Temple was seventy-eight years old, he
officiated at the wedding of the eldest granddaughter of Mrs Ilbert,
and after the ceremony, as he sat down by her on a sofa at Speaker's
Court, he was heard saying (to the great edification of younger
guests), 'And now, Rose . . . I *may* still call you Rose, mayn't I? . . . .'
Nobody who knew her could forget the peculiarly happy and childlike smile that wrinkled her upper lip, or her long white side-curls
à la Mrs E. B. Browning.

Equally inseparable from Rockhill was Aunt Helen, ready to take
any trouble in so far as the old lady was capable of giving trouble
of any kind. Aunt Helen was essentially—one might almost say,
desperately—gregarious. Knowing from childhood everybody all
round, great and small, she struggled untiringly to keep pace with
the steadily growing influx of visitors, down to' (or up to) the
bungalow folk that grew up round the golf course. On our way
home from a long afternoon walk, it was fatal to meet anyone with
whom she had not exchanged chats for a week or more. Hunger
and weariness were forgotten—or, more strictly speaking, she felt
none herself and forgot such possible frailty in us—until the whole
bag of talk had been emptied on either side. So also with Uncle
Donald, who might have sat to Addison for Will Wimble. After
an adventurous life, he had come down to bachelor days with the
old folk at home. He was more irresistibly sociable, if possible,
than his sister, and more ubiquitous, until after his threescore years
and ten, when lameness began to plague him in consequence of a
bullet received through his leg as trooper in the Canadian Rebellion
of 1870. Another mishap of that same time illustrated his good-

nature. He had been stooping to groom his horse's foreleg, when the animal had plunged and broken his jaw. He never told the story with the least tinge of self-pity or blame for the animal: on the contrary, he would always end up with 'poor beastie!' He used to comb the beach, after or before his golf, with the eager minuteness of schoolboy days; thus he was forever bringing home prizes ranging from whole branches of green banànas, or cedar cigar-boxes, down to 'summer shells', a delicate and almost microscopic jetsam from warmer seas which can be found after certain winds upon Broadsands beach. Such finds, again, he utilized with schoolboy ingenuity.

The village thus enjoyed, to a high degree, those advantages of Church life which it will be one of the main problems of an unclerical age to supply. In any English village, the official incumbent still forms the natural nucleus of crystallization for all idealisms and healthy activities, except in that tiny minority of cases when his personal failings reduce him to a negative factor. Our Thurlestone of 1903 had an unusual advantage, in sixty-three consecutive years of exceptional capacity and activity. Mr Coope, the rector of our time, was a Trinity (Cambridge) man whose private means had permitted him to take a world tour between his degree and ordination, and whose library contained, among other valuable items, the great seventeenth-century folios of St Bonaventura's complete works. He manipulated the church services enthusiastically, but not violently, in that Anglo-Catholic direction which was favoured by most of the summer visitors, by a few of the gentry, and even by one or two of the labouring families. When he built the new schoolroom, and planted on its gable the Cross of Constantine, ☧, the captious village critics spied in this monogram some furtive homage to the reigning Pope, Pius X.

This, then, became a second home to me, and a third workshop. My wife had agreed from the first that the family budget should be charged with £30 yearly for books, including subscription to the invaluable London Library.[1] Coope's *Bonaventura*, studied and

[1] When we settled in Cambridge, I eased financial pressure by dropping this subscription, but often found reason to regret the step; for that Library has a good many books lacking to our University. I seize this opportunity of paying homage to an institution which, in its own way, is perhaps unrivalled in the world.

digested day by day in the Rockhill Peggotty arbour made out of an old boat, kept me employed for a great part of these Devon holidays. We had many interesting visitors: a judge from Cyprus, a retired mining engineer from Australia, the widow of a Professor of Philosophy and her son, now risen himself to the Professorate. We had our own artist, whose abode in 'Sleepy Hollow' was perfect in its wild beauty. Other artists often came to this parish which in times past had attracted the great Turner with its grand rollers over the bar at Bantham, and whose famous arched rock he had portrayed in 'Ulysses Deriding Polyphemus'.[1]

Thus, with Eastbourne in Term-time, Pentney and Thurlestone for holidays, I was far more fortunate than any freelance could expect for his share of luck. Eastbourne itself furnished a whole set of the Rolls Chronicles in its Public Library. At Pentney, I was within reach of Lynn, where the Stanley library possessed, among others from St Margaret's Church, the four priceless folios of Gerson's works. Every now and then, we squeezed out money for the rail fare to the British Museum, where we transcribed together by day, and spent a night or two at an admirable lodging which we had discovered close by. More rarely, I could get an hour or two with Rashdall at Oxford.

All this time, it fortified my soul to know that H. W. Fowler was fighting his own way through, even though the seas divided us now. He came over from Guernsey to be best man at my wedding, a great sacrifice on the altar of friendship, for he posed, at any rate, as the most confirmed of bachelors. But we flattered ourselves that our own example had not been without influence on the contents of a postcard which I received from him some years later, and which ran: 'I didn't write before lest you should send me a present, and I write now lest you should learn it first from the papers, that to-morrow, on my 50th birthday, I marry Miss Jessie Marian Wills, aged 46.'

Thenceforward, there was a friendly rivalry between the married couples, even more healthy than there had been between the two bachelors. But I never reached, on paper, to the epigrammatic

---

[1] In the National Gallery, if indeed it survives the war. *Thurlestone* means 'holed stone', from the same root as the *tril* in *nostril* ('nose hole') and the miner's mechanical *drill*.

felicity of Fowler's description, in one of his yearly wedding odes,
of that diversity of natural temperament in his household which
contributed to perfection of married harmony. It began

> My wife and I, we disagree
> On every mortal matter;
> The Spratts, 'tis said, were odd; but we
> Are infinitely Spratter.

and ended:

> A crowning discord only can
> Solve discords so inhuman;
> She says the world's to her's one man—
> To me it is one woman.

Yet we could boast some contrast of that kind when we compared
the Pentney of my early years with this Thurlestone of my wife's.
And certainly both places were to us what F. W. Robertson once
wrote to a friend, when business led him to exchange the smoke and
wealth and noise of upstart Brighton for one brief glimpse of un-
spoiled country: 'I spent some hours in the village of Lindfield
itself, where I strongly felt the beauty and power of English country
scenery and life to calm, if not to purify, the hearts of those whose
lives are habitually subjected to such influences. Not that human
nature is better there, but life is more natural, and real nature I hold
to be the great law of our life, both physical and religious.'[1] The
ideal of one heart and one soul was as easy to realize in Devon as in
Norfolk.

Yet here also, as elsewhere, I left what my friend Scott used
jestingly to call 'the trail of the serpent'. I preached the Swiss
Army in a little village hall at Bantham, under criticism from a local
Colonel who—like Sir Ian Hamilton and Colonel Maude in those
same days, and Captain Liddell-Hart of *The Times* nowadays, and
other Colonel Blimps in the possible future—was indignant at the
slur cast upon our Volunteers by demanding that they should be
better trained and equipped than God and the War Office had made
them. Like them, this Colonel felt that the British Generals would
be rather embarrassed than assisted by the multitudes who would
be thrown on their hands, if ever service under stress of war became
a regular legal incident of British citizenship.

[1] F. W. Robertson's *Life and Letters*, ed. Stopford Brooke, vol. 1, p. 350.

CHAPTER XXXI

FIRST BOOKS

ENGAGEMENT and marriage brought me a very healthy reminder of life's realities. Those family obligations set a definite frame for my work. Controversy, as I shall try to explain in a later chapter, had already done much to call me from thought to action. Yet, even so, all might have ended as it did in the case of that Oxford scholar whose long-drawn preparations and irresolutions came to so lame a conclusion that his example stimulated Creighton to immediate production.[1] What saved me from that was the humdrum necessity of earning money, now and without delay. I remember that P. G. Hamerton, in his *Autobiography*, confesses the same.

During the first days of my 'new life', at Lausanne, in my little 'poële' at 25 francs a month on the fringe of the old town walls, I had read Meiners' discursive and antiquated work with the vague ambition of writing, at some distant day, a fairly comprehensive history of social life in the last few centuries of the Middle Ages. This, of course, was very much like 'the old woman who bought a raven to see whether it would live a hundred years',[2] and in any case the scheme would have broken down with its own weight. But I might well have gone on indefinitely reading Dugdale and Matthew Paris 'with my feet on the fender', at Eastbourne or elsewhere, until the Lucretian spectre, and the night wherein no man can work, should have found me still unready to render my final account.[3] Now, however, I saw at once, if I had not realized it before, the truth of Dr Johnson's remark that a man is seldom more innocently employed than when he is making money. For in fact money, in spite of its many obvious abuses, still stands, in the main, as the product and token of honest work.

Hitherto the wind had blown very much where it listed. I was

---

[1] *Life and Letters of Mandell Creighton*, vol. I, p. 186.
[2] *Letters of William Stubbs* (ed. W. H. Hutton), p. 99.
[3] *De Rerum Natura*, III, 959:
　　'Et nec opinanti mors ad caput adstitit ante
　　Quam satur ac plenus possis discedere rerum.'

born with a plentiful share of natural curiosity, which might easily
have degenerated into vulgar inquisitiveness but for my father's
example, freedom of discussion at home, and the mental discipline of a good school, and, above all, the teaching of Hardy and
Vaughan. Among our bedroom books at Lynn were half a dozen
clear-printed and convenient little volumes of *The Percy Anecdotes*,
that plentiful and genial miscellany which we owe to the diligence
of two monks at Fort Augustus. Again, in our family den down-
stairs, we could sprawl on the hearthrug with whatever volume my
father had taken out from the subscription library, not excepting
even such luxury volumes as Gould's *Birds of Europe*, or *Modern
Painters* or *The Stones of Venice*. In those Ruskins, there was always
the interest of speculating why this specimen from Turner was held
up to our admiration, or poor Cuyp gibbeted for our scorn. Thus
the child had been father of the man; and, even here at Eastbourne,
well past middle life, though my reading was no longer quite aimless,
yet still the central purpose was too indefinite. Not, however, but
that I had drifted in more purposeful fashion than might have been
apparent. Under the mere instinctive routine which I shared with
the bee or the coral insect, there was a real core of purpose, of my
own purpose and not anybody else's, partly inherited but in great
part maintained, if not actually created, by a sheer effort of will.
That was what St Thomas Aquinas might have called the true spark
of me, my 'scintilla'; or the 'godly purpose' of Juliana of Norwich.
That scintilla utilized my natural sensitiveness to local associations:
the sudden flash of 'Here is something you have come across before':
with a restless urge to catch and recall this half-forgotten image.
Such are the clues which lead us on from the merely arithmetical
to the geometrical stage of thought: the little floating germ takes
stature and shape from this logical association with its new fellow.
But those flashes of memory were in my case capricious and undisci-
plined. Some things had stuck and many others had perished, at
the mercy of a natural selection over which I had exercised too little
conscious control. When, only the other day, I read that the North
Sea had at last yielded up a piece of amber enshrining a flea of
geological antiquity, this smote me at once with Horace's application, 'There you have your own story!' My Heidelberg employer,
Armitage, had once burst out to me, 'My dear fellow, you have the

biggest collection of perfectly useless knowledge I ever came across !'
That had tickled me with pleasant self-conceit at the time; but in
1903 it faced me rather as a spectre. Not even a wilderness of fleas
in amber would help me towards what had now become my main
purpose in life. How could I extract coin of the realm from this
accumulation of rough ore and dross?

When it came to this practical point, I found a certain reasonable
confidence within myself. Even in more irresponsible days, reading
purely at random, but referring sometimes to contemporary writers,
I found myself a specialist here and there in matters which they were
content to take at second hand from each other. It was as though
a man should have haunted the countryside for more than half a
lifetime with gun and rod, until, in response to some urgent and
unexpected call, he should discover in himself a stock of accumulated
rural observations sufficient for starting him as a landscape painter.
And this became my solidest ground of confidence as the years went
on. Work grew into life, and life grew into work, and now in retrospect I see it all as if it were still present. Here in Canada, on these
January nights, with the crisp turf of the University Campus underfoot and the splendid frosty starlight above, I feel a physical analogy
with my mental standpoint during all those fighting years at Eastbourne. There as here, above and around me, were lights all the
more inspiring because they were too high to be reached, while my
feet were steadily planted upon solid earth.

Rashdall once said to me, 'I dare say I ought to be most concerned
with the great men of antiquity, but, somehow, I never could get
up the same interest for those people that I feel instinctively for those
of the Middle Ages'. In these words I saw exactly my own case.
Beloe, and the relics around us in almost every street at Lynn, had
sowed the first seed. When old White took me in his gig, one Sunday
of 1871, to the hamlet of Denver, where he regularly took Sunday
duty and ate Sunday dinner, I remember holding forth to him on
the crime of sixteenth-century vandalism, and the different Norfolk
we might have had if those monastic buildings had been taken over
by State and town for schools or hospitals. There was probably
something priggish in my unction here, and certainly it left him
cold. At Felsted, I utilized *The Felstedian* for pointing out that the
present existing buildings of Leighs Priory had nothing monastic

Plate X.   View from the author's rooms at St John's College, Cambridge (see p. 311)

Plate XI.   Signing the records at Queen's University, Kingston, with the Cardinal Archbishop of Quebec, after presentation for the degree of Doctor of Laws

about them, in spite of the pious belief of my House Master, who was as unsympathetic as White had been. Here again, I improved the occasion by adding a few words of righteous reprobation for the destructive work of Henry VIII. The restoration of Dunmow Priory was a fascinating work to watch. Some of us used to walk over regularly while the masons were there, at an age when we began to outgrow the tyranny of mere sporting interests; so that the ruined beauty of that minute surviving fragment penetrated us with a sense of personal loss. So also did the destruction of the wall-painting in the parish church, almost inevitable as it was. At home, in Norfolk, monastic ruins had been round me everywhere. I had taken a kitchen cinder shovel to Castleacre and unearthed, with the help of my sister Beatrice, not only a great many fragments of stained glass, but also a charming little angel's head in stone; far better than anything that fell to the lot of Sir William Hope's authorized excavations in later years. Those, and a hundred other insignificant details, had determined my bent; and it was almost inevitable that my first attempt to catch the public ear should have been connected with monastic life. That has become my main burrow into Antiquity. But, with regard to the original shape and direction of that burrow, I am often reminded of the text in Ecclesiastes: 'Thou knowest not what is the way of the spirit, nor how the bones do grow in the womb of her that is with child:...' our birth is but a spark and a begetting. But the moral of this is here, as there: 'In the morning sow thy seed, and in the evening withhold not thine hand: for thou knowest not whether shall prosper, either this or that, or whether they both shall be alike good.'

From very early South Lynn days, I had followed a rigorous index system with my numerous references and extracts. These latter amount by now to some 250 small volumes, the contents of which are indexed in one general ledger under very numerous rubrics, and in two exclusively monastic ledgers in greater detail. Thus I have been able, nearly always, to lay my hand after a brief search upon every piece of evidence which has ever struck me as of real importance. A few ghosts flit about in my memory, of striking passages which I neglected to fix and pin down at once, and which I dare not quote now from recollection only; but, on the whole, I owe immensely to this system, which seems to me better than the ordinary card index. For in some cases I possess page after page, consecutively, transcribed by myself or my wife or one of my copyists, always at hand within a few minutes of the immediate need.

As it was natural that my first serious essay should be in monastic history, so also I took what seemed the most natural line of approach, through contemporary biography. Autobiographies had always had special fascination for me. I had even once contemplated a bibliography of autobiographies, but desisted very soon in face of an immense task which only ignorance could ever have suggested. From St Augustine's to Mark Pattison's and Darwin's, these life stories had attracted my warmest sympathy, and seemed to bring me into closest familiarity with the writer's times. With advancing age, this has gone far to blunt my taste for fiction, except the lightest and most entertaining. Not, of course, that there is a hard-and-fast line between autobiography and fiction: the very title of Goethe's *Dichtung und Wahrheit* warns us there. But in the attempt to disentangle what a man was from what he would have liked to be and what he shows to the world, there is, to my mind, more interest and profit than in meditating over the characters and the problems even of so fine a novel as Mr E. M. Forster's *Passage to India*. Not only in the ponderables, but in imponderables also, I cannot help preferring the autobiography or intimate biography. As early as Heidelberg days, I had formed a plan for competing with fiction by writing a series of brief biographies founded on those memoirs which are now forgotten because their very bulk and multitude discourage the modern reader, but which are full of striking literary possibilities. I began with the *Autobiography* of Johann Gottfried Seume, whose *Tramp to Syracuse* had much attracted me; and these beginnings are somewhere among my papers. Mr Lytton Strachey's brilliant volumes, and even those of his imitators, have shown now what possibilities lie in that direction; and it would not be surprising if, fifty years hence, a body of brief biographies should have been created which could compete on equal terms with the novels of that future day. Now, therefore, I decided to take an autobiography as my main theme, and fill it out into a volume which might have been called *Salimbene and his Circle*. But, as Salimbene was then almost unprocurable and unknown, I called the book *From St Francis to Dante.* For in fact this frank and well-informed friar, born in 1221 and writing his last words about 1288, goes very far to fill one of the most remarkable centuries in Italian and European history. It is not altogether creditable to our Universities that, amid their countless pupils' monographs, they have still produced no exhaustive study either of Salimbene's *Chronicle* or of the contemporary *Diary* of Odo Rigaldi, Archbishop of Rouen (1248–69), or of Johann Busch in the fifteenth century.

In the face of my past experiments, it was a bold adventure to publish this volume of nearly 450 close-printed pages at my own risk. But those earlier attempts had neither made popular appeal nor expected commercial success. On the other hand, here at last was a subject which might reasonably hope to furnish a few hundred readers with interesting stuff not easily obtainable elsewhere. I therefore approached David Nutt, publisher and conspicuous member of the Folklore Society. He was to advertise for subscriptions through that Society, and to take one-third of the money that thus passed through his hands. I printed only 500 copies, and soon regretted my timidity. The subscription price was 8*s.* 6*d.*; non-subscription 12*s.* 6*d.*, I think. The 500 copies (*minus* those sent to reviewers) were soon sold out; and I then printed a second edition, slightly enlarged, of 2000 copies. These have sold slowly but steadily from year to year, and there are very few now left.

About the same time I published my brief fantasia, *Friar's Lantern.* This taught me the fate to be expected of a novel, printed without advertisement or patronage from any publisher, as opposed to a solid book for which subscriptions can be solicited. My sister Beatrice generously undertook to meet the printer's bill for this small volume. Sales in the ordinary way, during the first ten years or so, did not amount to a hundred copies; so this is one of my few volumes which have finally come down to the 'remainder' class.

My next ventures were still aimed at unloading rapidly what had long been accumulating. *Chaucer and his England*, following close upon Salimbene, contained the substance of one course of my University Extension lectures. This I wrote for Methuen & Co. at a royalty of 10 per cent: it is now in its seventh reprinting. A year afterwards, I published at my own risk *A Medieval Garner*, collecting, and translating where necessary, the episodes which I had marked in my reading as illustrating all sides of social and religious life. For this volume Nutt at first, and Constable afterwards, stood sponsors, selling the printed and bound volumes and taking a little more than one-third of the published price. The edition of 1000 was finally exhausted in 1932, when the Cambridge University Press reprinted it in four separate volumes under the title of *Life in the Middle Ages*. My next anthology was the most successful of all. This was when I was settled at Cambridge. The University now possessed, by Lord Northcliffe's endowment, a Professor of English Literature, in the person of Sir Arthur Quiller-Couch. Under his and Professor H. M. Chadwick's direction, a Faculty of English was established; and it was agreed that each period of English literature should be studied in conjunction with the social life of that time. I was commissioned to make a collection of extracts for this purpose, *Social Britain from the Conquest to the Reformation*. In spite of the World War, and the book's bulk, it sold surprisingly well. Thenceforward, as I calculate, my writings have brought me a steady average, per hour, equal to the compositor's wage for setting up the type. I make this comparison in no invidious sense, nor will anybody so interpret it who has watched a first-rate compositor at work, and taken account of the combined mental and manual qualities which go to the perfect management of his machine.

Meanwhile, at Eastbourne, with my crammer's wage as a solid foundation, and Pentney or Thurlestone for the holidays, we managed to pay our £30 a year for books, and almost as much for copyist and secretarial work beyond what my wife's time and energy could do. The daughter of our greengrocer, a very intelligent girl of thirteen or fourteen, was glad to earn 4*d.* an hour in her evenings; and I sometimes wondered whether I could equally well justify my own fee of 4*s.* an hour from Scott. With the daughter of our next-door neighbour, now Mrs Montagu Wilson, we were still more fortunate afterwards. She had just qualified herself as a typist; the convenience of work at her own door, and mainly at her own convenience, as compared with slightly higher pay under uncongenial conditions in the town, made her ready to accept 6*d.* an hour for her occasional help; and, when she passed on to more important work, we felt that we were parting from a real friend. But my wife's memory, like my own, dwells most happily upon our married partnership in a house just big enough for us and our two girls, and with just enough money to keep it going, and just enough literary and domestic work to balance the budget without too depressing drudgery.

Thus we enjoyed something of that artistic equilibrium which, as some folk would fain persuade us, the modern world has lost for ever, but which, like everything else, is generally accessible to those who are willing to pay God's market price for it. This is formulated in Descartes' rule of limiting one's desires rather than pressing the world to satisfy them, and Goethe's 'entbehren sollst du, sollst entbehren!'[1] A friend sent us at that time a little Japanese calendar, with a charming coloured woodcut for each month. One of these woodcuts perished somehow in the nursery, and I have since tried in vain to get it or borrow it for reproduction, whether from the British Museum Print Room or from private collectors. It showed the interior of the artist's own bamboo cottage. He was cutting a woodblock; his wife, squatting on the floor, was colouring prints with a stencil, and the baby, with a bristly little head like a black hairbrush, was packed in a bag at her back and looked over her shoulder. In those days I was publishing a series of home-made *Medieval Studies*. Nearly all were reprinted from the different reviews. I had found, not without difficulty, a London wholesale bookseller who was willing to print the titles in his catalogue and hand the copies over the counter at a commission of $2\frac{1}{4}d$. per six-penny pamphlet. These little sales brought me in sometimes as much as £2 a year: and when, some dozen years ago, the agent broke off our relations as no longer worth his while, I found myself reduced thenceforth to giving away the greater part of my pamphlets. The printed sheets came at a cheap rate straight from the workshop of the periodical, and I folded and stitched them into brown paper covers, printed with a woodcut which I had cut upon a block from one of our old Pentney pear trees. The process was very simple; one inked the block, laid it upon the carpet with a duly soaked sheet of brown paper, and stood upon it for half a minute, jigging a little to increase the pressure. Sunday afternoons, offering unusual quiet from work or visitors, were natural for this sort of job. But one summer Sunday, when some kind friend had taken the babies out,

[1] 'Thou shalt renounce, renounce!'

there dropped in upon us a literary lady who, with comfortable private means, occupied a much larger house in more fashionable surroundings than ours. She wrote with facility, and had a sort of tacit agreement with a well-known publisher to furnish him once or twice a year with some volume which commanded a satisfactory sale. But our relations were still rather conventional, when she suddenly came in upon us on this Sunday afternoon in summer. I was shirt-sleeved in the drawing-room, doing the habitual jig upon my block; papers were drying not only over that floor, but even in the little entrance passage and all up the stairs. But we found her a seat after a few minutes; and she sat out her visit with something of the painful fascination of a kind-hearted but inexperienced lady compelled to realize, for once, how the poor live.

CHAPTER XXXII

CAMBRIDGE AGAIN

HERE I have more than once anticipated chronologically. Let me therefore come now to my second Cambridge life, after just thirty years during which the little I had seen of any university had been almost always at Oxford.

It was in 1911 that we definitely left Eastbourne for Cambridge. That autumn I went down to the river on a bright October afternoon for the four-oared races. At Ditton Corner, waiting for the boats to come in sight, I found myself next to a grizzled beard which bespoke a probable contemporary. My natural remark was, 'It is just thirty years since I last saw this race'. He replied, 'Thirty years ago, I was in the winning boat'. Rapidly abstracting his beard, I said, 'Then you are J. J. Lister, of St John's'. I had never spoken to him; but on the towing-path men get to know each other by sight; and Lister, who was nephew to the famous physician and an excellent scientist himself, had stroked the Lady Margaret boat, through many races, with a mechanical steadiness of swing and a fixed resolve in his straightforward eyes which made him one of the most recognizable figures on the river. Almost as he spoke now, the boats began to show round Grassy; and in a few minutes we were following them up the Long Reach. The sun, at that time of year and day, shines almost directly along the Reach; so that they were soon rowing directly into it. There they were in 1911 as I had watched them for three consecutive years in the old days, when my blood was warm within. The two boats plunged into the sun, and onward through that sea of glory. Victor and loser were alike transfigured: it seemed no human struggle; splendid young limbs swung splendidly through the bewildering flash of oars and the dazzle of sun among those quicksilver eddies, while the spray splashed higher and faster as the fight became more desperate, until the final pistol shots divided winner and loser. Here was all the old excitement of sunlight and breathless suspense. Heraclitus was a liar; into this same river these same eyes had plunged again with the same old fascination! And this was only part and token of the one great miracle, that my

Tripos death of 1881 was now swallowed up in the victory of 1911, and I was once more a chartered freeman of this lost Paradise.

That had come about partly through two old friends of under-graduate days at St Catharine's: C. R. Haines, retired from his Uppingham Mastership, and H. J. C. Knight, who was now Fellow of Corpus and Principal of Westcott House. Haines suggested, and Knight promised to support, my candidature for the Birkbeck Lectureship in Ecclesiastical History at Trinity. This is a foundation of £30 per annum for two years; the beneficiary to give a minimum of six lectures. Rashdall wrote on my behalf to his old Harrow Master Montagu Butler, at that time Master of Trinity. James Gairdner, with whom my relations were almost exclusively con-troversial, generously added his weighty recommendation; and, to my unspeakable delight, the College finally elected me to an office immeasurably more important in its dignity than in its emoluments. I was allowed to give the lectures grouped in pairs, thus minimizing my travelling expenses. The whole series ran to twelve, upon Monastic History in the later centuries of the Middle Ages. They aimed at blocking out the whole picture which I have since striven to fill in with my *Five Centuries of Religion*. I had bought seven years earlier, for £3, an unbound copy of Dugdale's *Monasticon*, with only two or three parts missing; upon this I had thus been able to browse steadily by my own fireside; and now, in the months before the actual lectures, I set myself to go through all that was left, for the sake of more completeness and proportion in my general survey. Thus at last I could have claimed to 'have turned over every page' of those seven bulky folios, annotating and indexing as I went along. It had been hard work; but it gave a sureness of touch, within my own limitations, which has helped me much in later years.

The lectures were successful, and friends advised me to try my fortune altogether at Cambridge. I might take pupils there, use it as my base for Extension Lectures, and finally, perhaps, get a Lecture-ship at my old College, or elsewhere. Scott was now thinking of retirement into parish work. With his blessing, therefore, I had wound up my bargain with him, and taken my wife, my two daughters and my books to Cambridge by Easter, 1911. We were lucky enough to get a suitable house facing Parker's Piece, one of a row belonging to Jesus College. It was large enough for resident pupils, and I soon had three. Next session, I gave a course of University lectures on Life and Thought in the Middle Ages. Then came a wider opportunity; for Professor Gwatkin's infirmities compelled him to give up his larger classes, and Z. N. Brooke and I were simultaneously invited to take the long three-term course on Medieval Outlines, attended by nearly all first-year History men. This meant classes of sixty or seventy each; and in those days the lecturer was paid with a considerable proportion of the pupils' fees; so that I was already somewhat better off than at Eastbourne. I could thus drop the private pupil business, and move to a cottage at Great Shelford, where G. C. Macaulay was my neighbour. During the World War we all fell upon lean years; but by that time I had in my class nearly all the Girton and Newnham History pupils, not only for Medieval Outlines and for the Special Subject (St Francis and the Franciscans) but sometimes also for extra courses on medieval English literature. Thus, with Extension Lectures and a little examination work, especially in Oral French at different schools, we managed to balance our budget and pay education insurance for the two girls.

With the Armistice came a rush of prosperity. So many men came up to make up arrears of education, that classes were larger than ever, and lecturers were still paid according to their pupils' fees. A little later, when the Universities' Commission had done its work, this was changed; the Faculty Board paid us at a flat rate per lecture; thus, while I now received more for my Special Subject with from twelve to twenty pupils, I got much less for my Outlines, with perhaps as many as eighty. On the other side, the Faculty of English was now founded, and in 1919 I was appointed to the official University Lectureship in English, which poor G. C. Macaulay's sudden death had vacated. This meant at first a little less than £110; but soon came the liberal government subvention which increased enormously the funds of all Faculties, and led to a corresponding adjustment of many salaries. By this arrangement, the salary of the Lectureship in English was increased to £400 a year.

Then came my final stroke of economic luck. One morning my breakfast-post brought me two letters from St John's. One was from J. R. Tanner, of whom I had seen a good deal, and enjoyed something of that friendly warmth which he diffused all round. The other was from T. R. Glover, soon to be Public Orator, and already known for some years past as one of the most stimulating Classical lecturers. I had met him once or twice in the University Library, and exchanged views on Church History. Both wrote to the same generous effect: the College Council was offering me a Research Fellowship on the most honourable terms. I was bound to nothing but my own self-imposed tasks: 'Come and do your work here in the College among us.' I cycled upon air to my nine o'clock lecture, and thence to lay before the Master my most grateful acceptance. As H. F. Stewart put it, from his rooms at Trinity, I was now Fellow of 'a College second to none for disinterested scholarship'. Thus began another Vita Nuova, of unbroken help and harmony to the present day.

Apart from this substantial addition to my income, there now came more royalties from the University Press. For, during the next few years, I published a series of bulky volumes which, on the whole, have been more profitable commercially than can generally be expected of history that tries to grapple seriously with special problems. For one definitely peak year—perhaps about 1925—I paid income tax on £1500. But those bulky volumes, involving disputed questions of historical method, must be dealt with in my next chapter.

Not less pleasant than this affluence in the years before my super-annuation under the New Statutes, were the invitations to lecture before other audiences: Lowell Lectures at Boston (Mass.); a similar course at Aberystwyth; Ford Lectures at Oxford and Rhind Lectures at Edinburgh; and a paper at the Congrès Loisy, held at Paris in honour of the veteran's seventieth year by the Société d'Histoire des Religions. On this last occasion, each delegate in turn was com-missioned to say a few words of homage to Loisy. An old pupil of mine, employed at Geneva on the League of Nations, happened to pick up an evening paper and sent me a description of my person and speech as mirrored in the mind of a lively Parisian journalist. I have the cutting somewhere and think I can give the earlier sentences verbally: 'Imaginez-vous l'apparition la plus cocasse, la plus sau-grenue! La figure écarlate; la taille démesurément élongée; les vêtements trop courts et trop étroits; le geste embarrassé; un col et une cravate à faire mourir de rire!—et vous avez là l'honorable Coulton.'[1]

Here (I felt) was a journalist who had caught something of the Cambridge spirit. From my first days of return in 1911 to the present moment, I have been more and more ready to subscribe to what Leslie Stephen said in connection with Henry Fawcett, and F. W. Maitland, in later years, à propos of both. 'He would say that Cambridge is almost the only place where a man won his position exclusively on his merits. . . . The little world of Cambridge had the republican spirit in the best sense of the word.'

One of my first meetings in this new Cambridge life was with Housman, who had just been elected to the Latin Professorship, and by whose side I had the good fortune to find myself once at dinner in the Hall of Trinity. I had the temerity to plead that I had been one of the earliest readers of *A Shropshire Lad*. He replied, from behind his sardonic mask: 'I am told that it appeals especially to the criminal classes.' Then he unbent, and explained that three copies in succession had been stolen from the University Library. The temptation to pocket so tiny and comparatively high-priced a volume had proved overwhelming. One other incident may be worth recording. Housman and Harker of St John's, one year his junior, met first at a Commemoration Feast in St John's Hall when each, as events proved, had only a year or so to live. I was curious to see how this chance collocation would work; for Harker was one of the most taciturn of men. I could only see their backs; but that was enough; it was plain from first to last that each had entered into the spirit of the occasion: "Tis merry in hall when beards wag all'. One could see that there was no more talkative pair in the whole assembly. Next day I asked Harker what so inspiring subject they had found in common. He answered in one word, 'Dickens'.

If I had time to waste in vain regrets, it would be that my father did not live to see me established at Cambridge, where he had spent hard-earned money to plant me thirty years earlier, nor my mother to greet my Fellowship. Where is it that Ruskin deals with the man

[1] 'Imagine the queerest and most absurd figure! A scarlet face, a disproportionately lanky body, clothes too short and too tight, awkward gestures, and a collar and necktie to make you split with laughter—and there you have the honourable Mr C.'

whose success comes late in life?—'Let him lay the wreath on his mother's grave.' One of her favourite poems in later life was Matthew Arnold's *Cadmus and Harmonia*, the two Aged Snakes basking out their days in the sun. I see them both by the winter fire, my father devouring it with outspread hands, reading past years in its flickering flames, and saying, for the fiftieth time, with magnificent poetic licence: 'My children have never given me any anxiety in all my life.' It need hardly be said that the building-up of that fire became one of the main passions of his last years. I can hear my mother protesting: 'Eh, James, it's too hot already, and you're putting on a log that isn't dry.' The answer was punctuated with a vicious thrust of the poker: 'My dear, you wouldn't like to be so dry as that log will be in ten minutes time.'

CHAPTER XXXIII

HISTORY AND CONTROVERSY

AN AUTOBIOGRAPHY is nothing unless it represents the personal point of view; yet I am trying in this chapter to write also *sub specie aeternitatis* concerning things of fundamental interest for all writers and readers of History. Without exactly adopting Obermann's motto 'Eternity, be thou my refuge!' I am yet under the sobering thought of standing on the brink. Moreover, I can refer to printed records for some facts which might otherwise seem too strange for belief. In the minority of cases, where no full printed record exists beyond what I write here, readers must estimate my accuracy by what they find for themselves (supposing that anyone does take that trouble) in the documents to which I do refer them.[1]

I at first entered the historical field frankly as an amateur; and academic officials had every right to receive me critically. Nor can I ignore the generosity with which, on the whole, I have been treated by reviewers. But I feel now from inside, even more strongly than when I wandered outside the precincts, that History suffers more than any other Faculty from academic conservatism and pedantry.

Benedetto Croce says truly: 'History is Experience'. Thus, just as we cannot escape from experience in our daily lives, so also we cannot in History. The letter of thanks we write after a visit, recounting briefly our journey home and what we found there, is as truly history as a chronicle of the Norman Conquest; and it calls for similar methods of interpretation. The fact that different readers may read different things into it does not essentially alter the matter. It is merely a question of degree. No two minds form the same impression; each man's 'experience' of past events is personal; yet, among those who really want the truth, there is in the end far more agreement than difference. As Descartes said, the first factor in

---

[1] My controversial pamphlets have been tied together in sets; and a complete set, so far as they are still in print, will be sent to any Librarian of any Public Library who cares to send 1s., or 25 cents, for packing and postage to Miss D. R. Hodder, 90 Kimberley Road, Cambridge, England.

successful search for truth is the real desire to arrive at the truth: seek, and ye shall find. And in History, as elsewhere, our first guide should be common-sense. Not, of course, what we here call *common* is therefore *frequent*; far from it, the pettiest temptations and the most childish moods will sometimes banish it. But it is a sense which in various degrees is common to all men, just as error in its various degrees is common to all. 'By an admirable disposition of Nature, the things which mankind possesses in common are essential, and their differences comparatively slight: yet, on the other hand, their differences go a long way to modify their similarities.'[1] Common-sense prompts the real truth-seeker to use all his powers of observation and imagination. It spells final success, up to the point of which the man's faculties were capable of success, both for the financier and for the cobbler. Without having read Bishop Butler, each knows that Probability is the Guide of Life, and each throws all his energies into the search for probabilities. That is the successful business method, and it should be also the foundation of Historical Method. All discussions and theories are mischievous which, by representing Historical Method as something esoteric, tend to obscure this truth. That which we label as peculiar to the specialist is in danger of becoming peculiar to a clique. The more we divorce History from the common life of ordinary men, the more we strangle its own vigorous life.

The self-taught student is no doubt prone to exaggerate this; but University Professors are tempted to neglect it; and on this issue I have found myself at odds with some of my most dignified reviewers. While admitting the abundance and general accuracy of my facts and references, they have accused me of confusing the picture by indiscriminate appeal to widely different dates or countries. Again, I am said to have sinned against the canon 'Thou shalt not judge'. And, thirdly, I have given the public mere controversy where it wanted sober facts.

The first count I deny altogether; I have vainly challenged those critics to produce specific instances. They have, as I believe, read too hastily to note my logical sequences. The public at which I have aimed—mainly professional or business men or artisans who have leisure for solid reading in the evenings—can always judge for them-

[1] *Œuvres choisies de Rivarol*, ed. Lescure, 1880, vol. II, p. 239.

selves, since I make a point of showing my dates as I go along.
If a reader finds that, after citing an event from 1450, I go back to
note that we get the same phenomenon in a more rudimentary form
two centuries earlier, he will see the obvious logical reason for
breaking, at this point, my chronological sequence. As to foreign
countries, although the essential plan of my work was to cover all
Europe so far as time and energy permitted, yet in my own mind
I have always discriminated, and for my readers I have often paused
to note differences due to various climatic, racial, or political causes.
And here I must retort upon my accusers. Why was it left to me to
incur this reproach of doing badly the thing which neither they nor
their friends had done at all? Nowadays, I find a chorus of reviewers
insisting upon the special value given to the new *Cambridge Economic
History* by this common-sense plan of embracing all Europe, and
thus utilizing one country's experience to throw light upon another's.[1]
How can we explain the habit of treating English monasticism otherwise, except by that same indolence which has led us, with the world's
richest documentary sources in this field, to neglect them until recent
years? Even to the present moment, among the scores of subjects
for research which professors give out to their pupils, there is
scarcely one which leads them on to this, one of the most richly
documented and most disputed fields in history. If, as scholars are
agreed, the Reformation gave a fateful turn to European civilization,
whether for good or for evil; if, again, that revolution must to some
extent stand or fall by its treatment of the ancient monasteries; if,
moreover, the monastic Rules were so uniform from country to
country, and human nature so nearly the same at bottom everywhere, then what excuse can be found for always studying those
Rules piecemeal, and for neglecting the lessons that can be learnt
from a diversity of nations, whether in their obedience or in their
disobedience to their common profession? The final volume of my

---

[1] Compare Hume, *Inquiry Concerning the Human Understanding*, sect. VIII,
pt. i, where he insists upon this general truth, and makes the necessary modification afterwards: 'Would you know the sentiments, inclinations and course of
life of the Greeks and Romans? Study well the temper and actions of the French
and English. You cannot be mistaken in transferring to the former most of the
observations which you have made with regard to the latter. Mankind are so
much the same, in all times and places, that history informs us of nothing new
or strange in this particular.'

Five Centuries of Religion, which exists in three MS. copies on different sides of the Atlantic, and may or may not ever come to print, struggles to fill this gap. I there rehearse, chronologically and geographically, the different reforms attempted during the two centuries preceding the Dissolution. I try to do justice to those orthodox reformers, who were often veritable heroes, while noting the transitory nature of most of their reforms. In a supplementary chapter, I show how far these same difficulties persisted in those countries where the monastic system survived the Reformation. I have, in my turn, examined my critics in sufficient detail to feel sure that, if they have never met my challenge, it is because they have not found sufficient evidence. Bored by the multiplicity of my dates and places, and disconcerted by the frequent incompatibility of my conclusions with their own ideas, they found it easier to suspect jugglery among my details than to confute me by marshalling serious counter-testimonies. Rashdall gave me the wholesome warning that I sometimes 'expatiated too much'. Again, it was a sin against psychology, and therefore against common-sense and historical method, to call the reader's attention in my second volume, by heavy type, to what I looked upon as the key passages. It was in the now defunct *Athenaeum*, I think, that a reviewer described me as producing quotations, for whatever might be my immediate purpose, with the facility of a conjuror producing rabbits from his hat.

The next bone of contention is that of judgment in History. While trying to see both sides, I have striven also to face questions of good and evil, and to express in those matters my own 'experience', that is, my personal reaction to what I seemed to find in the records. Here again, as in my marshalling of evidence, I fear I may sometimes have expatiated too much. But, as against critics who exaggerate in the other direction, telling us that the historian who judges ceases at that point to be an historian at all, I am all the more impenitent because I have never met anyone who really practised that precept. In its mildest form, it runs: 'The historian's business is not to judge but to understand.' But, under analysis, this is meaningless; for *judge* and *understand*, so far from being exclusive contradictories, are in fact complementary ideas. How can we understand anything without taking pains to judge it? And, although our critic may plead that he is speaking only of moral judgment, and that he would only exclude ethical questions from what ought to be a plain narrative of events, yet that distinction is academic, and it breaks down in practice. Even if it did make for the advancement of learning that we should judge men's characters and motives without considerations of good and evil, and judge events without reference to their ethical results, in practice the thing is impossible. The idea is even more mischievous than the pedantic emphasis on 'historical method', as apart from common-sense. It is responsible for much of that separation of Academic History from daily life, which Professors C. H. Firth and G. M. Trevelyan, from different standpoints, have noted with regret.[1] We are told that the historian must relate 'the thing in itself', 'just as it actually happened,'—as though 'things' were really separable from their context, and as though 'actual happenings' could be presented with mathematical accuracy! Men have held Ranke up to us as a model, yet without reading him with real care; for Ranke does in fact judge Henry VIII, however briefly, with 'mingled aversion and admiration'. He decides for us which races of men are fit to survive, and which are unfit. He has afforded a specious excuse to a modern Nazi editor for claiming, 'Here comes out clearly his kinship with Otto v. Bismarck and Adolf Hitler!' In the same breath in which he disclaims judging, Ranke condemns Macaulay for judging; and his lengthy appendixes are in effect judgments upon his own predecessors. That, in fact, is an inescapable thing; the man who most austerely repudiates judgment upon dead men's actions is often most dogmatic in praising or blaming the documentary sources. Professor Collingwood has noted this practically universal infraction of the writer's own law: those who warn us off from judging Julius Caesar are most unsparing in their condemnation of Mommsen's conception of Caesar: yet 'if I may think a German Professor wrong, why not a Roman General?'[2] We cannot eliminate judgment without emasculating history; the mere

---

[1] G. M. Trevelyan, *Clio, a Muse* (1914), p. 8: 'Of recent years the popular influence of history has greatly diminished. The thought and feeling of the rising generation is but little affected by historians.' C. H. Firth, *Commentary on Macaulay's History of England*, p. 1: 'The art of telling a story seems almost lost in England now.'

[2] See Ranke, *History of England*, vol. I, p. 169, and introd. to Bk I; vol. IV, pp. 363–70; Preface to the Abridgment of Ranke's *Weltgeschichte* by Kurt Walter-Schomburg (1936); R. A. Collingwood, *Autobiography*, p. 272.

attempt betrays confusion of thought. Whenever I have heard the subject discussed, it has finally settled down to a mere question of degree. By all means let them warn us against too frequent and intensive judgment, and especially against bias and the censorious spirit. But the idea that judicial history ceases to be true history has proved always, under analysis, to be an attempt to jump away from one's own shadow. In the name of science it cherishes a super-stition from which the Physical Sciences have broken free. Judg-ment is necessitated, from the foundation upwards, if only in the selection and presentation of our material. Darwin wrote to the economist, Henry Fawcett, in 1861: 'How profoundly ignorant B [who had said that Darwin should have published facts alone] must be of the very soul of observation! About thirty years ago there was much talk that geologists ought only to observe, and not theorize: and I well remember someone saying that at this rate a man might as well go into a gravel pit and count the pebbles, and describe the colours. How odd it is that anyone should not see that all observation must be for or against some view if it is to be of any service!'[1]

The discussion on this subject of judgment between Acton and Creighton is seldom studied, so far as my experience goes, with close attention to all the relevant documents. It began with Acton's review of Creighton's later volumes in his *History of the Papacy*. The review pointed out that Creighton had sometimes overdone his detachment, to the extent of ignoring indefensible wrongdoing. Creighton answered with what Schopenhauer ungallantly calls 'the lady's argument' ('My dear, the soup is lukewarm'—'Did you want to scald your mouth, then?'). Acton wrote: 'The Reign of Sin is more universal, the influence of unconscious error is less, than historians tell us.' Seven years later, Creighton gave his Hulsean Lectures on Persecution, and said, 'It is a thought borne home to the mind of anyone who reflects upon the past, that the sphere of human *error* in matters of morality is smaller than is generally supposed, and the sphere of *sin* is greater' (italics his). Next year Acton was created Regius Professor of History at Cambridge, and spoke in his Inaugural Lecture that sentence which has become a household word both for approvers and for disapprovers: 'The weight of opinion is against

---

[1] *Life of Henry Fawcett*, by Leslie Stephen, p. 100.

me when I exhort you never to debase the moral currency or to lower the standard of rectitude, but to try others by the final maxim that governs your own lives, and to suffer no man and no cause to escape the undying penalty which history has the power to inflict upon wrong.'

The question of Impartiality, again, is often treated with a pedantry which exaggerates healthy reverence into idolatry. The exaggerated stress which is laid upon this word *impartial*, while the thing itself is, in many cases, notoriously impossible of attainment, is apt to confuse the real issue. It renders men more afraid of the criticism 'You are biased', than of ignoring vital points in awkward historical questions. As G. M. Trevelyan says: 'Dispassionateness—*nil admirari*—may betray the most gifted historian into missing some vital truth in his subject. In Creighton's treatment of Luther, all that he says is both fair and accurate, yet from Creighton alone you would not guess that Luther was a great man or the German Reformation a stirring and remarkable movement.' Rather than the word *impartial*, then, should we not use *judicial*, which is far more exactly correspondent with realities? The historian, like the judge, should begin with as little bias as is humanly possible: but gradually, as the evidence unfolds itself, he forms a hypothesis more favourable to one of the contending parties than to the other. Further development of the evidence may balance his mind more in favour of the other party. But his continual effort is towards a definite choice between one party or the other; and if, at the end, he can give no guidance to the jury, there must be a certain sense of frustration and disappointment. He began with indifference between the parties: but he ends, perhaps, by adjudging almost a hundred per cent to the one, and zero to the other. Moreover, if he had to sit down now and give the history of the case, that story would no longer be written with complete impartiality. He would write in the light of what he now feels to know; the narrative would present his 'experience', and his method would justly aim at presenting the truths to his readers in the order and proportion best calculated to bring out this, his final decision. For *impartiality*, in the unthinking mind, too often connotes *indecision*. Yet surely it is one function of the true historian to discover those differences which, in all probability, do actually lurk behind conflicting and confusing testimonies. Why should not even the most scientific historian content himself with Goethe's confession of faith: 'I can promise to be sincere, but not to be impartial'?

Few men had a wider and juster reputation for impartiality than the philosopher Henry Sidgwick. As Tutor of Trinity, Cambridge, he bore part responsibility for rejecting the two best candidates, perhaps, who ever failed for one and the same Fellowship. Nobody can blame the electors for choosing the philosopher James Ward; yet this involved the rejection of F. W. Maitland, future historian of Law, and William Cunningham the Economic historian. All three had been Sidgwick's pupils, and I had a portion of the inner story from Professor H. S. Foxwell.

To him, another and younger pupil, Sidgwick once explained what went a long way to influence his decision. He said, 'I was so impressed by Maitland's thesis that this, in itself, rendered me cautious. I found myself so often saying, "This is just what I should have written myself, if only I could have put it half so well", that I suspected a hidden share of partiality for a pupil whose ideas agreed so exactly with my own.'

Something of the same moral transpires from a story which Dr Montagu Butler, Master of Trinity, told in a lighter vein, concerning the three Tutors of his own undergraduate days in the fifties. In those days there were no entrance scholarships, but an examination at the end of the men's first year. 'There was the good Dean Peacock, so sensitively conscientious that nothing could ever tempt him to vote a scholarship to one of his own pupils. Next, there was X, so devoted to his pupils that he could never bring himself to vote for anyone else. And lastly, there was Dr Whewell, who voted with the utmost impartiality, because he did not know his own pupils by sight.'

Moreover, there are subtle snares in virtue herself; and a man's belief in his own impartiality may become a partiality all the more fatal for being unconscious. I seem to have noticed this very clearly among pacifists, whose creed demands the utmost impartiality. I once heard this exemplified among a group of historians at a public dinner. The most noted among them for his impartiality—and, I hasten to add, justly noted—happened to mis-hear his neighbour, and to give him credit for advocating an injustice against which, in fact, he was protesting. At two words which caught his ear, he flared up immediately. The other tried vainly to explain that he also was reprobating those two words; that, in fact, such flat disapproval was the whole point he was trying to express. Even if the impartial man listened to the explanation, it conveyed nothing to him in his then state of excitement. His face flushed, the veins swelled on his forehead, and his voice was addressed to the whole end of our table. He was a man so just, and so confident in his own justice, that the mere sound of an unjust phrase put him beyond comprehension of the actual words in their actual context. That, in my experience, has been only a very conspicuous example among many; and I have often wondered what sort of civilization might be developed in some new island under the dictatorship of a committee of picked 'impartial' men.

This brings me to the still more vexed question of Controversy in History. I entered upon my more solid volumes with a consciousness of the self-taught man's limitations. But I saw also that the field which interested me most was one which offered, side by side with new truths, an abundant crop of inveterate errors. Therefore, from the first, I employed destructive criticism for clearing the way to my constructive object. And, since such criticism would necessarily provoke counter-criticism, I resolved to guard myself and my readers, as far as possible, from errors of actual fact. With all my own large-scale volumes, and with those which the University Press has allowed me to edit under the title of *Cambridge Studies in Medieval Life and Thought*, I have undertaken to publish, with as little delay as possible, errata sheets acknowledging all corrections of fact brought to my notice. With regard to other more definite controversies in the press, I have nearly always followed a similar policy, at considerable expense of time and money. For I have offered to print all that an adversary could say against my own assertions and inferences, often to a very considerable waste of ink and paper, and to publish it within the same covers as my own words. My best friends have often regretted this; it has naturally excited a certain amount of harmless merriment. I cannot claim to have done the right thing always in the right way: but, that it was right for someone to appeal in the press against the falsehoods which were commonly put before the public—falsehoods beginning in ignorance but hardening into impenitent obstinacy even after full exposure—I have never doubted. Such an attitude has its dangers, of course. It is not the highest ideal; but for myself, in my own particular circumstances, I still believe it to have been best. It has sometimes brought me into contact with strange wayfarers; but it is the Open Road.

Naturally, however, this has suggested more bias on my part than I myself am conscious of. It is easy, in every dispute, for the onlooker to assume 'six of one and half a dozen of the other'. But, in actual life, it often transpires that the true ratio is far more unequal; and, meanwhile, those who have consistently proffered evidence for such a disproportion will have seemed bigots. The best way out of this difficulty is that of healthy public discussion; in one word, of Controversy, as defined by the Pocket Oxford Dictionary: 'Argument conducted in the press or by other printed publications between opponents.' In 1932, when I was privileged to give the Raleigh Historical Lecture before the British Academy, I chose this for my text. I cited great men who have sinned against the light on specific historical points and never retracted—Luther, Calvin, and Bossuet, for instance. I argued that these literary infidelities would have been far more difficult if the matters had been discussed with antagonists under the ordinary rules of public debate. Thence I concluded that what History needs is not less but more controversy; only controversy rendered respectable by purgation from its too frequent excesses. A stricter public attitude on this point might raise the standard of factual truth among historians to something which should at least approach that of our law courts. In short, we want not less quantity of controversy, but far better quality. The acting chairman on that occasion, as soon as I had ended, rose to say, 'I cannot feel that controversy can *ever* be respectable', and left the chair. It was impossible for me to point out to a chairman that he himself had avoided controversy only by giving the audience his own highly controversial opinion *ex cathedra*, and thus excluding forcibly any 'argument conducted between opponents'. I have no hesitation in quoting this public incident, since he was a scholar well known for his sincere and lifelong attachment to good will all round, and this *obiter dictum* evidently represented his own instinctive reaction, typical of academic orthodoxy in such matters. In any other context, he would have been among the last to forget

that Lessing spent more than half of his life energies in controversy;
that Socrates was perhaps the arch-controversialist of all time; and
that even the Gospels and the Acts are full of controversy, sometimes
in very plain language. It is natural that abusive freedom or unfairness of criticism should have given this kind of thing a bad name
in common speech; but that affords no valid excuse for the formal
and sweeping condemnation of things which are reprehensible only
in their abuse. So long as Historians, while condemning 'judgment',
are found under examination to mean only 'the misuse of judgment';
so long as they condemn 'controversy' in words which apply
properly only to its misuse, so long must they be content with a
definitely second place in comparison with chemists and physicists,
who define their terms with scrupulous accuracy and reason from
them with rigorous logic.

Let us have purer controversy, then, but more of it, for civilization's sake, on all highly contentious topics. Why, indeed, are those
topics contentious, except for the double reason that they excite
passionate interest, and are complicated enough to have resisted
hitherto the separate arguments of advocates on either side, each
preaching from his own particular pulpit and tempted to ignore the
other's inconvenient counter-pleas? Does not common-sense suggest that the two parties might be brought together into a single
court, where the judges—that is, the public—could with equal ease
hear both sides, and where the advocate who indulged in unreasonable inaccuracy or exaggeration would risk immediate exposure?
It is a commonplace that the present plight of the civilized world
is to a great extent due to sheer ignorance or misunderstanding of
plain facts, on one side or the other. Could this evil possibly have
reached its present pitch if our official historians had taken ordinary
scientific precautions in proper time? We had men on both sides
whose words commanded world-wide attention, and who could be
depended upon for able and temperate exposition, each of his own
country's case: Balfour, for instance, and Stresemann. We have our
University Faculties, our Royal Historical Society, and our British
Academy. Why did none of these suggest or encourage such an
official marshalling of pleas and counter-pleas on the Origin of the
War, or on the Versailles Treaty, not as a *status quo* but as a foundation for gradual better settlements? Between two such antagonists,

how could the most thoughtless mind condemn 'argument in the public press between opponents' as an essentially disreputable thing? Even as a commercial proposition, such a book would have outsold Mr J. M. Keynes. Friends often told me that it was mere wishful thinking to suppose that men were ever converted by argument; and I had not forgotten H. W. Fowler's postcard: 'Most convincing— by which of course I don't mean that it will ever convince anybody of anything'. Yet, at the worst, even if this reed had broken under the strain, it could not have wounded the hand of Peace so desperately as did the collapse of those slogans which historians, though well aware of their falsehood, have yet supinely permitted to become household words among credulous millions: 'Nothing worth having was ever gained by war'; or, 'Don't think of war, and you won't get war'.

CHAPTER XXXIV

AN EXTREME CASE

THIS brings me to the most critical point of all. It is not only that nearly all my work has had this controversial tinge, and that my avowed aim has been destruction for construction's sake. I must also meet the objection that, for nearly thirty years, I concentrated criticism so steadily upon a Cardinal of the Roman Church as to arouse a natural suspicion, except among the few who knew me in private life, that I had some personal grudge to pay off. The *doyen* of Roman Catholic apologists in Britain, Fr. H. Thurston, S.J., took mainly this personal line against me, tacitly abandoning most of the strictly historical ground. He wrote once: 'His position, it seems to me, entitled him to a certain measure of consideration and indulgence even from his adversaries, a consideration which I should always show in writing about an Anglican Bishop during his lifetime.' I replied: 'If ever you or your friends find an Anglican Bishop, or a University teacher, as habitually (and impenitently, which is far worse) inaccurate as Cardinal Gasquet, by all means expose them in the plainest language. St Bernard quotes from St Gregory, if my memory serves me, "*melius est ut scandalum oriatur quam veritas relinquatur*".'[1]

My personal contact with the Cardinal was simply that of an ordinary reader who exercises his right of asking an author civilly for straightforward references, in the face of apparently incorrect assertions. Behind this, lay no prejudice against the man as apart from his writings. On the contrary, I studied his face with great interest at the British Museum and the International Historical Congress, wondering what was going on within. It was handsome, with the added dignity of a man who had lived consistently in view of a not ignoble ideal, and who was accustomed to represent that ideal officially in all his public words and actions. It reminded me

---

[1] See my *A Premium upon Falsehood*, p. 23: 'It is better that scandal should arise than that truth should be deserted.' Fr. Thurston's 'during his lifetime' is characteristic.

of a stanza in George Herbert's *British Church*, where he characterizes her Roman rival:

> She on the hills . . .
> Hath kissed so long her painted shrines
> That even her face by kissing shines
> For her reward.

Moreover, an American scholar told me once, from behind the scenes, the tangled story how Gasquet missed his election to the Archbishopric of Westminster; a story which, so far as it went, was altogether honourable to him. But in his face there was also a plain note of personal vanity; something of the 'proud prelate' after Wolsey's pattern. Such was the man to my bodily eyes: one whose whole life had been moulded by the spirit which inspired Leo XIII's famous warning to the priesthood: 'Those who study [History] must never lose sight of the fact that it contains a collection of dogmatic facts which impose themselves upon our faith, and which no man is permitted to call in question.'[1] And, in increasing proportion as I studied him more closely, this religious apologist stood out as a living example of what Pascal records with lapidary precision: 'Jamais on ne fait le mal si pleinement et si gaiement que quand on le fait par un faux principe de conscience'.[2] Lord Acton said much the same concerning the Jesuits of the seventeenth century: 'It is this combination of an eager sense of duty, zeal for sacrifice, and love of virtue, with the deadly taint of a conscience perverted by authority, that makes them so odious to touch and so curious to study.'[3]

Gasquet had considerable literary ability, and had been laborious in his own way: but from the first he was superficial, and inaccuracy grew upon him like a crust, especially after the remarkable success of his two-volume *Henry VIII and the English Monasteries*. Creighton pointed out in *The English Historical Review*, first, that there was little original work in this book, and, secondly, that no vouchers were given for what was perhaps the most important pillar

[1] Encyclical of 1899, to the Clergy of France.

[2] *Pensées*, ed. Brunschvicq, III, 328: 'Never does a man do evil so fully and so lightheartedly as when he does it on a false conscientious principle.' Compare Huxley's verdict as recorded above in my chapter 'A Bee in the Bonnet'.

[3] *Letters to Mary Gladstone*, p. 142.

of Gasquet's whole case, viz. his statement that the healthy moral condition of the monasteries was established by the Episcopal Registers, of which only a fraction were as yet published. During the remaining forty years of Gasquet's life, marked by numerous editions and translations of his book, and other historical publications, he never took notice of this very broad hint; and Creighton's remaining years were too soon diverted to episcopal administration. Meanwhile other critics, and especially James Gairdner, whose word carried real weight, had hailed the book as epoch-making. Gairdner was an enthusiastic Anglo-Catholic, by revulsion from his early Presbyterianism; and the book so exactly suited the views of this party, as well as of Roman Catholics, that its commercial success could have been assured even though its faults had been worse. It was therefore the first of the kind that I took seriously in hand for my project of constructive criticism. I had not read Creighton's reviews; but I knew already enough of the Registers, both in print and in MS., to pitch at once upon that particular point. I could see through Gasquet's scanty references that he was borrowing at second-hand from Oliver's meritorious, but antiquated and sometimes very untrustworthy, book on the Exeter Registers. I found in addition so many mis-statements and garbled quotations in Gasquet's book, and it was still enjoying so much popularity and laudation, that I took the privilege of all serious readers, and wrote civilly to him in March 1901 for the references which were lacking in his book. With apologies for troubling him, I asked him to grant me, literally, only a few minutes. I enclosed a list of all the printed Registers known to me, and asked him, first, to initial those upon which he would rely for his testimonial to monastic morality, secondly, to cross out those upon which he did not rely, and thirdly, to add any titles of Registers, printed or MS., which might be missing from my list.[1] This, if he had had any straightforward and adequate reply, would have taken him just about what our medieval ancestors defined as 'a paternoster-while'. Yet I had to write three

---

[1] Fr. H. Thurston, S.J., asserted publicly, in defence of his colleague, that I had begun with incivilities which naturally moved the great man to contemptuous silence. I therefore published the whole correspondence at once in extenso (*A Premium upon Falsehood*, App. A). This reduced my accuser to silence, but he offered no apology.

times, always enclosing this list to spare him trouble; and I received only two curt replies to the effect that 'it would take me more time than I can spare to go through my collections'—a trouble which, of course, I had thrice carefully abstained from suggesting, lest excuse should be given for any such evasion. The book itself, just about this time, was appearing in a cheap and revised edition; yet the author refused to recognize his responsibility for even specifying the sources upon which he professedly based a judgment absolutely fundamental to his whole apologia!

Thenceforward it was clear that he meant to brazen it out, and that he deserved no quarter. Again, not long afterwards, the Anglican *Church Quarterly* exposed mis-statements of fact in Gasquet's new book on *The Old English Bible* which were even more inexplicable than any in the *Henry VIII*. One, indeed, was as indefensible as though he should have built a theory upon the denial that his own name began with a G.[1] Yet in a second edition, five years later, he not only reprinted unchanged those assertions but also the arguments drawn from them, without even the excuse of stereotype plates: the falsehoods were deliberately set up afresh by the typographer.

An old Balliol chum of my friend H. W. Fowler, orthodox Catholic but well-read and fairly open-minded, was naturally shocked when I showed him chapter and verse for this. At the same time he warned me: 'You mustn't try to bully a Catholic Prelate; you will gain nothing that way.' Yet to me, that seemed, all the more clearly, the one thing necessary for clearing a path through this jungle of lies.[2] I here use that invidious word advisedly, because there is a stage of impenitence at which what was mere mis-statement must be christened *falsehood*, and a still further stage of hardened deliberation when the only fitting word is *lie*. Lord Acton observed this distinction in that letter in which he characterized those of his fellow-Catholics—'the insolent and aggressive faction', as Newman had called them—who worked by crooked means to engineer the Infallibility Decree of 1870. He wrote: '[Ultramontanism] not only promotes, it inculcates distinct mendacity and deceitfulness. In certain cases it is made a duty to lie. But those who teach this doctrine

---

[1] I give full details on pp. 5 ff. of my booklet, *Sectarian History.*
[2] Or, as Pascal put it in his *Provinciales, mentiris impudentissime.*

do not become habitual liars in other things.'[1] It was precisely this which made Gasquet's apologetic strength, but rendered his literary dishonesties so mischievous, not only among his own party but also among the general public, unwilling to believe in a prelate's eclipse of conscience. A man's historical vices are harmful in direct proportion to his private virtues. I pleaded this point before the British Academy in 1932.

With Gasquet, the temptation was overpowering. By nature he was as described by his apologist, Fr. H. Thurston, S.J., 'most regrettably impatient of anything like revision'.[2] Then he leapt into fame with a book which, though fundamentally partisan and shallow, wore superficially a learned and dispassionate style, admirably calculated to impress candid readers. Even the garbled quotations themselves were perhaps not of his own garbling, but of the sort which are very commonly passed from hand to hand, without verification, among apologists in his Church. Meanwhile he was rapidly rising in the hierarchy; and thus, to the temptation of personal infallibility, was added the further temptation of class loyalty. An Abbot-General of the English Benedictines must not don the white sheet for errors which in a novice might earn the birch.[3] The further he had slipped away from the truth, and the faster his book sold, the greater were his difficulties when once he had set his face against frank confession and amendment. It is a weakness inherent in every centralized and strictly disciplined religious organization to exaggerate human frailty in this matter: 'My own church, right or wrong!' St Bernard, writing to his pupil, Pope Eugenius III, branded unsparingly that atmosphere of 'you absolve me, and I will absolve you' which, even then, was spreading from Rome over Christendom. The result was 'Impunity, child of carelessness and mother of insolence, root of impudence and nurse of transgression'.[4]

Temptations to error lie everywhere around us; but it is not everywhere that error is so easily condoned. Let us imagine as near a parallel as we can in the Physical Sciences. It is conceivable that a

[1] *Correspondence*, ed. Figgis and Laurence, p. 14.
[2] *A Premium upon Falsehood*, p. 23.
[3] Paul Desjardins, a Liberal Roman Catholic, complained about this time that the higher a man's hierarchical rank, the less we can believe his word.
[4] *De Consideratione*, IV, v. 20.

militarist organization might find profit to itself in the falsification of certain chemical facts, and that a popular and otherwise estimable general might succumb here to a narrow feeling of class loyalty. His fellow-militarists might back him through thick and thin, and the War Office authorities might give him what honours were at their disposal; but how long could he count on immunity among his fellow-scientists, outside the small circle who were already pledged to partisan support? And if his military bias in that case, even as the man's religious bias in this, had led him into mis-statements so flat and indefensible that an intelligent elementary schoolboy, put once upon the track, could run them all down in a morning's work, how many scientific friends would be betrayed into giving him special public favours? We have sometimes heard of scientists faking their experiments, but they are pilloried as examples. A barrister may allow himself great latitude of argument for his own case; but, if he is found to falsify actual facts, he is a marked man. Why should historians be content that their own field, as compared with others, should be a happy hunting-ground for irresponsibles who can count upon personal popularity in Clubland?

The Cardinal, however, was not only tolerated but encouraged. Every step made it harder for him to abandon this policy of dignified official impenitence; and, for a long time, verily it had its reward. Professor Tout tried to dissuade me from attacking him on the ground that 'the man is not worth powder and shot'. Yet Gasquet's *magnum opus* was selling, not among sectarian readers only, in numbers which neither Tout, nor any other professor of those years, could distantly approach. It was advertised how Gairdner, the Anglican scholar best qualified to judge of Gasquet's period, 'wrote that the charges against the English monks and nuns at the time of the Reformation "are now dispelled for ever"'.[1] When Gasquet was raised to the Cardinalate (1914) he publicly ascribed this dignity to his historical writings. A dinner was got up in his honour, and attended by an imposing company of historians and *littérateurs*. He was elected to the Athenaeum under the rule of Special Distinction. The Pope appointed him President of the Commission for Vulgate Revision; then, Prefect of the Vatican Archives; and finally Chief Librarian.

---

[1] *Life* of Gasquet in *D.N.B.*, by his Downside colleague, Abbot Butler, who gives no hint whatever of Gairdner's later doubts and recantation, in proportion as he gradually learned the truth from study of the original documents.

At an International Historical Congress, in 1921, he was naturally on the platform; and the chairman, a scholar of austere intellectuality, went out of his way to turn round and compliment the Cardinal: 'A great historian'; and then, after a pause, turning to the audience with special emphasis: 'A *very* great historian!'

It is true that, from the peak years of his *Henry VIII* onwards, his writings began to command less attention, and ominous whispers went round even among the faithful. When, to both editions of my *Ten Medieval Studies*, I added two appendixes with full details of nearly two hundred serious mis-statements, blunders in Latin, etc., which I had noted during the perusal of about half his output, then significant notes of warning were sounded by two papers usually favourable to him. Both pointed out that, for his own credit, he ought now to meet accusations which, at first sight at least, were so damaging.[1] He still took no notice; but readers gradually did, and sometimes, privately, even within his own Church. Gairdner, when he first saw my strictures, wrote to me that they formed 'a powerful indictment'; and, as time went on, he became increasingly disillusioned. In 1906 he allowed me to publish a letter of partial retractation. In 1912, when I sent him fresh exposure of garbled texts in Gasquet's recently published *Abbot Wallingford*, he replied, 'Abbot Gasquet does surprise me, and I do not wonder at your severity'. One of the last things he ever published (*Nineteenth Century*, July, 1909) amounted to a general retractation of his earliest favourable judgment. And his last letter to me described how he had just discussed the Wallingford book with Gasquet at the British Museum, with the result (I quote from memory) that 'I hardly knew whether I stood on my head or my heels'. A little earlier, there had been a scene at the Athenaeum which was described to me by one of the bystanders, T. Bailey Saunders, who had been Secretary to the London University Commission. He was much attracted by Gasquet, who, hearing that he had read my earlier strictures, took him to his rooms in Great Ormond Street and showed him, by way of self-defence, an imposing row of notebooks filled at the British Museum. In one of our walks at Eastbourne, he told me what he had seen and heard a day or two before. Pius X had just published

---

[1] *The Times Literary Supplement*, September 23, 1915; *Church Times*, July 15, 1921: 'Silence seems no longer possible after Mr Coulton has repeated the charge.'

his Encyclical *Pascendi*. Gasquet wrote twice from the Athenaeum to *The Times*, emphatically denying (what even the *Osservatore Romano* half admitted to be true) that this decree struck at Newman's Doctrine of Development. Saunders found himself among a group in the Athenaeum listening to Sir Rowland Blennerhassett, Lord Acton's friend, and, like him, of old Catholic ancestors. Sir Rowland laid *The Times* down, and said, with public and indignant emphasis: 'The man is lying, and he knows he is!' We must make allowance, of course, for freedom of speech in Clubland.[1]

In all this, the exposures received no help whatever from what might be called Official History. Naturally enough, my own persistence here, with its 'damnable iteration', seemed to many people the behaviour of a Protestant bigot; so that a brilliant journalist, in the Roman Catholic *Universe*, was able to condemn me offhand as a person who in the Roman religious press was regularly styled 'the notorious Dr Coulton'. I do not know of a single historian who has taken the trouble to verify Gasquet's incriminated passages sufficiently to pronounce judicially between him and me. The two persons who have come nearest to that standard are both Roman Catholics, amateurs in History, who began by sending me accusing letters, and ended by looking into the facts and warmly taking my part, even in the public press. One, I regret to say, who was Professor at a well-known Theological Seminary, has since been removed from his post and transferred to a country rectory. It was he who wrote publicly: 'I told Dr Coulton some time ago that I would resign from this discussion [of G.'s literary methods] if there was a plain declaration from the ecclesiastical authorities that the common herd of Catholics, to which I belong, may not discuss the faults, however plain and public, of the higher clergy. If the Cardinal Archbishop [Dr Hinsley] is prepared to make a declaration of the kind, we shall know where we stand.'[2] But, in my eyes, the one reason which makes it here worth while to tell this story, with all the detail which was necessary if it were to be touched at all, lies in its implications for the notorious neglect of History as compared with the Physical Sciences. Doubtless it was very human in so many official teachers that they should shirk the task of adjudicating among the sordid details of a violent dispute, partly in the public

---

[1] I give much fuller details in my *Premium upon Falsehood*, App. H.
[2] *Premium upon Falsehood*, p. 12.

press. What is more, there was in it a true touch of human generosity, and of sympathy for a respectable religious minority. But, from the plain business point of view, it is equally human for readers to prefer those studies in which they can trust the most distinguished specialists to look to the purity of their own wares. Generosity at the public expense is not among the highest virtues; and sympathy, again, if it takes the form of mere sufferance and protection from open criticism, is far from complimentary to those to whom we thus condescend.

The total warfare of to-day is teaching us to reverse old-fashioned proverbs. Nowadays we are learning to transform what was nobody's business into everybody's business. Wherever individualism is found to be developing a selfishness detrimental to the common good, there a wise collectivism must step in. This is Utopian not in the common depreciatory sense, but in that of St Thomas More himself, who showed the world how a six-hour working day would suffice if only we had conscription all round, of man-power and woman-power and wealth. He insisted that his ideal republic had discovered nothing which might not be done in other countries. The Utopians may not be so clever as the Europeans: 'Yet in study, in travail, and in laboursome endeavour they far pass us.' Whatever common-sense demands is undertaken by all Utopians in common, so that it is 'with marvellous speed despatched' by 'an innumerable company of people'; thus the work is completed 'in less time than any man would believe.'[1]

I shall not live to see it myself, but I am credulous enough to believe in the final victory of reason, however tardy, and to imagine a world in which the healthy initiative of writers, and the willing response of readers, will make cheating in History as disreputable, and therefore as rare, as cheating at cards. Half the evil lies in the torpor of public opinion: hence we have St Bernard's 'impunity, the child of carelessness'. We may attribute to all true democracy that which Osten-Sacken said to me in 1888 concerning American society, and what Lord Tweedsmuir has put with epigrammatic precision.[2] The first step on this ladder is that of honest publicity: if need be, of conflicting and complementary publicities. Christianity, the one force that lived and grew while the civilization of Imperial Rome decayed, was born in Controversy.

[1] *Utopia*, ed. J. R. Lumby, pp. 65, 69, 85, 141, 169.
[2] *Pilgrim's Way*, p. 269: see above, chapter xx, 'Heidelberg'.

CHAPTER XXXV

SOUL'S EASE

THERE is at Thurlestone a quiet lane leading past Court Barton Farm, down to the brook which opens out finally into The Lea and The Sands. Here lay a fallen tree that tempted one to sit in the sun; and here, in the late summer of 1918, my wife and I took a momentous decision which seems now inseparable from that tree. It was already possible in those days to hope that the end of war might be in sight; and then Cambridge would at last elect a successor to Gwatkin in the Chair of Ecclesiastical History. We agreed not only that I should stand, but also that I should clearly mark my standpoint. Gwatkin had been elected as a layman, and there ought to be no doubt that I reckoned myself in that same category. I would therefore give half a dozen public lectures which should show beforehand that I claimed the utmost historical freedom within the religious field. Rashdall would fain have dissuaded me; but I liberated my soul, and have never had reason to suppose that it influenced the result either way. Certainly it introduced no regrettable rivalries. For twenty years Professor Whitney and I worked harmoniously and in growing sympathy of companionship, if not in close scientific agreement. He became a generous supporter of the friendly subscription which paid my fees for the Doctorate; it was to him that I dedicated the little reprint of my *Two Saints* in 1932; and it was about that time that he too became involved in the Roman controversy, through his unsparing exposure of the exaggerated legends of English episcopal dependence upon Rome. My religious position has altered so little since then, though I have tried to keep an open mind in face of many other changes, that this present chapter will be, in effect, a brief summary of those lectures [1] and of the article which, at the editor's invitation, I contributed to *The Realist* for December, 1929, under the title of 'Modern Faith'.[2]

But, first, I must go back for a moment to Herefordshire, where the 'blue remembered hills', the 'spires', the 'farms', are no less

---

[1] *Christ, St Francis, and To-Day* (Camb. Univ. Press).
[2] Reprinted at 1*d.* by the Orpington Press, Orpington, Kent.

worthy than Shropshire to have inspired Housman's *Land of Lost Content*. It was in 1885, on the grass of the rectory orchard at Coddington, one warm afternoon of early September. I had already quitted my curacy; in a few days I was bound to travel still farther westward for my new work in Wales; the time and the place invited meditation. There I lay as in Andrew Marvell's Garden, 'ripe apples dropped about my head', and I found still more enchantment in the masses of autumn crocus, known hitherto only in the pages of Matthew Arnold's *Obermann*. Thrushes and blackbirds revelled among the fruit; the jay's scream from the spinney was mellowed into harmony; everything breathed a quiet Wordsworthian pantheism. But my thoughts wandered back inevitably to Mrs Curtis' mingled pity and horror of a few hours before, when I had told her my reasons for leaving parish work. Her plain reaction to the news had been that of a convinced Evangelical: Could she only make me realize the peril of eternal misery! For, with all her native breadth of mind and charity, she kept still from her early training too much fundamentalism to shake off those crude ideas of heaven and hell which dominated so many earnest minds, from General Booth at one extreme to Cardinal Newman at another.[1] Her passionate pleadings of that morning, in contrast with this deep peace of nature all around me, challenged unshrinking thought; and, the further I went, the more explicitly did reason reinforce my instinctive resistance to doctrines which would base God's justice upon what, in man, would seem most glaringly unjust. I saw how little Bible evidence there was to support the detailed and systematic horrors of that creed which was 'orthodox', nominally at least, among both

[1] A Belgian Redemptorist priest, Fr. F. X. Godts, has collected exhaustively the judgments of medieval theologians as to the small number of mankind who shall get to heaven (*De Paucitate Salvandorum*, Roulers, 1899). He writes: 'It is vain to seek even a single Saint who has taught that the number of the elect forms a majority.' St Alfonso Liguori [1750] confesses that 'the more general opinion is that the greater part even of the Faithful [Roman Catholics] are damned'. St Thomas Aquinas himself, for all his moderation, contrasts the 'few' saved with the 'very many' damned (*Summa Theol.* pars I, Quaest. XXIII, art. 7). Medieval preachers put the proportion at one in a thousand, or even in ten thousand. On the other hand, at Heidelberg, Mr Armitage often told me how his own father, a successful Yorkshire wool-merchant and orthodox Evangelical, passed his last years of retirement at Cheltenham in those mental agonies which Luther describes in his monastic cell.

Catholics and Protestants. And, now that decision was thus forced upon me, that which in early days had perhaps been mainly wishful thinking became demonstrable both in reason and in morality. I felt that this doctrine would bow us down to a wicked human imagination, and that atheism itself was preferable in many ways to this sort of cacotheism. As Plutarch said: 'I would rather a man should deny the existence of Plutarch, than that he should credit me with doing the things which are told of our gods and goddesses.' I had not then met with the still more emphatic protest of the medieval heretic;[1] but I did know my *Sartor Resartus*, and I rose up from those rectory apple trees and crocuses with his Everlasting No in my heart. Thus, so long as I retain my human reason and human feelings, it will be unthinkable to accept official responsibility for any religious organization committed to doctrines of heaven and hell which have contaminated 'orthodox' thought in the Middle Ages and beyond. It was just about this Coddington time that Dean Farrar raised a storm in Anglicanism by preaching, not against hell itself, but against that doctrine of an Everlasting Hell, which had forced other preachers, for so many centuries past, to draw the most appalling logical conclusions.[2]

Groups, like individuals, have souls of their own, following much the same laws when allowance is made for different circumstances. Therefore a Church, like a Churchman, needs Confession and Restitution for its spiritual health: such was the early Christian habit of public confession and effectual visible restitution. No religious community can afford, in this modern world, to traffic with ideas derived far less from the Gospels than from a bitterness

[1] It was testified before the Inquisition at Toulouse, in the thirteenth century: '*Item*, the said Peter said that, if he could lay hands on that god who, among a thousand men he had created, saved one and damned all the rest, he would tear him and rend him with tooth and nail as a recreant, and would hold him for false and perfidious, and would spit in his face' (C. Douais, *Documents, etc.*, vol. II, p. 100).

[2] Berthold of Regensburg, perhaps the greatest of all medieval mission preachers [1250], tells his audience to imagine themselves at white heat in a white-hot universe, during as many years as there are grains in the sea-sand, or hairs that have grown on all the beasts of the world since the Creation: 'and even then, you are only at the beginning; as far from the end as when you first started.' Yet Berthold was a Franciscan friar, kind-hearted and well versed in human nature.

engendered by persecution, mingled later with the crude fancies of half-converted barbarian races.

My Everlasting Yes, naturally, crystallized far more gradually than this Everlasting No. Starting from the Gospels, I realized how 'modernist' the earlier Church often was. When John the Baptist sent his disciples to ask Jesus, 'Art thou he that should come, or do we look for another?' (Matt. xi, 3), Christ's answer was different from what we commonly get nowadays from official Christianity in any of its organized denominations. He did not put before those enquirers a Confession of Faith; not even anything like the so-called Apostles' Creed. He did not reply with a clear definition *ex cathedra*: 'The answer to your first question is in the affirmative; to the second, in the negative.' His answer here, in effect, was identical with that other exhortation to the disciples themselves: 'Seek, and ye shall find; knock, and it shall be opened unto you.' Look round, collect fully and sincerely all the evidence you can find, and judge for yourselves. Religion, like History, is Experience.

'Christians are not born but made.' So wrote Tertullian some two centuries after the Crucifixion: and St Jerome, two centuries later again, said much the same.[1] St Augustine, in his *Soliloquy*, expresses the same struggle: 'I desire to know God and mine own soul.' 'Nothing more?' 'Nothing whatever.' This same sense of personal struggle and personal appropriation comes out in the recent confessions of a man who was no less remarkable as writer than as artist, and whose pen is as frankly unconventional as his chisel. Eric Gill is recounting his own conversion from Agnosticism, and he writes: 'I told you I invented a new religion and found it was an old one. In effect, I invented the Roman Catholic Church....I found a thing in my mind and I opened my eyes and found it in front of me. You don't become a Catholic by joining the Church; you join the Church because you are a Catholic.'[2]

Thus, Religion, like History, must necessarily differ from man to man; that is what the most elaborate formulas will never prevent. We may frankly accept this necessity, and yet believe firmly that the differences are comparatively irrelevant: that, in essentials, all

[1] Tertullian, *De Testimonio Animae*, § 1, and Hieronymus, *ep. ad Laetam* § 1: '*Fiunt non nascuntur Christiani.*'
[2] *Autobiography*, p. 70: cf. all the preceding pages from 64 onwards.

true seekers do find enough to live by. To-day, this is practically admitted even by some orthodox Roman Catholic theologians. For fourteen centuries that Church had interpreted literally the adaman- tine pronouncement of St Cyprian: 'Outside the Church there is no salvation.' That was one of the main pillars of Inquisitorial theory. But at last, about 1650, when the bloody religious wars had shown the impossibility of imposing one faith by force over all Europe, a Jesuit Cardinal can be found arguing that, to every soul which attains to reason in this life, God gives light sufficient for its salva- tion. All philosophies and creeds contain some element of truth: thus the soul that seeks God in good faith shall, by divine grace, find saving truth therein. This pronouncement is now seized upon by enlightened Roman Catholics and represented as the true meaning of St Cyprian's formidable text.[1] After so many centuries of mis- understandings and bloodshed, we are now at last permitted to believe in the whiteness of what seems plain black, and has been steadily denounced as black by medieval saints. By God's grace, each man may be saved through such grains of truth as are contained in his own creed. We may even maintain, with the earliest of great Christian apologists, that to seek the truth wholeheartedly is to be Christian in essence, if not in name.[2] Again and again, Religion is Experience. It is, for each man, the sum total of that man's truth- seeking: in each soul it bears its own stamp, none the less genuine for being individual, of the truth that makes us free. It gives each man the right to say with Luther after searching his own conscience: 'Here stand I, I can no other.'

Most instructive, in this connection, is the long and dignified dis- cussion between Bossuet, Hammer of Protestants, and the Protestant philosopher-mathematician Leibniz. Bossuet argued: 'Permit me to beg you once again, in conclusion, to examine seriously, in the

---

[1] See Karl Adam, *The Spirit of Catholicism*, chapter x, and especially p. 168.
[2] Justin Martyr, *First Apology*, § 46. 'We have already proved him [Christ] to be the firstborn of God, the Logos, of which mankind have all been par- takers; and those who lived by reason were Christians, notwithstanding they were thought to be atheists. Such among the Greeks were Socrates and Hera- clitus, and those like them.' Compare St Gregory the Great (*Moral. in Job*, lib. xxviii, c. vii, § 16). 'John the Baptist died not in the direct confession of Christ, but for telling the truth in a matter of righteousness; yet, seeing that Christ is truth, therefore in dying for truth he died for Christ.'

face of God, whether you have any sound means of preventing the
Church from becoming eternally variable, on the supposition that
it is possible for her to err, and to change her decrees on matters of
faith?' Leibniz replied: 'We prefer, my Lord, to be members of
such a Church, always moving and eternally variable.'[1] For he,
when confronted with other men's different religious experiences—
even when they differed so far as to seem flatly contradictory—could
fall back upon Christ's words: 'What is that to thee? follow thou
me' (John xxi, 22).

Those last three words give us the conclusion of the whole
matter. The Christian is the follower of Christ; and, as there are
many degrees of fidelity in following, so also are there many mansions in Christianity. There exists no Christian community so pure
that it has not, in the course of centuries, nourished many most
anti-Christian doctrines and practices. On the other hand, the body
which makes least explicit formal pretensions does nevertheless rank
among the highest in what are generally counted as the chief Christian
virtues. Each of us puts his own religious denomination first; but
many, on mature reflection, would give the second place to the
Society of Friends. It is one of the grossest historical errors to
define Christianity in blind accordance with the popular ideas of our
own or any other day, even though 90 per cent of the multitude
should share those ideas. All off-hand attempts to exclude this or
that other community from the title *Christian* are ruled out by plain
recorded facts. Whereas Roman Catholicism, at the Council of
Trent, pronounced the Holy Scriptures to be inerrant, yet it was
only then, after fifteen centuries of discussion, that she finally defined
which were those inerrant books; and her then definition was irreconcilable with the judgment of countless Fathers in earlier centuries,
including that of St Jerome to whom she owes her own official
Vulgate. Even the Divinity of Christ, after ten generations of
Churchmen had thought it out and discussed it, was still so doubtful
a point that the decision of the majority at Nicaea finally asserted
itself only after quarrels which embittered Europe for many genera-

---

[1] *Œuvres de Leibniz*, ed. A. Foucher de Careil (1860), vol. II, introd. lxxviii ff.
and text pp. 385 ff. That is the first edition which contains Leibniz's final letter;
Bossuet's nephew suppressed this in order to make it appear that his uncle had
had the last word.

tions to come. Down to the present day, no exact definition of the word *Christian* has commanded anything like universal consent. The plain historical standpoint is expressed in *The Catholic Dictionary*, commenting on Acts xi, 26: 'And the disciples were called Christians first in Antioch.' The term *Christian* was parallel to Pompeiani (followers of Pompey), and to the modern *Gladstonian* or *Darwinian*. Followers, that is, to whatever extent; for here, as with such equally important words as *Truth* or *Good*, there are naturally infinite degrees. No Church has ever felt sufficiently sure of herself to attempt any scientific and authoritative formula here.[1]

But we must turn again to the John Baptist episode; for there are other crucial words to be faced. Jesus appeals there to 'those things which ye do hear and see: the blind receive their sight, and the lame walk, the lepers are cleansed, and the deaf hear, the dead are raised up, and the poor have the gospel preached to them.' Let the enquirers seek sincerely, and they will find convincing miracles.

St Gregory the Great, preaching in St Peter's at Rome at about the time he was sending his missionaries to England, took his text from Mark xvi, 14–18, those words which so closely resemble Matthew xi, 5–6. His theme was the comparative cessation of such miracles as had marked the earliest Christian beginnings. The people of Rome, he saw, could no longer expect any frequency of '*corporeal*' (or, as we should say, *physical*) miracles. These had, indeed, been necessary to the earliest generations, and believers had received divine powers to work them for the conversion of unbelievers. But 'now, my brethren, seeing that ye work no such signs, is it that ye believe not?' Not so; 'for Holy Church worketh daily now, in

---

[1] Addis and Arnold, *Catholic Dictionary*, 3rd ed., p. 158: 'Probably the heathen at Antioch mistook *Christus* for a proper name, and called the disciples *Christiani* just as they called those who adhered to Pompey's party *Pompeiani*. . . . In later times the word has been used (1) for those who imitate the life as well as hold the faith of Christ, (2) for Catholics, (3) for baptized persons who believe in Christ, (4) for all baptized persons.' Aquinas in one place solemnly adopts the first of these definitions, in a form which would exclude our calling even the Pope a Christian, unless his personal life were such that he could truly be said 'to have crucified the flesh, with the affections and lusts thereof' (2a, 2ae, Quaest. CXXIV, art. 5, m. 1). But in his discussion of the distinction between heresy, Judaism, and paganism, he implies adherence to the last and most usual definition, that all baptized are Christians (2a, 2ae, Quaestt. X, XI). Compare *The Catholic Encyclopaedia*, vol. III, p. 720: 'Christian baptism constitutes membership in the Visible Church; the state of grace, membership in the Invisible.'

the spirit, whatsoever the Apostles then wrought in the body....
And indeed these miracles are all the greater for being spiritual: all
the greater, as uplifting not the bodies but the souls of men.' Christ
warned us that even wicked men can sometimes work bodily miracles
(Matt. vii, 22–23). 'Wherefore, my beloved brethren, love not those
signs which ye may share in common with the reprobate, but love
such as I have already said, miracles of charity and piety, which are
the more secure as they are more secret, and whose reward from God
is by so much the greater as their glory among men is less.' In other
words, the greatest of Christian miracles is the Christian Church
itself, despite all its human imperfections. Nearly two centuries
earlier, this had been put with epigrammatical exaggeration by
St Augustine: 'If [our adversaries] believe not that the Apostles
wrought any such things for confirmation of the resurrection of
Christ, it is sufficient then that the whole world believed them without miracles, which is a miracle as great as any of the rest.'[1]

Thus, once again, Religion is Experience. If, in fact, corporeal
miracles come within our experience, then we welcome them: to
deny their possibility a priori would be inverted dogmatism. But
we need not lament their absence; for we have always the spiritual
miracle under our very eyes:

> Une immense espérance a traversé la terre,
> Malgré nous vers le ciel il faut lever la tête.[2]

The belief in a Crucified Carpenter has taken more men out of themselves, and further out of themselves, than any other event in the
records of this half of the globe whose history we know with any
intimacy. Next to the life and death of Jesus himself, there is no
episode in all our history more remarkable than that evolution which
Lessing summed up in his Education of the Human Race. No book
has had so great an influence as that Bible which leads us from a
small seed of monotheism to the sufferings and steadfast faith of
that handful of disciples who inoculated mankind with the conviction
that Death, in face of the unconquerable human mind, may be

---

[1] De Civ. Dei, bk. xxii, ch. 5. Dante borrows this and pitches it one key
higher, 'the others are not worth the hundredth of it' (Parad. xxiv, 106).
[2] A. de Musset, Nuit d'Octobre: 'A vast hope has swept over the earth;
despite ourselves, we must needs raise our eyes to heaven.'

swallowed up in Victory. In the mental stocktaking which is imposed upon me at the end of a book like this, I can trace nothing more constant than my feeling that Reginald Stuart Poole was right in his insistence upon the New Testament as a book unique in spiritual interest and in the conscious authority with which it leads our thoughts upwards. Marcus Aurelius wrote: 'The poet hath said *Dear City of Athens!*, but wilt not thou, my soul, say rather: "*Dear City of God?*"'[1] Those words from the learned and pious Emperor surprise us with their modernity: they would seem more natural from one of those Galilaean fishermen of whom the assembled rulers and elders and scribes 'took knowledge that they had been with Jesus' (Acts iv, 13). If I quote these texts which I have met with in later reading, it is not that they have revealed so much as they have reinforced. From Llandaff days onwards, I have tried to read the Bible records as historical documents, in the light of their own times. From them, and from human nature in myself and in the rest of the world, I have gained support for my own pilgrimage and sympathy with fellow-pilgrims. Common-sense (so it seemed) suggested certain interpretations; and further reading has sometimes supplied that which Carlyle hailed so enthusiastically: the discovery that another man, from a different age and a different angle, has thought the same. If all this is old-fashioned, it may wear all the better for being genuine home-spun. Agnosticism, in my undergraduate days, was being thought out by advanced intellects; but to the undergraduate of these days it is rather a line of least intellectual resistance. The more thoughtful of the younger men are more willing to face the importance of the imponderables in life and thought.[2] There is even a reaction towards Roman Catholicism or Anglo-Catholicism. But such reaction, to be solid, must be based on personal experience: and this, in proportion as it is real, must soften the angles as it did in Eric Gill's case. The convert brings his own particular drop into the great ocean. I met once at a Swiss hotel a young French Professor who had emerged from the last war with a strong tinge of mysticism. He expressed surprise at another convert who had said, 'Only two things matter to me, the Mass and Confession'. I said, 'But, in the war, surely those did brace your

[1] *Meditations*, IV, 23.
[2] Compare among Pascal's *Pensées Diverses* the paragraphs headed: 'Différence entre l'esprit de géométrie et l'esprit de finesse.'

soul: when the whistle came, you could go over the top with the
conviction that you were in a state of grace and fortified by the
Church's rites'. 'No, that isn't how I thought. I thought "God
is just, He will forgive me".' 'Then you felt as a Protestant might
feel?' 'Precisely.' Many men, while paying homage to most strict
and definite creeds, have made for themselves a religion of their own;
'un paradiso in mezzo al Paradiso', as Aleardi would have said.
And it is thus that the world has settled down to some approximate
ideal of *live and let live*, not from want of real faith but through the
realization that true faith is far more than words can express.

What, after all, is the Christian faith? The classical passage is in
the eleventh chapter of the Epistle to the Hebrews, where faith is
first defined and then illustrated by a multitude of concrete instances.
That definition suggests no conflict between faith and reason; and
the instances are compatible with the highest reason. It was by faith,
for instance, that Moses' mother hid the child and risked Pharaoh's
anger. Common-sense suggests that this was a prompting of
motherly instinct; but why should not an act of motherly instinct
be an act of faith? Analysis will show, I think, that faith as conceived
by this writer to the Hebrews, who had probably seen Jesus in the
flesh, is really the operation of the man's inmost Self, calculating
things in relation to the whole Not-Self (God and the Universe)
in so far as our Self can realize them. Face to face with any particular
problem of life, faith is the courage which applies to that particular
case those laws which, in so far as the thinker knows, are true for
the universe in general. It is right that the human race should continue; few people seriously doubt that; therefore it is right to
protect child life even at the risk of one's own. No doubt it would
have been an even higher act of faith for the woman to have saved
some other child, or, again, that a bachelor personally indifferent
to children should have risked his own life for the sake of this little
worm which might, after all, grow up into an unredeemed villain.
But this in no way excludes the fact that the woman's act, such as
it was, was a real act of faith. Such, again, it is for one man to risk
his life when an armed robber holds up a whole train; so it was in
thousands of cases in the Great War: 'If this is really a fight for
freedom, then even my death will be a step towards a better world.'
It is faith which applies to the individual case, in spite of all that the
individual himself risks by its application, the law which is un-

doubtedly a law of life in general. It is unfaith which says, 'That may be all very well in theory, but I am not going to risk it in practice'. If this be true, then we have something of a real criterion between faith and superstition.

Faith is the courageous and unflinching application of principles which the man has real reason to hold as true; superstition has no such anchorage. No anchorage is absolute. But this only means that faith is no more infallible than any other human faculty.

It is in no way incompatible with the root idea of a reasonable universe, in which things pass gradually to higher order and, with this, to greater satisfaction. We find so much order in it already that it is far from unreasonable to suppose hidden order in the complications which, at present, baffle us completely. We can live, as Dante did, in the conviction of an immeasurably great Not-Self, whose will is our peace.[1] The problem, here again, is not fundamentally altered if we suppose that this apparent order is not in the universe itself, but is created by our own searching minds; for, even then, we still have the human mind searching for order, and capable to a great extent of finding order even in disorder. If the universe outside us is not yet reasonable, at least we are making it more reasonable by our own mental effort, for our minds are part of the universe. Thus there is ample ground for the conviction which, more or less distinctly, presses itself intuitively upon large numbers of thinking men, that this life is a time of trial, in which every choice has its significance: that the good choice is that which is in harmony with the spirit of the whole, and which therefore leads on to further harmony; and that, gradually, the preponderance of good over bad, however small, is tending towards a future harmony greater than we can conceive at present. Faith (using the word in that most real and fundamental sense in which the early Christians used it) moves the world. There is a great truth in that sentence which Lord Acton once quoted from Fénelon: 'He who fears excessively to be duped deserves to be duped, and he nearly always does get grossly duped.' There are contingencies in which scepticism is the mark of fear, belief the mark of courage. What and when those contingencies are, each man must judge for himself in his most secret conscience.

And so there are, and always will be, men who take risks of belief far beyond what mere reason can urge, though not incompatible,

[1] En la sua voluntate è nostra pace (*Parad.* III, 85).

in any real sense, with even the strictest reason. These men see that, in so far as we can trace it, man differs from beast mainly in this habit of foresight, and in the self-control which foresight commands. They feel that, though no reason can decide between the hopeful and the unhopeful view of life (for here we are dealing with ultimates), yet it is more human and less beastlike to hope; that hope is not a fugitive and cloistered virtue, but masculine and active and dignified. And, as they grow older, experience seems to show them that here is a hope which maketh not ashamed.

The subject is inexhaustible; yet some such details were needed to explain the standpoint from which my bulky volumes have been written. I felt, and feel still, that there was much unreality in the work that was being done on the Middle Ages, and even, in some conspicuous cases, scandalous literary dishonesty under the excuse of religious conviction. It was difficult, therefore, to avoid that my own books, taken by themselves, should give something of a one-sided picture. A cyclist, in a strong side wind, must needs lean consciously against the blast, and may well be betrayed into over-doing it. My friends have sometimes told me so; and he who held the highest official place among them, while admitting that readers might learn a good deal from my labours, felt nevertheless constrained to warn me against my 'unhistorical mentality, [my] constant shriek of *écrasez l'infâme*, [my] utter incapacity to see anything spiritual or progressive or attractive in medieval civilization'. 'It is not, to put it bluntly, history at all. It is an able and eloquent anticlerical pamphlet on a colossal scale.'[1] Yet within myself I am conscious of having striven, through Fortune's buffets and rewards, to see both sides, and to record sincerely my own personal experience as globe-trotter among the Shades. Mabillon himself, that model monk whom all recognize as the Father of Monastic History, insisted even to exaggeration that we must be more careful to record the failings of great men than their virtues.[2] It is only thus that we pay to their greatness the tribute of sincerity; for nothing short of this can bring out their full stature. We falsify the height of the mountain when we disguise the lowliness of the plain. Wherever the evidence is

---

[1] *Scottish Hist. Rev.* July 1923, p. 319; April 1928, p. 206.
[2] *De Studiis Monasticis*, pars II, c. viii, §§ 11 and 12. Compare Acton's approving comment in his *Historical Essays and Studies*, p. 465, and also Pascal's *Pensées*, ed. Brunschvicq, No. 352.

abundant, it nearly always shows that some of the saint's greatest difficulties were with his or her own kindred and neighbours.

Common-sense suggested to me from the first that *homo sapiens* is, on the whole, an improving animal, and History has seemed to confirm this probability more and more. There is no horror even in 1942, so I believe, which cannot be outmatched from the records of distant centuries. Man is not a fallen angel; the facts concordant with saner faith tell us that we have struggled painfully upwards, and exhort us to struggle still.

In that faith I have continued half a century, practically unchanged. Civilization, when all additions have been made for non-ecclesiastical contributions, and all deductions for ecclesiastical failings in teaching or practice, still owes a heavy debt to that great procession of Christian Churches which marches through the pages of history. So at least I feel, and more strongly from day to day. Nor is this weakened, but rather strengthened, by friends who avoid or repudiate the name of *Christian*, yet who show (as it was said of Henry Sidgwick) every Christian virtue except faith. The Cambridge philosopher McTaggart claimed the title of Atheist. It is relevant here to repeat what I printed once in reviewing his *Life* by Lowes Dickinson.[1] At a sitting of the Eranus Society some philosophical problem was being discussed, with McTaggart in his common attitude of abstract meditation. Suddenly he roused himself to say, 'The longer I live, the more I am convinced of the reality of three things, Truth, Love, and Immortality'.

In spite of all the seeming caprice of memory, to me it has never been the crude hazard of Christina Rossetti's 'Haply I may remember, and haply may forget'. Remembrance is a possession which the pessimist cannot take away from us: moreover, it is greatly subject to our own will. If, as I believe, this thing called 'I' survives bodily dissolution, and can still choose in the future as it has chosen in the past, then it shall rescue from that shipwreck the things and the friendships that have been most real. In so far as man differs from beast, it must surely be through some such exercise of will; and only thus can we say with Wordsworth:

> The thought of our past years in me doth breed
> Perpetual benediction.

[1] *The Times Literary Supplement*, January 7, 1932, p. 7.

APPENDIX

I should be ungrateful indeed if I did not here spare a few words of heartfelt thanks to Abbé J. P. Migne.

The prose of his life is told briefly by Christopher Wordsworth, nephew to the poet and afterwards bishop, in his *Diary in France*, under date of August 14, 1844. At his 'grande Imprimerie', a few hundred yards beyond the Barrière d'Enfer, Wordsworth found 'a vast establishment directed entirely by the Abbé himself. It contains all the processes necessary for printing, as type-founding, stereotype, *satinage, brochure, et reliure*, with the exception of paper-making. It is indeed a very wonderful institution, especially considered as created and governed by one single clergyman, whose previous studies could not have been very favourable to such an enterprise. It was stated to me that there were 200 workmen employed on the premises....[1] He is evidently born with a genius for command. His principal aim is to give to the world a complete collection, in a very portable form, and at a very economical rate, of all the Greek and Latin fathers of the Church. He said that he had long had this plan in his mind, and had never rested till he had begun to put it into execution. "And with what means did you begin?" "With nothing", he replied, "but *la bonne volonté*; a man, sir, could build a church like your St Paul's or Westminster Abbey if he had but a *good will* to do it." "But you had friends to support you?" "No, I had many *opponents* and enemies." "But the Bishops of your Church?" "They, sir, at first, were *all against* me; but seeing that I was in earnest, they have now come round and support me."...It ought to be mentioned, as a reason which I have heard assigned for the prelate's reluctance in the first instance to give his formal sanction to M. Migne's bold undertaking, that some other French ecclesiastics had formerly engaged in literary enterprises in which they had failed, and that he was apprehensive that the Abbé might add to the number of unsuccessful ecclesiastical speculators....If the undertaking should prove successful, it will tend, perhaps, more than any design of the present day to familiarize the mind of the literary public with the great writings of Christian antiquity, and will supply a popular library of patristic theology for the use of parochial divines, as well as academic students: and thus it cannot fail to render signal service to the cause of Christianity.'

Between 1844 and 1864, Migne printed a *Patrologia Latina* containing

[1] *The Catholic Encyclopaedia* says 'more than 300'.

217 volumes, with four volumes of indices, together with two series of his *Patrologia Graeca* in 161 volumes. Yet even these 382 volumes formed, in bulk, scarcely half of his total output. A disastrous fire consumed his whole establishment in 1868. He began rebuilding at once; but then the War of 1870 threw him back again. In 1875 he died, fighting still but practically bankrupt. Meanwhile, however, he had supplied medievalists with texts whose price made them accessible even to struggling scholars. They ranged from 7 to 8 francs a volume—roughly, 6s. or $1.50. They were reprints of standard old editions, mainly from those stately folios which Gibbon quotes in order to contrast the intellectual fertility of French monasticism with the barrenness of his own 'monks of Magdalen'.[1] The historical value of the stuff itself, in those 382 volumes, as apart from the editing, exceeds even the *Monumenta Germaniae* or our own *Rolls Series*. In the editing itself there is far less fault to be found than is often hastily assumed. Scholars, like other folk, hurry sometimes to the cheap conclusion that cheap things are therefore nasty. Even if the volumes had cost double their actual price, we should rather have reason to wonder at their comparative accuracy on the whole. Moreover, they have the enormous advantage of a uniform and encyclopaedic series. There must be few seats of higher learning which have not, or cannot at least borrow easily from a neighbouring University, any volume that may be required. Here in Toronto (but that is exceptional) I have one set within five minutes' walk, and another within ten, at the University Library or that of the Institute of Medieval Studies. A reference to Migne, therefore, is far more convenient to students in the ordinary way than one to a later and more scientific edition, which may indeed exist, yet be out of easy reach. Moreover, there is an educative value, especially for younger students when once they have been warned, in looking out for textual criticism as they go along. Finally, we have the immense advantage of a price that enables us to buy for ourselves; to read and digest and annotate at leisure, picking the book up for friendly consultation at any moment, as against our piecemeal interviews with some expensive edition in a library which opens for so few hours as is customary in England. 'We shall never understand those people of the past' unless we go out into

[1] *Autobiography*, ed. Birkbeck Hill, p. 56: 'The shelves of their library groan under the weight of the Benedictine folios which have issued from the single abbey of St-Germain-des-Prés at Paris.' My own Guibert was reprinted from the folio of 1651, and contained 550,000 words, or nearly four times as many as this present volume.

their highways and hedges: and that is what Migne's *Patrologia* enables us to do at the price of a couple of concert tickets.

So much for the prose of Abbé Migne, and now for his tragedy. The brothers Edmond and Jules de Goncourt made a characteristic entry in their *Journal* for August 21, 1864: 'A queer figure is this Abbé Migne, this manufacturer of Catholic books. He has started printing-works at Vaugirard, crammed full with priests who are under interdict, unfrocked rascals, devil-dodgers, fellows lost to all grace. If ever a police-officer appears, there is a stampede for the door. Migne has to shout out: "Don't budge! This doesn't concern any of you; the man has come to see me about some infringement of copyright!" From this press come forth orthodox encyclopaedias, collections of the Church Fathers in a hundred volumes: and at the back of this trade, he has another. He gets the curés to pay for his books partly in Mass cheques [*bons de Messe*], countersigned by the Bishop. These, taking one with another, cost from eight sous apiece [4*d.* sterling or $0.8] and he sells them again for forty in Belgium, where the clergy are not numerous enough to keep up all the Mass foundations left from the days of Spanish domination.' The Goncourts were not men to stick at embellishing a good story;[1] but the *Catholic Encyclopaedia* may be trusted for avoiding exaggeration in that direction. We read there (vol. x, p. 291): 'But difficulties accumulated. The Archbishop of Paris was averse to the commercial elements in the work, forbade the continuance of the business, and, finally, suspended the publisher from his priestly functions. The Franco-German war of 1870 inflicted great losses; then from Rome came a decree condemning the misuse of Mass stipends for the purchase of books, and Migne was especially named in connexion with this abuse. He died without ever having regained his former prosperity.' Professor Alphandéry, at the Congrès Loisy, told me how Migne, naturally enough, became a sort of Micawber, drifting from embarrassment to embarrassment. His priestly workmen were more embarrassed still; unscrupulous and sometimes desperate. Such men drift to the capital; and nobody, I believe, has attempted to deny what A. Houtin wrote in his autobiographical *Une Vie de Prêtre*, that at any given moment there are more priests at Paris on the streets—*sur le pavé*—than in regular pastoral employment. Therefore, according to Alphandéry, whenever Migne had to quit his establishment

---

[1] We can test them by their version and Professor Will Rothenstein's of a story in which Swinburne figures: *Journal*, vol. ix, p. 205 (April 6, 1894); Rothenstein, *Men and Memories*, vol. i, p. 235.

in the dusk, and to pass by a certain half-glazed door of the work-room, he always took the precaution of holding before him his walking stick, adorned with hat and overcoat, by way of lightning-conductor against stray pistol shots.

Be all that as it may, Migne's assistance to scholars was magnificent; the man's business flair and courage and tenacity put him by the side of Joseph Wright with his *Dialect Dictionary*.

INDEX

Abbeville, 226, 263
Abbey-Dore, 133, 146
Abbot Wallingford, see Gasquet, Cardinal
Abercorn, Duke of, 25
Abergavenny, 133; Sugar-Loaf, 133, 173
Abergwili, 171, 255
Aberystwyth, 182, 314
About, Edmond, 76
Abraham, Ernst, 164, 198, 199
Abrahams, the, 186
Academica, see Cicero
Acton, Lord, 138, 322, 330, 332, 336, 348, 349 footnote
Acts, the, 327
Adam, James, 121
Adam, Karl, 342 footnote
Adams, gardener, 65, 66
Addison, 298
Adelboden, 284, 286, 293, 294
Ad Eundem dinner, 110
Aegatian Isles, the, 81
Aen., see Virgil
Aeneas, 130 footnote
Aeschylus, 81, 95
Africa, 267; South, 32, 261
Agamemnon, 95
Ailsa Craig, 232
Ainslie, 217
Albergo Sirena, 241, 242
Albert Thomas, 272
Alderley, 144
Aldgate Station, 37
Aleardi, Aleardo, 235
Alexandra, Queen, 10
Alexandra Dock, 53
Algiers, 3, 89, 90
L'Allegro, 75
'Allen's House', 29
Alleyn, 218, 219, 220
Allinson, Anthony, Dr, 14, 15, 29, 65
Allinson, Calthrop, 16
Alp(s), 249, 265
Alphandéry, Professor, 353
Alpine climber, 109; Lakes, 290
Amalfi, 230, 236, 239, 240, 241, 243, 244, 246
Amaryllis, 53
America(n), vii, 58, 193, 196, 197, 207, 229, 230, 246, 274, 288, 330; Civil War, 193

Amiens, 187, 226
Amours de Voyage, 287 footnote
Anatomy of Melancholy, see Burton
Ancient Mariner, The, 207
Anecdota Literaria, see Wright, Thomas
Angell, Norman, Sir, 277, 278
Anglican(s), 182, 332, 334; Church, the, 22, 93, 137, 147, 148, 151, 153, 162, 340; Bishop, 329; priest, 164
Anglo-American Club, 198
Anglo-Catholic(s), Anglo-Catholicism, 30, 134, 138, 215, 299, 331, 346
Anglo-Franco-Russian relations, 196
Anglophil Frederick III, 198
Annales, see Baronius
Annals, see Tacitus
Antioch, 344
Antipodes, the, 172, 219
Antiquarian Society, the, 210
Anti-Saxons, 172
Antwerp, 37, 156, 187
Apocalypse, the, 45
Aquino, 246
Arabia Deserta, see Doughty, C. M.
Arbois, 251
Arcadia, 199
Arians, the, 106
Aristotle, 123
Armistice, the, 26, 313
Armitage, Alan, 187, 303
Armitage, F. A., 188, 189, 339 footnote; Mrs, 188, 190, 195
Armitage, Lionel, 191, 198
Arnold, Matthew, 85 footnote, 168, 211, 220, 241 footnote, 262, 316, 339
Arnold, Thomas, 128, 141, 215
Arques, 44
Arran, 232
Arras, 46
Art and the Reformation, 74 footnote, 233 footnote
Ascent of Mont Blanc, see Smith, Albert
'Ash Grove, The', 178
Ashton, A. J., 84, 85, 86, 276
A Silvia, see Leopardi
As I Went On My Way, 84 footnote, 276
Asquith, Mr, 270, 271, 272
Assisi, 132, 213
Athenaeum, the, 334, 335, 336
Athenaeum, The, 320

Athenaeum Plain, 25
Atlantic, the, 99, 162, 193, 229, 320
Aubrey, 32
Audley Cottage, Grantchester, 123
Austin Canons, Priory of, 61
Austin Friars, 2, 28
Austin Street, King's Lynn, 2, 7
Australia(n), 219, 300
Austria(n) dungeon, 235
Authorised Version, the, 53
Autobiography, see Hamerton, P. G., 302
Autobiography and Letters, see Tyrrell, Father
Autobiography of Abbot Guibert de Nogent, 248
Autotype Company, 161
L'Avare, 53
Avebury, Lord, 202
Avernus, 232
'Azoöphags', 59

Babylon, 147; Modern, 58
Backhouse, J. H., 78, 82
Backs, Cambridge, the, 122
Bacon, 189
Baedeker, 201
Baker, 'Bos', 51
Baker Lane, King's Lynn, 37
Balaam, 114
Baldwin, Lord, 272
Balfour, A. J., 161, 327
Ballot Act, 23, 24
Baltic Provinces, the, 194, 208
Balzac, 127
Bampton Lectures, see Liddon
Bangor, 182
Bank House, 29, 39
Bantham, 297, 300
Bantock, 30; 'Commodore', 30
Barcola, 248
Bardell, 28
Bardolph's nose, 75
Barker, 'Jas', cobbler, 73
Barnes, C. L., 206, 207
Barnett, Canon, 211
Baronius, 237
Barrow, Isaac, 68
Barzillai, 115
Baschkirtseff, 194
Baschkirtseff, Marie, 207
Basel, 286
Bastien, 40, 45, 47
Bateson, Mary, 104
Bateson, William, 104
Bath Cottage, Malvern Wells, 132
Baugh Fell, 213

Bavarian peasant, 191
Baxter, 149
Bayle, 168
Beaconsfield, Lord, 65
'Bear Hotel', Berne, the, 293
Beatrice, 86
Bebel, 273
Bedford, 21, 211, 212
Beerbohm, Max, 128
Beevor, Hugh, Sir, 70
Beevor, Ralph, 71, 78
Belchen, the, 186
Belgian Professor of Economics, 93; Redemptorist priest, 339 footnote
Belgium, 272
Bell's Life in London, 87
Belloc, Mr, 147 footnote
Beloe, Mr, 48
Beloe, E. M., 74, 304
Benedictine(s), 333; edition of St Bernard, 156; folios, 352 footnote; monks, 30; notes, 156; Origen, 164
Benjamin, 145
Bennett, H. S., viii, 173
Bensly, Professor, 202
Benson, Archbishop, 128
Benson, R. H., Father, 141
Bentley, Master of Trinity, 102
Bergstrasse, the, 187
Beringtons, the, 139
Berlin, 164, 186, 199, 265; University, 193
Bermuda, 266
Berne, 272, 286, 292, 293
Bernese, châlet, 289; Oberland, 186; rolls, 288
Berryman, 185
Bersaglieri, 232
Berthold of Regensburg, 155, 340 footnote
Bevan, Edwyn, 106
Bible, the, 79, 151, 172, 345, 346; English, 149
'Bible of the Poor, the', 74
Bieneman, G. A., 208
Bilney, 154
Birch, Canon, 158
Birch, Mr, 158
Birds of Europe, see Gould
Birkenhead, Lord, 126
Birkenhead School, 221
Birmingham, 2, 127, 163, 172; King Edward's School, 127, Headmaster at, 128; Small Arms Co., 256
Bishop orders his Tomb, The, see Browning, Robert
Bishop's Stortford, 88

Bismarck, Otto v., 196 footnote, 321;
  anti-, 197
Bismarcksbeleidigung, 196
Black Forest, the, 186, 249
Black Mountains, the, 133
Blackbrough, 61
Blackfriars, 28
Blaenos hill, 173
Blakesley, Dean, 108
Bland, C. C. S., 111, 114, 123, 259 footnote
Blennerhassett, Rowland, Sir, 336
Blimps, Colonel, the, 301
'Blonde Beast', 191
Blundell's School, 297
Boar's Hill, Oxford, 86
'Bocksbeutel', 195
Bodleian, the, 210
Boer(s), 261, 285; War, 266
Boethius, 223
Boger, 254
Bombay, University of, Vice-Chancellor
  of, 83
Bonderspitz, the, 288, 289, 291
Bonney, 102
Book of Margery Kempe, The, see Kempe,
  Margery
Booth, General, 339
Borngiesser, 49
Borrow, George, 180, 291
Bosanquet, Bernard, 221
Bossuet, 326, 342, 343 footnote
Boston, 20
Boston (Mass.), 314
Boucherie Hippophagique, 44
Boulogne, 39
Bourbons, the, 242, 243
Bourke, Mr, 25
Bowen, 161, 202
Bradby, Dr, 202
Bradford, 83
Bradley, G. G., 82, 85, 168
Bradman, 74
Bradmoor, 63
Braintree, 90
Brancaster, 62
Brandon, river, 140
Braxted, 2
Braybrooke, Lord, 97
Brecon Beacons, the, 173 footnote, 177
Bredon Hill, vii, 129
Brest-Litovsk, 272
Breydon Water, 140
Briggs, 40 footnote
Brighton, 208, 301
Brill, 210
Brillat-Savarin, 109

Brisbane, 248
Bristol, Recorder of, 276
Britain, British, 22, 24, 26, 128, 130,
  136, 189, 192, 199, 238, 262, 265, 266,
  267, 269, 270, 271, 272, 273, 274, 275,
  280, 288, 292, 301, 329; diplomats,
  256; education, 212; Generals, 301;
  Minister, 292; railways, 284
British Academy, the, 326, 327, 332, 333
British Church, see Herbert, George
British Museum, 160, 164, 196, 221, 223,
  285, 300, 329, 335
Broad Street, 285
Broadsands, 299
Bromsgrove School, 133, 206, 207
Bronsil Castle, 133
Brooke, Z. N., 313
Brother Vita, 178
Brown, Langdon, 137
Brown, Mrs, 252
Browne, G. F., 121
Browning, E. B., Mrs, 135, 298
Browning, Robert, 85, 137, 230, 276
Bruce, G. N., 212
Bruges, 187
Brussels, 187
Bryce, James, 287
Bryn Mawr University Library, 230
Buchan, John, 197 footnote; *see also*
  Tweedsmuir, Lord
Buckle, 83, 84, 163
Bucolics, 57
Buddha, 225
Bunsen, R. W. v., 193, 198
Burgh Castle, 140
Burgundy, 47, 141, 249, 250
Burney, Dr, 31
Burnley, Bishop of, 88
Burns, 74
Burtersett, 1
Burterside, *see* Burtersett
Burton, 187
Busch, Johann, 307
Bush, Mrs, 13
Bute, Marquis of, the, 146
Butler, Abbot, 334 footnote
Butler, Bishop, 318
Butler, H. Montagu, Dr, 91, 117, 142,
  201, 312, 324
Butler, Samuel, 103, 142
Butter Canal Street, Antwerp, 37
Byron, 3, 243

Cadmus and Harmonia, see Arnold
  Matthew
Caesar, Julius, 321

Caesarius of Heisterbach, 259 footnote, 260

Calais, 39, 40, 263, 286, 293

Calcutta, 58

Caliban, 81

Calthorpe, *see* Calthrop

Calthorpe, Lord, 39

Calthrop, 2, 39

Calthrop, Gordon, 69

Calthrop, Henry, 2, 3

Calthrop, Louisa, 90

Calthrop, Richard, 3, 89, 90

Calverley, C. S., 53, 117, 238, 254 footnote

Calvin, 326

Calvinistic Methodist, 172

Cambridge, vii, 2, 3, 14, 26, 28, 33, 38, 59, 72, 82, 86, 88, 91, 92, 93, 94, 99, 100, 101, 105, 110, 113, 114, 115, 120, 122, 123, 125, 127, 135, 141, 145, 155, 177, 190, 193, 204, 207, 214, 226, 230, 233, 238, 252, 257, 259 footnote, 263, 283, 284, 299 footnote, 308, 311, 312, 315, 338; All Saints Church, 91, 92; Anglo-Saxon Chair, 119; Birkbeck Lectureship, 312; Blues, 126, 176, 253; Christ's College, 111, 113; Clare College, Fellow of, 210; Corpus Christi College, 94, Fellow of, 2, Master of, 3, 94, 95, Scholar, 96, Fellows' Garden war, 96, Fellow of, 312; cricket, 111, 122, 258; Downing College, 97, 98, Fellow of, 98; Ecclesiastical History, Professor of, 105, 106, 338; Emmanuel College, 68; English Literature, Professor of, 308; Faculty of English, 308, 313; football at, 111; footpath, 123; Girton College, 313; Gonville and Caius College, 12, 100, 122, 123; Jesus College, 91, 92, 313; King's College, Fellow of, 33, 97, 101, 113, 219; Lady Margaret Professor, 118; Latin Professor, 59, 315; Magdalene College, 97, Fellow of, 118; mathematicians, 100; Mathematics, Professor of, 68; May Races, 111; Newnham College, 97, 313; Norrisian Professor, 118; Peterhouse, 93; philosopher, 350; Prize winners, 126; Professors, 161, 200, 202, 219; Public Orator, 314; Queens' College, 97, 122; Regius Professor of History, 322; rowing, 152; St Catharine's College, 88, 90, 94, 96, 97, 98, 111, 113, Chapel, 113, 114, 115, 117, 118, 119, 121, 122, 125, 126, Commemoration Feast, 115, Fellow at, 127, 151, 312; St John's College, 27, 49, 92, Fellows of, 92, 97, 103, 104, 263, 297, 311, 313, Master of, 97, 98, 101, 102, 103, Library, 102, 103, 206, Chapel, 104, 106, 160, 188, 193, 206, 209, Commemoration Feast, 315; Senate House, 95 footnote, 98, 117; Sidney Sussex College, 97, 109, 111, 174; Sports, 100; Trinity College, 69, 87, Chapel, 91, Master of, 68, 91, 94, 102, 106, 142, 312, 314, 324, Statutes of, 94, 95, 97, 101 footnote, Library, 107, Nevile's Court, 108, 109, Fellow of, 120, 123, 141, 144, 299, 312; Trinity Hall, 86, Fellowship at, 49, 87, 103, Fellow of, 201, 222, 283, 315; University Library, 314, 315; University Press, 308, 314, 325; Vice-Chancellor, 107; Volunteer Corps, 266, 277; weekly paper, 107; Wrangler at, 36, 49, 103, 104, 121, 159

Cambridge Bible for Schools and Colleges, The, 120

Cambridge Economic History, 319

Cambridge Memories, see Thorneley, T.

Cambridge Modern History, 92 footnote

Cambridge Studies in Medieval Life and Thought, 325

Camden Medal, 106

Camden Society volume, 156

Camembert, 250

Camorra, the, 244

Camp Hill, 134

Campbell, Lewis, 282

Campbell, Robert, 49, 282, 283, 291, 293

Campbell, Thomas, 282

Canada, vii, 5, 36, 197, 259, 295, 304; French, 56

Canadian Rebellion, 298

Canonical Scriptures, the, 164

Canterbury, Archbishop of, 141, 203; St Augustine's, Principal of, 122

Capitol, the, 247

Cappuccini, the, 240, 243

Capri, 238, 239

Capucin monastery, 240

Cardiff, 144, 145, 146, 176, 182; Mayor of, 142

Carlisle, Bishop of, 36

Carlyle, 84 footnote, 193, 229 footnote, 346

Carlyle in Old Age, see Wilson, D. A.

Carmarthen, 171, 175; Bay, 183; Vans, 173, 179, 181, 184

Carnegie Endowment, 34

Carr, Edwin Trevor Septimus, 113, 114, 120, 121, 125
Case for Compulsory Military Service, The, 270 footnote, 277 footnote, 281 footnote
Castleacre, 37, 61, 305
Castle Rising, 1, 2
Catechism, Shorter, the, 161
Catholic Dictionary, The, 344
Catholic Encyclopaedia, The, 351 footnote, 353
Caux, 227
Caxton Hall, 199
Celtic architecture, 146; romance, 148
Cenis, Mt, 131, 230
Censeur, the, 40, 45
Cerrig-Cennen, 183
Chablis, 250, 251 footnote
Chadwick, H. M., Professor, 308
Chamberlain, Austen, 273 footnote
Chamberlain, Joey, 110
Chamberlain, Neville, 272
Chamier, 253
Channel, the, 40, 250
Chantilly, 263
Chapman, A. P. F., 178
Chapman, F. E., 175, 178, 185
Chapman, John, pedlar, 62
Charing Cross, 220, 223, 293
Charles XII, see Voltaire
Charrington, 258
Charterhouse, 158
Château des Comtes, 37
Chaucer, 58, 229; language of, 116
Chaucer and his England, 283, 307
Chaucer's Mill, 100
Cheapside, 89, 223
Chelmer, the, 75
Chelmsford, 69, 151; solicitor, 77
Cheltenham, vii, 107, 130, 339 footnote; Headmaster of, 253
Chepstow, 133
Chester, Bishop of, 181
Chesterfield, 165 footnote
Chesterton, G. K., 284
Childers, Mr, 158, 159
Chilterns, the, 151
China, 197, 295
Chinese pagoda, 64
Chipping Campden, 89
Chipping Hill, 89, 90
Chipping Ongar, 89
Cholmondeley, 20
Chorley Wood, 161
Christ, 151, 155, 162, 172, 247, 341, 343, 345, 346, 347

Christ, St Francis, and To-Day, 338 footnote
Christendom, 333
Christianity, Christian(s), 274, 275, 337, 341, 342, 343, 344, 345, 347, 349, 351; apologists, 342; early, 278, 340, 348
Christmas, 10, 45, 53, 186
Christmas Eve and Easter Day, see Browning, Robert
Christ's Hospital, 111, 112, 113
Chronicle, see Salimbene
Church Inn, Thaxted, 75
Church Quarterly, The, 332
Church Stretton, 135
Church Times, The, 141, 335 footnote
Churches of Lincolnshire, The, 89
Churchill, Winston, Mr, 76
Cicero, 81, 123, 244 footnote
Cistercian ruins, 43
Citizen Militia, 269, 278
Civil Service, the, 24
Clairmarais, 43, 44
Clare, Earls of, 133
Clark, Albert, Professor, 210
Clark, J. W., 3
Claughton, Bishop, 151
Clerical Disabilities Act, 94, 208, 209
Clifton, 188, 193
Clio, a Muse, 321 footnote
Clough, A. H., viii, 167, 287
Clyde, Firth of, 231
Cobbett, 73
Coch Castle, 146
Cockernhoe, 151, 152, 154
Cocumella, the, Sorrento, 236, 238
Coddington, 107 footnote, 133, 135, 136, 137, 339, 340
Colborne, G. F., 81, 82, 86, 88
Col de Balme, 227
Col de Jaman, 227
Col de la Forclaz, 227
Colenso, Bishop of Natal, 103
Coleridge, 175
Colet, John, Dean, 143
Collections and Recollections, see Russell, G. W. E.
Collingwood, R. A., Professor, 321
Collins, C. A., 47
Cologne, 38, 187
Colosseum, the, 247
Colson, F. H., 284
Colwall, 133, 135, 137; Church, 137; Ghost, 134
Comely Bank, 193
Commedia, see Dante

Commentary on Macaulay's History of England, 321
Commentary on the Book of Daniel, see Pusey
Commentary on the Galatians, see Luther
Confessions, see St Augustine
Congrès Loisy, the, 314
Conservatives, 94, 272
Constable, 308
Constantine, Cross of, 299
Contemporary, The, 264
Contra Celsum, see Origen
Coope, Mr, 299
Cooper, Thomas, 262
Cope, 123
Copeland, 5
Copenhagen, 89
Coriolanus, 239
Cork, 76
Corn Exchange Street, Cambridge, 59
Cornaro, 59
Cornelius Nepos, 53
Cornhill Magazine, The, 14
Cornwall, 291
Corpus Poetarum, 82
Correspondence, Acton, Lord, 333 footnote
Corsair, see Byron
Costigan, Captain, 37
Cotman, 249
Cotswold Hills, vii, 130
Coulton, Beatrice, 10, 65, 305, 307
Coulton, Edmund, 7, 10, 14, 17, 55, 57, 64, 90, 187, Pl. iii
Coulton, Ellen, 3, 60
Coulton, Etta, 186, Pl. iii
Coulton, Ewan, 1
Coulton, 'Grandmamma', 3
Coulton, James (Jim), 4, 17, 48, 53, 57, 58, 67, 139, 140, 204
Coulton, James, the Rev., 1, 2, 48
Coulton, John, 6
Coulton, John James, senior, 1, 2, 3
Coulton, John James, junior, 2, 3, 6, 266, Pl. v
Coulton, Mary, viii
Coulton, Priscilla, 3
Coulton, Richard, 4, 7, 17, 26, 39, 41, 42, 46, 53, 55, 140, 187, 211, 225, 266, Pl. iii
Coulton, William, 1
Counts Palatine, 188
County School, the, King's Lynn, 57
Courcy-le-Château, 226
Court Barton Farm, 338
Coverley, Roger de, Sir, 262, 297

Cowbridge, 200
Cowley, A. E., 210, 213
Cowper-Temple clause, 212
Cox, Mr, 73
Cramb, J. A., 270
Cranford, 297
Crawshay-Bailey, 177
Creighton, Mandell, 105, 106, 302, 322, 323, 330, 331; Mrs, 106
Cresswell, George, 39
Crimean War, the, 196, 197
Croad's School, King's Lynn, 8, 9, 39
Croce, Benedetto, 317
Crockford's Clerical Directory, 153, 209
Cromwell, Oliver, 26; Richard and Robert, sons of, 68
Croxley Green, 158
Cruise upon Wheels, A, see Collins, C. A.
Crystal Palace, the, 26, 285
Culley, E. H., Professor, 178, 183
Cunningham, W., Archdeacon, 98, 324
Curtis, Lionel, 135, 136, 267
Curtis, Reginald, 135; Mrs, 135, 136, 137, 166, 175, 339
Custance, Parson, 136
Custom House, King's Lynn, 32
Cut Bridges, the, 36
Cuyp, 303
Cwmamman, 184
Cymmrodorion Society, 181
Cymric, 172; preacher, 171
Cyprus, 300

Dachshund, 130
Dale, A. W. W., 278 footnote
Dale, R. W., 278
Danbury Hall, bishop's palace, 151, 156
Danbury Park, 151
Danglars, 242
Dante, 66, 86, 131, 184, 225 footnote, 237, 248, 345 footnote, 348
Dart, the, 179
Dartington, 295
Dartmoor, 296, 298
Darwin, 280, 306, 322, 344
Dauber, see Dawber
David, King, 115
David Copperfield, 9, 51, 81
Davidson, Randall, Archbishop, 141
Davies, Llewelyn, 144
Davies, Peter, 47
Davies, W. H., 181
Dawber, John, Colonel, 134
De Amicitia, 140
Dean, Martin, 30
De Civ. Dei, see St Augustine

Decline and Fall, see Gibbon
De Consideratione, 333 footnote
Defoe, 108
de Goncourt, Edmond, 353
de Goncourt, Jules, 353
De Imitatione Christi, 156
Delgado, 42, 43
Delmé-Radcliffe, 152
de Mably, Monsieur, 251
Deniseau, Monsieur, 242
Dent, 213
Dent, Mr, 213
Dent du Midi, 227
Denver, 304
De Paucitate Salvandorum, see Godts, F. X., Fr.
De Quincey, 190
Derby, Lord, 271 footnote
Derbyshire spinners, 135
De Rerum Natura, 302 footnote
Descartes, 165, 225, 227, 275, 309, 317
De Senectute, 140
Désiré, 40, 44
Desjardins, Paul, 333 footnote
De Studiis Monasticis, 349 footnote
De Testimonio Animae, see Tertullian
Devil's Alley, the, 32
Devonshire, 283, 286, 287, 291, 296, 298, 300, 301
Dialect Dictionary, 354
Dialogues, see Caesarius of Heisterbach
Diary in France, see Wordsworth, Christopher
Dichtung und Wahrheit, 306
Dickens, 49, 155, 200, 315
Dickinson's paper mills, 161
Dictionary of National Biography, 136
Dictionnaire, see Bayle
Dido, 130 footnote
Dieppe, 226
Diercks, 238
Dijon, 226, 263
Discours de la Méthode, see Descartes
Disestablishment, 172, 173
Disraeli, 23, 24, 87, 146
Dissolution of the Monasteries, the, 30, 68, 320
Distinguo, 44
Ditton Corner, 311
Division du Travail Social, see Durkheim
Doctrine of Development, 336
Documents, etc., see Douais
Dolau Cothi, 184
Dominicans, the, 28
Doncaster, 141, 142
Donne, 225

Doorn, 198
Dorset, vii, 200
Dotheboys, 51
Douai, 39
Douais, 340 footnote
Doughty, C. M., 262
Dover Castle, 263
Downham, 33
Doyle, Conan, 217
Drake's pottery yard, King's Lynn, 7
Druidic figure, 149
Dublin hood, 153
Dubois, Paul, Monsieur, 76, 77
Dugdale, 302, 312
'Duke's Head', the, King's Lynn, 29
Dulwich, vii; College, 120, 209 footnote, 217, 218, 219, 220, 221, 222, 224, 263, 285
Dumas, 242
Dunbar, 62 footnote
Dundee marmalade, 59
Dunmow, 69, 73, 78, 79; Priory, restoration of, 305
Dunn, A. T. B., 176
Dürer, 5
Durham, 113; Dean of, 108; hood, 153; University, 183
Durkheim, 99
Dutch consul, 148
Dyer, 179
Dynevor, 179

Earlom and Smith, 5
Early Victorian Cambridge, see Winstanley, D. A.
East Anglia, 20, 70
East Anglian fens, 133
East Gates House, King's Lynn, 33
Eastbourne, vii, 159, 224, 226, 230, 249, 251, 254, 259, 262, 263, 283, 284, 300, 302, 303, 304, 308, 311, 313, 335; Public Library, 300
Eastern Counties, 130; schools in, 69
Eatanswill, 23
Ebbw, 181
Ebury, Lord, 158
Eclogues, 53, 227
Eddystone Rock, 296
Edgehill, 130
Edinburgh, 191, 214, 314; Academy, 193
Education Act, the, 154; Bill, 211
Education of the Human Race, see Lessing
Edward VI, 200; commissioners of, 48
Edward VII, King, 9, 10, 53, 158, 296
Edwards, A. G., 170

Egyptian donkey, 109; Premier, 255
Eiger, the, 286
Elijah, 120
Elisha, 120
Elizabeth, Queen, 92, 142
Elizabethan Settlement, 92
Elliott, E. W., 127
Ellis, Havelock, 136
Elysium, 235 footnote
Encyclical, of 1899, 330; *Pascendi*, 336
Encyclopédie, grande, La, 280
'Ends', 151
England, vii, 10, 40, 42, 61, 62, 69, 85, 93, 129, 175, 191, 199, 230, 245, 288, 344, 352; agricultural, 135; Bank of, Governor of, 158; Church of, 118; conversion of, 39; northern, 6, 213; scholarship in, 162; schoolmasters in, 85
English, Englishman, Englishmen, 33, 39, 138, 161, 172, 181, 184, 191, 197, 229, 240, 247, 265, 280, 319 footnote; Benedictines, 333; books, 41, 195 footnote; Church, 189, 338; education, 41, 42, 47, 52, 129, 203, 216; history, 103; language, 47, 63, 78, 92, 103, 117, 122, 171, 172, 175, 182, 188, 289, 291, 313; life, 239; literature, 308; monasticism, 319, 334; peer, 158; Perpendicular style, 38; philosophers, 221; poem, 106; pupils, 39, 176; scenery, 301; social life, 262; teaching, 175, 212, 218; town life, 29; translation, 53; traveller, 47, 243; venison, 109; village, 298
English Dialect Dictionary, 189
English Historical Review, The, 330
English Works of St Thomas More, 262
ep. ad Laetam, see Hieronymus
Ephesians, 157
Episcopal Registers, the, 331
Eranus Society, the, 106, 107, 350
Erasmus, 29, 122; portrait, 122
Eryx, 81
Essay on the State of German Literature, see Carlyle
Essays, see Macaulay
Essays and Reviews, 183
Essex, 53, 68, 70, 84, 86, 90, 151; Hall, 221
Essex, see Morant
Essington Hotel, Malvern Wells, 129
Eton, 53, 101, 153, 202, 219, 252; master at, 53, 285; scholars, 97; Etonian, 33, 159, 201, 260
Eu, 226
Eugenics Review, The, 277 footnote

Eugenius III, Pope, 333
Europe, European, 196, 197, 200, 240, 280, 281, 319, 337, 342, 343; affairs, 158; city, 232; history, 176, 307; University life in, 91
Europe's Apprenticeship, 92 footnote
Evangelical churchman, 158
Evangelicalism, 135, 144, 339
Evenden, 257
Everard, 53
Exchange and Mart, The, 256
Exeter, 86, 283, 284, 291, 293; Bishop of, 297
Exeter Registers, the, 331

Faerie Queene, see Spenser
Fanshawe, 97
Far East, the, 172
Farewell to Love, see Campbell, Thomas
Farnleyberg, 190, 199
Farrar, Dean, 202, 341
Farringdon Street, 38, 168
Father Rhine, 261 footnote, 264
Fathers, the, 164, 343, 353
Faulkbourn Hall, 89
Faust, 55, 59
Favre, Camille, Colonel, 267
Fawcett, Henry, 315, 322
Fawcett, Mrs, 159
Feldberg, the, 186
Fell, Judge, 1
Felsted, vii, 34, 37, 41, 57, 68, 69, 70, 71, 72, 73, 74, 75, 76, 77, 78, 80, 81, 82, 83, 86, 88, 89, 127, 133, 141, 146, 214, 266, 282, 284, 304; Debating Society at, 83; Library, 84; Speech Day, 89, 90
Felstedian, The, 83, 304
Feltoe, C. L., 210
Fénelon, 348
Fenland, 10
Fens, the, 124
Ferrar, Nicholas, 138
Ferry Lane, King's Lynn, 32
Field, The, 258
Fioretti di San Francesco, 131
First Apology, see Justin Martyr
Firth, C. H., Professor, 321
Fischer, Kuno, 193, 194
Fisher, H. A. L., 161
Fishguard, 103
'Fishy Water', 225
Fitzwilliam Museum, the, 128, 258
Five Centuries of Religion, 312, 320
Fleet, the, 11, 12
Flemming, Professor, 61

Florence, 62, 132, 229, 230
Florentine picture gallery, 237
Folklore Society, the, 307
Fontainebleau, 263
Food Reform Shop, 59
Forclaz, 228, 289
Ford Lectures, 314
Forster, E. M., 306
Fort Augustus, 303
Fortnightly Review, The, 157
Foster, Gertie, Miss, 157
Fowler, F. G., 111, 112
Fowler, H. W., 111, 215, 216, 217, 255, 270, 300, 301, 328, 332
Fox, George, 1
Fox, J., 33
Foxwell, Ernest, 27
Foxwell, H. S., Professor, 324
France, 39, 40, 55, 187, 198, 249, 263, 272; clergy of, 330 footnote
France, 201
France, Anatole, 194
Francis, 12
Franciscans, 155, 182, 289, 313, 340 footnote
Franco-German War, 239, 353; Declaration of, 55
Frankfort, 117
Frankfurter Zeitung, 196
Franklin, Benjamin, 5
Frederick, E. P., 139
Free Church, 137; Minister, 144
French books, 41, 156, 188, 190; courtesy, 47; ecclesiastics, 351; language, 47, 52, 53, 109, 113, 127, 131, 176, 194, 208, 265, 269, 285, 313; monasticism, 352; national anthem, 43; professor, 346; Proverbs, Old, 157; schoolfellows, 41, 46, 129; sky, vii; soldiers, 77; teacher, 1; teaching, 76, 78, 175, 201, 209
Frenchman, Frenchmen, 46, 176, 193, 195, 226, 319 footnote
French Method, see Ollendorff
Friar's Lantern, 264, 397
Frogs, The, 82
Froissart, 184
From St Francis to Dante, 306
Froude, J. A., 163, 164, 172, 295
Frutigen, 286, 292, 293
Fry, C. B., 126
Fulford, 210
Fuller, Ned, 75

Gaetani, Signor, 242, 243, 244, 245
Gairdner, James, 312, 331, 334, 335

Gale, 70, 71
'Gallant Sailor', the, 33
Galleywood Common, 69
Galloway, 232
Gallus Gallo lupus, 46
Gamlyn, the elder, 52
Gamlyn, William, 51
Gardner, Alice, Miss, 97
Garland, Mr, 29
Garrett, A. E., 159, 168
Garrett, Rhoda, Miss, 159
Garrett-Anderson, Mrs, 159
Garrod, Miss, 32
Garth, hill, 146, 148
Gascoigne Minor, 191
Gasquet, Cardinal, 329, 330, 331, 332, 333, 334, 335
Gaywood, 55
Gedge, William Wilberforce, the Rev., 127, 128, 129
Geldart, E. M., 16
Genesis, 103
Geneva, 47, 229, 248, 251, 272, 314; International Labour Bureau at, 272
Georg., see Virgil
George V, King, 92
Gepp, Hubert, 212
German(s), 190, 191, 195, 197, 232, 238, 321; agriculture, 192; architecture, 38; army, 198; language, 52, 76, 89, 168, 173, 176, 187, 190, 194, 198, 201, 212, 292; literature, 193; Press, 196; Reformation, 323; Reichstag, 280; rusk, 14, 28; scholarship, 162; schoolfellows, 129; teaching of, 76, 78, 201
German-Swiss, 49
Germany, 55, 169, 186, 187, 192, 197, 198, 199, 211, 239, 272, 273, 277, 278, 281; Church of, 192
Gerson, 300
Gerusalemme Liberata, 236
Ghent, 37
Gibbon, 2, 84, 88, 93, 96, 229, 352
Gibbon, Hôtel, 229
Gidding, Little, 138
Gilbert, W. S., 161
Giles, Peter, 121
Gilkes, 209 footnote, 218, 219, 220, 221, 222
Gilkes and Dulwich, see Leake, M.
Gill, Eric, 341, 346
Girls' High School, King's Lynn, 32
Gladstone, Mary, Lord Acton's letters to, 138
Gladstone, W. E., 61, 84, 158, 159, 194, 273, 344

'Glorious Seven', the, 152
Gloucester, vii, 130
Glover, T. R., 314
Godts, F. X., Fr., 339 footnote
Goebbels, 49, 52
Goethe, 50, 59, 126, 173, 186, 187, 190, 236, 261, 306, 324
Golconda, 35
Golden Grove, 179
Golden Valley, the, 133
Goliardic songs, 156
Gooch, 217
Goodwin, Harvey, 36
Gordon, Mary, 3
Goschen, 276
Gospels, the, 327
Gotha Gymnasium, 198
Gothic Architecture, see Rickman
Gothic art, 187
Gough, 26
Gould, 303
Grammar School, the, King's Lynn, 8, 16, 39, 48, 49, 50, 57, 95; Masters at, 49, 53; speech days, 53
Grand Combin, 227
Grand Pont, 226
Grand Tour, the, 243
Grant, 214
Grantchester, 100, 123, 124; 'Grind', 100, 109, 122
Granville, Lord, 158
Grassy, 311
Gray, 189
Great Eastern Railway, the, 15, 25
Great Ormond Street, 335
Great War, the, 270, 272, 273, 281, 308, 313, 347
Greek, 50, 52, 59, 80, 85, 87, 115, 143, 144, 155, 206, 218, 219, 220, 319 footnote, 342 footnote; blood, 130; fathers, 351; Professor of, 282, 288; Testament, the, 53, 143, 157; verses, 83
Green, J. R., 78, 85, 158
Greenbank School, 217
Greenland, 95, 96
'Greens', 151
Gregory VII, 233
Gretel, 176
Greyfriars, 28; convent, 37
Greyfriars' Tower, King's Lynn, the, 7, 12, 18, 33, 49
Griffin, 221
Grignon, W. S., the Rev., 69, 70, 76, 82, 83
Grimm, 177, 272
Grimm's Law, 190

Grindelwald, 293
Grongar Hill, 179
Gross-Lohner, the, 290
Gruyère cheese, 44
Guanock Bridge, 12
Guernsey, 300; vest, 31
Guibert, 352 footnote
Gunning, 93
Guthrie, T. Anstey, 87 footnote
Gwatkin, H. M., Professor, 103, 104, 105, 106, 142, 313, 338; Mrs, 106
Gwent, 181

Haddon, T. W., 82, 84, 86
Hades, 130 footnote
Hadow, Henry, Sir, 138, 210
Hafod, 184
Haggard, Miss, 63 footnote
Haileybury, 76, 202, 211, 214
Haines, C. R., 111, 114, 120, 312
Haldon Terrace, Exeter, 283
Hale, Matthew, Sir, 90
Hall, Bishop, 120
Hamerton, P. G., 302
Hamilton, Claud, Lord, 25
Hamilton, George, Lord, 25
Hamilton, Ian, Sir, 301
Hamlet, 184
Hammond, J. L., 211
Handel, 199
Handschuchsheim, 196
Hanno, 81
Hansell, H. P., 176
Harding, Stephen, 200
Hardt, the, 190
Hardwick, Alan, 51, 52
Hardy, E. G., 86, 88, 109, 170, 201, 209, 303
Hardy, Thomas, 209 footnote
Harker, 315
Harkness Tower, viii
Harnack, 262
Harpenden, 151
Harper, Dr, 200, 201, 202, 203, 214
Harrow, 117, 142, 147, 153, 157, 161, 201, 202, 252, 312; Headmaster of, 127, 141
Hart, Henry, 213, 214, 216, 217
Hart, Mrs, 285
Harvard, 200
'Harvest Moon', 121
Hassall, John, 189
Hauptmann, Gerhart, 239
Headington, 84
Hebrews, Epistle to the, 233, 347
Hector, 41

Heidelberg, vii, 148, 185, 186, 187, 189, 190, 191, 192, 193, 194, 195, 196, 197, 198, 201, 211, 222, 226, 233 footnote, 239, 265, 293, 303, 306, 337 footnote, 339 footnote; Castle, 186, 187
Heidentum in der Christlichen Kirche, see Trede
Heiliggeistkirche, Heidelberg, 186
Heine, 36, 169
Heitland, W. E., 83, 92, 103, 104, 107, 117, 118, 168
Henley, 152
Henn, Mathematical Tutor, 87
Henn, Henry, 87, 88, 103
Henry VIII, 20, 49, 68, 305, 321
Henry VIII and the English Monasteries, see Gasquet, Cardinal
Henslow, Professor, 95
Heppenstall, 213, 214
Heptarchy, the, 24
Heraclitus, 342 footnote
Herbert, George, 330
Hercules, 87
Herder, 190
Hereford, Herefordshire, 136, 338; Beacon, 133; Bishop of, 133; Cathedral, 132, 173
Herne Hill, 222, 285
Herodotus, 80
Hertfordshire, 147, 151, 210; parson, 87
Hibbert Journal, The, 224 footnote
Hickson, G. F., 284 footnote
Hieronymus, 341 footnote
Highland Reaper, see Wordsworth, W.
Highlands, the, 108
High Street, King's Lynn, 10, 37, 63
Hill, Edward, Sir, 168
Hills, R. P., 255
Hills-Johnes, James, Sir, 184; Lady, 184
Hinsley, Cardinal Archbishop, 336
Hirst, F. W., 126
Hist. de France, see Michelet, J.
Historical Essays and Studies, see Acton, Lord
Historische Vergleichung, 227
History of Civilization, see Buckle
History of England, 321 footnote
History of the Papacy, see Creighton
History of St Catharine's College, see Jones, Dr
History of Sherborne, see Wildman
Hitchin, 151, 153, 156, 157; Priory, 152, 153
Hitler, Adolf, 321
Hobbes, philosopher, 32, 138
Holbein, 2

Holborn Viaduct, 285
Holy Orders, 3, 94, 106, 139, 182, 208
Homeric feast, 6; meal, 152; scholar, 110
Home Rule, 142
'Honest Lawyer', the, 4
Honeybourne, *see* Hunnybun
Hook, Dean, 118
'Hoos', 151
Hope, William, Sir, 305
Hope End, hill, 135
Hopkinson, Austin, 267 footnote
Horace, 57, 64, 81, 122, 178, 303
Hornigolds, Hornyolds, 129, 139
'Hornyold Arms', the, 129
Hort, Professor, 202
Houbraken, 5
Hound of Heaven, see Thompson, Francis
House of Commons, the, 2, 21, 22
Housman, A. E., Professor, 113, 121, 133, 206, 207, 262, 315, 339
Houtin, A., 353
Hubbersty, 120
Hügel, Von, 262
Hughes, George, 152
Hulsean Lectures, 322
Humanité, L', 273
Hume, 319 footnote
Hunnybun, nurse, 11
Hunstanton, vii, 9, 20, 127; railway line, 13
Hunter, Dr, 15
Huntington, H. E., 127, 129, 130, 131, 132, 134, 138, 155, 224, 230, 246; Mrs, 130, 131
Huxley, Thomas, 163, 276, 280
Hyacinthe, Père, 255
Hyperion, see Longfellow

Ibsen, 207
Iceland, 287
Idylls, see Tennyson
Ilbert, Courtenay, Sir, 71, 106, 286, 287
Ilbert, Miss, 286, 287, 289, 293, Pl. vii
Ilbert, Mr, 295
Ilbert, Mrs, 295, 297, 298
Ilbert, Rose, 298
'Ilbert Bill', the, 286
Iliad, the, 41
Ilmenau, see Goethe
India(n), 83, 247; Civil Service, 254; Mutiny, 268; self-government, 286
Infallibility Decree, 192
Inferno, see Dante
Ingram, D. S., 83
In Memoriam, see Tennyson
Inniskilling Dragoons, the, 261

Inquiry Concerning the Human Understanding, 319 footnote
International Arbitration League, 277
International footballers, 70
International Historical Congress, 329, 335
Internationalism, 80
Inverness cape, 153, 284
Ipswich, 159
Ireland, Home Rule for, 142–3; Protestant Church in, 24
Irish Melodies, see Moore
Irishmen, 4, 114, 188
Ischia, 231, 236
Isle of the Sirens, 239
Israel, 120
Italian(s), 229, 235, 240, 248; art, 196; bishop, 244; blood, 130; dishes, 242; engravings, 114; history, 307; hostelry, 307; journey, 246; language, 130, 233; schoolfellows, 129; servants, 130
Italy, 47, 131, 187, 213, 226, 229, 230, 234, 235, 237, 248, 249, 284; North, 33
I walked by Night, see Rolfe

Jackson, Cyril, 212
Jackson, Henry, 92, 106, 107, 108, 109, 110, 111, 123, 142
'Jacobin' and 'Jacobite', 85
Jagg, Elizabeth, 28
James, 'Stiggins', 253
James, William, 72
Jargonel pears, 14
Jary, 51
Jaurès, 272
Java, 148; Dutch consul in, 148
Jayne, Bishop, 181
Jeeves, 248
Jerusalem, 65, 238
Jessopp, Dr, 61
Jesuit(s), 138, 165, 193 footnote, 330; Cardinal, 342; scholar, 59
Jewish, 238, 265; face, 65; family, 186; refugees, 212
Jocelyn, Lord, 23
John Bull and his Island, 77
John Inglesant, see Shorthouse
John the Baptist, 341, 342 footnote, 344
Johnson, Dr, 31, 50, 302
Jones, A. V., 76, 128, 206, 254
Jones, G. Hartwell, 176, 218, 219
Jones, Mr, 180
Jones, 'Vinegar', 82
Jones, W. H. S., Dr, 113, 119, 121
Jones, Willoughby, Sir, 143

Jorrocks, 152
Journal de Genève, the, 267
Journal des Goncourt, 194
Journal of Last Expedition, see Scott, R. F., Captain
Journal of Philology, see Shipley, Arthur
Jowett, 86, 276
Judaism, 344 footnote
Juliana of Norwich, 303
Jungfrau, the, 286
Jung-Stilling, 173
Junker, 196
Jupiter Tonans, 13
Jura, the, 251
Justin Martyr, 342 footnote

Kaiser, the, 191, 198, 239, 272
Kander, the, 286
Kandersteg, 290
Kapurthala, the Rajah of, 247
Kaufmann, 117, 123
Keble, 149
Kehl, 174
Keiller, Messrs, and Sons, 59
Kemp-Welch, 297
Kempe, Margery, 30
Kendon, F. H., viii
Kennedy, Benjamin Hall, 103, 109, 142
Kensington High Street, 273
Kent, 16, 153, 285
Kentish orchards, 263; railways, 27
Kershaw, Mr, 53
Keynes, J. M., 328
Kickleburys on the Rhine, The, 283
King brothers, the, 70
King Lear, 57
King Street, King's Lynn, 29, 32
King's College School, 269
King's Cross, 156
King's English, The, see Fowler, H. W.
King's Lynn, vii, 1, 2, 5, 7, 9, 13, 20, 21, 22, 23, 24, 25, 28, 29, 30, 31, 32, 34, 35, 36, 37, 38, 53, 55, 56, 57, 60, 63, 65, 66, 73, 74, 124, 140, 176, 296, 300, 303, 304; cheeses, 15; Mayor of, 48; Stanley Library, 300
King's Parade, Cambridge, 100
King's Staith Quay, King's Lynn, 37
Kings, Book of, 120
Kingsbridge, 296
Klose, Dr, 188
Knight, A. M., Bishop, 122
Knight, H(enry) J. C., Bishop, 105, 120, 121, 312
Knox, John, 49, 161
Korthals, Mr, 148

Krakatoa sunsets, 148
Kynaston, 253

Labour Party, 273, 278
Lady Bridge, 11
Lady Margaret Boat Club, 101, 311
La Fontaine, 9, 57
Lamb, Charles, 86, 151
Lampeter School, 170, 177, 178, 182, 183; Principal of, 181
Lancashire, 5, 213; cookery, 55; dialect, 66
Lancaster, William, Sir, 48
Lancing College, 214, 215, 216
Land of Lost Content, 339
'Land of my Fathers', 178
Landon, H. J., 74, 75
Landor, Walter Savage, 230, 294
Langland, William, 133, 139, 150
Langwade, 8
Lankin, Sergeant, 283
Laon, 226, 286, 293
La Riccia, 237
Latham, Henry, the Rev., 86, 87
Latin, 50, 53, 59, 80, 81, 87, 92, 115, 117, 122, 139, 140, 155, 156, 168, 201, 202, 218, 220, 244 footnote, 285, 335; civilization, 229; fathers, 351; Professor of, 176; verse, 54, 82, 106, 107 footnote, 116
Latin Dictionary, Thomas Cooper's, 262
Latin Prose Composition, see Bradley
Latouche, Rose, 184
La Touche, 114
Lausanne, 208, 226, 228, 302
Lawrence, Alick, 285, 286, 287, 288
Lawrence, Henry, Sir, 285, 292
Lawrence, Lady, 291, 293, 294
Lays of Ancient Rome, see Macaulay, T. B.
Lea, The, Thurlestone, 338
League of Nations, the, 314
Leake, M., 218 footnote
Leamington, 5, 6
Ledbury, 135
Lee, Prince, Bishop, 127
Leeds, 2; Theological College, 118
Lees, Beatrice, 5
Lees, Elizabeth, 5
Lees, Samuel, 5
Lee-Warner, Henry, 106, 107, 108, 297
Leghorn, see Livorno
Legrand, Monsieur, 41, 42, 46
Leibniz, 342, 343
Leighs Priory, 68, 304

Leland Stanford University, 277
Lenin, 272
Lenna Episcopi, 20
Leo XIII, 330
Léone Léoni, see Sand, George
Leopardi, 89 footnote, 131
Lerici, 132
Le Roux de Lincy, 157
Lessing, 164, 190, 229, 327, 345
Lessius, 59
Letters of William Stubbs, 302 footnote
Letters to Mary Gladstone, 330 footnote
Levin, 98
Liber Studiorum, see Turner
Liberal Party, the, 13, 14, 22, 23, 24, 25, 95, 197
Liberal(s), 270, 271, 273
Liddell-Hart, Colonel, 301
Liddon, 162, 163
Liebknecht, 273
Life, see Dale, A. W. W.
Life and Letters, see Creighton, Mrs
Life and Letters, Robertson, F. W., 301 footnote
Life and Letters of Mandell Creighton, 302
Life and Sermons, see Robertson, F. W.
Life and Thought in the Middle Ages, lectures on, 313
Life in the Middle Ages, 308
Life of Fawcett, see Stephen, Leslie
Life of Gasquet, 334 footnote
Life of Leslie Stephen, see Maitland, F. W.
Life of Lord Birkenhead, 210 footnote
Life of Macaulay, see Trevelyan, G. O., Sir
Lightfoot, Bishop, 128
Lille, 286
Lincolnshire, 2, 89
'Lindenbaum', 199
Lindfield, 301
Lindsell, 74
Lister, J. J., 311
Literary Reminiscences, see Payn, James
Little Mudbury, 128
Liveing, G. D., Prof., 97, 98, 102
Liverpool, 217, 231
Liverpool Street, 15, 37, 156
Lives of the Painters, see Vasari
Lives of Twelve Bad Men, see Seccombe, Thomas
Livorno, 130, 230, 248
Livy, 81
Llandaff, 145, 146, 148, 149, 151, 164, 168, 169, 176, 346; Cathedral school at, 141; Dean of, 142

Llanddeusant, 179, 184
Llandingat, 182
Llandovery, 173, 176, 177, 180, 182, 183, 185, 202, 210, 214, 218; fair, 180; Headmaster of, 170, 185
Llanelly, 172, 177
Llanfair, 182
Llanidloes, 146
Llantarnam, 181
Llanthony Priory, 133
Llanwrda, 185, 187
Llanwrtyd, 173, 181
Llewelyn, Dean, 183
Lloyd George, 172, 173, 273
Loisy, 314; Congrès, 353
London, 4, 15, 21, 35, 62 footnote, 67, 69, 132, 144, 145, 153, 154, 156, 158, 159, 160, 161, 170, 174, 193, 194, 204, 209, 211, 217, 220, 222, 223, 230, 234, 259, 261, 270, 274, 284, 295; Bishop of, 74; Bridge, 40, 62; City of, School, 82; Greater, vii; Library, 299; North, 121; University, 335, Professor at, 161, 200; suburb, 158
London on the Thames, Canada, 5
London Road, King's Lynn, 28
Long Reach, Cambridge, the, 311
Long Retrospect, see Guthrie, T. Anstey
Longfellow, 186
Lonsdale, Lord, 1
Loom of Youth, The, see Waugh, Alec
Lorenzo de' Medici, see Roscoe
Loretto, 214
Lothair, see Disraeli
Lothbury, 223
Lotze, 208
Loughborough Junction, 285
Louis XIV, 43
Lowell Lectures, 314
Lowes Dickinson, 350
Lowry, 253
Loyola, 164
Lucas, 157
Lucknow, 285
Lucretius, 82, 302
Ludgate Viaduct, 285
Ludlow, 133, 135; castle, 173
Lumby, Joseph Rawson, the Rev., 113, 118, 119, 120, 337 footnote
Luna, hotel, Amalfi, 243
Lundy Island, 184
Lunn, Henry, Sir, 284, 286, 287, 288, 289, 292
Luria, see Browning, Robert
Luther, 138, 151, 323, 326, 342
Luton, 21, 63, 151; hat factories, 154

Lycée Impérial de St Omer, the, 39, 40, 41, 43, 45, 46, 47, 53; diet, 44
Lynn, see King's Lynn
Lynn Advertiser, The, 13
Lyttelton, Alfred, 254
Lyttelton, Edward, 254
Lyttelton, Lord, 141

Mabillon, 349
Macadam, 4
MacArthur, D. W., 84 footnote
Macaulay, G. C., 313
Macaulay, T. B., 7, 24, 84 footnote, 85, 156, 321
Macbeth, 56
Mackery End, 151
Macready, 201
McTaggart, 106, 107, 350
Maddison, Fred, 277
Magdalen, 'monks of', 352
Maher, James, 4
Mahogany Tree, 294
Main Illusions of Pacificism, The, 277 footnote, 281 footnote
Maitland, F. W., 98, 111 footnote, 195 footnote, 209 footnote, 283 and footnote, 315, 324
Malacca cane, 100
Malaga, 130
Malaprop, Mrs, 291
Malory, 125
Malvern, vii; Beacon, 173
Malvern College, 130, 131, 132, 141, 210; handwriting, 129
Malvern Wells, 127, 129, 130, 133, 134, 139, 147, 148, 155, 256, 284; Great, 127, 134, 139; Little, Court, 139; water, 128
Manchester, 2, 84, 85, 205, 206, 238; Bishop of, 128; Grammar School, 84; Recorder of, 84
Manchester Guardian, The, 196, 275, 277
Mannheim, 186
Manon Lescaut, 210
Manzoni, 138
Marcus Aurelius, 111, 346
Margate, 35, 40
Marham, 61
Marius the Epicurean, see Pater, Walter
Marlborough, 71, 82, 85, 202
Marlburian, The, see Ilbert, Courtenay, Sir
'Marseillaise', the, 43
Marshall, Willie, 64
Mart, the, at King's Lynn, 66
Martial, 157

Marvell, Andrew, 339
Masefield, John, 133
Mason, Peter, 101
Massachusetts, 20
Massingham, H. W., 25
Matthew's shop, Cambridge, 97
Maude, Colonel, 301
Mayflower celebration, 58
Mayor, 'Johnny', Latin Professor, 59, 60, 124
Mayor, Robin, 59
Mecca, 186
Medieval Garner, A, 307
Medieval Outlines, 313
Medieval Panorama, 179 footnote
Medieval Studies, 309
Meditations, see Marcus Aurelius
Mediterranean, the, 231, 240, 245, 246, 249
Meech, S. B., 30 footnote
Meiners, C., 227
Melanchthon, 262
Melrose, 37
Memoirs, see Pattison, Mark
Memoirs of a Brother, 152
Memorial Day, viii
Memory hold-the-door, see Buchan, John
Men and Memoirs, see Rothenstein, Will, Professor
'Men of Harlech', 178
Mendip Hills, the, 168
Mercer's Row, King's Lynn, 37
Meran, 260
Merry, W. W., 110
Mesopotamia, 84
Messiah, see Handel
Methuen & Co., 307
Metropolitan life, 161; Railway, 158, 161
Micawber, 353
Michael, see Wordsworth, W.
Michelet, J., 175, 250 footnote
Mickle, Mr, 20, 21
Micklethwaite, 20
Middle Ages, the, 17, 20, 22, 91, 200, 224, 302, 304, 312, 349; Fair in, 66; peasant farmer of, 56; universities in, 92
Middle Level Drain, the, 8
Migne, J.P., Abbé, 248, 351, 352, 353, 354
Milan, 229
Mildenhall, 153
Mill, J. S., 270, 271
Millbank, 148
Milner, 267
Milton, 37, 199, 206, 290
Milton's mulberry tree, 14

'Mitty', *see* Coulton, Elizabeth
Modern English Usage, see Fowler, H. W.
Modern Languages, teaching of, 80
Modern Painters, see Ruskin
Moffatt, 121
Môle, the, 248
Mommsen, 83, 84, 321
Monastic History, 312
Monasticon, see Dugdale
Mönch, the, 286
Monmouth, 183
Montaigne, 226, 227 footnote
Mont Blanc, 227
Monte Cristo, 212
Montgomery, Robert, 49
Montreux, 227
Monumenta Germaniae, 352
Moody, Thomas, 31
Moonstone, The, 47
Moor Park, 158
Moore, 185
Moore-Smith, G. C., Professor, 102
Moorish pirates, 245
Morant, 74
More, Thomas, St, 68, 337
Morgan, Frank, 175
Morghen, Rafael, 114
Morning Post, The, 270, 271
Morpeth, 1
Mothers' Union, 35
Moule, Charles, 97
Much Hadham, palace of, 74
Mulciber's palace, 37
Müller, 191, 192
Muller hat, 40
Municipal Reform, 21
Murdstone, Mr, 81
Murray, 285
Muslims, 262
de Musset, Alfred, 220, 345 footnote
Myddfai, Physicians of, 179
Myers, F. W. H., 106, 107, 108, 297

Nansen, 212
Naples, 37, 226, 230, 231, 232, 233, 234, 235, 246; Bay of, 231, 239
Napoleon, 33
Napoleon III, 43, 44
Napoleonic foresight, 256; wars, 245
Nar, river, 56, 61, 140
Narborough, 56, 60, 62; Hall and Manor of, 62
Narford, 62
Nation, The, 271
National Gallery, the, 122, 148, 234, 300
National Service League, the, 199, 270

Nazi editor, 321
Neckar, the, vii, 188, 189
Neckargemünd, 187
Neckarthal, 187
'Nellie Gray', 131
Nelson, Lord, 131, 140
Nelson Street, King's Lynn, 32, 33
Neuenheim College, 188, 189, 190, 191, 195, 198
New Conduit Street, King's Lynn, 33, 36
Newhaven, 248
Newman, Cardinal, 65, 147, 162, 211, 332, 336, 339
Newmarket, 125
Newport (Mon.), 81
New Zealand, 295; Bishop of, 104
Nicaea, 343
Nichols, F. P., 252
Nietzsche, 191
Night Side of Nature, The, 16
Nineteenth Century and After, The, 277, 335
Nisida, 231
Nogent, Guibert de, Abbot, 248, 249
Norfolk, 1, 57, 62, 89, 108, 136, 144, 246, 297, 301, 304, 305; angel roofs, 62; bloaters, 34; cookery, 55; dialect, 34, 116; dumplings, 291; 'Holy Land of', 61; jacket, 289; poppies, 64; squire, 143
Norman Conquest, the, 200, 317
Norman doorways, 74
Normandy pippins, 40
Northamptonshire, 58
Northcliffe, Lord, 308
North End, the, King's Lynn, 15, 23, 24
Northey, A. E., 147, 153, 154, 156, 157, 164, 166; Mrs, 154
North Sea, the, 36, 303
Northwood, 158, 161
North Wootton, 1
Norway, 216
Norwich, 55, 59, 116, 176; Bishop of, 20, 143; Cathedral, 30; Juliana of, 303
Nubar Pasha, 255
Nuit d'Octobre, see Musset, A. de
Nürnberg, 186, 187
Nürnberg Chronicle, 186
Nutt, David, 307, 308

Oates, Laurence, 260, 261
Oates, Titus, 103
Oberland, the, 286, 289, 293
Obermann, 317
Obermann, see Arnold, M.

Obstetrical Society, the, 159
Odell, Mrs, 162
Odgers, Blake, 204
Oedipus Tyrannus, 282
Oeschinen See, the, 290
Œuvres choisies de Rivarol, 318 footnote
Œuvres de Leibniz, 343 footnote
Offin, 71
Offley, 63, 147, 151, 152, 154, 155, 156, 157, 158, 160, 161, 163; Hall, 152
O'Grady, Mr, 76
Okehampton, 184
Oldham, 1, 5
'Old Tower, The', King's Lynn, 28, 49
Oliver, 331
Ollendorff, 41, 52
Ollivant, Alfred, 262
Olten, 286
On the Creed, see Pearson, Bishop
'Ophelia' roses, 56
'O'Rell, Max', 77, 176
Oriental, Orientalists, 238; philosophy, 162; studies, 210
Origen, 164, 168
Osservatore Romano, the, 336
Osten-Sacken, C. R. von der, Baron, 194, 195, 196, 197, 237, 337
Oundle, 219
Our Lady of the Stiletto, 232
Ouse, the, 8, 11, 140; Little, 140
Overstolzen-Haus, 38
Ovid, 91
Owd Bob, see Ollivant, Alfred
Owen, Ernest, 98, 127, 130, 135, 139, 141, 284
Owen, John, 170, 171, 172, 174, 175, 182, 184
Owen, Rose, 295, 297
Oxen-born Bees of the Ancients, see Osten-Sacken, C. R. von der, Baron
Oxford, 5, 83, 86, 93, 106, 107 footnote, 121, 126, 130, 131, 138, 144, 145, 156, 170, 171, 175, 177, 183, 184, 189, 193, 194, 204, 207, 209, 210, 212, 215, 217, 224, 262, 270, 293, 300, 302, 311, 314; All Souls, Fellow of, 135; Balliol College, scholar of, 16 footnote, 84, 105, 183, 206, 286, Fellow of, 287, 332; Bishop of, 35; Blue, 177, 189, 217; Clarendon Press, 312; Exeter College, 295; football at, 70; Jesus College, Fellow of, 86, Principal of, 200; Keble College, 131, 134, 175; Law Professor at, 16 footnote; Magdalen College, President of, 175, 193; Magdalen College School, 210;

Oxford (*cont.*)
    Martyrs' Memorial at, 91; 'monks of
    Magdalen', 93; New College, 183;
    Oriel College, 208, 217; prizes, 107,
    286; Queen's College, Fellow of, 214;
    rowing, 152; Savilian Professor at,
    68; Taylorian Reader, 198; Taylorian
    Scholarship at, 130; University Col-
    lege, Scholar of, 82, 83; Wadham
    College, 83, 84, 86, 126, 210; Wor-
    cester College, 188
Oxford Dictionary, Pocket, the, 326
Oxford English Dictionary, The, 85 foot-
    note, 217
Oxford Magazine, The, 217
Oxford Street, 168

Paddington, 293
Paganism in the Christian Church, see
    Trede
Paget, Dr, 35
Palestine, 158
Palmerston, Lord, 103, 297
Pantheon, the, 247
Papal Infallibility, 244
Paradise Lost, 37
Paris, 44, 131, 226, 242, 249, 263, 273,
    314, 352; Archbishop of, 353; exhi-
    bition, the, 47; Siege of, 109
Paris, Matthew, 302
Parker, Lady, 2
Parker, Louis Napoleon, 207, 208, 217
Parker's Piece, 101, 312
Parliament, 2, 94, 266, 267, 286, 297
Parliamentary Reform, 21
Parochial and Plain Sermons, see New-
    man, Cardinal
Partington, Mrs, 162
Pascal, 330, 332 footnote, 346 footnote,
    349 footnote
Pascal, Newman and Loisy, see Williams,
    W.
Pas-de-Calais, the, 39
Passage to India, A, see Forster, E. M.
Pasteur, 280
Pasteurian-Listerian gospel, 124
Pater, Walter, 210
Patrologia Graeca, see Migne, J. P.,
    Abbé
Patrologia Latina, see Migne, J. P., Abbé
Pattison, Mark, 83, 123, 162, 307
Paul, Mr, 58
Paul et Virginie, see St-Pierre
Payn, James, 254 footnote
Payot, 226
Peace Pledge Union, the, 274

Peachey, the innkeeper, 74
Peacock, Dean, 324
Peaks, Passes and Glaciers, 109
Pearson, A. C., Professor, 219
Pearson, J., Bishop, 162, 163
Peddar's Way, 62
Pedlar, at Swaffham, 62
Pelly, 77 footnote
Pembroke Street, Cambridge, 59
Pen-Allt-Mawr, 133
Pen-y-Cader Fawr, 133
Pen-y-Cerrig Calch, 133
Pennines, the, 213
Pensées, see Pascal
Pentney, vii, 26, 55, 57, 58, 61, 62, 63,
    64, 65, 67, 136, 139, 154, 171, 211,
    285, 293, 300, 301, 308, 309; 'Abbey',
    61, Plates iv, vi
Percy Anecdotes, The, 303
Perowne, E. H., 95
Perse Grammar School, the, 101, 213
Perugia, 132
Pesto, 243
Petit Séminaire d'Issy, 149
Petworth, 148
Phillimore, 107, 181
Pickwick Papers, The, 23
Piers Plowman, see Langland
Pietro, 248
Pilgrim Mothers, the, 58
Pilgrim's Progress, 19
Pilgrim's Way, 197, 337 footnote
Pisa, 132, 230
Pitt, the elder, 22
Pius X, Pope, 299, 335
Plague, see Defoe
Plato, 88, 111, 123, 144, 155, 156, 214,
    241
Ploeck, the, Heidelberg, 188, 192
Plutarch, 340
Plymouth, 284
Poetae Scenici, 82
Poles, 212
Poligny, 141, 251 footnote
Pollock, 283
Pompeii, 234
Pompey, 344
Ponte Vecchio, 62
Pontypridd, 144
Poole, 22
Poole, Reginald Stuart, 164, 346
Pope, 100
'Porte d'Or', the, 45, 47
Portsmouth, 261; Dockyard, 160
Posilipo, 232
Positano, 239

Postern, King's Lynn, 12
Pound, the, King's Lynn, 29
Power, Eileen, 265
Pozzuoli, 232
Praeterita, see Ruskin
Premium upon Falsehood, A, 329 footnote, 331 footnote, 333 footnote, 336 footnote
Pre-Raphaelite school, 47
Presbyterianism, 331
Pressland, A. J., 191, 193
Pretor, Alfred, 117, 120
Pretoria, 285
Priory Lane, King's Lynn, 30
Private Secretary, The, 153
Procida, 231
Promessi Sposi, see Manzoni
Propertius, 97 footnote
Protagoras, see Plato
Protestant, 197, 336, 340, 342; Church, 24, 342, 347; controversialist, 192; Protestantism, 138
Proverbs, the book of, 48
Prussia(n), 238
Public Library, King's Lynn, opening of, 34
Public School Modern Language teaching, 78
Public Schools, 285
Public Schools and Public Needs, 80 footnote, 264
Puck, 36
Punch, 103, 109 footnote
Purbeck marble, 25
Purg., see Dante
Pusey, 162
Puteoli, *see* Pozzuoli

Quaker, 157, 218, 276, 278; prosperity, 1
Queen Street, King's Lynn, 29, 48
Quella Graciosa, 243
Quiller-Couch, Arthur, Sir, 308

Rachel Ray, see Trollope
Radicals, 21, 72, 271, 272
Radley, James, 5, 6
Radley, Mary Ann, 6
Radley, Sarah, 6
Radley, Sophia, 5
Radnor Forest, 173
Raglan, 133
Raleigh Historical Lecture, 326
Rangoon, Bishop of, 122
Ranke, 321
Raper, R. W., 107
Rapson, Professor, 160

Rashdall, Hastings, 160, 183, 210, 224, 300, 304, 312, 320
Ravello, 245; Cathedral, 244
Raven, Tancred, 83
Ravenna, 37
Realist, The, 338
Recollections of a Bishop, The, see Browne, G. F.
Red Mount, the, 12; Chapel, 26
Rees, Aneurin, 179, 180
Rees of Ton, 179
Reformation, the, 92, 118, 319, 320, 334
Regensburg, Berthold of, *see* Berthold
Rehbraten, *see* Tyrolese venison
Reid, J. S., 123
Reid, Mayne, 41
Reims, 226
Reine Pédauque, La, 194
Reinkens, Bishop, 192
Religio Militis, see Hopkinson, Austin
Reminiscences, see Clark, J. W.
Reminiscences, see Gunning
'Renaissance' and 'Renascence', 85
Renan, 147, 162, 164, 227
Republic, see Plato
Revue des Deux Mondes, 227
Rhetoric, see Cope
Rhind Lectures, 314
Rhine, river, vii, 186, 187, 190, 223, 261
Rhoades, James, 208
Rich chapel, the, Felsted, 73
Rich, Richard, Lord, 68
Richards, 179
Richards, James Brinsley, 252
Richter, Herr, 280
Rickman, 74
Rickmansworth, 155, 157, 158, 161, 168, 189; Park, 158
Rigaldi, Odo, *Diary*, 307
Riley, Athelstan, 215
Ripon School, 111
Rising Castle, 26
Roberts, Lord, 184, 270, 273
Robertson, F. W., 164, 301
Robinson, 113, 121; Mrs, 113
Rochdale, 193
Rochefort, Abbé of, 1
Rochester, Bishop of, 131; See of, 142
Rock of Twm, 180
Rockhill, 295, 296, 300
Rogers, Henry, 151
Roi des Montagnes, see About, Edmond
Rolfe, the poacher, 58, 63
Rolls Chronicle, the, 300
Rolls Series, the, 352

Roman(s), 319 footnote, 321, 330; Mass, 163; religious press, 336; road, 62; tourist, 236; walls, 140

Roman Catholic(s), 129, 191, 192, 194, 197, 329, 331, 332, 333, 336, 339 footnote, 340, 341, 342, 343, 344, 346, 353; Church, 118, 137, 341; controversy, 338; convert, 141; historians, 138; priest, 155, 192; seminary, 44

Roman Catholicism, 138

Romanticism, 197

Rome, 237, 241, 246, 247, 333, 338, 344, 353; Imperial, 337; St Peter's at, 344

Rome, the Church of, 22, 52, 138, 147, 192, 262, 329, 333, 335, 342, 343, 344, 346

Roscoe, 85

Rosmersholm, see Ibsen

Ross, 133

Rossetti, Christina, 350

Rossetti, D. G., 146

Rothenburg, 186, 187, 188, Pl. vii

Rothenstein, Will, Professor, 353 footnote

Rotterdam, 186, 187

Rouen, 37, 187; Archbishop of, 307

Round Table, The, 135

Rousseau, 1, 241, 250, 251, 263

Routh, 102

Rowe, A. W., 80, 81, 82, 83; Rowe's House, 71

'Rows', the, Yarmouth, 35

Royal Commissions, 93, 94, 95

Royal Society, the, 68

Roydon, 1

Rugby, 128, 141, 144, 170, 201, 203, 216, 297; Head of, 76

Rushmore, F. M., 126

Ruskin, 14, 27, 73, 184, 226, 230, 237, 251 footnote, 261, 263, 285, 303, 315

Russell, Bertrand, 280

Russell, G. W. E., 143, 144

Russia(n), 194, 195, 202, 212, 272; retreat from, 33; Revolution, 272

Sabatier, 224

Sabellianism, 164

St Albans, Bishop of, 151

St Alfonso Liguori, 339 footnote

St Andrew, 245

St Andrew's Day, 259

St Andrew's Street, Cambridge, 98

St Andrews University, 282

St Anne's Hill, 260

St Asaph, See of, 170

St Augustine, 151 footnote, 156, 306, 341, 345

St Bees, 1

St Bernard, 156, 329, 333, 337; letters of, 224

St Bonaventura, 155, 299

SS. Cosma e Damiano, 247

St Cyprian, 342

St David's, Bishop of, 170, 173, 184; day, 179

St Francis, 313

St Francis, see Sabatier

St George's Hall, King's Lynn, 37

St-Germain-des-Prés, 352 footnote

St Gregory, 329, 342 footnote, 344

St James' Street, King's Lynn, 9, 10, 13, 23, 36, 49

St Jerome, 341, 343; letters by, 156

St John's Church, King's Lynn, 8

St-Julien, 250 footnote

St-Julien-du-Sault, 249, 250

St Katharine's Dock House, 211

St Katharine's Wharf, 40

St Margaret's Church, King's Lynn, 10, 12, 25, 300; Churchyard, 30

St Nicholas Church, King's Lynn, 23, 29

St Nicholas Street, King's Lynn, 24, 33

St Omer, vii, 39, 40, 41, 43, 46, 53, 55, 69, 89, 127, 286; Cathedral, 43

St Paul, 106, 143, 232; Pauline texts, 143, 149, 164

St Paul's, Canon of, 121; Cathedral, 285, 351; Dean of, 143

St Paul's School, 176, 269

St Peter's, Rome, 247

St-Pierre, 41

St Thomas, 151

St Thomas Aquinas, 155, 156, 246, 303, 339 footnote, 344 footnote

St Thomas More, 262

Salcombe, 295

Salerno, 239, 243, 245; Cathedral of, 233

Salimbene, 178, 230, 244 footnote, 248, 306, 307

Salimbene and his Circle, 306

Sand, George, 127, 210

Sanderson, 219

Sandford, 52

Sandhurst, 220

Sandringham Hall, 9, 53

Sands, The, Thurlestone, 338

San Gimignano, 132

Sankey, Lord, 171

Sankt Anna Kapelle, Heidelberg, 192, 193

Sta Agata, 232
St Agostino alla Zecca, 232, 233
Sant' Angelo, Monte, 237, 238
Sta Caterina, 240
Saracen marauders, 245
Sartor Resartus, 340
Sarzana, 248
Saturday Night, 16
Saturday Review, The, 158
Saunders, T. Bailey, 261, 335, 336
Schmidt, 192
Schopenhauer, 322
Schubert, 199
Scotch woollen pedlars, 34
Scotland, 6, 74, 171, 191, 259; North, 161
'Scots Grey', the, 28
Scotsman, 112, 161, 177, 191, 255
Scott, Gilbert, Sir, 73, 92, 104
Scott, H. v. E., 111, 121, 125, 185, 224, 226, 251, 252, 253, 254, 255, 256, 257, 258, 259, 260, 261, 268, 283, 286, 301, 308, 313; his brother, 259; Mrs, 256
Scott, R. F., Captain, 261
Scott, master at Felsted, 77
Scottish Hist. Rev., 349 footnote
Scottish poetry, 62
Scottish students, 121
Scribes and Pharisees, 136
Seccombe, Thomas, 12, 133
Second Empire, the, 41
Sectarian History, 332 footnote
Sedbergh, 206, 212, 213, 214, 215, 216, 217, 222, 285
Sedbergh Fells, the, vii
Seebohm, 157
Selby, F. G., 83, 85, 86
Selwyn, Bishop of New Zealand, 104
Sens, 249
Sept Écluses, 44
Serm., *see* St Augustine
Sesenheim, 186
Seume, Johan Gottfried, *Autobiography*, 306
Seven Years at Eton, *see* Richards, James Brinsley
Several of My Lives, *see* Parker, L. N.
Severn, the, 127, 130, 132, 181
Shakespeare, vii, 217, 218, 220, 285; Sonnets, vii
Sheffield, 2, 102; cutler, 161
Shelford, Great, 100, 313; Little, 114
Shelley, 132, 248
Shepherd's Sabbath Hymn, the, 169

Sherborne, 83, 128, 175, 189, 200, 201, 202, 203, 204, 206, 207, 208, 209 footnote, 210, 211, 213, 214, 216, 217, 220, 284; School Charter, 201
Shipley, Arthur, Sir, 194 footnote
Shoreditch, 15
Short History of the English People, *see* Green, J. R.
Shorthouse, 138, 139
Shouldham, 61
Shrewsbury, 83, 101, 103, 105, 218; Headmaster of, 142
Shrimpton, 217
Shropshire, 133, 135, 218
Shropshire Lad, A, 315
Siamese kitten, 58
Sidgwick, Arthur, 76
Sidgwick, Henry, 94, 324, 350
Siena, 132
Sigg, Jean, 272
Simon, John, Sir, 126, 271
Simond, Ami, Monsieur, 269
Sinclair, F. E., 70, 71
Sion Catti, 180
Skeat, 119
Sketches from Cambridge, by a Don, *see* Stephen, Leslie
Skirryd, 133
Slasher, Tipton, the, 87
'Sleepy Hollow', 300
Smith, Adam, 270
Smith, Albert, 41
Smith's Prizeman, 36
Snodgrass, 28
Snow, 253
Snowden, Lord, 270
Snowdonia, 133, 148, 171, 172, 173
Social Britain from the Conquest to the Reformation, 308
Socialist(s), 272, 272; the *Westminster Gazette* and, 271
Société d'Histoire des Religions, the, 314
Society for Pure English, the, 215
Socrates, 82, 214, 327, 342 footnote
Soliloquy, *see* St Augustine
Solomon, 1
Somerville College, 5
Somme, the, 226
Son of Belial, A, *see* Geldart, E. M.
Sophist, 214
Sophocles, 81
Sorrento, 230, 236, 237, 239, 240, 289
Soul's Tragedy, A, *see* Browning, Robert
South Gates, the, King's Lynn, 4, 28
South Kensington, 182

South Lynn, 252, 253, 256, 257, 259, 260, 263, 267, 268, 283, 305; Church, 28; Vicarage, 16
South Polar Expedition, 261
Southend Pier, 40
Southward, 113, 120
Southwark, 285
Souvenirs d'Enfance et de Jeunesse, see Renan
Spain, 238
Spaniard(s), 42, 238, 266
Spanish Armada, 296; chestnuts, 158; domination, 353; leather, 29
Sparta(n), 213; diet, 69
Speaker's Court, 298
Spenser, 236
Spezia, Bay of, 246
Spirit of Catholicism, The, see Adam, Karl
Sporting Times, 255
Spragg, Solomon, 28
Spratt, A. W., 113, 115, 116, 117, 118, 120, 122, 123, 124, 125
Stable, Alfred, 16, 133, 134, 141, 248
Stable, J. J., Professor, 248
Stanley, A. P., 141, 142, 144
Stanley, Lord, 25, 53
Stanley Public Library, the, King's Lynn, 21
Star, the, 140
Starr, Jordan, Dr, 277
Staunton, 4
Stebbing, 74
Steerforth, 9, 51
Steinwein, 195
Stephen, 6
Stephen, Leslie, 49, 87, 93, 94, 158, 195 footnote, 209 footnote, 221, 254 footnote, 259 footnote, 283, 315, 322 footnote
Stephenson, George, 13
Stewart, H. F., 314
Stewart, J. M. A., 111, 112, 113
Stokesay Castle, 173
Stonegate Street, King's Lynn, 11, 12
Stones of Venice, The, see Ruskin
Strachey, Lytton, 306
Strafford, 103
Strassburg, 186, 187
Stratford-attë-Bowe, 49
Stresemann, 327
Strong Army in a Free State, A, 264, 272 footnote
Stuart times, 68
Stubbs, William, Bishop, 184
Stubenvoll, Pastor, 192, 233 footnote

Studies in Medieval Thought, 92 footnote
Study of British Genius, A, see Ellis, Havelock
Subasio, Monte, 132
Suffolk, 12
Sullivan, Arthur, Sir, 161
Sully-Prud'homme, 250
Sumatra, 148
Summa Theol., see St Thomas Aquinas
Sunda Straits, 148
Surrey, 27, 176
Sussex Downs, 257; roads, 257
Swaffham, 61–2
Swansea, 177
Swansea Schools case, 255
Swinburne, 202, 230
Swiss, 208, 228, 253, 272, 289, 292, 346; army, 292, 293, 301; militia, 265, 285
Switzerland, 208, 226, 263, 266, 268, 269; German, 211

Tacitus, 285
Taff, the, 141
Taine, 227
Talbot, E. S., Bishop, 131
Taliesin, 148 footnote
Tammany, 244
Tanner, J. R., 313
Tasso, 236
Tasso, see Goethe
Tauchnitz, 121, 230
Taylor, Jeremy, 175, 179
Temple, Frederick, Archbishop, 192, 203, 205, 297, 298
Temple, Major, 297
Temple, the, 293, 294; Master of the, 141, 142, 143
Ten Medieval Studies, 335
Tennyson, 116, 125
Tertullian, 341
Tewkesbury, vii, 130, 133
Thackeray, 37, 158, 250, 283, 294; relation of, 253
Thames, the, 40, 253
Thaxted, 74, 75
Theatre Plain, King's Lynn, 7, 9
Thelema, Monks of, 287
Thew, J. D., 13
Thew, Mr, 12, 18
Thirlwall, Bishop, 184
Thirty-nine Articles, the, 163
Thompson, Francis, 164
Thompson, the Misses, 11, 12
Thompson, W. H., 91
Thomson, J. J., Sir, 94, 95, 97, 99, 100

Thoresby, 48; School, 4, 48
Thorneley, T., 87
Thornton, 121
Thousand and One Gems, The, 282
'Three Pigeons', the, King's Lynn, 10, 30
Thring, Dr, 69
Thucydides, 81, 115
Thun, Lake of, 284, 286
Thurlestone, 295, 297, 299, 300, 301, 308, 338
Thurston, H., Fr., 329, 331 footnote, 333
Tiber, the, 247
Time and Tide, 275
Times, The, 275, 301, 336
Times Literary Supplement, The, 335 footnote, 350 footnote
Tintern, 37, 133
Titterstone Clee, 133
Tityrus, 53, 64
Tiverton, 297
Todhunter, 259 footnote
Todtnau, 186
Tolbooth arches, King's Lynn, 33
Tom Brown's School Days, 152
Tonbridge, 263; Headmaster of, 253
Toronto, 277, 352; City Library at, 276; University Library at, 276, 352
Torquay, 284
Tory Party, the, 13, 20, 21, 22, 24, 25, 98, 203, 286
Totnes, 179
Toulouse, Inquisition at, 340 footnote
Tout, Professor, 160, 334
Tower, Bernard, 214, 215, 216
Tower House, 7, 29, Pl. iii
Tower Place, 12, 16, 28, 29, 33
Town Hall, the, King's Lynn, 9
Towy, the, 179, 181, 184, 222
Toynbee, Arnold, Professor, 15
Toynbee Hall, 211, 212, 213
Tramp Abroad, see Twain, Mark
Tramp of Syracuse, see Seume, Johan Gottfried
Trede, 192, 233 footnote
Tregaron, 180
Trendelenburg, 193
Trent, Council of, 343
Trevelyan, G. M., Professor, 93, 321, 323
Trevelyan, G. O., Sir, 84, 117, 156, 224
Trient, the, 227, 228
Trifan, 173 footnote
Trinità del Monte, Church of, 247
Troed-y-Rhiw, 180
Trollope, 23 footnote, 25 footnote, 152

Troy, 17, 18, 19
Trumpington, 100
Trumpington Street, Cambridge, 151
Tudor ancestors, 26; monarchy, 92
Tuesday Market Place, the, King's Lynn, 2, 20, 24, 29, 37, 39
Tuke, 157
Turnbull, 120
Turner, 148, 183, 300, 303
Twain, Mark, 19, 192, 198 footnote
Tweedsmuir, Lord, 197, 337
Two Saints, 338
Tyrolese venison, 109
Tyrrell, Father, 192, 255 footnote, 262

Uhland, 168, 169, 187
'Ulysses Deriding Polyphemus', 300
Union Library, the, Oxford, 156
Unitarian minister, 16 footnote
United States, the, vii, viii, 16
Universe, The, 147 footnote, 336
Universities, medieval, 92
Universities of Europe, see Rashdall, Hastings
University Calendar, the, 107, 124
University Fellowships, 3
University Librarian, assistant, 12
University Preacher, 36, 104
University Reporter, the, 121
Unto this Last, see Ruskin
Uppingham, 69, 312
Upsala, 212
Upward Anguish, The, see Wolfe, Humbert
Upward Struggle, The, see Wolfe, Humbert
Utopia(n), 337
Utopia, 337 footnote

Vancouver, 32
Vansittart, A. A., 109
Vasari, 156
Vatican Council, 244
Vauban, 43
Vaughan, C. J., Dean, 117, 127, 141, 142, 143, 144, 145, 146, 147, 149, 150, 166, 170, 220, 303; Mrs, 142, 143
Vaughan, David, 144
Vaughan, E. T., 151
Velan, 227
Venables, 158
Venetian senator, 59
Venn, Henry, Dr, 100
'Veritas', 108
Versailles, 274; Treaty, 327
Vesuvius, 232, 236

Vetii, House of the, 234
Vice Versa, see Guthrie, T. Anstey
Victoria, Hotel, Heidelberg, 198
Victoria, Queen, 3, 9, 92, 159, 183, 287; Jubilee of, 183, 184, 222, 228, 247, 261
Victoria Station, 263
Victorian architects, 73; board-school boy, 17; dress, 289; education, 72, 80, 85; England, 61; Lynn, 20 ff., 28 ff.; obedience, 31; quarrel, 94; times, 63, 200, 215; tradition, 60, 92; type, 128
Victorian Schoolmaster: Henry Hart, A, 213 footnote
Vie de Jésus, see Renan
Vie de Prêtre, Une, 353
Village Labourer, The, 211
Virgil, 17, 53, 57, 64, 81, 102 footnote, 130, 230, 232, 237; tomb of, 232
Vita Nuova, see Dante
Volga, the, 205
Voltaire, 41, 174
Voyage, see Montaigne

Wade, 219
Wagg, Benjamin, 28
Wagner, 139
Wales, 168, 171, 172, 176, 177, 179, 339; hills of, 133, 150, 188; North, 171; South, 103, 177, 181; Wild, 148
Wales, Prince of, 53, 158, 176; marriage of, 9
Walker, Headmaster of Manchester, 85, 205, 206
Walker, Fred, 121
'Walks', the, King's Lynn, 12, 13
Wallingford, 335
Wallis, John, 68
Wallis, Mr, 51
Walpole, Sir Robert, 20, 219
Walters, 175
Walter-Schomburg, Kurt, 321 footnote
War of 1914–18, the, 93, 126
War Memories, see Lloyd George
Ward, James, 324
Warren, Herbert, Sir, 175, 193, 194
Wash, the, 13, 25
Washington, 194
Waterloo, 33, 292, 295, 296; port, 36
Watford, 161
Waugh, Alec, 207 footnote
Waveney, the, 140
Way of All Flesh, The, see Butler, Samuel
Weekly Register, see Cobbett
Wellesleys, the, 158
Wellington, Headmaster of, 131

Wells, 168; Cathedral, 169, 233 footnote
Wells, H. G., 225
Wells, 'Joey', 210
Wells House, Malvern Wells, 127, 132, 135, 141
Welsh, 175, 180, 200; education, 182; language, 171, 175; manuscripts, 180; scenery, 173, 179
Welsh Marches, 133
Welsh valleys, vii
Welshman, 172, 174, 187
Weltgeschichte, 321 footnote
Wensleydale, 1
Westacre, 61, 63
Westcott, Bishop, 128, 202, 209
Westcott House, Cambridge, 312
Westminster, 295; Abbey, 221, 351; Archbishopric of, 330; Deanery of, 144
Westminster Gazette, The, 57
Westminster Review, The, 199
Westmorland, 213
Whewell, Dr, 87, 119, 142, 324
Whigs, 20, 23
White, 304, 305
White, Thomas, the Rev., 48, 50, 52, 53; Mrs, 51
White Chief, see Reid, Mayne
White Company, The, see Doyle, Conan
Whitefriars, King's Lynn, 28; Monastery, 28
Whitehead, A. N., Professor, 200
Whitney, Professor, 338
Wickham, Headmaster of Wellington, 131
Wildman, 200 footnote
Wildstrubel, the, 290
Wild Wales, see Borrow, George
Wilhelm I, 239
Wilhelm II, 198
William, *clericus,* 133
Williams, Rowland, 183
Williams, W., 262
Williamsburg, 11
Wills, Jessie Marian, 300
Wilson, Bernard, 214
Wilson, C. P., 176
Wilson, D. A., 84 footnote
Wilson, K. P., 176
Wilson, Montagu, Mrs, 308
Wimble, Will, 298
Winchester, 202
Winder, hill, 213, 214
Windsor, 2; Duke of, 176; Queen's Page at, 153
Winstanley, D. A., 99, 101 footnote

Winter, master at Llandovery, 174
Wisbech, 4, 21, 22
Wisden, *Cricketer's Guide*, 258
Witham, 89
Wolfe, Humbert, 83, 84, 210 footnote
Wolsey, 330
Woman in White, The, 47
Wood, master at Felsted, 78, 79
Woodard Schools, the, 215
Woolcott, J., 111, 112, 113
Woolwich, 220, 267
'Woolwich Infant', 267
Worcester, 127, 163, 173; Cathedral, 130, 173
Wordsworth, Christopher, 351
Wordsworth, William, 1, 2, 32, 132, 238, 250, 263, 339
Wormegay, 61
Wrekin, the, 133
Wren, 254
Wright, Joseph, 189, 354
Wright, Thomas, 230

Würzburg, 186
Wye, the, 132
Wykehamists, 168
Wymondham, 20

Yarmouth, 13, 23, 27, 34, 35, 36, 40, 140, 246
'Yearning', 235
Yeovil, 204
Yorkshire, 1, 339 footnote; Fells, 213; West Riding, 178
Yorkshireman, 124
Young, 25
Young, Ben, 65
Young, E. M., 201, 202, 203, 204, 205, 206, 252
Young, Lady, 202
Yverdon, 269

Zion, songs of, 131
Zulu chief, 103
Zunftwesen, 197

CAMBRIDGE: PRINTED BY W. LEWIS, M.A., AT THE UNIVERSITY PRESS